BUSINESS ISSUES, COMPETITION AND ENTREPRENEURSHIP

HRM AND MARKETING ORIENTATION IN THE NEW ERA

BUSINESS ISSUES, COMPETITION AND ENTREPRENEURSHIP

Additional books in this series can be found on Nova's website under the Series tab.

Additional e-books in this series can be found on Nova's website under the e-book tab.

BUSINESS ISSUES, COMPETITION AND ENTREPRENEURSHIP

HRM AND MARKETING ORIENTATION IN THE NEW ERA

PANAGIOTIS KYRIAZOPOULOS, PH.D.
EDITOR

nova publishers
New York

For permission to use material from this book please contact us:
Telephone 631-231-7269; Fax 631-231-8175
Web Site: http://www.novapublishers.com

Library of Congress Cataloging-in-Publication Data

ISBN: 978-1-62808-959-2

Published by Nova Science Publishers, Inc. † New York

CONTENTS

INTRODUCTION

Dear Readers,

This book is devoted to the role of Human Resources in today's post-industrial era. As we leave the 2nd Industrial Revolution, we are entering the 3rd Industrial Revolution, which is characterized as 'the Information Society and network.' In this time of transition, in some countries, Human Resources is often seen as software that can be amended at relative ease in order to achieve the optimum cost, whereas other countries theorize that it resembles more of a piece of hardware that cannot be upgraded but only replaced.

This book covers these aspects, addressed through research by the authors in individual subject areas. It is my expectation that this research and the ensuing findings will prove to engage readers in a stimulating and thought-provoking discourse.

Prof. P. Kyriazopoulos (Ph.D.)
Chief Editor

In: HRM and Marketing Orientation in the New Era
Editor: Panagiotis Kyriazopoulos
ISBN: 978-1-62808-959-2

Chapter 1

COMPLEXITY AND HUMAN RESOURCES MANAGEMENT IN BRAZIL

Lina Nakata[*]
University of Sao Paolo, Brazil

ABSTRACT

Organizations may be viewed as organisms whose complexity varies depending on internal and environmental factors. This view appears reasonably commonsensical, but it is also explored by authors who couple complexity theory with organizational studies, such as Richardson (2005), Battram (2002), and Sterman (2000). With this assumption as its starting point, the present study seeks to correlate different organizational characteristics with the complexity of human resources management, using an empirical survey of 150 Brazilian companies as its dataset. The survey was carried out in 2008; our sample consisted of companies of different locations, sectors, and sizes operating in the Brazilian market. Compensation of the organization's head HR executive was used as a proxy for HR management complexity. We tested six characteristics: gross earnings; total number of employees; number of facilities; level of employee education; average wages; and HR budget. Four of these were found to be most relevant in explaining the compensation of head HR executives, which we chose as a proxy for management complexity: number of employees, number of facilities, average wages, and percentage of employees with an undergraduate or graduate education. This exploratory study warrants further confirmation of its findings, but we believe our results indicate that it is possible to associate management complexity with company characteristic variables. The four variables chosen in this study were found to explain 26.9% of the salary of head HR executives in our sample.

Keywords: Complexity, people management, HR executive

[*] E-mail: linankt@gmail.com

1. INTRODUCTION

The management of complexity requires a combination of multidisciplinary knowledge, flexibility, and competencies consistent with each context. In the search for organizational solutions, management professionals are frequently faced with issues involving aspects that are both difficult to understand as a whole and influential in decision-making and its consequences. Managers deal constantly with market changes, and time and again new challenges arise: the more complex the characteristics of their organizations become, the less predictable and calculated do their actions.

Organizations may be compared to living organisms, made up of millions of cells – a quantitative phenomenon, but also a qualitative complex, as its constituent parts are neither arranged according to a simple, orderly pattern, nor are they disordered as the molecules of a gas (Morin, 1974). The interaction among these parts is complex, nonlinear, poorly predictable, and in a constant state of flux. The cells that make up natural organisms may be compared to persons and to the internal constituents of a social organization: these constituents are constantly interacting, and it is the pattern of their relationships that defines the essence of the organization that comprises them (Cilliers, 2005).

From this perspective, one may state that complexity and people management, though little explored, are worthy of the attention of organizational theory and its scholarship. Depending on their intrinsic characteristics and on interaction with the environment, organizations may become high-complexity systems (Richardson, 2005). It is reasonable to assume that organizations that cross this threshold will also undergo an increase in the complexity of how it manages one of the most essential resources of any business (Prahalad, 1995): people. This raises the possibility that one may refer to certain organizations as having complex people management systems, which are placed under the responsibility of professionals notable for their management competence in a certain market.

Nonetheless, one question remains: what defines the complexity of an organization's HR management? This study seeks to contribute to the investigation of possible answers to this question. In order to do so, we put forth a few hypotheses on characterizing variables that could define greater or lesser HR management complexity. These hypotheses were developed on the basis of the most recent theories on organizations and management of complex systems and then submitted to a group of HR managers for qualitative validation. These six variables (gross earnings, total number of employees, number of facilities, level of employee education, average wages, and HR budget) were then correlated with the compensation of the company's head HR executive. We found that four of these variables had greater power to explain the compensation of sample professionals, which may indicate that these organizational characteristics require more complex people management systems.

2. Conceptual Framework

2.1. Complexity

Being complex is not the same as being complicated: while complexity implies complicatedness, it is a broader concept than the latter. According to Morin (1990), the word complex should be understood in its literal sense of complexus, *a whole made up of interwoven parts*. Complex thought is fundamentally that one which deals in uncertainties and is able to conceive organization; it is the thought that can bring together, contextualize, and globalize, but also recognize the individual; it is something that communicates with itself, as a loom brings threads together (Morin, 1990).

Maturana and Varela (1972), in turn, address the matter of complexity from a biological standpoint through use of the term *autopoiesis*, which may be defined as "self-production" or "self-organization". An autopoietic system is a unity organized "as a network of processes of production (transformation and destruction) of components which: [...] through their interactions and transformations continuously regenerate and realize the network of processes (relations) that produced them" (Maturana, and Varela, 1972).

According to Morin and Le Moigne (2001:20):

> "Complexity is a fabric of inseparably associated heterogeneous components: it poses the paradox of the one and the multiple. It is, in fact, the fabric of happenings, actions, interactions, feedbacks, determinations, chance occurrences, that make up our phenomenal world. But complexity thus shows the disquieting features of confusion, inextricability, disorder, ambiguity, uncertainty... Hence the need, for knowledge purposes, to order phenomena by rejecting disorder, driving away what is uncertain, that is, to select elements of order and certainty, to remove ambiguity, to clarify, distinguish, hierarchize..."

Morin and Le Moigne believe knowledge should organize everything that goes on within an organization, as the organization needs to avoid chaos and maintain a categorization of its parts in order to function. Complexity must be perceived as a phenomenological factor, and organizations should not attempt to avoid it as if it were an obstacle to management. According to Morin (1974), the sphere of complexity includes organization of diversity.

More concisely, Giovannini (2002) defines complexity in the literal sense of the word: something that encompasses or includes many parts; a set of interconnected things, facts, or circumstances. Complexity is therefore understood to be that which is not simple, and is not a unitary, indivisible element (Morin, 1974).

Cilliers (2005:8) believes complexity theory "has implications for the way we conceive the structure of an organization, as well as for the way in which complex organizations should be managed". The author defines eight essential general characteristics of a complex system:

1. Complex systems consist of a large number of elements which in themselves can be simple.
2. The elements interact dynamically by exchanging energy or information. These interactions are rich [...] the effects of these interactions are propagated throughout the system.
3. The interactions are nonlinear.

4. There are many direct and indirect feedback loops.
5. Complex systems are open systems – they exchange energy or information with their environment […].
6. Complex systems have memory, not located at a specific place, but distributed throughout the system […].
7. The behavior of the system is determined by the nature of the interactions, not by what is contained within the components […].
8. Complex systems are adaptive. They can (re)organize their internal structure without the intervention of an external agent.

Using the definitions put forth by Cilliers (2005) and other authors in the same school (Goldstein, 2005; Lawrimore, 2005), one may characterize an organization as a complex system: it comprises many components (the more, the stronger characterization can be); the exchange of energy and information among components is intense and dynamic; interactions are nonlinear and high-feedback. In their adaptive course in relation to the environment, these organizations self-organize themselves, adopting difficult-to-predict behavior, which privileges notions of emergence and self-organization. That is, complex systems are characterized by predominantly emergent behavior and a tendency to self-organization that sediments itself in a system-wide memory.

Recognizing complexity does not imply adopting a vague, indeterminate, incomprehensible, or even chaotic notion of the organization. It is a new framework of analysis capable of dealing with contemporary organizational phenomena, the correct understanding of which requires new constructs.

Complexity, emergence, and self-organization also do not mean management is impossible; they do mean that the use of standardized models and prescriptive management solutions is not feasible. These alternatives are incompatible with systems that comprise highly diverse elements with inconstant behavior (Giovannini, 2002).

Therefore, complexity may certainly be managed, as long as management follows its particular logic. Managers must first and foremost understand that they are part of a broader system (Salthe, 2005:88); only then will they be able to regulate or control limited aspects of this system. Furthermore, complex systems are always immersed in larger, equally complex systems, forming a hierarchy; managers must know this hierarchy if they are to act within it, but they should not have pretensions of shaping it to their intentions.

The concepts of emergence and self-organization place managers in the role of conducting complex social processes in which agents are endowed with self-determination. Managers must be influential, encouraging the exchange of information and energy, and attempting to lend it direction; however, they must be aware that the definitive character of this direction cannot be pre-established. In a complex organizational environment, prescriptive actions give way to directive interaction of the relationships established within the company. As noted by Hunsberger, human performance is reflected in the cognitive capacity of complex thought; that is, it is up to managers to exercise systemic thought, the only way to understand and actively participate in complex phenomena (Hunsberger et al., 1992).

The identification and measurement of complex systems is no easy task, and does not have tried-and-true methods for it. Although complexity theory provides important contributions to observation and measurement at the organizational level (Dent, 2005), the identification of complexity depends on creating specific measures for each case. Certain authors go as far as claiming that it is impossible to generically measure the complexity of an organization or of a given system.

Nevertheless, attempts at measuring system complexity have been made. The first qualitative analyses were carried out in the 1970s, in the computer science field (McCabe, 1976), seeking to identify computerized systems of greater or lesser complexity. As Richardson (2005) notes, computers are tools that allow construction of complex representations and exploration of the behavior of complex systems. Ironically, the very technology responsible for much of the complexity of modern life created new means of understanding it.

As some researchers in the computer science field have found, the complexity of a system increases with the elaborateness of its structure, not with the number of variables with which it operates. It is precisely the nonlinearity of interactions between the system's components and the system and its end result that makes the system more or less complex.

People management in organizations is part of a wider system; its component elements are diverse and vary according to the variation in the rest of the system. In the absence of universal mechanisms to identify and measure complexity, we had to choose a proxy variable to stand for it. Many identifiable factors amenable to research could be considered; we felt the most adequate proxy would be the compensation of each company's head HR executive. This follows the principle of agent rationality: companies seek to optimize their financial resources, so it is only reasonable to assume that the most complex and critical systems of an organization are entrusted to its highest-paid professionals.

Several studies on HR management, careers, and compensation suggest that contemporary organizations have sought to connect recognition and compensation to competencies and work complexity (Hipólito, 2002; Dutra, 2004). Towards this end, organizations invest in distinctive management models, in which the identification of competencies and their application to performance assessment, promotion, and selection processes plays an essential role. In such models, the complexity of one's work is one of the main criteria to set apart various performance levels and career stages.

Further evidence of how work complexity ties in to people management may be detected in studies on compensation of HR professionals. A salary survey conducted in northeastern Ohio found that median pay for HR executives increased 23% in 2003, and 30% in 2004. This increase was attributed not only to an improving economy, but also to "the new skill levels needed to keep up with the increasing importance and complexity of employee relations issues" (Prisinsky, 2005).

As we have seen so far, the concepts of complexity and complex systems make up an adequate analysis structure for understanding people management within organizations. Due to their growth in both number and diversity of components and their fostering of increasingly intense internal and external information and energy exchange, these organizations have become more complex. The people management models they adopt must have followed a similar trend. The following section provides an in-depth discussion of the concept of people management, and evidence of how it may relate to complex systems.

2.2. People Management Models or Systems

To Fischer (1998:22) the traditional concept of an HR management system describes a management function that seeks to "obtain and maintain a workforce – composed of diligent, capable, competent, solidary, cohesive, motivated and perfected individuals – that is enthusiastically dedicated to contributing with its finest efforts". This comes down to a set of procedures that seeks no more than process efficiency. Milkovich and Boudreau (2000:19) justify the essential nature of human resources, arguing that HR management is "a series of integrated decisions that form the employment relationships"; it is directly influenced by the capacity of the organization – and its employees – to meet corporate goals.

A people management model may therefore be characterized as the manner through which a company organizes itself to guide human behavior in the workplace. By means of management strategies, policies, or processes, companies implement guidelines and guide managers in their relationship with employees (Fischer, 2002). One may thus state that contemporary people management is more complex, as it goes beyond traditional HRM practices. It focuses more heavily on less predictable, emergent, and self-organizing components and results, such as the way a company gets employees involved in defining strategy. The behavior of employees before stakeholders, the absorption of new technology, and the development of an innovative product or process – all now fall under the purview of people management (Ulrich, 1997; Huselid, 2005). This widens not only the scope of people management, but also the very idea that HR is a closed system, a set of interconnected and systemically organized processes and tools (Fischer, 1998).

Albuquerque (2002) notes a similar advancement within the view of strategic HRM. In taking on such a role, people management would begin to recognize the impacts of the external organizational environment, of competition, and of market dynamics. The focus of HR shifts to the long run, given the need of engaging all employees in corporate strategy and not just the top brass. The concepts of emergence, distributed intelligence, distributed memory, and self-organization surface once again, as characteristics that provide complexity to strategic people management systems.

Another relevant aspect of the contemporary HRM model concerns its sharing tasks with an ever greater number of other organizational systems. The main such component consists of line managers. Milkovich and Boudreau (2000) argue that people management responsibilities now extend to all executives in the organization, as the literature long proposed they would. People management experts remain in a consulting capacity, providing technical support and guidance; employee training, development, creativity, and satisfaction, however, are ultimately under the responsibility of team leaders (Milkovich, and Boudreau, 2000).

As shown in Illustration 1, executives and employees throughout a company's many departments may be considered *clients* of the HR function. One of the primary functions of a people manager is being a service provider, and this may be considered a lower-complexity activity. Performing as an agent of change, however, involves greater uncertainty and interaction, and demands more complex tasks, for which managers must make use of more sophisticated competencies. The following section will discuss complexity as it pertains to people management.

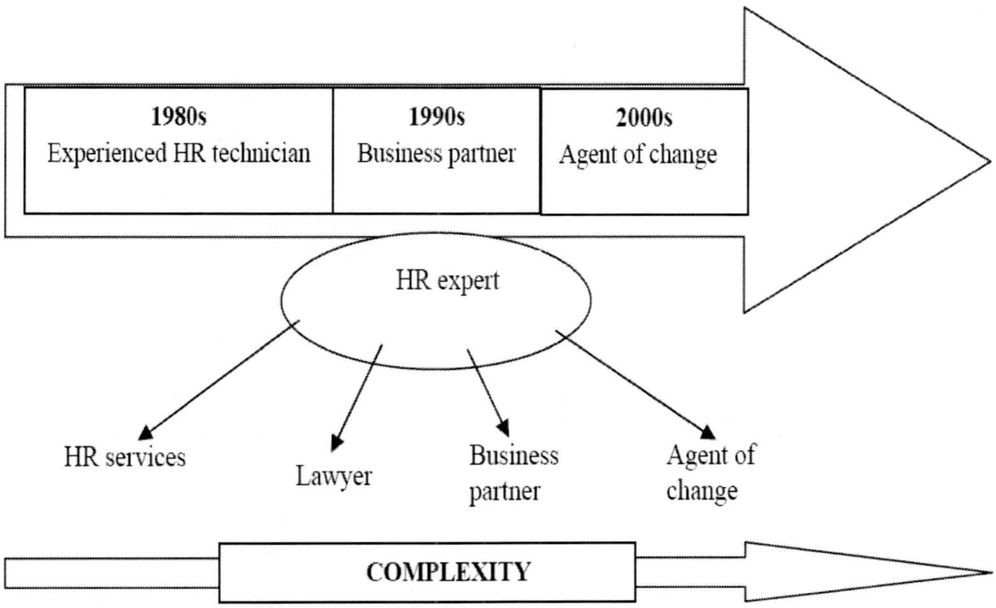

Source: adapted from Milkovich and Boudreau (2000).

Illustration 1. Evolution of the role of the people manager.

2.3. Complexity and People Management

Vasconcellos (1979) believes that, as an organization grows, so does the difficulty of top management maintaining previous levels of centralized authority; this leads to diversification of technical and administrative issues and an increase in their complexity. Certain decisions which would have been made by the company's top echelons are now distributed among its lower hierarchical levels, making the organization more dynamic.

People management is a complex subsystem, which is part of even broader and more complex system (the organization). Several schools have different views on complexity, which may be applied to each people management model, as shown in the following table (Giovannini, 2002:86; Maximiano, 1997):

The relationships among schools, models, and stages of complexity shown in Table 1 may be explained by Morin (1974), who defines the complexity of complexity. It is a hierarchy, a structure of stacked systemic levels, in which the general properties that emerge at a certain level become basic elements of the following one.

This transition shows that the world has undergone several changes, and increasingly deals with the dynamism of the whole and the parts. These changes may be summarized as greater flexibility, dependence on more sophisticated competencies, and systemic thought. They are important to understanding that HR management must take these factors into account, and that people must somehow keep up with this evolutionary movement.

Authors such as Colbert (2004) directly associate complexity with the evolution of people management models, stating that a high degree of institutionalization of complexity principles in the HR system is associated with better organizational performance.

Table 1. Relationship among school, human resources model, and complexity vision

School	People management model	Outlook on complexity
Classic school	Traditional model	System elements are self-similar and interdependent
Human relations at work	Motivational model	"Human being" and "organization" are respectively the singular and plural forms of the same phenomenon
Strategic management	Strategic HRM	Unpredictability, self-organization restrict planning
Participative management/ entrepreneurial management	Competence-based management	Participation presumes understanding and incorporation of characteristics of the whole; creativity is a natural characteristic of dynamic, nonlinear systems

Source: adapted from Giovannini (2002).

Table 2. Complexity and societal changes

From	To
Geared at low complexity	Geared at hypercomplexity
High individual specialization	Low individual specialization; versatility
Strong hierarchical relationships	Weak hierarchical relationships
High level of centralization	Decentralization
Programs directed at individual behavior and social action	Heuristic strategies are more relevant than programs
Little individual autonomy; coercion	Much individual autonomy; freedom
Stringent restrictions	Mild restrictions
Little communication and interaction between people and between subsystems	Extensive communication and interaction between people and between subsystems
Suppression of uncertainty, nuisances, and disorder	Disturbances and disorder
Stability and little room for invention and evolution	Instability and much room for invention and evolution

Source: adapted from Morin (1974).

Another factor must be taken into account: the increasing complexity of work itself. With the advent of information technology and automation, simple, routine tasks are being assigned to machines, making room for much more complex work to be executed by humans. In modern organizations, "complexity is not in situations *per se*, but in what situations require of people" (Dutra, 2004:41). Each organizational reality must live with complexity and deal with ever higher demands. Freedom is therefore the development of the ability of a self-organizing entity to use uncertainty autonomously and in a random manner; this is a consequence of complexity, not the foundation on which complexity is built (Morin, 1974).

Lawler and Elliot (1996) also believe that organizations start managing people through a logic of complexity. They believe work has been increasingly characterized by extremely complex issues, which require precise, well-thought out decisions. The solution would consist of classifying employees' positions according to their skill levels, providing evolution as occupations change to entail more experience, responsibility, and multitasking activities.

According to Dutra (2004), the concept of complexity has become important to understand the reality of people management in organizations. Hipólito (2001:68) agrees, stating that the association between salary brackets and added value of work is only natural, because jobs are tied to contracts through which the organization "appropriates the value generated by a certain type of work, for a set number of hours per week, in exchange for pay". Two trends therefore appear to contribute to the high complexity of people management models and systems. On the one hand, they start to become part of and meet the demands of more complex organizations; on the other, they serve to manage work that has been growing intrinsically more complex. In the present study, we will attempt to investigate the former trend, seeking to identify organizational variables that could explain the complexity of human resources management models or systems.

3. Methods

Data collection for our study consisted of a survey, applied to a group of companies that take part in an annual nationwide survey carried out to identify organizations in Brazil with exceptional workplace quality. From the 500 organizations that applied for the survey in 2008, we chose the top 150. Companies respond to a 36-question quantitative questionnaire that elicits data on the company's characteristics, its workforce, and the makeup of its people management model. Although the sample consists of nationally renowned organizations influential in their respective markets, it should be considered a purposive nonprobability sample (Selltiz et al., 1987): it provides a well-delimited population but does not necessarily ensure proportionality or representativeness.

Our data collection instrument (Marconi, and Lakatos, 2003) consisted of a form to be filled by the respondent's HR representative. The instrument was pre-tested in a standard organization and adjusted as needed. Questions included data on gross earnings (in Brazilian reais, presented in U.S. dollars in our results), number of employees, number of operating facilities with ten or more employees (branches, plants, factories, or production units, but not departments, areas etc.), average employee wages (in Brazilian reais, but shown in dollars), level of education (percentage of employees who, respectively, completed elementary school, high school, undergraduate studies, or graduate studies), and HR budget (in Brazilian reais, but shown in dollars; this variable does not take payroll into consideration). Furthermore, one of the questions requested that respondents provide the nominal monthly pay and annual variable compensation and/or bonus of the company's head HR executive.

The people management literature shows that compensation (fixed or variable) takes into account the competencies required of and developed by people within an organization.

Each of the aforementioned variables was validated by a twenty-member board consisting of the head HR executives of nationally renowned organizations. These professionals were invited to take part in group dynamics and encouraged to take part in an activity that sought to identify the principal relationships established between an organization and the variables that could identify it as being more or less complex. The variables selected by the group may be seen in the following schematic (Illustration 2), as may our research problem. We proceeded to data treatment, and our results are discussed in section 4. The following topic will present our results and analyze its main points, towards answering the proposed research question.

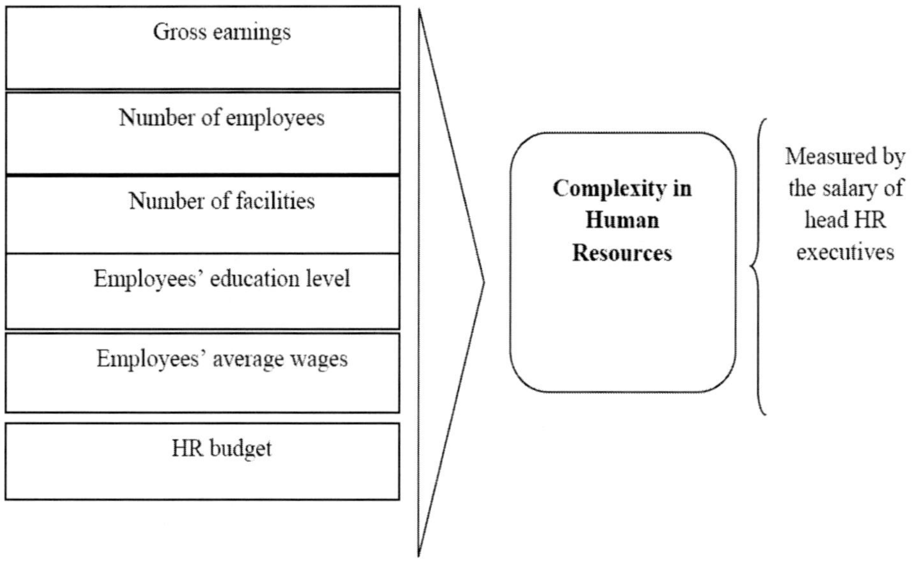

Illustration 2. Research problem variables.

4. Presentation and Analysis of Results

The companies that make up our study sample are described in Table 3 below.

The companies' characteristics vary considerably in many aspects. It is also important to verify that the means are higher than the medians, indicating that some companies have much larger values in the presented variables. They belong to various sectors and are diversified.

Given the above organizations, Wooldridge (2006) states that a variable may vary as a function of other factors, generically represented as follows:

$y = f(x_1, x_2, x_3...)$
y = dependent variable
x_1, x_2, x_3 = factors influencing the dependent variable

For the present case, we expect people management complexity to vary with the company's earnings, its number of employees, number of facilities, average wages, level of employee education, and HR budget. This relation may be expressed as follows:

complexity of people management = f (gross earnings, employees, facilities, average wage, education, HR budget)

Information on earnings (gross earnings), number of employees (employees), number of facilities employing ten people or more (facilities), nominal average salary in each company (average wage) and budget allocated to the human resources function (HR budget) are provided as gross values and were taken directly from questionnaire answers.

Table 3. Descriptive analysis of organizations included in the survey

Size	No. of companies
Small (100 to 500 employees)	30
Medium (501 to 1.500 employees)	39
Large (1.501 or more employees)	31
Number of employees	Amount
Mean	4.909
Median	1.338
Minimum	144
Maximum	99.306
Gross earnings	USD
Mean	1.003.503.863
Median	461.964.500
Minimum	174.166
Maximum	18.566.099.200
Number of facilities	Amount
Mean	53
Median	6
Minimum	1
Maximum	1.748
Average wage	USD
Mean	1.148
Median	2.394
Minimum	124
Maximum	4.442
HR budget	USD
Mean	2.102.432
Median	600.380
Minimum	2.000
Maximum	31.424.800
Employees with a post-secondary education	%
Mean	48,3
Median	49,0
Minimum	2,0
Maximum	100,0
Annual salary, head of HR	USD
Mean	128.861
Median	92.860
Minimum	4.127
Maximum	552.000

The *education* variable considered the percentage of employees with a post-secondary education (undergraduate studies, complete or incomplete, and/or graduate studies), on a scale of 0 to 100. For example: a company that had 31% of employees with an undergraduate education and 9% with a graduate education (master's, doctorate etc.) would be assigned a scholarship score of 40.

We adopted compensation of the company's head HR executive as a proxy variable for complexity in people management. Wooldridge (2006) defines a proxy variable as one that best approaches another whose measurement is impossible or non-trivial.

For the purposes of this study, we understand compensation, whether fixed or variable, to be mostly based on the complexity managed by the head of human resources in the course of his or her work. We do recognize that many other factors influence or could measure the complexity of people management; however, as it would be impossible to identify and quantify all of these factors, we must simply recognize the limitations of our study. We therefore note that our results are valid *ceteris paribus* – all other relevant factors remaining the same (Wooldridge, 2006:13). When a variable may be explained by other factors, it is termed a dependent variable; the factors that attempt to explain it are explanatory variables. It is important to note that econometric models, such as the one used here, attempt to establish a causal relationship: explanatory variables cause of explain the dependent variable, even if partially.

In brief, the purpose of this study is to identify the extent to which the six aforementioned variables, *ceteris paribus*, explain complexity in people management (represented by the proxy variable of head HR executive compensation). The model may be represented as follows:

$$salary = \beta_0 + \beta_1\, gross\ earnings + \beta_2\, employees + \beta_3\, facilities + \beta_4\, average\ wage + \beta_5\, education + \beta_6\, RH\ budget + u$$

According to Wooldridge (2006), the u term contains all unobserved factors and measurement errors. Even if other factors that help explain the wage phenomenon are added to the model, u can never be completely eliminated. This term is known as the error term or disturbance term. The constants β_0, β_1, β_2, β_3, β_4, β_5, β_6 are the model's parameters; they describe the directions and forces of the relation between salary and the factors used to determine it in the model (Wooldridge, 2006).

Prior to data tabulation, we eliminated outliers, such as null values or those exceeding plausible levels. Our results are shown in Table 4 below. We must stress that companies excluded from the sample are no less important or relevant than those included; they are simply cases that could introduce bias into the model due to their discrepancy.

The results of regression analysis show that 30.24% (R^2 = 0.3024) of the head HR executive's wages is explained by the four variables considered. Wooldridge (2006) defines the R^2, or coefficient of determination, as the explained variation rate compared with total variation.

Table 4. Results from the econometric test, with six variables

Variable	Coefficient	Std. Error	t-Statistic	Prob.
C	62811.91	47803.49	1.313961	0.1921
GROSS_EARNINGS	-9.19E-07	5.99E-06	-0.153409	0.8784
EMPLOYEES	22.36155	6.204211	3.604253	0.0005
FACILITIES	-1236.623	332.8971	-3.714729	0.0003
AVG_WAGE	34.79128	13.20753	2.634201	0.0099
EDUCATION	1858.161	952.8242	1.950162	0.0542
HR_BUDGET	0.003651	0.002654	1.375708	0.1722
R-squared	0.302406	Mean dependent var		309049.8
Adjusted R-squared	0.257400	S.D. dependent var		240768.5
S.E. of regression	207480.4	Akaike info criterion		27.39089
Sum squared resid	4.00E+12	Schwarz criterion		27.57325

Another definition is the fraction of sample variation that is explained by explanatory variables. After analysis of the above results, we excluded the variables gross earnings, education, and HR budget, for comparison purposes, as their p-values, although adequate, were outliers when compared with those of the other variables. Stern (2008:26) defines the p-value as “the probability of getting a sample is more extreme than the one we got”.

The new model, no longer considering gross earnings, and HR budget, may be represented as follows:

$$salário = \beta_1\ employees + \beta_2\ facilities + \beta_3\ average\ wage + \beta_4\ education + u$$

Results obtained with the new model (no longer considering gross earnings and HR budget) are shown in Table 5 below.

The new regression shows that 26.90% ($R^2 = 0.2690$) of the head HR executive’s wages is explained by the variables employees, facilities, average wage and education, which is nonetheless a relevant finding.

Table 5. Results from the econometric test, with four variables (without *c*, *gross_income*, and *hr_budget*)

Variable	Coefficient	Std. Error	t-Statistic	Prob.
EMPLOYEES	26.62563	5.169485	5.150538	0.0000
FACILITIES	-1338.907	305.9397	-4.376377	0.0000
AVG_WAGE	40.81650	12.89161	3.166131	0.0021
EDUCATION	2522.041	802.6624	3.142094	0.0022
R-squared	0.269003	Mean dependent var		309049.8
Adjusted R-squared	0.246160	S.D. dependent var		240768.5
S.E. of regression	209044.7	Akaike info criterion		27.37766
Sum squared resid	4.20E+12	Schwarz criterion		27.48187

S. E. of regression showed no significant loss of information, even after the exclusion of an explanatory variable. Fava (2000) claims that, when comparing two models, the best is that producing the lowest S. E. of regression (Anderson, Sweeney, and William, 2002; Gujarati, 2000; Pindyck, and Rubinfeld, 1991; Vasconcellos, and Alves, 1999).

From our results, we may conclude that six variables – gross earnings, number of employees, number of facilities, employee education, and HR budget – would explain 30.24% of people management complexity. Furthermore, when earnings and HR budget were excluded, the remaining variables still explained 26.90% of people management complexity, as measured by compensation of the head HR executive.

6. Final Thoughts

Organizations are part of increasingly dynamic and competitive environments; they must therefore manage the complexity they deal with. Attempts to reduce complexity are fruitless, as they would make a few tasks easier, but would in no way contribute to solving challenges.

Our data showed that six characterization variables explain 30% of people management complexity, while only four of these variables explained up to 27% of the salary of a head HR executive. This is quite an expressive result when one considers that myriad conditions influence the compensation of a professional charged with managing such an important system. Our finding shows that total number of employees, average wages, percentage of employees with an undergraduate or graduate education, and HR budget are factors that may be used to measure management complexity, as a company's compensation system embodies the complexity of a certain job.

We believe that this study contributes to the theory in its approach to the matter of complexity and people management, a theme that has been widely cited but little explored in empirical studies, particularly through qualitative approaches. One of the limitations of this study is its use of a non-probability sample; we recommend that, in future, a more representative sample be chosen. The use of a proxy variable to represent complexity, as deduced from the reflections of other authors, may also have limited our results. One further restriction may have been determined by our choice of explanatory variables; other company characteristics could have been considered, such as sector, origin of capital, applied technology etc. and were not used simply because we chose to use a previously established database as our reference.

References

Albuquerque, L. G. 2002. A gestão estratégica de pessoas. In Fleury, M. T. L. (Org.) *As pessoas na organização.* São Paulo: Gente.

Anderson, D. R., Sweeney, D. J., and William, T. A. 2002. *Estatística Aplicada à Administração e Economia.* 3. ed. São Paulo: Pioneira Thomson Learning.

Battram, A. 2002. *Navigating complexity.* London: Industrial Society.

Bussab, W. O., and Morettin, P. 2002. *Estatística Básica.* 5. ed. São Paulo: Saraiva.

Cilliers, P. 2005. Knowing Complex Systems. In Richardson, K. A. *Managing Organizational Complexity:* Philosophy Theory and Application. Information Age Publishing Inc.

Colbert, B. A. 2004. The complex resource-based view: implications for theory and practice in strategic human resource management. *Academy of Management Review, 29, 3, 341-358.*

Dent, E. B. 2005. The Observation, Inquiry and Measurement Challenges surfaced by complexity theory. In Richardson, K. A. *Managing Organizational Complexity:* Philosophy Theory and Application. Information Age Publishing Inc.

Dutra, J. S. 2004. *Competências:* conceitos e instrumentos para a gestão de pessoas na empresa moderna. São Paulo: Atlas.

Fava, V. L. 2000. Testes de raízes unitárias e cointegração. In Vasconcellos, M. A. S., and D. Alves. *Manual de econometria.* São Paulo: Atlas.

Fischer, A. L. 1998. *As mudanças no modelo de gestão de pessoas na década de noventa – um estudo sobre as empresas brasileiras consideradas exemplares.* Tese de doutorado apresentado à Faculdade de Economia, Administração e Contabilidade da Universidade de São Paulo, São Paulo.

Fischer, A. L. 2002. Um resgate conceitual e histórico dos modelos de gestão de pessoas. In Fleury, M. T. L. (Org.) *As pessoas na organização.* São Paulo: Gente.

Giovannini, F. 2002. *As organizações e a complexidade:* um estudo dos sistemas de gestão da qualidade. Dissertação de Mestrado apresentado à Faculdade de Economia, Administração e Contabilidade da Universidade de São Paulo, São Paulo.

Goldstein, J. 2005. Emergence, Creative Process an Self-Transcending Constructions. In Richardson, K. A. *Managing Organizational Complexity:* Philosophy Theory and Application. Information Age Publishing Inc.

Gujarati, D. N. 2000. *Econometria Básica.* 3. ed. São Paulo: Makron Books.

Hipólito, J. A. M. 2001. *Administração salarial:* a remuneração por competências como diferencial competitivo. São Paulo: Atlas.

Hipólito, J. A. M. 2002. Sistema de recompensas: uma abordagem atual. In Fleury, M. T. L. (Org.) *As pessoas na organização.* São Paulo: Gente.

Hunsberger, B., Lea J., Pancer, S. M., Pratt, M., and McKenzie, B. 1992. Making Life Complicated: Prompting the Use of Integratively Complex Thinking. *Journal of Personality, 60, 1, 95-114.*

Huselid, M. A. 2005. *Strategic Human Resource Management:* Theory And Practice. Sage.

Lawler, J. J., and Elliot, R. 1996. Artificial intelligence in HRM: an experimental study of an expert system. *Journal of Management*, Spring.

Lawrimore, B. 2005. From excelence to emergence: The Evolution of management thinking and the influence of complexity. In Richardson, K. A. *Managing Organizational Complexity:* Philosophy Theory and Application. Information Age Publishing Inc.

Marconi, M. A., and Lakatos, E. M. 2003. *Fundamentos de metodologia científica.* São Paulo: Atlas.

Maturana, H. R., and Varela, F. J. 1970. *Autopoiesis and cognition:* the realization of the living. Dordrecht: Reidel.

Maximiano, A. C. A. 1997. *Teoria geral da administração:* da escola científica à competitividade em economia globalizada. São Paulo: Atlas.

McCabe, T. J. 1976. A Complexity Measure. *IEEE Transactions on Software Engineering, 2, 4, 308-320.*

Milkovich, G. T., and Boudreau, J. W. 2000. *Administração de recursos humanos.* São Paulo: Atlas.

Morin, E. 1974. Epistemology: complexity. *International Sociological Science Journal, 26, 4, 555-584.*

Morin, E. 1990. *Introdução ao pensamento complexo.* Lisboa: Instituto Piaget.

Morin, E., and Le Moigne, J. 2000. *A inteligência da complexidade.* São Paulo: Petrópolis.

Pindyck, R. S., and Rubinfeld, D. L. 1991. *Econometric models and economic forecast.* 3. ed. McGraw-Hill.

Prahalad, C. K. 1995. *Competindo pelo Futuro.* Rio de Janeiro: Campus.

Prisinsky, D. 2005. HR execs see salaries soar. *Crain's Cleveland Business, 26, 14, 3-4.*

Richardson, K. A. 2005. *Managing Organizational Complexity:* Philosophy Theory and Application. Information Age Publishing Inc.

Salthe, S. 2005. An Aproche to Causality in Organized Complexity. In Richardson, K. A. *Managing Organizational Complexity:* Philosophy Theory and Application. Information Age Publishing Inc.

Selltiz, C., Wrightsman, L. S., and Cook, S. W. 1987. *Métodos de pesquisa nas relações sociais.* São Paulo: E.P.U.

Sterman, J. D. 2000. *Business Dynamics: Systems Thinking and Modeling for a Complex World,* McGraw-Hill/Irwin.

Stern, J. M. 2008. *Cognitive constructivism and the epistemic significance of sharp statistical hypotheses.* São Paulo: IME-USP.

Ulrich, D. 1997. *Human Resource Champions:* The Next Agenda for Adding Value and Delivering Results. Boston, MA: Harvard Business School Press.

Vasconcellos, E. P. G. 1979. Centralização x descentralização: uma aplicação para laboratórios de instituições de pesquisa e desenvolvimento. *Revista de Administração da USP, São Paulo, 14, 2.*

Vasconcellos, E. P. G., and Alves, D. 1999. *Manual de Econometria.* São Paulo: Atlas.

Wooldridge, J. M. 2006. *Introductory econometrics:* a modern approach. 3. ed. Cincinnati: Thomson-South Western.

In: HRM and Marketing Orientation in the New Era
Editor: Panagiotis Kyriazopoulos
ISBN: 978-1-62808-959-2

Chapter 2

EPIONE: THE PAN-EUROPEAN HEALTHCARE OBSERVATORY FOR KIDS: KNOWLEDGE MANAGEMENT, INTELLECTUAL CAPITAL, SOCIAL NETWORKS AND SEMANTIC WEB TECHNOLOGIES TO THEIR FULL POTENTIAL FOR PERSONALIZED HEALTHCARE SERVICES

Patricia Ordóñez de Pablos[1]*, Jingyuan Zhao[2] and Jose Emilio Labra Gayo[3]

[1]Dept. of Business Administration, The University of Oviedo, Faculty of Economics, Spain

[2]Harbin Institute of Technology, School of Management Harbin, Heilongjiang, China

[3]Department of Computer Science, University of Oviedo, Oviedo, Spain

ABSTRACT

The strategic objective for a unified European Union requires many initiatives in Pan-European level. Especially in the Health Domain many things have to be done towards the establishment of effective, personalized, and functional services for all the European citizens. In this article we exploit the promises of Intellectual Capital and Knowledge Management disciplines, targeting to the justification of a Pan-European Healthcare Observatory for kids (EPIONE).

The EPIONE Observatory and the underlying Managerial and Technological infrastructure are analysed in this article, and provide an excellent showcase for how emerging technologies can develop excellent capacities for the management of Knowledge and Intellectual capital and the support of high performance health care services.

---

* Corresponding autor: Email patriop@uniovi.es

Keywords: Health, Knowledge Management, National Healthcare Systems, Advanced Infrastructures, Intellectual Capital

1. Introduction

In the Ancient Greek Mythology, EPIONE, the goddess of the soothing of pain, the wife of the medicine god Asklepios, and the mother of a number of minor healing gods, including Hygeia (Good Health), Panakeia (All-Cures) and Iaso (Healing), in her appealing image and the corresponding myths reflected the need of people for Health and recovery. In our modern societies, Healthcare represents one of the critical pillars of social coherence. It is also a context where the quality of civilized world is judged. At the Pan-European level, local differences, significant gaps in the performance of National Healthcare systems, poor performance of IT infrastructures and isolated management of critical clinical and health related knowledge set a "Tower of Babel" context. Additionally it is also recorded a very slow responsiveness of Healthcare Institution to "special needs/emergency cases" and this has a critical impact in the loss of human lives.

From the other hand in the Scientific World, Research and Development summarizes the collective effort for innovative solutions, new approaches, and adoption of technologies.

In this article the main purpose is to present the main ideas and propositions supporting EPIONE an FP7 proposal for Personalized Healthcare Services. It is organized as follows. In Section II, we provide the key aspects of the challenges for the health domain in Europe by exploiting a knowledge management. We present some characteristic real world scenarios and highlight the key points of missing performances. An integrated discussion of these two provide a justification for the rationale and strategic mission of EPIONE at Pan-European Level.

In section III, we provide the theoretical background and the key innovative aspects of EPIONE as anchored in Intellectual Capital and Knowledge Management state of the art and latest developments. The development of a matrix of key research issues and Strategic Propositions of KM and IC towards high performance organizations and "human networks" is used for the a roadmap towards the development of the key components of EPIONE.

In section IV, the discussion is concentrated on the detailed presentation of the innovative aspects of EPIONE. Very briefly, six major technological streams set the backbone for personalized services, namely:

- Semantic Web [for Ontological Engineering]
- Open Source Software [for the development of tools and extensibility]
- Social software, Web 2.0 [for the design, and operation of online communities]
- Web Services [for the package of II-enabled intelligence and services]
- Ubiquitous and Mobile Technologies [for the provision of Smart Cards, and Mobile Devices tagging the Digital Health ID of Kids]
- E-learning technologies [for the establishment of flexible, dynamic, personalized learning spaces]

In Section V, we present the EPIONE architecture and main services and also a draft of its Business Model.

Finally at the Section VI we promote the real challenges for the adoption of EPIONE in the context of the European Level and we conclude with a roadmap for political consultation at a high level for the Adoption of Emerging Technologies for Health.

2. Personalized Healthcare Services: A Knowledge Society Primer

Beyond Local Boundaries

The integration at the European level requires key initiatives aiming to demolish local boundaries as imposed by local inefficiencies. From this perspective the vision of European Integration needs to be reflected in various rational strategic actions.

In a strange way very often the strategic objectives at a high political level require time and significant resources till the moment they will be beneficiary for the European citizens. In such context the vision of the Knowledge Society challenges the designs, implementation and support of advanced personalized healthcare services.

The knowledge society is often treated as a utopia, where optimistic considerations for the role of new technologies envision unrealistic value-adding services for citizens, and knowledge is purported to create dramatic economic advances.

In the last years, several scientific disciplines have initiated debates on the characteristics of the knowledge society and the required consultations towards the establishment of "managing bodies", the crafting of strategies and policies as well as the specification of action programs.

Given the significance of the knowledge society as a new context of our living era, four significant objectives formulate the challenges of the EPIONE at a “high political level” for the health domain at the European level:

1. The need to investigate the "soft" and "hard" aspects of the knowledge society in the Health Domain, with the aim of providing organizational and strategic frameworks as well as infrastructures enabled by the evolution of information technologies.
2. The need to support a manifesto for sustainable development for the European Healthcare based on collaboration, knowledge and learning exploitation, and personalized healthcare services for all.
3. The need to anchor government policies in scientific evidence concerning the characteristics of the emerging knowledge intensive economy and social environment, with emphasis to humanistic visions.
4. The need to investigate the key priorities of the knowledge society in terms of critical aspects of human life.

Knowledge and Learning Management

Within this context, the last years the evolution of Knowledge and Learning Technologies is truly amazing. Excellent approaches, sound theoretical propositions, state-of-the art systems are here ready to provide a new level of sustainable development.

Today, national healthcare systems provide the contexts for the applications of Knowledge and Learning Technologies. Several committees of technologists and experts of the Health, clinical and pharmaceutical domain are trying to find the right balance, and to implement knowledge –enabled, learning-aware, technology-enhanced systems. But there seems to be a problem!! A significant gap between technological possibilities and technology adoption, as well as a lack of fantasy with respect to the ways in which new technologies can open up new roads for provision of personalized healthcare services, community building and effective knowledge transfer. Billions of euros are spent for new technologies at every level of health, but unfortunately, in many cases the investments seem to be a waste of money. It is not a problem of availability of technologies but rather a problem in terms of tight linkage to the old and inefficient healthcare provision paradigms. We must investigate new roles towards a new era of healthcare services, away from the inflexible characteristics of the past, and we must take steps towards open collaboration and synergies exploitation (Ordóñez de Pablos et al., 2010; Rodriguez et al., 2009; Zhao and Ordóñez de Pablos, 2010, 2011).

With the shift towards the knowledge society, the change of working conditions and the high-speed evolution of information and communication technologies, peoples' knowledge and skills need continuous updating (Labra et al., 2010; Zhao, Ordóñez de Pablos, 2009). Learning, based on collaborative working, creativity, multidisciplinary, adaptiveness, intercultural communication and problem solving, has taken on an important role in everyday life and especially in the Health Domain. The learning process is becoming pervasive, both for individuals and organizations, in formal education, in the professional context and as part of every aspect of the HealthCare domain's reality. Learning and Knowledge can be the basis for new healthcare personalized services that should be accessible to every citizen, independent of age, education, and social status and tailored to his/her individual needs (Lytras and Ordóñez de Pablos, 2009, 2010).

Knowledge Networking, Advanced Semantics, Social Networks

Knowledge Artifacts, New Roles, and new connections in the Healthcare domain bring forward the requirement for *Knowledge Networking* and *Knowledge Routing*. Towards this direction it is extremely important to research and to advancing the knowledge on design variables and conditions for social networks in health. Knowledge Management and Semantic Web provide the technological lenses for the specification and analysis of these variables towards a new era of social interactions and human experiences with computers. As semantic technologies prove their value with targeted applications, there are increasing opportunities to consider their application in social contexts for the provision of health care services (Barranquero et al., 2010).

The role of semantics for information integration and analysis has been studied for a long time. In the context of the recent activity in the Semantic Web, the availability of methodologies and tools for ontology development has allowed knowledge representation to make practical inroads through successful development of large numbers of domain ontologies. Use of ontologies to develop new classes of semantic applications is particularly evident in the fields of life sciences, health care, government and technology-intensive sectors. Increasing adoption of W3C recommendations such as RDF, and to a lesser extent

OWL, has allowed emerging as well as mainstream industry to bring new tools and products, as exemplified by RDF support by Oracle.

As semantic technologies prove their value with targeted applications, there are increasing opportunities to consider their application in Health enablers. Knowledge management has been accepted as a critical enabler aiming to increase organisational performance by better use of intellectual assets, in addition to which many organizations are forced to increasingly deal with knowledge services that form larger parts of the global economy. Thus there are recent examples of applications of semantics for empowering knowledge management or better supporting knowledge services. In the context of knowledge management and services, organizational and human issues are of equal if not higher importance than the technical issues that have tended to receive the bulk of attention in the past. Consequently, integrated approaches that touch these aspects, or those that extend technical and domain knowledge to services or organizational and people issues are especially sought. This is intended to initiate a dialog between the organizational, human and technical views of the field.

One critical aspect of exploitation of SW and KM technologies for health relate with the design and support of Social Networks.

"NEW HORIZONS for a NEW GENERATION of Healthcare services at European level". This is the ultimate objective of the application of knowledge and learning technologies in the European HealthCare system. New contexts, new models and new service designs that promote the vision for high performance healthcare services provision.

3. EPIONE UNIQUE VALUE PROPOSITION: BEYOND PERFORMANCE GAPS

The previous section contributed significantly to our objective to highlight the main areas of EPIONE societal value. In this section we will go deeper in our analysis and we will summarize some key missing performance gaps in the provision of personalized healthcare services to kids.

The overall strategy concerning personalized healthcare services for Kids as proposed by the EPIONE Observatory is anchored to the following strategic statement:

> "No Personalization of healthcare services can happen without an intensive analysis, development, maintenance and continuous management of a HEALTH IDENTITY, a collection of critical tacit and explicit knowledge related with each European citizen".

The emphasis of our approach to KIDS health identity provides a mean for a long-term management of critical health, clinical, psychological and development knowledge of kids that can be used as the basis for various personalized services.

In the domain of HealthCare, things are extremely complex:

- *Knowledge is a key pillar and a key enabler of performance.* Knowledge in various forms from "scientific artifacts" and "well documented know how" to "common sense" and "discourses", requires the establishment of formal and informal management and diffusion channels. Knowledge management has been used as a high-promise business concept. In an era of business transition, the effective management of knowledge is proposed as a strategy that exploits the organizational intangible assets. We recognize knowledge management as a socio-technical phenomenon where the basic social constructs such as person, team and organization require support from ICT applications. An integrated analysis at artifact, individual, team, organizational, inter-organizational and global level is required. In the current state at European level is really disappointed the fact that we don't have mechanisms for the acquisition and exploitation of this kind of knowledge. Isolated efforts for the management of personal healthcare record are really out dated.

- *Hundreds of specialized and non-specialized Communities of Experts and Communities of Practice define a dynamic context of knowledge networking.* Doctors, Patients, Health Policy Makers, Pharmaceutical community, Government Officers, Researchers are only a few of the critical peers within the Healthcare network. Within such "rich" environment in terms of "relationships" healthcare domain requires emphasis on the "individual unit". The vision of personalized healthcare services and patient-centric healthcare information systems in fact must exploit a huge knowledge-networking infrastructure aiming to act in prevention and treatment through well-justified Knowledge Strategies. The Community / Collaborative Perspective poses many challenges also to the management of HEALTH personal IDENTITY. In most of cases we miss the opportunity to enrich the "personal health records" with knowledge provided by various stakeholders. In EPIONE this is considered as one of the greatest challenges. The development of KIDS ontology will be used for the annotation of kids' health identity and in this process the role of the surrounding EPIONE Network is really critical. Several stakeholders, experts, through well-defined services will populate and enrich the Identity of Kids.
- *Knowledge Strategies* at healthcare domain transform key "political" objectives to functional processes aiming to support the daily "battle" for the provision of health services of high quality to citizen. Unfortunately nowadays very poor performance is recorded related with the clear connections between the provision of services and the underlying knowledge components required for the performance of critical health processes.
- The *different beneficiaries groups* of healthcare services require a multilevel analysis for the requirements towards design of personalized healthcare services. In EPIONE the emphasis is paid on KIDS.
- The *anarchy in the way that Healthcare information systems developed* in the past decades requires significant investments in Enterprise Application Integration and Interoperability. And unfortunately in the current efforts the emphasis is not paid on the "knowledge components" integration but rather on a simplistic integration at transfer and connection level. We have a critical absence of Business Integration.
- The *Health Identity* needs extensive analysis in terms of knowledge items that it incorporates and also in terms of provision and maintenance at European level. In EPIONE the development of the Identity will be based in a collaborative KIDS ontology, which while provide a common consensus for the key themes that matter for the health and the development of kids. For sure such approach can have

significant implications also for the deployment, since there will be a "protected personal health identity" of employees in later years.

- The mobility of European Citizens requires flexible and *interoperable healthcare infrastructures* that exploit "local" knowledge in "global" contexts.

For sure this is an endless list of challenges for the adoption of emerging technologies in the context of Healthcare Domain towards personalized health care services.

In the next figure we summarize the main theoretical and technological foundations of EPIONE as well as its contribution and innovation aspects.

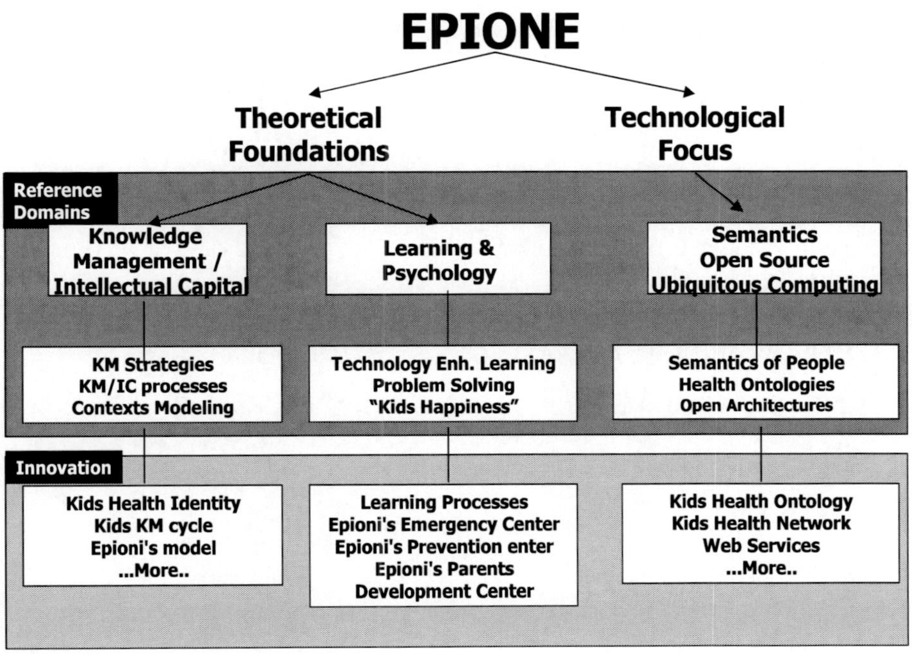

Theoretical Foundations And Technological Focus

Concerning the theoretical foundations the overall idea is the exploitation of state of the art and innovative approaches of knowledge management, intellectual capital, learning and psychology domains.

The technological emphasis of EPIONE is anchored in 5 pillars:

- Semantic Web [for Ontological Engineering]
- Open Source Software [for the development of tools and extensibility]
- Social software, Web 2.0 [for the design, and operation of online communities]
- Web Services [for the package of II-enabled intelligence and services]
- Ubiquitous and Mobile Technologies [for the provision of Smart Services over handheld devices]
- E-learning technologies [for the establishment of flexible, dynamic, personalized learning spaces]

A more detailed discussion of key themes that will be investigated concerning the theoretical and technological foundations is given below.

KM Strategies Exploitation

A systematic analysis of knowledge management strategies at artefact, individual, team, organizational and inter-organizational /network, societal level will result to an understanding and justification of the required knowledge elements of a Kids Health Identity. In parallel the in depth analysis of contexts of potential exploitation for personalized healthcare services, will be documented in a KM cycle, which will be used for the structuring of a business model for the Observatory. In simple words the overall discussion concerning KM strategies will be based on the following pillars:

SECTION A: ARTIFACT LEVEL

- Managing Documents
- Managing Metadata and Semantics
- Managing Taxonomies

SECTION B: INDIVIDUAL LEVEL

- Constructing Yellow pages of experts
- Managing individual profiles
- Managing Tacit Knowledge

SECTION C: TEAM LEVEL

- Managing Workflows
- Managing Discussion Forums
- Exploiting Collaborative Work Systems
- Managing Team Dynamics

SECTION D: ORGANIZATIONAL LEVEL

- Building Best Practices
- Developing Knowledge Maps / Ontologies
- Managing Competencies
- Managing Organizational Memory

SECTION E: INTER - ORGANIZATIONAL LEVEL

- Managing inter-organizational network
- Managing Projects
- Future Technologies

Semantic Social Networking

From the other hand EPIONE exploits innovative approaches that will be justified concerning new modes of semantic social networking. Towards this direction the following are the key pillars of an extensive literature review that will be undertaken in order to summarize the unique value proposition concerning new modes of learning and social networking in the health domain:

- Social network analysis as applied to the Web
- New forms of interaction in social systems
- FOAF and other metadata schema describing individuals and social ties
- Folksonomies, tagging and other collaboration-based categorisation systems
- Sharing contents in on-line communities
- Blogging as a social activity and approaches to semantic blogs
- Wikis, semantic Wikis and other collaborative knowledge creation systems
- Collaborative filtering in social settings
- Analysing social interaction for finding knowledge on Web users
- Design variables and conditions for knowledge sharing and creation systems
- New forms of interaction in knowledge sharing and creation systems
- Collaborative filtering
- Semantic Desktops
- Social Network Analysis to support implicit learning and sharing within educational environments
- Analysis of Large Online Communities for Building Intellectual Capital
- Web Communities of Practice for Sharing, Creating, and Learning
- Implicit, Formal, and Powerful Semantics in Communities of Practice
- Metadata and Annotation Techniques for Automated Support of Collaborative Learning

Semantic Web and Social Networking Advanced Themes for Health

A more focused exploration of literature concerning the exploitation of Semantic Web and Social Networking will be performed covering topics like:

- Semantic Networking for Health, pharmaceutical and clinical Information systems.
- Knowledge Management supported ubiquitous and pervasive applications for health, pharmaceutical and clinical sectors.
- Knowledge Portals/Spaces and Grids for health, pharmaceutical and clinical sectors.
- Knowledge Management for Reference Health Information.
- Knowledge Management for Evidence based Medicine.
- KM for Clinical Decision Support.
- Knowledge Acquisition and Authoring of Clinical Guidelines and Rules.

- Knowledge Maintenance and Versioning of Clinical Knowledge such as Order Sets and Templates, Clinical Documentation Templates, Clinical Rules, Reminders and Alerts, etc.
- Ontology-based Knowledge Management as applied to Clinical Practice.
- Discovery of Knowledge in Clinical Databases as applied to Knowledge Management.
- Meta-information descriptions for the management of clinical information assets and its applications to learning and practical use.
- Knowledge and Learning Management Applications for life long learning in health sectors.
- Mobile Knowledge Agents for health services.

Semantic Knowledge Management

- Use of Semantics in Knowledge Services and Service Science (where the technical, human and organizational aspects of services are considered)
- Engineering of ontologies for Knowledge Management and Services
- Architectures, Algorithms and representations for Semantic Web approaches to Organizational Information Systems
- Organizational knowledge integration or organizing domain knowledge using ontologies, semantic metadata and other semantic capabilities
- Design and modelling of Semantic Web Resource or Service repositories and distributed knowledge-based systems in the organizational context
- Business Modelling and Business processes as mediated by Semantic technology with support for technical, human and organizational components
- Ontologies related to organizational and people/participants, including competencies and competency description standards and schemas, and their application to organizational memory and organizational learning, and productivity or collaboration enhancements
- Practical frameworks of organizational value as associated to Semantic Web technology
- Semantic Technology in the framework of organizational learning and organizational behaviour.
- Use of semantic technology to enhance knowledge access and re-use
- Use of semantic technology to promote knowledge sharing and collaboration

4. The Pan-European Healthcare Observatory: Architecture, Services, Business Model

EPIONE summarizes leading edge theoretical and technological, approaches and will exploit a sustainable business model. One of the most disappointing realities in 5th and 6th Frameworks of the European Commission is the termination of offered “services” of funded projects after the completion of their duration. It seems that the exploitation frameworks are so weak that cannot find “anchors” to the society and the business to capitalize on the promises of sound propositions and innovations.

In EPIONE the sustainable model is based on the line of SOCIAL RESPONSIBILITY and with an multidimensional sponsoring program the services of EPIONE will be supported from pharmaceutical companies, government organizations, IT companies and Non Government Organizations.

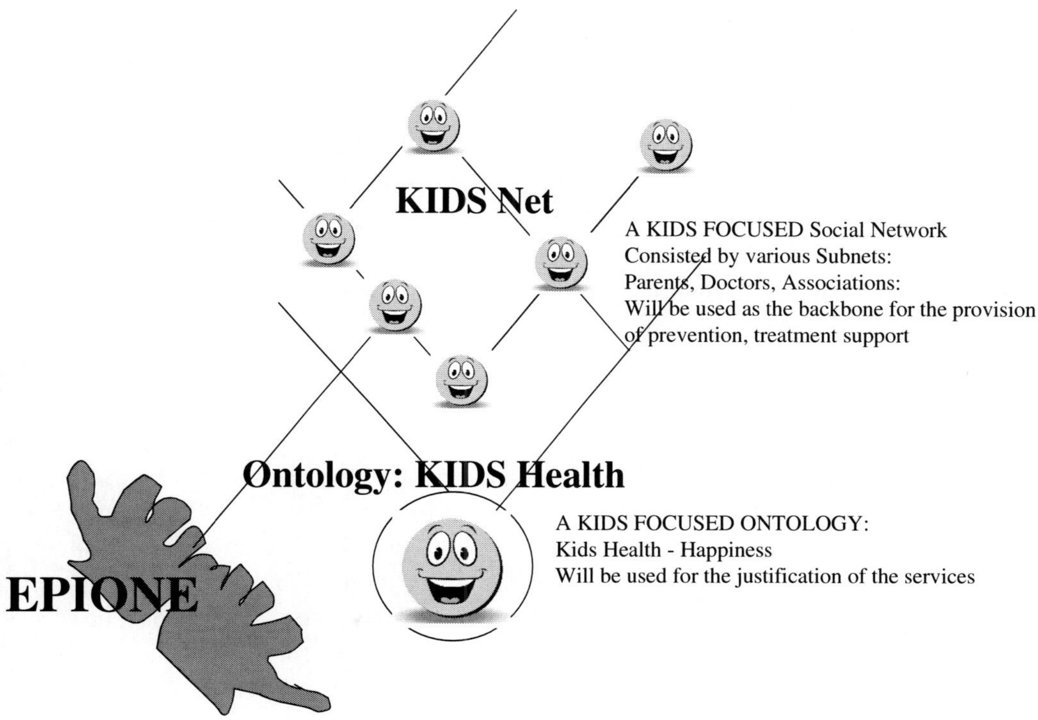

Concerning the value offering and the unique value proposition of EPIONE we will summarize the key deliverables in the next paragraphs.

In fact there are a number of social challenges that go beyond the scope of this paper.

Knowledge Level

KIDS Ontology: All the knowledge codification will be build on the top of a kid’s ontology, which will summarize all the concepts related to the health and psychology of kids. In a way the Kids Health and Psychology Identity will be exploit KIDS Ontology and will provide a long-term knowledge asset. The challenging aspect of kids ontology is the “modularity” where specific sub-ontologies will summarize the knowledge aspects of sub domains like diseases, prevention, treatment, drugs, doctors, etc. These basic constructs will be used as the basis for the justification of personalization. In simple words the exploitation of the concepts and relations in Ontology will be used for the design and support of meaningful knowledge Transfers.

KIDS Consultation, Prevention, Treatment, Support and Emergency Network: One of the greatest challenges of EPIONE relates with the design and management of a European

Technological Enabled Social Network aiming to bring together several stakeholders and to provide significant services to various beneficiaries. By exploiting leading edge approaches in Semantic Social Networking the EPIONE's network is a knowledge intensive network where knowledge creation and use are promoted with a service-oriented perspective. Within this network several "entities" provide the critical backbone:

- Doctors
- Parents [And Parents Associations]
- Psychologists
- School Authorities
- Associations
- Experts [e.g. related with special care needs e.g. Dyslexia, etc]
- Government Policy Makers
- Health Managers
- Health Organization Representatives
- Pharmaceutical Representatives
- Non Government Organizations
- … [more]

The main characteristic of the EPIONE social network is the orientation to kids. Each of these categories contributes to the discussion and collaborative building of kids ontology contributing to the "agenda" of the issues that summarize the KIDS health entity. So in fact a kind of a *Consultation, Prevention, Treatment, Support and Emergency Network* with thousands of peers give to EPIONE an excellent capacity for addressing general or special issues. Towards this direction the EPIONE's Observatory set services, technologies and managerial processes as well as a business model aiming to:

- To increase the knowledge performance towards excellent quality health services to kids at Europe
- To increase the efficiency of learning for individuals and groups
- To facilitate transfer and sharing of knowledge
- To contribute to a deeper understanding of the learning process by exploring links between human learning, cognition and technologies

Technology Level

To meet the various social challenges is a leading issue of research in EPIONE on the use of technology to support health and personalized services. According to Lytras and Sakkopoulos (2007) the exploration of SW and KM for health can be organized according to the following pillars.

Knowledge Management Key themes:

- Social Networks/Knowledge Networking
- Context-Awareness
- Ubiquity and Pervasiveness
- Open Source Software
- Intelligent knowledge and learning infrastructures

Semantic Web Key issues:

- Semantics
- Ontological Engineering
- Semantic Web Services
- Intelligent Agents / Interoperability
- Rules/Logic/Trust
- Emerging Topic

Develop an ontology that will be the specification of a conceptualisation of the knowledge domain of European HealthCare for Kids. This ontology, or schema, will aggregate in one place knowledge from several European countries. This requires a deep study of HealthCare. The ontology will capture aspects of real-world or domain semantics, as well as represent ontological commitment forming the basis of semantic normalization. This effort will include the development of controlled vocabularies that describe services and products, and will involve developing tools to create, maintain, and use distributed ontologies. Significant effort will be paid also in Ontology integration, Ontology merging, Ontology alignment. It is also required to de define new engineering methods for the construction and maintenance of distributed ontologies.

Technology Level

Personalized Services

Kid Level:

- Registration, and update of Kid Health Identity
- Consultation, Prevention, Treatment
- Personal Development, Surveys on Psychographics
- Diagnosis of early childhood special needs
- Learning by Doing, Interacting and Collaborating [Virtual Space for constructive activities
- Personal Development Plans and Activities
- Protection [ubiquitous monitor of kids presence – a simple system for monitoring losses, kids evanescence]
- Emergency System
- E-Ambulance

Parents Level:

- Consultation
- Personalized support
- Personalized advices for "Network"
- Communities of Interests
- Collaborative filtering
- Opinion Publication Network
- Personalized Learning Services

Doctors:

- Virtual Symposiums
- Collaborative authoring
- Wikis / Blogs
- Requests for advices
- Personalized Learning Services
- Dynamic Linkage of learning resources

Health Institutions:

- Alliance Programs
- Provision of Services
- Management of Health Identity

Government Organizations:

- Consultation
- Partnership programs

Associations /Non Government Organizations:

- On-demand Services [e.g. specific services for KIDs @ AFRICA]

Academia:

- Learning Services for Students in Medical Schools
- Open Knowledge/Open Access Journals

Press/Journalism:

- Open Knowledge/Open Access Journals

Table 1. A strategic map for policy consultation and government action in Health Domain

	Social Networks/ Knowledge Networking	Context-Awareness	Ubiquity and Pervasiveness:	Open Source Software	Intelligent knowledge and learning infrastructures
Semantics	Semantics of People (Liu et al, 2006) Description of Profiles and annotations of relations [Rafaeli et al (2007)]	Semantics of Contexts Analysis of requirements for the Semantics of the Business processes in Health [Carrion G. (2006)] Definition of Contexts in Semantic Terms [Hädrich T& Priebe T, (2005)]	Mobile Semantics Annotations of huge non textual clinical knowledge	Semantics on the move Exploitation of FOSS for the development of scalable, and economic solutions	Semantic annotations of learning content (Brusilovsky et al, (2006); Jonassen D. (2006); Andric M. et al (2007); Porto et al (2007),,] Integration of technology enhanced learning with key business systems (Ordonez de Pablos, 2006) [Lytras M., Pouloudi N., (2006)]
Ontological Engineering	Ontologies for Health Domain – Integration/development of a KM ontology for health [Cristani, M. and Cuel, R. (2005)]	Collaborative Modelling Conceptual Modelling	Building ontologies towards ubiquitous Electronic Health Records	Support for ontology handling within open data management systems [Hósemann, & Vossen (2006)]	Automatic ontology and learning objects matching (Jovanovic et al, 2006), (Tun et al, 2006)
Semantic Web Services	Semantic web services for health social networks – design of core capacities	Provision of semantic web services with emphasis on clustering and segmentation	Integration of Ubiquitous and pervasive computing with Semantic Web services	Web Services Semantic Description support Frameworks Open Approaches / Open Knowledge Services	Dynamic service composition based on learning semantics to support curricula and educational administration issues [Sheth A. & Lytras M. (2007)]

Table 1. (Continued)

	Social Networks/ Knowledge Networking	Context-Awareness	Ubiquity and Pervasiveness:	Open Source Software	Intelligent knowledge and learning infrastructures
Intelligent Agents / Interoperability	Personalized Health Services / Integration of the Supply and Demand for knowledge in Health [Bicer et al. (2005), Eichelberg, M. et al (2005), Shabo, A. & Hughes, K.S., (2005)]	Knowledge drilling across platform environments in health IS	Pervasive computing interoperability using semantic enhanced agent for autonomous machine communication (O'Sullivan et al, 2003)	Interoperability for description based consumption of services and remote objects	Multimedia learning objects for laboratory activities retrieval and integration (Hósemann et al, 2006); Dou W et al. (2007),
Rules/Logic /Trust	Trusted networks / Rule languages for the health domain/ Emphasis on clustering [Bassiliades et al (2006)]	Identity Management in Multiple Contexts / Integration and Reasoning	Pervasive Anonymity	Open Web Services licensing foundation and security infrastructure	Learning Designs and Learning profiles in Health Albano G et al (2006); Jeon S. et al (2007)
Emerging Topics	e-Health 2.0	Anonymity in context based knowledge mining	Ubiquitous e-health card Ubiquitous e-health social service id	Open Web Services embracement	Open Knowledge, Open content, Semantic Based Knowledge and Learning Infrastructures Global online learning communities Hill R. (2007) Inclusion

Examples

The following are very few services that can be build on the top of the previous mentioned capacities:

- Establish social networks for kids from different countries
- Establish social networks for parents with kids with the same diseases
- Establish social networks for doctors treating kids with the same diseases.
- Information on the treatments that kids need to receive in each European country
- Advice parents on what procedures need to be taken care of if moving inside Europe with kids.
- Determine which drugs are available in the origin country but not at destination.

A detailed Architecture and a Business Plan are currently under development. An FP7 Proposal is planned for submission in the 1st Call of FP7.

5. EPIONE for a Humanistic Vision: Health for All at a Fair Price

EPIONE has a great potential. But many times everything in our modern societies is a matter of good timing. We do believe that EPIONE is a timely proposition with critical social value, with capacities and services targeting in a long future provision and not at all an opportunistic gathering of capacities for funding.

We must proceed and we all must be "partners" in a humanistic vision:
Health For All at a fair price. A better world with kids in safe and health.

References

Albano G., Gaeta M., Salerno S. (2006), E-learning: a model and process proposal, *International Journal of Knowledge and Learning* 2006 - Vol. 2, No.1/2 pp. 73 - 88.

Andric M. Devedzic V. Hall W, Carr L. (2007), Keywords linking method for selecting educational web resources a la ZigZag, *International Journal of Knowledge and Learning* 3(1): 30 - 45.

Barranquero Tolosa, J., Labra Gayo, J.E., Martínez Prieto, A.B., Méndez Núñez, S. and Ordóñez de Pablos, P. (2010), "Interactive web environment for collaborative and extensible diagram based learning", *Computers in Human Behaviour*, Vol. 26, Issue 2, pp. 210-217.

Bicer, V.; Kilic, O.; Dogac, A. and Laleci, G.B., (2005), Archetype-Based Semantic Interoperability of Web Service Messages in the Health Care Domain, in *International Journal of Semantic Web and Information Systems* (IJSWIS), Vol. 1, Issue 4, pp: 1-23.

Cristani, M., Cuel, R. (2005), A Survey on Ontology Creation. Methodologies, in International Journal of Semantic Web and Information Systems (IJSWIS), Vol. 1, Issue 2, pp: 49-69.

Eichelberg, M., Aden, T, Thoben, W., (2005), A Distributed Patient Identification Protocol Based on Control Numbers with Semantic Annotation, in *International Journal of Semantic Web and Information Systems* (IJSWIS), Vol. 1, Issue 4, pp: 24-43.

Fabio Porto, Ana Maria De Carvalho Moura, Fabio Jose Coutinho Da Silva, Adriana Pereira Fernandez (2007), The ROSA project: leveraging e-learning to a semantic layer, *International Journal of Knowledge and Learning* 3(1): 46 – 75.

Hädrich T, Priebe T, (2005), A Context-Based Approach for Supporting Knowledge Work with Semantic Portals, in *International Journal of Semantic Web and Information Systems* (IJSWIS), Vol. 1, Issue 3, pp: 64-88.

Hill R. (2007), Reflections on resource-based learning environments: continuing the exploration of opportunities and obstacles, *International Journal of Knowledge and Learning* 3(1): 12 – 29.

Hósemann, B.; Vossen, G. (2006), "OntoMedia— Semantic Multimedia Metadata Integration and Organization", *International Journal on Semantic Web and Information Systems,* Vol. 2, No. 3, pp. 1-16.

Jonassen D. (2006), Accommodating ways of human knowing in the design of information and instruction, *International Journal of Knowledge and Learning* 2006 - Vol. 2, No.3/4, pp. 181 – 190.

Jovanovic, J.; Gasevic, D.; Devedzic, V. (2006), "Ontology-Based Automatic Annotation of Learning Content", *International Journal on Semantic Web and Information Systems,* Vol. 2, No. 2, pp. 91-119.

Labra Gayo, J.E., Ordóñez de Pablos, P. and Cueva Lovelle, J.M (2010): "WESONET: Applying Semantic Web Technologies and Collaborative Tagging to Multimedia Web Information Systems", *Computers in Human Behaviour*, Vol. 26, Issue 2, pp. 205-209.

Liu, H.; Maes, P.; Davenport, G. (2006), "Unraveling the Taste Fabric of Social Networks", *International Journal on Semantic Web and Information Systems*, Vol. 2, No. 1, pp. 42 – 71.

Lytras M., Pouloudi N., (2006), "Towards the development of a novel taxonomy of knowledge management systems from a learning perspective". *Journal of Knowledge Management,* Accepted for publication in Vol. 10(6): 64-80.

Lytras, M.D. and Ordóñez de Pablos, P. (2009): *Social Web Evolution. Integrating Semantic Applications* and Web 2.0 Technologies IGI-Global.

N. Bassiliades, G. Antoniou, I. Vlahavas (2006), A Defeasible Logic Reasoner for the Semantic Web, *International Journal on Semantic Web and Information Systems*, Vol. 2, No. 1, pp. 1-41, 2006.

Ordóñez de Pablos, P., Lytras, M.D., Lee, W-B. and Karwoski, W. (2010):"*Electronic Globalized Business and Sustainable Development through IT Management: Strategies and Perspectives",* IGI-Global.

Peter Brusilovsky, Judith Knapp, and Johann Gamper (2006), "Supporting teachers as content authors in intelligent educational systems", in the *Int. J. of Knowledge and Learning*, Vol. 2, No. 3and4, pp. 191 – 215.

Rafaeli S., Raban D., Ravid G. (2007), How social motivation enhances economic activity and incentives in the Google Answers knowledge sharing market, *International Journal of Knowledge and Learning* 3(1): 1-11.

Rodríguez González, A., Jiménez, E., Radzimski, M., Gómez, J.M, Alor-Hernández, G., Posada-Gómez, R., Labra Gayo, J.E. (2009b): Applying Caching Capabilities to

Inference Applications Based on Semantic Web. 1st International Conference on Collective Intelligence - Semantic Web, Social Networks and Multiagent Systems, Studies in Computational Intelligence 244 Springer 2009: 27-37, Wroclaw, Poland.

Rodríguez González, A., Labra Gayo, J.E, Alor-Hernández, G., Gómez, J.M. and Posada-Gómez, R. (2009a): ADONIS: Automated diagnosis system based on sound and precise logical descriptions. *Proceedings of the Twenty-Second IEEE International Symposium on Computer-Based Medical Systems,* August 3-4, 2009, Albuquerque, New Mexico, USA. IEEE 2009, 1-8.

Sanghyun S. Jeon, Gilliean Lee, Samsun (Sem) Lampotang, Stanley Y.W. Su (2007), An integrated e-learning system for simulation-based instruction of anaesthesia machines, *International Journal of Knowledge and Learning* 3(1): 106-120.

Shabo, A. and Hughes, K.S., (2005), Family History Information Exchange Services Using HL7 Clinical Genomics Standard Specifications, in *International Journal of Semantic Web and Information Systems* (IJSWIS), Vol. 1, Issue 4, pp: 44-67.

Sheth, A. and Lytras, M. (2007) Semantic Web-based Information Systems: State of the Art Applications (Advances in Semantic Web and Information Systems), Cybertech Publishing, Hersey, USA.

Sicilia M., Lytras M., Rodríguez E., García-Barriocanal E., (2006), Integrating descriptions of knowledge management learning activities into large ontological structures: *A case study, in Data and Knowledge Engineering,* Volume 57, Issue 2, pp: 111-121.

Wanchun Dou, Xiping Liu, Guihai Chen, S.C. Cheung, Shijie Cai, (2007), Knowledge flow management supporting complex problem solving: learning spectrum and its infrastructure, *International Journal of Knowledge and Learning* 3(1): 88-105.

Zhao J., Ordóñez de Pablos P. (2009) School innovative management model and strategies: The perspective of organizational learning', *Information Systems Management*, Vol. 26, Issue 3, pp.241 – 251.

Zhao, J. and Ordóñez de Pablos. P. (2010a). Analysis of cooperative mechanism of industry-academy RandD alliance lab and case study, *Human Factors and Ergonomics in Manufacturing,* March-April, Vol. 20, Issue 2, pp. 123-134-.

Zhao, J-Y., and Ordóñez de Pablos, P. (2011): "Regional Knowledge Management: the Perspective of Management Theory", *Behaviour and Information Technology*, Special Issue, forthcoming.

In: HRM and Marketing Orientation in the New Era
Editor: Panagiotis Kyriazopoulos
ISBN: 978-1-62808-959-2

Chapter 3

FACTORS INFLUENCE B2B RELATIONSHIPS IN MEDIUM-SIZED FIRMS: TRADITIONAL VS. E-COMMERCE

Irene Samanta*
University of the West of Scotland, UK

ABSTRACT

The advent of the internet has created numerous opportunities for marketing professionals to enhance current marketing practices, including electronic relationships. However, the investigation of e-relationships and the factors from the e-marketing point of view that influence e-relationships in an internet environment are scant. Furthermore, there appears to be no investigation of this phenomenon within the context of Greek Business to Business Medium-sized firms (MSF).

The literature does not investigate this research problem in any depth. However, a framework about the role of the business today in a changing globalized environment, the shift from 'old' to 'new' world of business B2B relationships in an e-business context, the strategic features of buyer-supplier relationships and relationship marketing in the existing literature were investigated.

To investigate these research issues, a quantitative research was contacted. The sample comprised of forty (40) companies. The split is as follows: twenty of them make use of e-commerce (20-e-commerce) and the remaining twenty do not (20-traditional). Amongst the 20-e-commerce companies, there are 10 that are buyers and 10 that are sellers/suppliers. We have the same type split amongst the 20-traditional companies. Data was analyzed and the hypotheses specified were tested using statistical techniques. The findings of this research have implications for the three research issues. The results of the research showed that moving on to the findings regarding the B2B relationships that are complemented by e-commerce practices, we understand that a number of our original hypotheses reject and in some cases, we see no divergence between traditional and e-commerce businesses. The conclusions of our research revealed that in post-industrial eRa MSFs' strategic objectives remain the same whether operating in an e-commerce or

* E-mail: isamanta@teipir.gr.

in a traditional environment. MSFs are differentiating their tactics and means used to face the intense competition which is characterized by the globalization of markets.

The main contribution of this research is the development and confirmation of a final theoretical framework about e- relationships in -sized B2B firms.

Keywords: B2B medium-size firms, relationships, e-marketing

INTRODUCTION

Nowadays, electronic business (e-business) includes thousands of companies which provide a tremendous number of products for electronic markets. Unlike the traditional markets, the electronic markets allow the participants to easily compare the offers and perform business processes faster. The adoption of e-business technologies and practices in firms has transformed the nature of business transactions. Many Business to Business (B2B) activities are shifting to the online environment, where stakeholders are enabled to access a variety of information and services which can be considered as a key element of their competitiveness (Chung et al., 2003). As e-business applications become commonplace and more sophisticated, B2B firms are facing the problem of software integration and the difficulty of efficiently designing and implementing their business process.

On the other hand, the use of the Internet is being increasingly expanded in B2B relationships in order to improve effective communication, distribution, and streamline processes with customers and stakeholders. As Chung et al (2003) stated, a firm going global through the use of the Internet should take into consideration some important factors defining an e-marketing strategy as well as redefining the organization's internal processes, since the Internet has changed the rules of traditional business.

Some scholars (Ratnasingam and Pavlou, 1998) have argued that the Internet has created a new marketing arena, by moving organizations closer to their customers. In the world of e-marketing, success is defined by the firm's ability to build long-term customer relationships that bring value to the customers and stakeholders and sustain profitability to the organization. Despite the fact that the Internet can enhance relationships, it can also have a detrimental effect on them if the appropriate strategy is not applied (Stahl, 2002). Technology alone cannot provide a magic solution that will immediately resolve all e-marketing challenges. According to Strauss et al. (1999), an important element in defining the strategy to adopt for e-marketing and e-business in general, resides in determining the company's initial level of commitment.

B2B Internet marketing includes the use of all three forms of e-commerce (Internet, Intranet and Extranet) for purchasing goods and services, buying information and consulting services, as well as submitting requests for proposals and receiving proposals (Zinchan, 2002). B2B Internet- based technologies provide effective and efficient ways through which corporate buyers can gather information rapidly about available products and services, evaluate and negotiate with suppliers, implement order fulfillment over communication links and access post-sales services (Wright, 2004). From the supplier's side, marketing, sales, and service information is also readily gathered from customers (Zinchan, 2002). This application of Internet-based systems for improving the supply chain performance forms the basis of B2B e-commerce. It could be suggested that pace of change in this area has been rapid, making it difficult for companies to examine thoroughly the advantages and disadvantages of different ways of managing inter-firm relationships.

Therefore, Business to Business Internet marketing has received widespread attention as one of the key drivers in sustaining an organization's competitive advantage. On the other hand, the development of Internet usage has experienced transformations particularly in the area of expectations of organizations for creating value within a supply chain. This allows businesses to extend their relationships with customers, suppliers, retailers, brokers, co-producers, employees and shareholders, and achieve a more personalized relationship with them (Stahl, 2002). The development of such personalized relationships is a key goal of marketing, because they tend to be more sustainable.

As a conclusion, the new economy seems to be changing the world dramatically. It creates new possibilities for development in countries such as Greece. It creates a global economy obliging everyone to be properly prepared to confront the pressures of international competition. The responsibilities of both state and the business world are immense and any delays will have a negative affect on both industry and government.

The main reason, therefore, behind the decision to adopt this topic is the belief that it may be valuable in Greece, by identifying that there is a lack of research to date in this studied area.

This research project aims to gain a generic understanding of practices of factors from the e- marketing point of view influence business-to-business relationships in Greece. In this significant part of the "brave new world", the businesses in Greece are asked to answer the call for further development and modernization of their practices. From this standpoint, specific information on B2B Internet marketing, and business-to-business relationships and processes will be gathered to provide a better understanding of the issues at stake. It will then be possible to devise a comprehensive framework, based on literature, and a review of the pertinent to arrive at partial answers to the research questions. Emergent concepts, theories or hypotheses from the research will be compared with the extisting literature in order to note consistencies with and departures from other findings.

LITERATURE REVIEW

Business to Business Relationships

Business-to-Business (B2B) relationships are widely researched in a marketing context. They are defined as markets where a business markets and sells goods and services to another business for use by the customer, or for resale to other customers (Amit and Zott, 2001). According to (Wang et al.2000), there are five groups of factors that need consideration in relation to business networks. These are:

a) Characteristics of the relationships and interactions in which a firm is involved
b) Characteristics of a firm's relationship partners
c) Characteristics of connected relations and their interactions
d) Characteristics of a firm's network positions
e) Characteristics of the network as a whole

These factors influence the potential success and longevity of a relationship. In general, business-to-business relationships tend to be relatively long-term and stable overall; it is the interaction of the stakeholders that impact on the exchange within the relationship (Stahl, 2002).

A prime objective of relationship marketing is to create superior customer value at the one-to-one level. The premise is that while it is impossible to have a relationship with a market or even a segment, it may be possible to establish a relationship with an individual customer or consumer (Wright, 2004). In B2B environments, there has been a noticeable trend towards customers seeking to do business with suppliers on an entirely different basis from in the past.

Historically, companies would have multiple suppliers so as not to keep in a long-term dependency while information sharing was minimal. Today, there are signs that this almost adversarial approach to buyer/seller relations may be changing. The emphasis now is on reducing the supplier base, moving sometimes to single sourcing for any one item; and working much more collaboratively, supported by transparent information (Wright, 2004).

Companies have changed their approach because they have realized that they can greatly enhance the efficiency and effectiveness of their supply chain through collaborative working (Hofacker and Jamie, 1998). Conventional supply chains are based upon each entity - whether buying or selling organization - seeking to optimize their own operations. Such approaches have led to resources and assets being duplicated, and have even resulted in sub-optimization across the chain as a whole. Conventional wisdom suggests that those companies with the greatest internal resources and capabilities will gain competitive advantage, but the new school of thought recognizes the mutual dependencies between organizations and the importance of leveraging the combined capabilities of the supply chain as a whole (Hofacker, 1998). Watson et al (2000) show that the relationships are defined by the ultimate success or failure of the standard of commitment, trust and cooperation of the partners. Thus, each participant must be tuned-in to their partner's needs and should bring into line its expectancies and objectives with its partners' expectations (Spekman et al., 1998).

Gummersson, (1987 recognized four forms of relationships and examined matters at a strategic and tactical level. At the strategic level, firms are encouraged to form partnerships, alliances, and networks (Palumbo and Herbig, 1998). From a tactical level, it is necessary for firms to engage in direct contact with buyers and sellers. Also, according to Naude and Holland (1996), in order to benefit, firms need to have a customer-oriented service system and to interact with each other on a one-to-one basis. Special emphasis was given to how cooperative relationships in networks, as opposed to adversarial relationships, can support companies to be centered on their core competence and raise their competitive advantage.

Consequently, the development of e-relationships in B2B industries has been accelerated by the up-growth of technology that joins organizations to their partners in their demand and supply chains. A link process among firms maximizes the creative value of information and communication exchanges which are unique and rich and are not easily replicated (Straus and Forest, 1999). The main aim of this thesis is to encourage B2B firms to develop successful e-relationships between buyers and sellers that have, or intend to adopt, an e-marketing philosophy and to implement these practices in order to satisfy the needs of both buyer and seller. Relationships are widely accepted to result in coordination and integration of a firm's electronic transactions (Straus and Forest, 1999).

In an ever changing and often unstable business, environment B2B companies must constantly challenge their own thinking. Ultimately, companies wishing to stay in the 'comfort zone' are not going to be around for long. Stagnation is, therefore, the ultimate threat for a B2B business, while the ability to reinvent the organization has become a main goal. As Peter Solvik, Senior Vice-President and Chief Information Officer of Cisco Systems, put it, "The new economy is about reinventing how business is conducted –in every single job, in every single corporation. There's a revolution going on, and we have to rethink every single relationship within the company and beyond" (Remeyni et al, 1998).

The extent to which the proposed strategy of the party taking the initiative in trying to set up a partnership is implemented is partly in the hands of the other party. Steps to promote and develop the relationship, together with the negotiation approaches employed, need to be adapted to the responses of the other party. Suppliers accustomed to traditional adversarial attitudes and negotiating stances may be suspicious and reluctant to change, at least at first (Remeyni et al, 1998).

Successful partnerships, are likely to occur when both sides have common 'hearts and minds', as well as their formal pronouncements, to making them work.

There does appear to be grounds for this apprehension, in the light of some experiences, in which a dominant party has used an apparent partnership policy. Some suppliers may retain fundamental objections to the more open methods of the partnership philosophy and prefer not to change their ways. Not all firms, therefore, will prove to be good candidates for a partnership arrangement. Buyers will need to decide whether there are more favorable alternatives or whether they will need to continue on a more traditional basis. The relative strength of a buyer's negotiating position in the supply marketing together with the negotiating ability of the buyer, will determine whether resistance of a reluctant supplier can be overcome and a genuine conversion effected (Lockett and Blackman 2001).

Business relationships play a significant role in the business enterprise arena. The former can even determine the degree of a company's success regarding its performance as the sale volume market shares growth and profitability.

Many of the aspects of supplier- buyer appraisal are neatly summarized by Christopher et al (1991) as the ten Cs of effective Supplier –Buyer relationships as follows:

1. Competence of the supplier/purchaser to undertake the tasks required
2. Capacity to meet the supplier/purchaser total needs
3. Commitment of the supplier/purchaser in terms of quality, cost driving and service
4. Control systems in respect of inventory, costs, budgets, people and information
5. Cash resources and financial stability ensuring that the selected supplier is financially sound and is able to continue in business into the foreseeable future.
6. Cost- commensurate with quality and service
7. Consistency –the facility of the supplier to deliver consistently and, where possible, to improve levels of quality and service.

Three further Cs identified by Carter (2001) are:

1. Culture –suppliers and buyers should share similar values
2. Clean –suppliers and purchasers should satisfy legislative and other environmental requirements

3. Communication – can the supplier communicate and receive information electronically?

B2B Relationships in E-Business Network

In Business to Business (B2B) transactions, Internet is a necessity as it enhances firm's corporate presence (Adam., 1998). Almost 90% of enterprises across Europe use their own web site to market their products (Eurostat, 2006).

Alternatively, e-commerce across industries (e.g manufacturing, banking and finance, wholesale and retail Distribution) reflects the ability of companies to increase profitability and productivity. That is why almost half of firms' purchases occur online in a European basis (European Commission, 2005). The main reason is that it improves communication among partners along a value chain business model (Adam., 1998) predicting market changes occurred by the increased competition in the same industry. This is also confirmed by a research conducted by Eurostat across Europe in 2005, which revealed that 36% of enterprises use Internet medium for buying goods and using services whereas 62% of enterprises are represented on the web chiefly for the purpose of marketing their products (Eurostat, 2006). The understanding of the changes from the business environment is becoming imperative, and has been defined as 'the subjective probability by which an organization believes that the underlying technology infrastructure and control mechanisms are capable of facilitating inter-organizational transactions' (Ratnasingam,1998).

Therefore, according to Berry (1983), the development of e-marketing strategies in B2B transactions has affected relationships quite drastically, allowing more competition and more control over processes and employees. According to Berry (1983), the rapid alterations of the business environment mainly influence B2B relationships and this thesis is an attempt to identify the firms' intentions to deal with these changes. Based on strategic issues focused on marketing, proportionately to the positive or negative response of B2B firms, we can then identify how firms move from the traditional to the new era in order to develop successful relationships. Deregulation of markets and increasing global competition are two factors that are associated with the global restructuring of companies. A major issue for most of these companies is the innovation and creation of better ways of doing business.

Business Internet marketing is one tactic used to achieve this objective and has emerged as one of the key drivers in sustaining a firm's competitive advantage. It means that the Internet has eliminated the barriers so that many firms can operate globally. B2B firms endeavour to improve the execution of business transactions by streamlining inter-organizational operations system (IOS) networks and applications. In order to face the influence of globalization, the intense competition and the new technologies in B2B electronic commerce, firms should redefine their strategy to increase customer satisfaction and to achieve better corporate decision-making, greater economic efficiency and more rapid exchange of information (Wang et al, 2000).

The business rationale for using B2B e-commerce can be explained by the simple equation: profit = revenue – cost. Therefore, businesses use technology to either lower cost or increase revenues in this changing business environment. Depending on how it is applied, B2B e-commerce can increase revenue by creating new profitable relationships in order to provide a better service to the customer (Wang et al, 2000).

With the increase in potential markets, however, come new challenges to the manager whose aim is to advance a firm's position. The advent of new competitors with globalization makes it difficult for managers to rest on their laurels and wait for their competitors to meet them halfway. This is especially important for managers in smaller firms, who are now facing competition from larger firms endowed with economies of scale. One thing managers need to initiate in global companies is establishing an element of trust within the company. While the customer is the most important part of any business, the employee should be viewed as the second most important part (Wang et al, 2000).

The Influence of B2B Electronic Exchange on Marketing

Wright (2004) has described the role of marketing in industries using the informatics technologies widely. The changes he suggested become feasible though the development of electronic expressions. Specifically, these changes include:

- Products adjusted to consumer's needs.
- Not linear, meaning not serially concomitant communication tactics.
- Electronic transfer of financial resources.
- Administration systems of databases for information management.
- Smaller distribution networks assigning major roles to the facilitators of
- Natural and information flow.
- Increased pressure to prices that lead to decreased prices.

These changes come from the development and the reinforcement of the competitive environment as well as from the introduction of informatics technologies. Straus and Frost (1999) schematized the alterations the marketing system undergoes so as to be evolved from the traditional form to the one depending on the electronic expression of the industry.

The electronic industry imprints that at the electronic market environment, the business activities and practices boosts the development and the administration of relationships with every customer individually, improving in this way, the focalization of the industry on the offer of more appropriate and more adjustable product solutions.

Informatics technologies have changed the nature of marketing dramatically. Hence, industries use informatics systems in order to accumulate data from selling points and telecommunication systems to establish the routes of the accumulated mass of information among the members of the supply net or among the supply chain and the distribution channel. The capabilities of the electronic linkage and distribution of information result in the acceleration and better time scheduling of the planning and producing procedures as well as of the natural flow of the products.

Internet allows the industries to address to the global market and not to be restricted to local or geographically defined markets. Information in reference to the purchasing behavior of the consumer is warehoused in knowledge bases. Knowledge bases are dynamic systems offering capabilities of completing and updating consumers' elements, data mining, formulating and extracting of conclusions, while it also has the capability of unimpeded and thorough disposal of such data to anywhere or anyone, according to the operational tactics of the industry. As a result, the knowledge bases allow the industries to create dynamic, adjustable profiles of departments of the market and the consumers, so as to derive information, which will allow them to plan more individually targeted or adjustable product solutions and better targeted communication plans (Zinkhan, 2002).

The combination of all of the capabilities given above create changes to the competitive environment and new occasional activity areas (Naude and Holland, 1996). Consequently, informatics technologies and internet allow the industries to readjust the business models and to differentiate their competitive practices.

RESEARCH METHODOLOGY

Sampling

In order to meet the above objectives, the quantitative approach was selected. The choice of representative probability simple random sampling is vital for this research in order to be achieved high degree of representative ness. The choice of probability sampling techniques is dependent on the feasibility and sensibility of collection data to answer research questions and to address objectives of the entire population. Furthermore, the results are projected to the total population, embodying the sampling error. The questionnaire is addressed to the high level management (i.e. CEO, general director, sales managers). The research intended to examine Greek businesses and the sample was formulated on the base of the 2342 Greek medium-sized companies according to the classification of Industrial and Commercial Chamber for 2004. The population of the MSFs (medium-sized firms) in greater area of Athens (Attica) comprises of 1525 firms.

We addressed 100 B2B firms and 40 companies responded. Therefore, our sample is comprised of forty (40) companies. The split amongst those is as follows: twenty of them make use of e-commerce (20-e-commerce) and the remaining twenty do not make use of e-commerce (20-traditional). Amongst the 20-e-commerce companies there are ten that are buyers and ten that are sellers/suppliers. We have the same type split amongst the 20-traditional companies.

Research Model

The companies filled out a 10-page questionnaire concerning their behavior either towards its suppliers or towards its clients. This sample of 40 volunteer companies is divided into 20 e-commerce and 20 traditional firms. The participants in the research hadn't expressed any difficulty in understanding the content, how to complete questions and easily responded. The aim of this preliminary research was to find out whether there are differences in behavior and how the companies treat suppliers and clients, depending on whether they are active in e-commerce or not. The questionnaire includes the following sections: The companies were asked to evaluate on a scale from 1 (zero significance) up to 5 (very significant) how important are the factors for the adoption of electronic business relations. The next two sections of the questionnaire are the selection criteria of buyers/suppliers and the characteristics of the selected client/supplier are described. Again, in a scale from 1 (zero significance) up to 5 (very significant), the companies were asked to evaluate the selection criteria and the characteristics of their partners in a five-degree scale where 1 is never and 5 is always. Also, the relationships with Buyers/Suppliers are examined and described on a scale from 1 (non influence) up to 5 (intense influence). Finally, the factors arising among seller/buyer in the various stages of electronic relationships are examined.

Research Hypothesis

The basic hypothesis of the research is to compare the answers of *e-commerce-buyers* and *e-commerce-sellers*: These are differentiations in e-commerce depending on whether they are sellers/suppliers or buyers. The same comparison is also made for the traditional firms.

Statistical Analysis

In the statistical analysis of the 40 companies, the descriptive statistics (the data was considered as numerical and proceed to the analysis of the mean values and standard deviation) and X^2 tests among the questions and the «*e-commerce*» - «*traditional*» were used. Finally, for the part of the questionnaire concerning the company relations among those using e-commerce and those who do not, the factor analysis was used. Factor analysis is a statistical method which aims to find common factors in groups of variables. Thus, by expressing those factors we reduced the problem's size. Instead of working with the initial variables, we work with fewer, since the factors are constructed in such a way so as to maintain, as possible, the information of the initial variables. We create new variables, the factors, in which in a subjective way, acknowledge some non-measurable variables such as intelligence in technology. Explaining the correlations in the data which we assumed are exclusively due to the existence of some common factors which created the data.

Research Findings

The companies were asked to evaluate on a scale from 1 (zero significance) up to 5 (very significant) how important are the factors (Table 1) to the adoption of electronic business relations.

From those 5 factors, we see that "pressure for lowering production costs" has the highest mean value - 4 (significant). The remaining factors are all above 3. Therefore, if we wanted to rank those factors based on the mean values, the first one would be "pressure for lowering costs", the next "lower price demand by clients"; something expected since clients always seek lower cost. Following are "globalization and market deregulation" and "competition".The last factor is "pressure from cooperators who have moved to e-commerce solutions", and its mean value is close to 3 which mean that this criterion may be considered indifferent for companies when deciding to adopt e-commerce.

In Table 2, we note that all criteria have a mean value higher than 4 and very close to 5. Also, all standard deviations are lower than 1 which means that there is no large deviation of the answers from the mean. This shows us that experience, solvency, cooperation, personalization and need satisfaction by the product are all considered significant up to very significant criteria. If we wanted to rank them, we could say that the most significant is the product satisfying the client's needs.

Table 1. Factors influence the adoption of electronic business relationships

Question		
	Mean score	Std. Deviation
Globalisation and market deregulation (q14)	3.73	1.086
Pressure by competition to the company (q15)	3.63	0.979
My clients ask for lower product prices (q16)	3.90	1.046
Pressure for lowering production costs (q17)	4.00	1.062
Pressure from cooperators who have moved to e-commerce solutions (q18)	3.28	0.987

Table 2. Selection criteria of buyers/suppliers

	Mean score	Std. Deviation
Product personalization to the clients' needs (q20.1)	4.20	0.823
Capability to satisfy exactly our specifications (q20.2)	4.63	0.490
Experience (q20.3)	4.36	0.707
Solvency (q20.4)	4.65	0.533
Cooperation (q20.5)	4.65	0.533
Product satisfying your needs (q20.6)	4.68	0.616

Followed closely by "solvency" and "cooperation", the same small difference follows the "capability of the product to cover absolutely our specifications". Experience as a criterion stands one place over the last criterion which is the product's personalization. From this ranking we conclude that the most significant characteristic for a product is to be able to satisfy the client's needs and the least important is to be personalized to the client's needs. One can draw the conclusion from this that clients prefer something ready that covers their needs than something that can be adapted to them.

Out of the 40 companies participating in the research, all have answered, and, in the third, 39 almost and, for all a majority record "very important". No company characterizes experience, solvency, cooperation, satisfaction of its specifications and needs as of no or little importance. We also note that "cooperation" and "solvency" have the same weight for the companies. Following is the "capability to exactly satisfy our specifications", then "experience" and finally, "personalization of the product to the clients' needs". As a conclusion, we may say that the most important is the product to satisfy their needs and of least importance is the personalization of the product to the clients' needs.

In the next section, the companies were asked for some characteristics of their selected client, if they are suppliers or their selected supplier if they are buyers. We see that there is considerable difference of the means depending on the characteristic. The first two *does the selected supplier/client fulfills his promises?* And *do you value his services?* Have a mean above 4, meaning often. Therefore, those are characteristics that the selected client/supplier should have. For the next characteristics, we see that the means are lower than 3 - specifically 2.5. This means that those are things that the selected client/supplier should do rarely or are indifferent (Table 3). From those 3 characteristics, the last in *order to achieve his own objectives, does the supplier/client fails sometimes to provide the appropriate support?* has a mean value of 2.58 – that is, close to 3 (indifferent).

Table 3. Characteristics of the selected buyers/suppliers

The selected client/supplier		
	Mean score	Std. Deviation
Is the selected supplier/client true to his promises?	4.10	0.591
Do you acknowledge his services?	4.30	0.687
Does the supplier/client modifies sometimes the agreed terms in order satisfy his objectives?	2.48	1.062
In order to satisfy his objectives, does the supplier/client promises sometimes things which eventually he does not realize?	2.48	0.960
In order to satisfy his objectives, does the supplier/client sometimes fails to provide the appropriate support?	2.58	0.958

Table 4 regards factors affecting company relationships with buyers/suppliers are being analyzed. The means and std. dev. of the eight most important factors according to the statistic results are shown. The factors *"Steady product quality in the long run"* and *"Consistency in product quality and specifications"* affect intensively the relations with buyers/suppliers. Followed with high influence are *"Forecast for shortening delivery times", "Timely product supply, as agreed", "Increased response to the supplier/buyer needs", "Improvement of the product's cost effectiveness" and "Lower prices when ordering higher quantities"*. We also note that influential of all factors is the company's fame. We notice that all means are higher than 3 with a lower value 3.25 and higher 4.33. The most important factors are the company's fame and the lower prices with a supply of increased products. Those factors have an intense influence on the relations developed among businesses. There follows the steady quality of the products in the long run, and after that, the improvement in cost effectiveness and the smaller delivery times. Timely supply and consistent quality have the same influence. None of the factors have zero influence. Therefore, they all contribute to the supplier/buyer relations.

Table 4. Factors influence B2B relationships

	Mean score	Std. Deviation
Forecast for shortening delivery times	3.73	0.716
Fame of the company for creating commercial relations	4.33	0.572
Steady quality in the long run	3.95	0.714
Timely product supply, as agreed	3.70	0.823
Consistency in quality and product specifications.	3.70	0.687
Increased response to supplier/client needs.	3.25	0.899
Improvement of product's cost effectiveness	3.83	0.931
Lower prices for increased quantity supply	4.13	0.833

The aim is to compare the answers of *e-commerce-buyers* and *e-commerce-sellers*: These are differentiations in e-commerce depending on whether they are Sellers/Suppliers or Buyers. The same comparison is also made for the traditional traders.

In (Table 5) we see the prices of X^2 tests among the questions and the "*e-commerce*" – "*traditional*". The aim is to compare the answers of *e-commerce-buyers* and *e-commerce-sellers* and the same comparison is also made for the traditional traders.

In the 2nd column, the value of the X^2 test statistic is presented and in the third column, we see the p-value for each. When this value is lower than 0.05 (we choose a significance level of 5%), then we accept that the variables are not independent. The Sig.value (p-value) in the 3rd column of the table is not lower than 0.05 in any question. Therefore, we accept the null hypothesis that the questions with the transaction type are independent. So, the factors affecting the adoption of electronic business relations have no correspondence to the fact that a company uses e-commerce or not.

Table 5. Factors influence the adoption of electronic business relationships between e-commerce - traditional B2B firms

Variables	(Q19) *e-commerce – traditional*	
	Pearson Chi-square	Approx. Sig.
Globalization and deregulation of the markets(q14)	9.424	0.051
Pressure of the competition to the company(q15)	1.905	0.753
My clients ask for lower product prices (q16)	6.041	0.196
Pressure for lowering production cost (q17)	3.059	0.548
Pressure from cooperators who have moved to e-commerce solutions (q18)	0.456	0.978

Table 6. Factors influence the adoption of electronic business relationships between e-commerce -buyers–e-commerce-sellers B2B firms (X^2 tests)

	Pearson Chi-square	Approx. Sig.
Globalization and market deregulation (q14)	7.705	0.103
Pressure by competition in the business (q15)	2.976	0.562
My clients ask for lower product prices (q16)	5.052	0.282
Pressure in order to reduce production cost (q17)	4.743	0.315
Pressure from cooperators who have adopted e-commerce solutions (q18)	2.500	0.645

Table 7. Factors influence the adoption of electronic business relationships between Traditional -Buyers–Traditional-Sellers B2B firms (X^2 tests)

	Pearson Chi-square	Approx. Sig.
Globalization and market deregulation (q14)	4.229	0.238
Pressure by competition in the business (q15)	4.152	0.245
My clients ask for lower product prices (q16)	2.667	0.446
Pressure in order to reduce production cost (q17)	0.800	0.670
Pressure from cooperators who have adopted e-commerce solutions (q18)	4.400	0.221

In (Table 6) we see the values of X^2 in column across the questions for the "*e-commerce-buyers*" and "*e-commerce sellers*" and in the following (Table 7), the comparison between "*traditional buyers*" – "*traditional sellers*". The value Sig. (p-value) in the 3rd column of the table is not less than 0. 05 for any question. Therefore, we accept the null hypothesis that the questions with the type of transaction (whether a company participates as buyer or as supplier/customer) are independent. Therefore, the factors affecting the adoption of electronic business relations have no connection with the fact that a company participates as Buyer or as Seller/Supplier. The same conclusion also arises among the traditional.

CRITERIA FOR THE SUPPLIER/CLIENT SELECTION

In order to examine the differentiations among the companies active in e-commerce and those who are not, for the criteria of supplier/client selection the statistical X^2 test is used (Table 8). The Approx. Sig. values are all higher than 0.05. We therefore accept the null hypothesis that there is no dependency among the questions and whether the companies undertake e-commerce or not. This shows us that companies doing e-commerce do not answer differently than those who do not.

The same test is also made for the supplier/customer selection criteria comparing "*e-commerce –buyers*"–"*e-commerce-sellers*". The values Approx. Sig. are all higher than 0.05. We therefore accept the null hypothesis that there is no dependence among the questions and whether the companies participate as buyers or sellers/suppliers.

Table 8. Criteria for the supplier/client selection between e-commerce-traditional B2B firms

Criterion	(Q19) *e-commerce – traditional*	
	Pearson Chi-square	Approx. Sig.
Product personalization to the clients' needs (q20.1)	1.250	0.741
Capability to satisfy exactly our specifications (q20.2)	0.107	0.744
Experience (q20.3)	2.316	0.314
Solvency (q20.4)	3.259	0.196
Cooperation (q20.5)	1.370	0.504
Product satisfying your needs (q20.6)	1.752	0.416

Table 9. Criteria for the supplier/client selection between e-commerce firms

	Pearson Chi-square	Approx. Sig.
Product personalization to the clients' needs (q20.1)	1.587	0.662
Capability to satisfy exactly our specifications (q20.2)	3.333	0.068
Experience (q20.3)	3.600	0.165
Solvency (q20.4)	1.562	0.585
Cooperation (q20.5)	0.220	0.639
Product satisfying your needs (q20.6)	3.325	0.333

This shows us that among the companies active in e-commerce, Buyers do not answer differently from Sellers/Suppliers (Table 9). We continue the analysis with the comparison among "*traditional*–buyers"–"*traditional-sellers*",The conclusion is the same among the companies using traditional ways of commerce of no significant difference (Table 10).

Table 10. Criteria for the supplier/client selection between traditional–buyers–traditional-sellers B2B firms

Criteria		
	Pearson Chi-square	Approx. Sig.
Product personalization to the clients' needs (q20.1)	5.778	0.123
Capability to satisfy exactly our specifications (q20.2)	0.220	0.639
Experience (q20.3)	0.573	0.751
Solvency (q20.4)	1.091	0.580
Cooperation (q20.5)	3.943	0.139
Product satisfying your needs (q20.6)	1.200	0.549

The Selected Client

The next step (Table 11) is to see whether the answers for the selected client/supplier are independent of whether a company makes e-commerce or not. All p-values are higher than 0.05. Therefore, the answers concerning the selected client/supplier are independent of the transaction type of the company (electronic or not).

Complementing this, X^2 tests were taken among the questions and the "*e-commerce-buyers*" – "*e-commerce-sellers*".The values are never lower than 0.05; therefore, the answers are not different among buyers and suppliers, given that both use the e-commerce. Proceeding with "*traditional–buyers*"–"*traditional-sellers*" comparisons again have no value lower than the test level (0.05). Therefore, we reach the conclusion that among the companies which do not use e-commerce, the answers of buyers and sellers/suppliers are also no different.

Table 11. Characteristics of their selected client between e-commerce – traditional

	Pearson Chi-square	Approx. Sig.
Is the selected supplier/client true to his promises?	1.034	0.793
Do you acknowledge his services?	1.048	0.790
Does the supplier/client modify sometimes the agreed terms in order satisfy his objectives?	5.213	0.157
In order to satisfy his objectives, does the supplier/client promise sometimes things which eventually he does not realize?	1.628	0.653
In order to satisfy his objectives, does the supplier/client sometimes fail to provide the appropriate support?	1.133	0.769

Relationships with Buyers/Suppliers

Regarding the transaction type of the companies (e-commerce-traditional) in Table 12 and the factors of question 22, there is a statistically significant (0.05) correlation only for factor *"Improvement of product's cost effectiveness"*. This conclusion comes out of the statistical check X^2. We compare the Sig. value with significance level 0.05.

It is necessary to define how strong or not is this link among *"Improvement of product's cost effectiveness"* and the "*e-commerce*" – "*traditional*". We shall use the Kendall's tau-c correlation coefficient which is for ordered data and nxm tables. The coefficient has a (0358) p-value 0.027(<0.05). We therefore do not accept the null hypothesis that the coefficient is not statistically different than zero. This means that the correlation among "Improvement of product's cost effectiveness" and the "*e-commerce*" – "*traditional*" is strong.

Table 12. Factors affecting B2B relationships between e-commerce – traditional

	Pearson Chi-square	Approx. Sig.
Forecast for shortening delivery times	7.619	0.055
Fame of the company for creating commercial relations	1.850	0.604
Steady product quality in the long run	0.582	0.748
Timely product supply, as agreed	2.727	0.256
Consistency in product quality and specifications.	0.373	0.830
Increased response to the supplier/client needs.	1.228	0.746
Improved product cost effectiveness	8.313	0.040
Lower prices when ordering higher quantities	5.315	0.150

Table 13. Factors affecting B2B relationships between e-commerce –Buyers and e- commerce-Sellers

	Pearson Chi-square	Approx . Sig.
Forecast for shortening the anticipated delivery times	2.091	0.554
Company fame for the creation of commercial relations	6.786	0.034
Product quality steady in the future	2.619	0.270
Timely product supply, within the time-frame agreed	1.111	0.574
Consistency in quality and specifications of the products.	5.590	0.061
Increased response to the supplier/client needs.	1.143	0.767
Improvement to the effectiveness of the product cost	5.757	0.352
Lower prices when supplying larger quantities	2.318	0.314

As above (Table 13), are made between "e-commerce buyers" and "e-commerce sellers" for the seven most important factors of question 22 using a X2 test, all results are insignificant with the exception of the criterion *"the fame of the business for the procedure of creating commercial relations"*. Therefore, the Buyers answer differently from the Sellers, given that both use e-commerce. For the Buyers, "*the fame of the business"* has some up to "high influence" in deciding to create business relations, while for the sellers/s suppliers, it has high up to intense influence. Therefore, for the sellers/suppliers it matters more compared to the Buyers.

In the "*traditional–buyers"–"traditional-sellers"* comparisons, there is no Sig value lower than the critical value (0.05). Therefore, we conclude that among the companies not using e-commerce, the answers of Buyers and Sellers/Suppliers are not different.

Factor Analysis

For the part of the questionnaire concerning the company relations among those using e-commerce and those who do not, the Factor analysis method was used. A basic condition for understanding factorial analysis is that the questions concerning the relations with Buyers/Suppliers have a strong correlation among them. The existence of strong correlations shows that there are some factors behind the questions which contain the information of the questions and at the same time, reduce the problem's size. If this condition is satisfied, we may proceed to Factor Analysis.

The Kaiser-Meyer-Olkin (KMO) Measure of Sampling Adequacy gives a value of 0.872 (quite above 0.5) which means that there are many correlations among the questions and we can apply a satisfactory model.

The Scree Plot (Figure 1) is a criterion for the multitude of the factors that are going to be used. We see that from the second eigenvalue, the graph starts turning into a straight line. That is, we can take the first two factors for the analysis of the data, and those suffice for the interpretation of questions 23-31.

Also, in the fluctuations table, we can see the ideal number of factors that can interpret the biggest percentage fluctuation of the variables. A good percentage is at least 65%. In the "Total Variance Explained" table, the two factors are able to interpret a 67.8% of the total fluctuation. For a better adaptation of the factors, the Varimax rotation method was used. Thus, we continue the analysis with two factors. The table "Anti-image matrices" has diagonal data over 0.05 and close to 1. The smaller value is 0.822 and the larger 0.922.

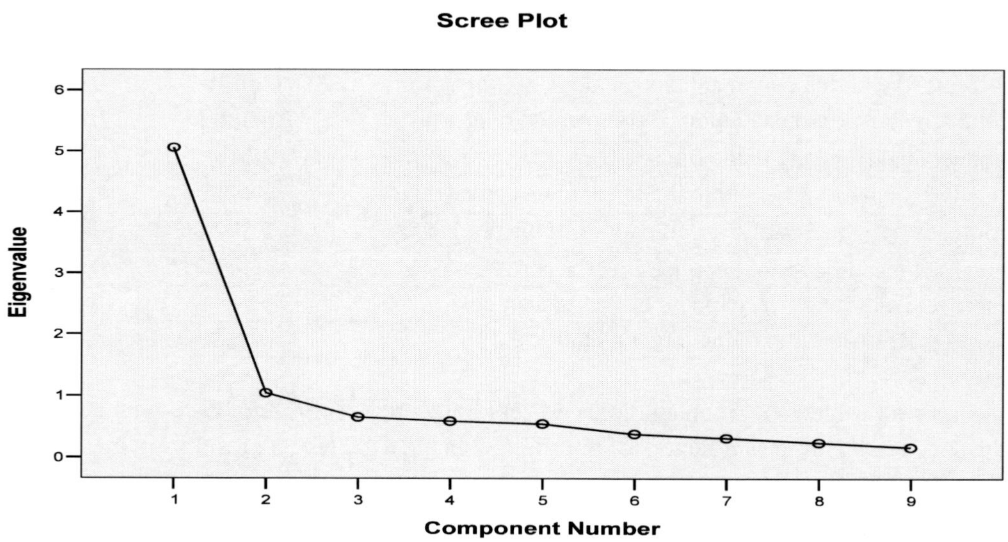

Figure 1. Scree Plot.

Table 14 shows the two factors which arose from the factorial analysis. In the first column are the factors and the name of each one. In the second column are the questions which interpret the factors and in the last column are the coefficients (the "weights") of each question.

Table 14. Factor analysis

Factors	Questions	*Coefficients*
Factor 1 Orders and transactions	Q23 Product variety	0.860
	Q24 Easy search and product selection.	0.801
	Q28 Fulfillment of your expectations by the new supplier compared to traditional suppliers	0.637
Factor 2 JiT	Q25 Easy ordering procedure	0.803
	Q26 Secure transactions.	0.678
	Q29 Issues in stock and production replacement.	0.832
	Q30 Effectiveness of replenishment chain	0.590
	Q31 Observance of agreed order delivery times and elimination of unnecessary expenses	0.795
	Q27. Premium consistency in delivery services.	0.702

Having reduced the problem's size into two variables, we continue the analysis. Through the use of those two factors, we want to compare whether there is differentiation between the e-commerce traditional companies. Since the factors are continuous variables, we shall use the t-test for two independent samples. In this case, the statistical hypothesis that we want to test is whether the mean values of the two company groups for each factor are equal. As before, we define a critical value of 5%.

Initially, we compare the e-commerce and traditional companies (Table 15). The sig. values are higher than 0.05. Therefore, there is no difference among e-commerce and traditional companies.

Table 15. T-test check among "e-commerce" and "traditional"

Factors	t-test	Sig. (2-tailed)
Factor 2 Orders and Transactions	-1.147	0.259
Factor 1 J iT	0.252	0.802

FACTORS ARISING IN ELECTRONIC RELATIONS AMONG SELLER/BUYER IN THE VARIOUS STAGES OF ELECTRONIC RELATIONSHIPS

This part of the survey is answered by all businesses, either active in e-commerce or not. As in the previous parts of the questionnaire, we are looking at whether there is a relation among those questions and the "e-commerce –traditional". Before the X^2 tests, we examine the answers for those questions of all 40 businesses participating in our research. In the introductory stage, the uncertainty, business risk and cooperation conditions are developed: expected when a new cooperation starts among companies which had no contact in the past. In the development stage, important factors are whether the co-operator is known, the adaptation to his demands, the obligations placed, and the understanding of his needs. In the maturity stage, the experience, the agreement for reducing prices, the signature for long-term trade agreements, the continuous product sale, and the information exchange are expected to be significant. Finally, in long-term relations, an important factor is the signature of long-term agreements and practices aiming to solve problems of the co-operator: expected since now the relation among buyer/seller focuses on the improvement of the existing relation (Table 16).

We conduct the X^2 test in order to see whether there is a correlation among the questions and the transaction type (use of e-commerce or not). We discover that there is a correlation with *"Knowledge of co-operator"* (ρ=0,024), *the "Information exchange"* (ρ=0.008) and the *"Co-operation problem resolving practices*"(ρ=0.004).

Table 16. Stages of electronic relationships

	Introductory stage	Development stage	Maturity stage	Transaction stage (termination of relation)	Long-term relation
1. Uncertainty	29 (72.5%)	2 (5%)	4 (10%)	5 (12.5%)	0
2. Business risk	15 (45.5%)	11 (33.3%)	3 (9.1%)	3 (9.1%)	1 (3%)
3. Knowledge of co-operator	8 (21.1%)	15 (39.5%)	12 (31.5%)	0	3 (7.5%)
4. Adaptation to his needs	2 (5.7%)	22 (55%)	5 (14.3%)	1 (2.9%)	5 (14.3%)
5. Obligations placed	4 (11.4%)	13 (37.1%)	11 (31.4%)	0	7 (20%)
6. Experience	0	6 (17.1%)	18 (51.4%)	1 (2.9%)	10 (28.6%)
7. Understanding of his needs	3 (8.8%)	15 (44.1%)	10 (29.4%)	1 (2.9%)	5 (14,7%)
8. Agreement for reducing prices	3 (8.6%)	10 (28.6%)	14 (40%)	2 (5.7%)	6 (1,1%)
9. Signature of long-term trade agreements	1 (2.9%)	3 (7.5%)	15 (42.9%)	1 (2.9%)	15 (42.9%)
10. Cooperation conditions	15 (41.79%)	14 (38.9%)	6 (16.7%)	1 (2.8%)	0
11. Continuous product sale	0	13 (36.1%)	14 (47.2%)	2 (5.6%)	4 (11.1%)
12. Information exchange	8 (22.9%)	8 (22.9%)	9 (25.7%)	2 (5.7%)	8 (22.9%)
13. Problem resolving cooperation practices	1 (2.8%)	14 (38.9%)	6 (16.7%)	0	15 (41.7%)

The next step (Table 17) is to see how strong those correlations are. Our variables are homogenous. The coefficient used in this case is the Kendall-tau-c coefficient. Values close to 0 show a weak correlation and values close to 1 show that the variables are strongly correlated. In the *"Knowledge of co-operator"* the coefficient has a value of -0.188 (ρ=0.298), in "*«Information exchange*", its value is 0.519 (ρ=0.003) and in *"Co-operation problem resolving practices"* it is 0.485 (ρ=0.004).

Table 17. Correlation among the questions of stages and the transaction type

	(Q19) *e-commerce – traditional*	
	Pearson Chi-square	Approx. Sig.
Uncertainty	4.823	0.185
Business risk	4.465	0.347
Knowledge of co-operator	9.433	0.024
Adaptation to his needs	3.496	0.476
Obligations placed	3.065	0.382
Experience	1.823	0.610
Understanding of his needs	2.768	0.597
Agreement for reducing prices	2,782	0.595
Signature of long-term trade agreements	2.974	0.562
Cooperation conditions	4.455	0.216
Continuous product sale	1.117	0.773
Information exchange	13.845	0.008
Cooperation problem resolving practices	13.569	0.004

The X^2 values between the questions and the "*e-commerce-buyers*" – "*e-commerce-sellers*" the value of the test statistic is not lower than 0.05 in all comparisons. Therefore, the answers are not different among buyers and sellers/suppliers, given that they both use e-commerce.We reach the same conclusions if we make the same tests for companies using traditional ways of commerce.

Prediction Model

In order to optimize the strategic decisions of a business, and providing that the constants of the sample fulfill the assumptions necessary to effect a linear regression, we created a multiple linear model with a dependent variable:

"*The positive experience of clients, the added value in the administrative chain, and the mix of marketing communication constitute the new marketing relationship mix in the relations of sellers-buyers*".

We tested the following independent variables because they are explaining better the dependent variable above:

- Product delivery within the timeframe expected by the customer;
- The qualitative punctuality of deliver services;
- The common planning of quality control systems between two businesses;
- Improved ability to perform deliveries on time (Just In Time);
- Achieving economies of scale through the supply of increased quantities in lower prices;
- Product variety;
- Ease of research and product choice;
- Ease in ordering process;
- Market research cost prior to each new order;

- Ordering cost for products/services;
- Resulting cost of inventories;
- Communication cost between business and supplier;
- Administrative cost of managing logistics;
- Supply of suitable information from the customer or supplier to our business;
- Working with customers/suppliers with regard to withholding inventories;
- Working with customers/suppliers with regard to process planning;
- Working with customers/suppliers with regard to prediction and production planning;
- Working with customers/suppliers with regard to products/services quality;
- Working with customers/suppliers with regard to product planning.

Using the variables above, we arrived at a model that contains "*the administrative costs of managing logistics*" and "*the resulting cost of inventories*" as well as the constant. The remaining variables were excluded from the model due to the fact that their coefficients were not statistically different from zero; as a result, they made no contribution to the interpretation of the dependent variable.

The method we used to arrive at the final model is "Forward Method". This method identifies amongst all independent variables, the one variable that is strongest with the dependent. As a next step, it elects the variable with the second highest correlation. This process continues until there are no more statistically relevant variables.

The Model:

The following model resulted using the Forward Method:

$$Q13 = b_0 + b_1{*}\ q8\_5 + b_2{*}\ q8\_3 + e$$

where Q13 stands for positive customer experience;
q8_5 stands for the administrative costs of logistics management;
q8_3 stands for the resulting cost of inventories;
and e stands for residuals;
b_1 and b_2 are the coefficients of the variables and b_0 is the constant.

The Coefficients table contains the factors' values (Table 18).
Coefficients (a)

Hence, the model stands as follows:

$$Q13 = 3.758 + 0.222{*}\ q8\_5 - 0.176{*}\ q8\_3 + e$$

Therefore, we see that the "administrative cost of logistics management" contributes positively to the "positive customer experience". We derive this conclusion by noting the positive sign of the coefficient. The administrative cost applies within an industrial unit (for immediately addressing orders, for minimizing cost, for storage conditions and re-test times).

Table 18. Factors' values

	Unstandardized Coefficients		Standarized Coefficients	T	Sig.	Collinearity Statistics	
	B	Std. Error	Beta			Tolerance	VIF
(Constant)	3.758	.222		16.928	.000		
Administrative costs of Logistics management	.222	.065	.715	3.401	.003	.689	1.452
Resulting cost of inventories	-.176	.075	-.496	-2.359	.028	.689	1.452

The above fact translates into: The recent innovations in integrating manufacturing have significantly reduced the overall costs of the entire system and simultaneously, increased customer service and system adaptability. Management costs have been reduced and increased output quality while decreasing process time. Such innovations have forced everyone in B2B firms to become more skilled themselves at integrating manufacturing and distribution processes. The core competence of process and systems integration has become a competitive driver in the market - a managerial path dependency.

These innovations help a business function in rapid response and includes tools such as: bar-codes, meters in sales outlets, electronic scanners, and electronic exchange of information. These tools offer certain benefits in inventorization (with a view to holding less stock), in reducing operational costs, reducing product returns and improving customer service.

Therefore, in B2B relationships, the administrative cost of logistic management contributes positive value chain and the marketing communication mix which reduce the cost for the client thus increasing customer choice and satisfaction.

On the contrary, the "Resulting cost of inventories" variable has a negative sign, which affects "Positive customer experience" negatively.

The Validity of the Model

For a regression model to be valid, apart from using coefficients different from zero, there are other conditions that have to be met also.

First, we check the analysis of variance (Table 19). The null hypothesis of coefficient F is that all coefficients of the model are simultaneously equal to zero. Since Sig equals 0.09, then at a confidence level equal to 0.05, we disprove the null hypothesis. Therefore, there is no chance for all coefficients to be equal to zero so the resulting model has validity.

Moving on, we check the rate of variation of the dependent variable that interprets the model. In the *Model Summary* (Table 20) we obtain information such as the value of R, of R^2 and R^2 Adjusted. R stands for the indication of the percentage of fluctuation of the dependent variable, which interprets the model. In our case, the model interprets 60% of the total variance of the sample. Values close to 1 indicate that the factors involved in the construction of the model are satisfactory for describing the movements of the dependant variable. R^2

Adjusted is also an indicator of the model's adjustment. The difference with R^2 is that R^2 Adjusted takes into account the multitude of factors that contribute to the model. For this reason, when we want to compare models with a different number of dependant variables, R^2 Adjusted is a more reliable index. Compared with the first model, we see that R^2 Adjusted has a greater value. Hence, the second model offers better explanation.

Table 19. The validity of the model

	Sum of Squares	df	Mean Square	F	Sig.
Regression	.662	2	.331	5.939	.009(b)
Residual	1.171	21	.056		
Total	1.833	23			

Carrying on, we check whether there are any problems with the residuals. The Durbin-Watson statistic demonstrates that if the residuals are independent to each other then the values of the Durbin-Watson statistic, (which is close to 2), confirms the independence hypothesis.

For the final model to be acceptable, we should not have a multi-collinearity problem. Multi-collinearity occurs when the independent variables involved in the model are linearly dependent each other. The condition index in (Table 21) below is used in order to identify any possible multi-collinearity problem.

Table 20. Model Summary

Model	R	R Square	Adjusted R Square	Std. Error of the Estimate	Durbin-Watson
1	.438(a)	.192	.155	.259	
2	.601(b)	.361	.300	.236	2.108

Table 21.Collinearity Diagnostics(a)

Dimension	Eigenvalue	Condition Index	Variance Proportions		
			Constant	Admin costs for logistics mgmt	Resulting cost of inventories
1	2.941	1.000	.01	.01	.00
2	.035	9.222	.69	.67	.00
3	.025	10.866	.30	.33	1.00

When the values of this index are greater than 15, then there is possibly a problem; values greater than 30 indicate a serious problem. In the case before us, the index has a value of 10, thus there is not even an indication of multi-collinearity.

Another indicator of multi-collinearity is the *Tolerance* index, which can be located in the *Coefficients* table. The values it takes vary between 0 and 1. When the index's value is close to 0 then the variable is the linear combination of the other. The value of the index for the two variables included in the model is close to one (0.689) and therefore, we do not have a problem of multi-collinearity and of being able to judge the independent impacts of each explanatory variable.

CONCLUSION OF THE RESEARCH FINDINGS

In the research conducted, we were looking to ascertain whether there are any differences between traditional buyers and traditional sellers as well as between e-commerce buyers and e-commerce sellers in order to verify the hypothesis below:

H1: Traditional Buyers and Traditional Sellers behave differently from E-commerce Buyers and E-commerce Sellers.

Firstly, we assumed that the factors regarding the adoption of e-commerce relationships (globalization and market deregulation, pressure by competition to the company, customers asking for lower product prices, pressure for lowering production costs, pressure from co-operators who have moved to e-commerce solutions) are equally important. In other words, both traditional buyers and traditional sellers regard the five factors above to be of equal importance. Subsequently, we make the same assumption for e-commerce buyers and e-commerce sellers.

As far as both comparisons go, the hypothesis we made is rejected. At the end of the day, these factors are equally important for both traditional buyers and traditional sellers as well as of equal importance for e-commerce sellers and buyers.

Furthermore, we assumed that for the variables relating to selection criteria relating to traditional sellers and buyers, they are different to e-commerce buyers and e-commerce sellers. As far as both comparisons go, the hypothesis we made is rejected. At the end of the day, these factors are equally important for both traditional buyers and traditional sellers as well as of equal importance for e-commerce sellers and buyers. Also, we assume that for the frequency that the selected sellers or buyers respond to the needs of their partners differentiate among to traditional sellers and buyers and e-commerce buyers and e-commerce Sellers.

As far as both comparisons go, the hypothesis we made is rejected. At the end of the day, the frequency that the selected sellers or buyers respond to the needs of their partners are equally important for both traditional buyers and traditional sellers as well as of equal importance for e-commerce sellers and buyers.

Moving on, we assume that for the factors influence the relationships of buyers and sellers are different. Also in this case, traditional sellers agree or disagree to the same extent.

The hypothesis is the same for e-commerce buyers and e-commerce Sellers.

Therefore our initial hypothesis is confirmed. This means that the correlation among "Improvement of product's cost effectiveness" and the "*e-commerce*" – "*traditional*" is strong. Also, the factors affecting the relationships between e-commerce buyers and e-commerce sellers are insignificant with the exception for the Buyers, "*the fame of the business*" has some up to "high influence" in deciding to create business relations, while for the sellers/s suppliers, it has high up to "intense influence". Therefore, for the sellers/suppliers it matters more compared to the Buyers.

Conclusion

The present research was conducted in 40 B2B firms in dyads to find out whether there are differences in behavior and how the companies treat suppliers and clients, depending on whether they are active in e-commerce or not.

The research was looking to ascertain whether there are any differences between traditional buyers and traditional sellers as well as between e-commerce buyers and e-commerce sellers. Examining B2B firms, which operate either in an e-commerce environment or in a traditional one, the factors affect their relationships, outline, it does not appear to differentiate their behavior. This means that the same factors that influence the exchange process of traditional B2B firms to the same extent influence firms which operate their business in an e-commerce environment. Important issues in B2B relationships such as communication from the information exchange, JiT, agreements, cooperation conditions, problem solving, adaptation to the customer needs to appear to affect firms to the same extent. These issues are grouped through a factor analysis in two main factors: 1. orders and transactions and 2. JiT. Certainly, there are some exceptions: it was found out that there is a strong correlation between e-commerce – traditional firms in *improved product cost effectiveness.* Thus, another important factor that seems to influence the relationships of e-commerce –buyers and e- commerce-sellers is *company fame for the creation of commercial relations.*

Specifically, there is a weak correlation from the *knowledge of co-operator through the information exchange* as well *B2B firms to implement practices for problem resolving.* These variables could facilitate relationships' development and success during the relationships life cycle.

Finally, the following model resulted from the analysis of the research findings modulates the marketing relationship mix in the relations of traditional sellers-buyers and e-commerce sellers-buyers*: the "customer experience" influence positively by the "administrative cost of logistics management" (unit (for immediately addressing orders, for minimizing cost, for storage conditions and re-test times).*

Discussion

The advantages from the development of electronic relationships according to our findings include better management of the supply chain, both for the supplier and the buyer, quicker adaptation to the changes in the demands they have of each other, a drastic reduction in administrative costs, the attainment of lower prices in relation to physical markets, as Rayport and Sviokla (1995) revealed in their own research.

This ascertainment is confirmed by Sawhney and Kaplan (1999a) who state the theory of reduced search cost which pushes down the prices of products in electronic markets. Rayport and Sviokla (1995) agree with the above view, pointing out that the most significant effect of electronic relations is the changes they make to the structure of transactions as regards the terms and cost elements that characterize them. Further benefits, such as the volume of information that the supplier collects and manages, contribute to the better regulation of production, and of the supply chain. Information completeness is something else situated between the supplier and the buyer and makes a decisive contribution to achieving successful relations.

The results of our survey confirm the findings of Spekman (1988) that the reduction in the costs of the supplier in physical and electronic markets is not the same for all companies active on the Internet.

Our survey showed that other cost factors participate in this philosophy and in this way, it was adapted and completed by the results of the survey concerning the comparison of the supplier's costs in physical and electronic markets. Technology on its own does not constitute a competitive advantage; it must be leveraged with the rest of the company's cost data in order for it to fully satisfy needs, a fact verified by Kleindl (2001).

Our survey showed the factors defining the suitability of activation in electronic markets for a company already active in physical markets. Thus, the characteristics were set out of companies that can survive in the environment of the New Economy from which it emerges that the changes brought about by electronic business can hardly be characterized as revolutionary, but are probably the product of entrepreneurial growth as the factors do not especially differ between the traditional and the electronic companies. Among the companies participating in the survey, it does not appear that there have been revolutionary changes in the companies active at the same time both in physical as well as in electronic commerce, as their behavior does not differ whether they are active in traditional commerce (with a tendency at some point in the future to go into electronic business) or in electronic commerce.

The findings also suggest that when it comes to B2B relationships development purposes, even in an electronic environment, the old rules retain their vitality. In fact, despite the innovative and quite different characteristics of the "market space", compared with the traditional marketplace, it maintains its robustness.

LIMITATIONS AND FUTURE RESEARCH

There are some limitations to consider regarding the results of this research. First, we offer the buyers' and sellers' view as a starting point to understand the determinants of the B2B relationships in e-business environment. The research relies on the responses of the buyers and sellers only from medium-sized firms in Greece, providing an incomplete view of the relationships.

Since the buyer–supplier relationships research in the electronic market context is still in an early stage (Morganand Hunt, 2003), we offer the buyer's and sellers' view as a starting point to understand how they can develop and adapt an e-marketing strategy (Anderson and Narus, 1990). Nevertheless, we strongly encourage future research in a bigger sample of separately from sellers' or buyers' view.

A second limitation regards the fact that the sample consists of participants firms from the area of Attica. Future research should include participants firms from a wide area in Greece. A third limitation is that our research sample didn't include the service sector. Fourth, the data is longitudinal. Future research could benefit from being tested not in a longitudinal design, as longitudinal studies provide stronger inferences while the external factors from the business environment are unpredictable and may influence the firms' behavior (Anderson and Narus, 1990; Morgan and Hunt, 1994). Fifth, a limitation may reside in the specific ness of the target of this study—Greek medium-sized firms. While enhancing the focus of this research, it may also limit the generalization of the results to some degree, at the same time creating the need for further studies in larger firms. Future research might explore, for example, how B2B firms learn about the features and services necessary to ensure success. It is hoped that by shedding light on the use of new information and communication technologies, this study will trigger further works to the improvement of B2B relationships theory and practices in a B2B e-context.

REFERENCES

Adam, S 1998, 'Electronic marketing and the internet: Measuring the IPOR gap', paper presented to Australia New Zealand Marketing Academic Conference, University of Otago, Dunedin, New.

Amit, R and Zott, C 2001, 'Value creation in eBusiness', *Strategic Management Journal*, vol. 22, pp. 483-520.

Anderson, JC and Narus, JA 1990, 'A model of distributor firm and manufacture firm working partnerships', *Journal of Marketing*, vol. 54, no. 1, pp. 42-59.

Berry, LL 1983, 'Relationship Marketing', in GLSGDU L. L. Berry (ed.), *Emerging Perspectives on Services Marketing*, American Marketing Association, Chicago.

Christopher, M, Payne, A and Ballantyne, D 1991, *Relationship Marketing*, Butterworth-Heinemann, Oxford.

Chung, A., A. Ephraim, P. Hechmann, T. Laseter, B. Long, K. Oliver, D. Schwarting, and T. Von Der Decken, (2001), *The e-Marketplace Revolution. Creating and Capturing the Value in B2B e-commerce,* Booz Allen and Hamilton Inc.

Gummesson, E 1987, 'The new marketing -developing long term interactive relationships', *Long Range Planning*, vol. 20, no. 4, pp. 10-20.

Hofacker, C. (2001), *Internet Marketing, 3/e,* John Wiley and Sons.

Hofacker, C. F. and M. Jamie (1998), World Wide Web Banner Advertisement Copy Testing, *European Journal of Marketing,* 32(7/8):703-712.

Kleindl, B. (2001), *Strategic Electronic Marketing: Managing E-business,* South Western College Publishing, Cincinnati, OH.

Lockett, A. and I. D. Blackman (2001), "Strategies for Building a Customer Base on the Web: Symbiotic *Marketing," Journal of Strategic Marketing.*

Morgan, R. M. and Hunt, S. D. (1994) 'The Commitment-trust theory of relationship marketing', Journal of Marketing, 58 (July), 20 – 38.

Naude, P, Holland, C, 1996, "*Business-to-business relationships*», Relationship Marketing, Theory and Practice, Paul Chapman Publishing, London.

Palumbo, F. arid P. Herbig (1998), "International Marketing Tool: The internet," *Industrial Management and Data Systems,* Vol. 6, pp. 253-261.

Palumbo, F., Herbig, P, 1998, International marketing tool: the Internet, Industrial Management and Data Systems, 98, 6, 253-61. partnerships', *Journal of Marketing*, vol. 54, no. 1, pp. 42-59.

Remenyi, D, 'How to build a successful e-business ', in possession of C. Perry, USQ. 2000.

Ratnasingham, P 1998, 'The importance of trust in electronic commerce', *Internet Research: Electronic Networking Applications and Policy*, vol. 8, no. 4, pp. 313 - 21.

Rayport, J. F. and J.J. Sviokla (1995), "Managing in the Marketspace", *Harvard Business Review,* Nov-Dec, pp. 141-150.

Sawhney, M. and S. Kaplan (1999a), "B2B E-commerce Hubs: Towards a Taxonomy of Business Models," URL: http://gsbwww.uchicago.edu/fac/sLeven.kaplan/research/taxonomy.pdf.

Spekman, R 1988, 'Strategic supplier selection: towards an understanding of long-term buyer-seller relationships', *Business Horizon*, vol. 31, no. 4, pp. 24-36.

Strauss, J and Forest, R 1999, *Marketing on the Internet: Principles of Online Marketing*, Prentice Hall, New Jersey.

Strauss, J. and R. Frost (1999), *Marketing on the Internet: Principles of Online Marketing,* Upper Saddle River NJ: Prentice Hall.

Stahl, B., 2002, From Product to performance: Creating business relationships, 18th IMP-Conference, Perth Urban, G.L.

Wang, F, Head, M and Archer, N 2000, 'A relationship-building model for the Web retail marketplace', *Internet Research: Electronic Networking Applications and Policy*, vol. 10, no. 5, pp. 374-84.

Watson, RT, Berthon, P, Pitt, LF and Zinkhan, GM 2000, *Electronic Commerce: The strategic Perspective*, The Dryden Press, Fort Worth. Web, *Harvard Business Review,* July-August, pp. 105-113.

Wright, R., 2004 Business to Business Marketing, A step by step guide, Prentice Hall, Essex.

Zinkhan, M. G. 2002, "Promoting services via the internet: new opportunities and challenges". Journal of Services Marketing, p.412-23.

In: HRM and Marketing Orientation in the New Era
Editor: Panagiotis Kyriazopoulos
ISBN: 978-1-62808-959-2

Chapter 4

Marketing Practices of Small Family Business in Greece

***K. Terzidis*[1] *and Irene Samanta*[2]**
[1]Graduate Technological Education Institute of Kavala, Greece
[2]Graduate Technological Education Institute of Piraeus, Greece

Abstract

The study refers to family businesses and identifies the marketing practices that are applied by the first and second generations who manage the firms. Data were collected from a database of Greek private family companies (n=380) using personal interviews to owner/managers. According to the findings, the owners of family businesses do not conform to conventional marketing rules since their implementation is haphazard and informal; they make most decisions on their own, respond to current opportunities and circumstances and, therefore, any decision-making occurs in a loose, unstructured, spontaneous way, according to personal and business priorities at any given point in time. Firms should focus on the services or products offer in order to create a competitive advantage and gain advantages in the areas where large businesses face problems, i.e. customer service, special relationships with the customers and suppliers and flexibility in providing services.

Keywords: Family business, marketing mix

Introduction

Family businesses constitute a dynamic segment of the economy that contributes to wealth creation, job generation and national competitiveness (Ward and Aronoff, 1990; Westhead and Cowling, 1995; Wang, 2002) and is a vital part of industrial change and innovation. Similar to all organizations, family firms have to make use of a number of organizational activities, structures and strategies in order to satisfy customers while overcoming competition. However, due to the fact that in this category of business the social and economic systems coexist and interact, these companies, while choosing the appropriate courses of action, have to face all the pros and cons of family businesses as well as all the positive and negative characteristics of economic firms in general. Consequently, the need for these firms to use marketing strategies is considered to be a necessity and not peripheral to their requirements. The owners have to plan for the future while dealing with essential daily matters from customer enquiries, production matters and financial control to employee recruitment and other operational details within severe resource constraints (Stanworth and Gray, 1991; Hogarth Scott et al., 1996).

The establishment of family business research as an academic field of study is relatively recent and even though a plethora of family businesses issues and marketing tactics exist there is a scarcity of both theory and practical implication in the use and impacts of marketing concept. According to (Stanworth and Gray, 1991) family business has not been explored as an independent sector. In Greece according to research conducted by (Grant Thornton 2003) family firms represent 80% of all business. It has not been explored to the extent it should have been nor has it been given the importance it ought to have. As a result it is very important to investigate the marketing tactics in the most vital sectors.

The aim of the research is to identify the impact that the marketing practices of 1st and 2nd generation has on family businesses in Greece. Furthermore, the current paper examines the marketing practices between the different sectors of activities, whether these companies attribute importance in understanding the market and competing at the same time.

LITERATURE REVIEW

Marketing Orientation of Family Business

Family firms could be defined as enterprises in which two different social systems, the business system and the family system intersect (Getz and Carlsen, 2005).

However, a commonly accepted definition for family businesses does not exist (Sharma et al., 1996 in Getz and Carlsen, 2005). According to (Yilmazer and Schrank 2006) family are the businesses, in which at least two family members work and the business is owned and managed by one of the family members. (Getz and Carlsen, 2005) on the other hand simply defines them as enterprises controlled by members of a single family. (Getz and Carlsen, 2005) state that by simply searching for the term ‘family business’ the many relevant references are not revealed as a great part of the literature is subsumed under another heading such as entrepreneurship and small business.

One of the main characteristic of a family business is the succession of ownership to the next generation. According to (Rosenblat et al., 1985) ‘succession in family businesses is important as it does not require only the transfer of ownership and control but also a number of changes in the business model’ and that the members of the next generation, who are usually more educated and innovating, must be so as to compete in the market place (Sharma et al., 1996). However, in the companies that display distinctive patterns of power and authority (Poutziouris, 2003), first-generation owners seem to be reluctant as they believe that despite the fact that decision-making within the business is affected by the entire family system, members of the next generation will not succeed in increasing the company’s size.

Getz et al. (2005) identified that the preparation level of owners and successors influences the transition and the future direction of businesses and has a significant impact on the firm's marketing concept.

It is well documented that small family businesses have unique advantages that differentiate them from conventional marketing in large corporations (Getz et al., 2005). These advantages may be determined by the inherent characteristics and behaviour of the family members or owners, and may be determined by the inherent size and stage of development of the enterprise.

Therefore it should be noted that the majority of family businesses, presents a significant lack in the ability of managing marketing techniques, technological advances and human resources. If the business size is not large enough to depend upon a large number of customers, the owners are not willing to take any risks.

These limitations can be summarized as:

1. Limited resources (such as finance, time and marketing knowledge);
2. Lack of specialist expertise (owner-managers tend to be generalists rather than specialists); and
3. Limited impact in the marketplace.

In addition, the owners of family businesses do not conform to conventional marketing rules since their implementation of marketing rules is haphazard and informal; they make most decisions on their own, respond to current opportunities and circumstances and, therefore, any decision-making occurs in a loose, unstructured, spontaneous way, according to personal and business priorities at any given point in time. Clearly, such limitations will influence, indeed determine, the marketing concept of such businesses.

Thus, these characteristics restrain the dynamism of this segment as well as its survival and entrepreneurial development across generations (Poutziouris et al., 2003). In addition, these constraints prevent family firms from maintaining business planning while conditions of uncertainty turn them away from strategic planning activities, (Bhide, 1994; Hill, 2001) thus making marketing an issue peripheral to their requirements.

Nevertheless, despite the fact that family businesses see marketing as an 'unnecessary luxury', as businesses move along the growth-life cycle the pressure for planning and implementing marketing strategies increases (Bruce, 1987, Kenny and Dyson, 1989; Scott and ; Watts et al., 1998). Family business owners have to develop strategies in order to allow the company to adapt to environmental changes, segmenting the market where it belongs, focusing on satisfying their customers as this is a major aim of the marketing concept.

This means that 1st and 2nd generation firm's main task is to determine the needs, wants and interests of the market's targets and to deliver the desired satisfaction more effectively and efficiently than competitors in a way that preserves or enhances consumers (Kotler, 2002) through the creation, distribution, promotion and pricing of goods, services and ideas.

It is therefore important that family management is fully committed advantages to the marketing concept and that it forms the basis for all goals decision within the company. According to (Carson, 1990) there are a number of issues relating to small firms' marketing. These include the constraints affecting this type of marketing, the extent to which the general principles of marketing can be applied to each particular situation, the role of planning in marketing and the evolution of firms through different phases of development. (Carson, 1990) emphasized the importance of marketing planning and how it must be adapted to the circumstances of the business. Carlson's models describe the constraints affecting the way in which small firms undertake marketing. Limitations are classified as minimal, limited and substantial; they relate to resources and are described in terms of time and money devoted to marketing. Carlson's models identify four stages of marketing from the date of its establishment to reactive, tinkering marketing, entrepreneurial and proactive marketing.

Environmental Scanning

Family businesses' first priority in order to adopt the marketing concept is to gain a full understanding of the market and the factors that influence it. Understanding the market by identifying opportunities that t hey can take advantage of, as well as threats that they must face, is crucial for this kind of business. Especially in today's competitive marketplace, identifying the size and features of competitors affects marketing decisions. Offering the product or service in a way that will outsell the competition is critical and so is the strategy that the company will choose to use in order to target the desired segments of the market (Watts et al., 1998).

Nevertheless, family business owners, especially those who founded the firm, find it difficult and believe it to be a waste of time, money and resources to be occupied in such a process. Unlike their successors that are, in general, more educated and make greater use of technology, founders believe that the best way to gain an understanding of the market to maintain close personal contact with clients. The characteristics of rival competitors and each one's experience, market position, staying power, strength and predictability. In addition it helps the company to find the most prosperous way to address a competitive market by relying on its strengths and on characteristics that competitors lack (McTavish et al., 1996).

In Greece, according to (Makridakis et al., 1997), any kind of planning is difficult since owners tend to concentrate on the short term. They intend, with their little or no formal marketing education and work experience, to practise a simplified marketing strategy that is customer oriented, due to the fact that part of their philosophy is to 'please everyone'. What the majority of family businesses really want, is to sell their products. In order to do so, at the first stages of the business life cycle, especially when entering the market, they target a single segment and use a simple strategy.

However, in extensive markets, a company cannot serve everyone as customers are numerous and diverse in their buying requirements. As a result, it researches its market to know how many potential customers it has, what their needs are and how to reach them (McTavish et al., 1996). Then it divides large, heterogeneous markets into smaller segments that can be reached and served more effectively (Kotler et al.,1999; Kotler, 2002).

However, while for the majority of large businesses the data for these segmentation variables are fairly readily available and it is easy for them to identify the segment or those segments for which they want to provide a product based on their objectives and their resources (McTavish et al., 1996; Kotler, 2002), for the majority of family firms this rarely occurs. This occurs because of financial restraints, lack of resources and technological innovation, low educational level of first-generation owners and lack of managerial skills makes segmentation for this type of company impossible.

Nevertheless, as the company moves on and looks for the potential to increase aggregate sales, the owner of the business should use differing marketing combinations to target multiple segments (McTavish et al., 1996). At the same time they should examine the interrelations of cost–performance–technology as well as deciding whether to follow an undifferentiated, differentiated or concentrated marketing, based on their resources, product variability, lifecycle stage and competitive marketing strategies (Kotler et al., 1999; Kotler, 2002).

RESEARCH METHODOLOGY

Sample Frame

The establishment of family business research as an academic field of study is relatively recent and even though a plethora of family businesses issues and marketing tactics exist there is a scarcity of both theory and practical implication in the use and impacts of marketing concept. In Greece it has not been explored to the extent it should have been nor has it been given the importance it ought to have. As a result it is very important to investigate the marketing tactics in the most vital sectors.

The research took place in the general area of Athens between December 2006 and March 2007. The sample that was used for the current research related to small family businesses that operate in Greece.

Primary data of a non-probability sample using respondents convenient to the researcher with the use of a structured questionnaire were collected. Data were collected from a database of Greek private family companies (n=380) using personal interviews to owner/managers of first- and second-generation family businesses.

We define a small family business as one that employs up to 50 employees. Eurostat's 2006 statistics show the dominance of small family businesses in Greece and the European Union. According to Eurostat's, the self-employed that are rated as a business occupies 50.4% of all businesses and 10% of the employment. The sample size was from a list provided by the Industrial and Commercial Chamber in Piraeus.

The survey team researched family businesses established 30 years ago and employing two officers or directors with the same last name. There were 380 companies that participated in the survey. The overall response rate was 47.5%.

Construct Measurement

A questionnaire was developed specifically to collect information among first and second-generation owners about the impact of marketing concepts in the family business. The questionnaire was based on a review by Hill, (2001). Drawing on the study of the literature above, the survey was devised with the three following research questions in mind:

1. Which factors in particular enhance the use of marketing practice in a family business?
2. Which limitations reduce the application of marketing techniques?
3. Where should the business focus in order to gain a competitive advantage?

Therefore, the questionnaire designed was divided into two sections each with its own subsections. Section A asked the respondents questions to state their opinions on the product, price, channels of distribution and promotion. Section B included general and external questions from the business environment The data base created specifically for this survey included owner-members of the first and second generation of family businesses.. The questions in each section were posed using the Likert scale. For instrument consistency, each scale included five items: 5=strongly agree, 4=agree, 3=neutral, 2=disagree, 1=strongly disagree.

To get answers to these questions, an interview based on a pilot questionnaire was conducted with five retail companies in Greece.

Demographic Characteristics

The majority of family firms (41. 67%) were established after 1980, with the remainder of the firms (26. 67%) before 1980. It appears that family companies are more prolific in retail trade (41. 6%) and services (26. 3%) and construction activities (9. 7%) and less prolific in wholesale trade (8. 2%).

Only 32.4% of family companies have a second-generation perspective and have experienced ownership change. The average percentage of sales from each market is 85% operate in the Greek market (50.6% local and 34.3% national) while the remainder operates on a global scale (15.69% of the respondents). About 43.2% of family companies have an annual turnover up to 100,000 euro, while 32.4% have up to 500,000 euro and a percentage of 8.2 surpass 1,000,000 euro.

Financial resources used by family business reflect a conservative borrowing profile. The sample companies' main characteristics can be summarized in (Table 1) as follows:

Demographic characteristics between 1st and 2nd generation regarding to the sector of activities most of them belong to the retailing sector, wholesale trade and construction activities. The majority of 1st generation annual turnover appear to be up to 100,000 euros while the majority of the firms of the second generation to be from 100000 to 500000 euro.

Table 1. Sample demographic characteristics

Variables	%
Age distribution	(41. 67%) were established after 1980 (26. 67%) before 1980.
Sector	Retail trade (41. 6%) Services (26. 3%) Construction activities (9.7%) Wholesale trade (8. 2%).
Business transfers	32.4% have a second-generation perspective
Average percentage of sales from each market	85% operate in the Greek market (50.6% local and 34.3% national) on a global scale (15.69%).
Turnover distribution	43.2% annual turnover up to 100,000 euro, 32.4% have up to 500,000 euro and 8.2 surpass 1,000,000 euro.

Data Analysis

As it can be seen in (Table 2), respondents relating to the level of education to family business generally tend to be closely related. A percentage of 36, 3 had relatively few years of experience outside the family business, whilst a 28, 2% had more than five years experience. The relation to outside experience to family business was identical 29, 7% and not related the 22, 9%. They had worked full-time in the family firm for an average of five years prior to assuming operational control. Most of them were encouraged by the preceding generation to access the business, but ultimately joined based on their own satisfaction to participate.

Table 2. Preparation levels of first and second generation

Variables	%
Relation to outside experience to family business	Not related 22,9 % Somewhat 12,6 % Related 29,7 Closely related 17,9 %
Years in family business prior to taking control	<1 43,2%, 1-5 30% 6-10 13,2% 11-15 9,4%
Relation of education to family business	Not related 21,3%, Somewhat Related 12,4%, Related 12,4, Closely related 24,5%
Preparation level of second generation at taking over the management of family business	Not at all prepared 2,1%, Somewhat prepared 8,5%, Neutral 33,1%, Well prepared 42,3%, Very well prepared 14,1%
Preceding generations encouraged in joining the business	Strongly discouraged 3,5%, Neutral 31,3%, Encouraged 39,7 %, Strongly encouraged 23,1%

The external environment takes a lead role in planning the family business' strategy (Table 3). The economic situation, where there is a recession which is developed through reducing demand, lowering prices, profits and revenues is a matter that concerns the majority of the businesses. Family businesses suffer through a lack of knowledge of the customer base, the market and the understanding of marketing practices (74.9%). Practices are often not suitable when adopted by family businesses.

Table 3. Internal and External environment

	Yes %	No %
The instability of economy affect family businesses	90,5	9,5
Changes in technology affect the way family firm do business	64,9	35,1
The changes of Government regulations affect family firms' marketing decisions.	63,5	36,5
Staff-members participate in marketing decisions	50,9	49,1
The firm have strategic writing plan	19,0	81,0

The result is often inadequate marketing and business mistakes. Moreover, marketing planning by family firms has limited adaptation. Technological advance is proved to be one of the most important problems for small family businesses owing to the lack of expenditure and specialization, and the limitations in expertise which outline the marketing background.

Management style can be described as self-assisted, where owners have taught themselves marketing through their experience in family business.

The changes of government regulations affect 1st generation family firms' marketing decisions in a higher extent than 2nd generation. Regarding the participation of the staff-members in marketing decisions there is not any difference between 1st and 2nd generation.

The Implementation of Marketing Practices between First and Second Generation

In order to analyze the relationships among the variables data is used table cross tabulation analysis. First (1st) and second (2nd) generation of family businesses appear that are not interested in international activity except for opportunities that arise in creating low-cost products. This is perhaps due to the first generation's business founders, who cannot adapt to an ever changing and global economic environment in order to perceive the international market as a united one and segment the market into various parts, in which to develop their activities. The international activity of the businesses that responded positively is developing towards achieving competitive costs (in order to face competition in a global economy) and logistics economies.

The majority of 1st and 2nd of owners identify the lack of renewal and the need for family firms to update their portfolios by adding new products. This is due to the pressure exerted by the external environment in which the firm operates and the restricted resources that a family business has at its disposal. The creation of a portfolio of products (enhancement of new products) could initiate conditions of enriched profitability. The majority state there are seasonal variations in sales.

In addition, those firms of 1st generation that include thinking about forecasting, developing low-cost strategies and relationships as marketing are clearly sales orientated towards planning decisions. The policy that 2nd generation implements to the forecasting is to investigate in detail the reactions of their competitors Table 4.

Management of 1st and 2nd appears to be satisfied with the business's current location. This means that either no significance is placed upon logistics or many problems are solved due to a special relationship between them and the suppliers. The evolution of marketing practices in the firm from the date of its establishment is the stage of entrepreneurial marketing that is carried out instinctively as the owner learns about marketing and recognizes its value in general. Owners often have a craft or production background, which can lead to an approach incompatible with the marketing concept.

Family business of 2nd generation state that there is flexibility to find suppliers as it is oriented from the logistics point of view. Therefore it seeks for new suppliers. From the other hand, 1st generation as it is sales oriented indicate a seasonal variation in their sales while the 2nd generation is presented to make an effort to have a rate demand. The competitor's actions influence 40.8% of small family businesses pricing decisions. As far as pricing policy is concerned, 2st generation of the firms pursue the liberation of standard mark-up, while the remainder of 1st generation deems it should remain as in a closed economy as is dragged by the competitors pricing policy.

Table 4. Differences in marketing practices between first and second generation of owners

There is a second generation of owners in family firms									
	First Generation			Second Generation			Total		
Variables	Mean	S.D.	N	Mean	S.D	N	Mean	S.D	N
Forecasting sales	3,86	257	790	3,82	123	713	3,84	380	765
Do you find out what your competitors are doing	3,44	255	898	3,63	123	793	3,50	378	869
Seasonal variations in sales	3,55	257	1,155	3,17	122	1,183	3,43	379	1,176
Are you satisfied from your business current location?	3,64	257	938	3,74	122	780	3,67	379	890
Do you find new sources of suppliers?	3,88	255	840	3,95	121	805	3,90	376	828
Competitor's actions influence pricing decisions	3,37	254	1,228	3,13	119	1,154	3,29	373	1,209
Use of advertising	2,58	257	1,312	2,51	123	1,133	2,56	380	1,256
The use of sales promotion	2,17	197	1,587	2,12	104	1,554	2,15	301	1,573
Have promotional efforts worked?	2,71	255	1,261	2,72	122	1,152	2,72	377	1,225
Do you give training your staff regarding personal selling?	3,17	218	1,097	3,16	108	,949	3,17	326	1,049
Do you conduct market research	3,28	246	1,187	3,38	123	1,068	3,31	369	1,148
Use of different selling techniques or promotional methods for older versus younger customers	3,31	257	1,300	3,36	123	1,174	3,32	380	1,259
Do you find new sources of suppliers?	3,17	253	1,201	2,85	123	1,185	3,07	376	1,204

Advertising campaigns through mass media are avoided from the majority of 1st and 2nd generation. Promotional activities are reduced in 1st and 2nd, even though they have formerly proved beneficial. The limitations here arise from the minimal impact on expenditure and expertise from the point where one firm spends the minimum amount of money necessary to communicate with its customers to the point where a firm and its products are known in the marketplace. Respondents determined that customers that are developed personal communication channels where people communicate directly with each other, including face to face, person to audience, telephone or mail and word of mouth are the advertising that works best and influences customers. In favor of the above, issues such as differentiation, management, innovation and technology are considered to be of secondary importance. Those who took part in research believed that quality combined with the creation of a long-term relationship with the customer and proper pricing policies are the main factors behind a family business's survival in a competitive environment. This situation describes a reactive marketing where all customers are personally known to the owner and business tends to develop through word of mouth recommendations based on product, price and delivery.

Table 5. Mann Whitney U Test of Significance

There is a second generation of owners in family firms			
Grouping Variable:There is a perspective of 2nd generation	Seasonal variations in sales	Competitor's actions influence pricing decisions	Use of different selling techniques or promotional methods for older versus new customers
Mann-Whitney U	12752,500	13118,500	13214,000
Wilcoxon W	20255,500	20258,500	20840,000
Z	-3,074	-2,147	-2,474
Asymp. Sig. (2-tailed)	002	032	013

A trained staff can prove beneficial and 2nd generation businesses invest in them in order to have customers' feedback. Many focus on the means of promoting sales and the employees that work in them. Family business of 1st generation don't have different selling techniques or promotional methods for older versus younger customers. Here it is confirmed that 1st generation is sales oriented as new and old customers are equally treated. In reverse 2nd general take into consideration new and old customers as accounts. It is easier for 2nd generation of business to retain customers than to attract new ones. This explains the focus on a more customer-orientated system.

In general, it should be noted that the majority of family businesses are thought of as rather conservative. This could be due to the culture of the first generation, who finds it difficult to absorb new economic condition.

Using the question *if there is a perspective of second generation* deal with two sets of sample data from two contrasting areas, area of first and area of second generation, with the aim of comparing them and demonstrating differences. Mann Whitney U Test of Significance was used in order to verify whether the differences between the two sets of sample data are truly significant or whether these differences could have occurred by chance.

The findings verify that the main differences between two generation which are focused in three crucial issues of marketing practices. First matter is in the seasonal variations in sales which first generation appears to follow this policy due to lack of flexibility to find new suppliers. Compare to the 2nd generation which implements a flexible strategy pursuing a rate demand of their products‘.

The second deep-going issue is the influence that impresses the competitor's actions to 1st generation pricing decisions. With a competition-based pricing policy, 1st sets its prices by determining what other companies competing in the market charge. This means that they set the prices higher than, lower than, or on par with the competitors based on the advantages and disadvantages of a company's product or service as well as on the expected response by competitors to the set price. This last consideration-the response of competitors-is an important part of competition-based pricing, especially in markets with only a few competitors. In such a market, if one competitor lowers its price, the others will most likely lower theirs as well. While 2nd generation implements different pricing policy in order to attract the customers which is based mainly in technocratic methods deal with customers in the wake of their results.

Finally the use of different selling techniques or promotional methods for older versus younger customers 2nd generation appears to follow this promotion policy in order to obtain information from their customers.

Cross Tabulations

A cross tabulation was conducted taking into consideration first and second generation in relation with the implementation of different sectors Regarding to the perspective of first and second generation in relation the sector of activity belong the family firms from the Table 6 below showed that retailing gathers most of the second generation followed by service sector and last the construction sector.

In the Table 7 the small family business to a great extent operate in the local market, to a certain extent in national level, while a small number of firms operate in the international market.

Table 6. Sectors of activity of 2nd generation

		There is a perspective of second generation		Total
		No	yes	No
Sectors	Construction	24	17	41
	Wholesale	23	8	31
	Retailing	105	53	158
	Services	78	23	101
	Technology	1	1	2
	Other	21	17	38
Total		252	119	371

Table 7. International activity

		There is a perspective of second generation		Total
		No	Yes	No
Market	100% Local market	115	53	168
	National Market	74	40	114
	International market	29	21	50
Total		218	114	332

In this case the firms which operate in an international level asked to respond in an open question *"What influence their decision for international exports?"*. They respond that the reasons they develop international activity in order to succeed economies of scale to face the competitiveness in the global economy and the firm achieve a low logistic cost (41 firms respond this matter).The second reason is the creation of a portfolio of products (enhancement with new products) which can increase the profit (34 firms respond).Finally, family firms don't interest to exploit the new opportunities emerged from the new economy (23 firms respond. The next open question refers to "*Family firms find new customers or continue with the current customers?*"Family firms responded that they sustain the current customers and create new ones. Consequently, family businesses are customer-centric oriented. The final open question is "*What type of advertising is more effective*" firms responded that don't invest for advertising but they are supported by their customers through the "word of mouth". The Table 8 presents the results according to the sector of activity that operate the most in the international market. The sector of retailing has the most of the international activity as well as in local and national market while the service sector which is next showed a weak presence internationally but equally presence in national and local level.. In Greece the majority of family business firms that exist and operate in an international market belong to retailing and service sector.

Taking into consideration that the majority of the family business belong in four main sectors an examination between different marketing practices with the four sectors was investigated.

The results of Table 9 showed that the four sectors seek to find new sources of suppliers. Especially the construction sector influenced more the pricing decisions from competitor's actions.Therefore the firms belong to the construction sector analyze the external environment to find out what their competitors are doing. The use different selling techniques or promotional methods for older versus younger customers is the same in all sectors as well as the sales forecasting. The use of advertising it is not successful as well as the promotional efforts where in the case of retailing sector doesn't work at all.

Table 8. Markets in relation to the family business sectors

Market			Construction	Wholesale	Retailing	Services
Market	100% Local market	Count	16	7	72	59
		% within sector categories	42,1%	24,1%	51,4%	68,6%
	National market	Count	15	15	44	22
		% within sector categories	39,5%	51,7%	31,4%	25,6%
	International market	Count	7	7	24	5
		% within klados categories	18,4%	24,1%	17,1%	5,8%
Total		Count	38	29	140	86
		% within sector categories	100,0%	100,0%	100,0%	100,0%

Table 9. Marketing practices implemented in relation to the for main sector

	Construction		Wholesale		Retailing		Services	
	Mean	Std. Deviation	Mean	Std. Deviation	Mean	Std. Deviation	Mean	Std. Deviation
Do you find out what your competitors are doing	3,66	,825	3,58	,720	3,46	,910	3,40	,829
Seasonal variations in sales	3,59	1,072	3,55	1,091	3,57	1,087	3,16	1,279
Are you satisfied from your business current location?	3,51	,810	3,81	,601	3,69	,957	3,65	,925
Do you find new sources of suppliers?	4,18	,747	3,68	,748	3,97	,859	3,82	,791
Competitor's actions influence pricing decisions	3,67	1,034	3,74	1,154	3,21	1,234	3,28	1,201
Sales forecasting	3,85	,760	4,13	,619	3,81	,799	3,81	,731
Use of advertising	2,71	1,250	3,00	1,342	2,41	1,211	2,74	1,286
Have promotional efforts worked?	2,13	1,497	2,37	1,573	1,95	1,477	2,13	1,614
The use of sales promotion are successful	3,38	,861	3,43	1,136	3,07	1,041	3,16	1,054
Do you give training your staff regarding personal selling?	3,25	1,104	3,26	1,032	3,39	1,163	3,23	1,188
Do you conduct market research	3,37	1,318	3,61	1,202	3,39	1,225	3,27	1,280
Use of different selling techniques or promotional methods for older versus younger customers	3,28	1,099	3,45	1,091	3,03	1,277	3,01	1,170

In general there are not concussive differences in marketing practices between small family business sectors. Firms don't implement based on a marketing plan or in an integrated marketing mix but they are focused in fragmentary marketing practices such as pricing and personal selling and reproduce the competitors' marketing policy. At the same time their promotional efforts doesn't have worked successfully.

Taking into account the above findings the implementation of marketing practices in family business of first and second generation in general (Table 10) can be assumed in the following:

Table 10. 1st and 2nd generation Family business marketing practices

Issues Marketing Practices	1st Generation Marketing practices	2nd Generation Marketing practices
(1) Marketing limitations in expenditure and expertise	Limitations of expenditure Limitations of expertise in marketing practices	Efforts to communicate with its customers but limited investments
(2) Unspecialized marketing practices	Follow the reactions of competitors in pricing policy	
(3) Composed planning versus operations	Developing strategies of low cost and relationship marketing,	There is a balance between planning and operations decisions
(4) Marketing planning adaptation	Sales oriented	Customer oriented
(5) Entrepreneurial tinkering	Spontaneous attempts to increase sales, through occasional local advertising and brochures. Seasonal demand	Occasional local advertising and brochures. Focus in selling techniques Rate demand

As we can see from the above Table 10 belongs the second generation of owners who have developed its own policy and implement different marketing practices from this of the first generation and don't depend from the competition. Specifically, they apply a sales policy which has affected a balance in quantities of good sold per year. The applied marketing practices are independent of competitors' policy. They don't use different marketing practices to old and new customers as it does first generation.

Conclusion

First and second generation of family businesses owners face in common a number of challenges in order to survive to the next generations. The transition speed of the buying habits of their customers is in many sectors rather large as the competition techniques of the large businesses are in position to shape market rules. The ever changing market policy of the suppliers in cost and condition issues and cooperation preconditions as well as the commercial consequences of technology advances means that a family business should be informed of market and customer trends. According to the findings, the owners of family businesses do not conform to conventional marketing rules since their implementation is haphazard and informal; they make most decisions on their own, respond to current opportunities and circumstances and, therefore, any decision-making occurs in an unstructured, way, according to personal and business priorities at any given point in time. Such limitations influence the marketing concept of such businesses. Firms are involved, these of first generation however, believed that quality combined with the creation of a long-term relationship with the customer and proper pricing policy are the main factors behind a business's survival in a competitive environment.

The value creation of family business in order to obtain Entrepreneurial performance through marketing practices is succeeded with the use of some essential factors.

The Factors that positively influence the implementation of marketing practices is the relation to outside experience to family business and the time which the members are employed in business prior to taking control. In addition the relation of education to family business consists a positive factor for the second generation as well as the preparation level at taking over the management. The encouragement of 1st generation from the preceding generations in joining the business is a basic incentive for them.

The above factors are required from either 1st or second generation to obtain the essential knowledge within industry related. The phases that firm need to acquire a marketing value are the specific capabilities beginning from the basic processes of marketing practices. The first generation of the owners of family businesses do not conform to conventional marketing rules since their implementation is haphazard and informal; they make most decisions on their own, respond to current opportunities and circumstances and, therefore, any decision-making occurs in an unstructured, way, according to personal and business priorities at any given point in time. They use unsuitable marketing techniques as they don't invest in time and money to devote to marketing. From the other hand second generation has higher capabilities in marketing decision option as they are willingness to take risks and enlarge the business. The main differences of 1st and 2nd generation in adoption of marketing practices present 1st generation to be sales oriented than second generation which is oriented according to the customer needs. Thus the implementation of a pricing policy by the 1st generation is based on competitors' reactions while the 2nd generation is based on the demand of products. Finally they follow a common marketing communication strategy with limited advertising. The only exception is that second generation use selling techniques and some promotional activities for older versus new customers.

Finally, family business managers should give emphasis and reputable to gain advantages in the areas where large businesses face problems, i.e. customer service, special and personal relationships with the customers and suppliers and flexibility and tailor-made in providing services/products.

References

Avramidis, N. (2007) "Issues and Necessities of Small and Medium Size Businesses". *Aluminium Profile Magazine*, Vol. 7. (15-17).

Bhide, A. (1994) "How Entrepreneurs Craft Strategies That Work". *Harvard Business Review,* Vol. March April pp150–61.

Carson, D. (1990) "Some Exploratory Models for Assessing Small Firms' Marketing Performance (A Qualitative Approach)". *European Journal of Marketing*, Vol. 24 (11-12).

Grant Thornton Research in *Alba Economic Post*, 12 April 2003.

Hill, J. (2001) "A Multidimensional Study Of The Key Determinants Of Effective Sme Marketing Activity: Part 1". *International Journal Of Entrepreneurial Behaviour and Research,* Vol. 7 (5) pp 171–204.

Hogarth Scott, S.; Watson, K.; Wilson, N. (1996) "Do Small Businesses Have To Practice Marketing To Survive And Grow?". *Marketing Intelligence And Planning,* Vol. 14 pp 6–18.

Kenny, B.; Dyson, K. (1989) "*Marketing In Small Business*". Routledge, London.

Kotler, P. (2002) "Marketing Management". Prentice-Hall, Inc. Pearson Education Company NY.

Kotler, P.; Armstrong, G.; Saunders, J.; Wong, V. (1999) "Principles Of Marketing Second European Edition". Prentice Hall Europe, London.

Kyriazopoulos, P.; Terzidis, K. (2000) *"Management SME in the 3rd Industrial Revolution "*. Sychroni Ekdotiki, Athens.

Makridakis, S.; Caloghirou, Y.; Papagiannakis, L.; Trivellas, P. (1997) "The Dualism Of Greek Firms And Management: Present State And Future Implications" *European Management Journal* Vol.15 (4-15).

McTavish, A. R.; Gunasekaran, S. G.; Yli-Olli, P. (1996) "Establishing A Strategic Framework For Improving Productivity*". Integrated Manufacturing Systems,* Vol.7 (4) pp 12–21.

Poutziouris, P. (2003) "The Strategic Orientation Of Owner-Managers Of Small Ventures Evidence From The UK Small Business Economy". *International Journal Of Entrepreneurial Behaviour and Research,* Vol.9 (5) pp 185–214.

Rosenblat, P.C.; De Milk, L.; Anderson, R. M.; Jhonson, P. A. (1985) "The Family In Business: Understanding The Dealing With The Challenges Entrepreneurial Families Face". Jossey Bass, San Francisco, CA.

Scott, M.; Bruce, R. (1987) "Five Stages Of Growth In Small Businesses". *Long Range Planning,* Vol.20 (3) pp 45–52.

Sharma, P.; Chrisman, J.; Chua, J. (1996) "A Review And Annotated Bibliography Of Family Business Studies". Kluwer, Boston, MA.

Stanworth, J.; Gray, C. (eds) (1991) "20 Years On: The Small Firm In The 1990s". Paul Chapman, London.

Wang, Y. (2002) "*Succession Issues And Business Performance: Evidence From UK Small And Medium-Sized Family Businesses",* Unpublished doctoral dissertation, Southampton Institute, Southampton, UK.

Ward, J. L.; Aronoff, C. E. (1990) "To Sell Or Not To Sell?". *Nation's Business,* Vol.78 (1) pp 63–64.

Watts, G.; Cope, J.; Hulme, M. (1998) "Anshoff's Matrix, Pain And Gain Growth Strategies And Adaptive Learning Among Small Food Producers". *International Journal Of Entrepreneurial Behaviour and Research,* Vol.4 (2) pp 101–111.

Westhead, P.; Cowling, M. (1995) "Employment Change In Independent Owner-Managed High-Technology Firms In Great Britain", *Small Business Economics* Vol.7 (2) pp 111–140.

Yilmazer, T.; Schrank, H. (2006) "Financial Intermingling In Small Family Businesses". *Journal Of Business Venturing,* Vol.21 pp 726–751.

In: HRM and Marketing Orientation in the New Era
Editor: Panagiotis Kyriazopoulos
ISBN: 978-1-62808-959-2

Chapter 5

MODELING THE HUMAN FACTOR OF MARRIAGE MARKET DYNAMICS THROUGH OPERATIONS MANAGEMENT TECHNIQUES: A CASE STUDY INVOLVING SOCIOLOGICAL AND PSYCHOLOGICAL ATTRIBUTES

Jacques-Antoine Gauthier*[*1], Nguyen Vi Cao[2], Marlène Sapin[3], Emmanuel Fragnière[4] and Eric Widmer[5]
[1]University of Lausanne, Switzerland
[2]Haute Ecole de Gestion de Genève, Switzerland
[3]Swiss Centre of Expertise in the Social Sciences, Switzerland
[4]University of Bath, School of Management, UK
[5]University of Geneva, Switzerland

ABSTRACT

What are the actual attributes of men and women that lead to the optimal couple matching? In fact, many research findings already enable researchers to assess the probability that a given couple will divorce or not over the life course. Typically, sociological as well as psychological variables (e.g. respectively level of education and mental health) significantly affect the longevity of unions. However, such type of assessment is complex as it should also take into account the combination of these factors. To address this issue, we have developed an optimization model that minimizes the number of divorces in a given society. We assume a theoretical model which states that a central agency knows exactly the characteristics of all potential mates and is in the position to decide how to match them. We have thus solved a Mixed Integer Program based on the linear assignment model to match two equal groups of men and women. Based on a representative and longitudinal sample of 1074 cohabitating and married couples in Switzerland, we estimate various objective functions corresponding to age,

* Address for correspondence: Jacques-Antoine Gauthier, University of Lausanne, Research Center Methodology, Inequalities and Social Change (MISC), Bâtiment de Vidy, CH – 1015 Lausanne, Switzerland. e-mail: Jacques-Antoine.Gauthier@unil.ch; Phone: +41 21 692 38 43 Fax +41 21 692 38 45.

education, religious affiliation and devotion, ethnicity, depression, and previous divorce experience based on all possible pairs of men and women belonging to the sample. Results show that the current state of marriages or partnerships is well below the social optimum. Of course this provocative stance does not support the idea that optimizing marriage is indeed possible or desirable. Instead, it shows that operations management techniques usually employed for solving production problems can also be used to better understand this crucial issue of social sciences.

1. Introduction

A large body of literature shows the economic, social, and psychological costs associated with divorce (Amato, 2000). Spouse separations exert adverse consequences on future generations because it causes significant negative effects on children's educational trajectories and therefore on human capital (Amato and Keith, 1991; Amato, 2000; Cherlin et al., 1998). From this perspective, a slight reduction of the frailty of couples might diminish the social and economic costs of family breakdowns (Becker, 1981). In a recent article that attracted much public and scientific interest (Cao, Fragnière, Gauthier, Sapin, and Widmer, 2010), we state that "men and women 'choose' their mates on the basis of feelings of love, physical attraction, similarity of tastes, beliefs, attitudes, and shared values. All of these determinants are supposed to help them be happy together (Berscheid and Reis, 1998; Yela and Sangrador, 2001; Hohmann-Marriott, 2006; Myers, 2006). However, research has shown that the longevity of marriages or partnerships also depends on objective attributes such as differences in age, family history, and educational levels (Bumpass and Sweet, 1972; Wagner, 1993; Kalmijn, 1994, 1998). Thus, how can we optimize romantic partner attributes, and how far from the optimum is the current situation" (Cao et al., 2010, p. 547)? Therefore, assessing the extent to which couples are paired optimally may be realized in the light of the minimization of divorces and separations. Unexpectedly, the publication of our results gave rise to numerous reactions and comments (http://www.edwidmer.org/page-pub4-100). Many claim that focusing exclusively on objective criteria was insufficient to explain the stability of marriage. Therefore this chapter aims at proposing a substantive enhancement and discusses the initial paper by integrating cultural and psychological variables within the mathematical approach developed in it. To this aim, we integrate cultural and psychological variables in a new empirical model. This mathematical approach reallocates spouses in order to reduce the likelihood of divorce within the set of constraints defining the marriage market. It is organized as follows.

In Section 2, we present research findings concerning the marriage market and divorces. In Section 3, we describe the sociological survey used to build the database and the optimization parameters developed through econometrics models. In Section 4, we describe the optimization model we developed. In Sections 5 and 6, we present, interpret, and discuss the results of our case study in light of the debate surrounding the initial paper.

2. Dynamic of the Marriage Market: What Makes Couples Split?

The marriage market is constrained by objective factors. Studies show that the tendency of similar individuals to match is overly dominant, a well known fact described by sociologists as "homogamy" (Blackwell and Lichter, 2004; Kalmijn, 1998). Spouses tend to be similar with respect to social characteristics such as social origin, education, race, ethnicity, religion, and age. Interaction opportunities in mate selection can be studied in a macro-level perspective. First, they depend on the relative size of the various groups present in a population, and second, on the distribution of social groups across space. Homogamy is stronger in large groups and in areas in which groups are dominant. The rate of heterogamy is directly related to the heterogeneity of the population (Blau et al., 1982; Blau and Swartz, 1984). Individuals belonging to small minorities are forced to marry out of their groups because few potential spouses are available in their own groups. Therefore, homogamy and heterogamy depend to a large extent on the homogeneity or heterogeneity of the society considered in terms of cohort sizes, educational levels, religious and ethnic composition, etc.

Homogamy has been hypothesized to affect conjugal satisfaction and divorce. Overall, it was found that heterogamous marriages or partnerships increase the probability of break-up. Indeed, cultural dissimilarities increase the likelihood of divorce (Price-Bonham and Balswick, 1980; Felmlee et al., 1990; Janssen, 2002). For age heterogamy, the likelihood of a break-up increases when the wife is older (Janssen, 2002). Couples in which one partner is divorced have a higher probability of breaking up (Cherlin and Furstenberg, 1994). The results for educational levels are more mixed. Some studies show that educationally homogamous marriages are more stable than educationally mixed marriages (Bumpass, Castro Martin and Sweet, 1991; Jalovaara, 2001; Tzeng, 1992).

2.1. Religion, Partnerships and Divorce

For many early sociologists, religion is a central institutional and moral force that protects the community against anomy (Durkheim, 2008[1912]). In the industrialized countries of late modernity, despite the overall decrease of traditional church attendance (Voicu, 2009), with the notable exception of the U.S., institutionalized religious values remain a central cultural reference because they still exert strong normative influences on individual orientations (Giddens, 2005). Everyday interactions and social practices are to some extent loaded with religious references as they happen in fields of symbolic power, concerning the properties regarding the judgment of taste, for instance (Bourdieu, 1979; Swartz, 1996). In other words, such "cultural norms consist of rules which detail acceptable ways to speak, think, feel and behave" (Fay, 1996, p. 56).

In the family realm, religious norms influence the ways in which conjugal and parental roles are defined and the extent to which these roles are interchangeable and gendered. The early internalization of such patterns of reference is therefore a key element on which homophily and homogamy may then develop (Reiss, 1960; Berger and Kellner, 1964). However, the survival of these widespread cultural norms in current Western countries is paralleled by a strong process of individualization that brings substantial changes in particular in the recognition of alternative groups and behaviors as well as in gender relationships, the sexual division of labor, and the value of marriage (Voicu, 2009; Whyte, 1990; Kohli, 1985). In this context, empirical research shows that couples with poor levels of cohesive strategies face more relational difficulties and are more likely to split than the others (Widmer, Kellerhals, and Levy, 2003, 2004).

Astonishingly, very few studies have addressed the relationship between religious factors and divorce (for a review see Vaaler, Ellison, and Powers, 2009). The available literature shows that at least two linked dimensions concerning religion play a role in marital dissolution: religious affiliation (Lehrer and Chiswick, 1993) and attendance patterns (Call and Heaton, 1997). Both dimensions reflect various functional configurations as denominational homogamy (i.e., partners belonging to the same religious community) supposes shared values between spouses concerning marriage, fertility, childrearing, gender roles, leisure activities, finance, and friendship choices, whereas attendance favors the enactment of the normative orientations supported by one's affiliation. Since it facilitates social cohesion (Coleman, 1988), the latter extends the values orientation of the couple to a broader community and improves the social resources available to couples (Bourdieu, 1980). However, these indicators reflect complex and interdependent social realities. The extent to which individuals evaluate and report their religious affiliation and the frequency of their religious attendance depends on many factors such as the context in which either spouses are embedded, the degree of conformity toward social desirability, and the amount of economic, social, and cultural capital available to them (i.e., types of social network composition, social support, social resources).

We may hypothesize on the one hand that the increasing variability of social configurations of reference favors conjugal conflict and separation because it is associated with a loosening of conjugal ties partly due to reduced solidarity with the community and to new challenges concerning couple power relationships. On the other hand, shared religious values may simply increase the social cost of divorce independently of the dynamic and quality of the conjugal relationships.

2.2. Depression and Divorce

It is not only cultural factors that are at play as far as conjugal satisfaction and divorce are concerned—psychological factors also have an impact. Research findings highlight the association between depression, marital distress, and divorce (e.g., Tschann et al., 1989; Mastekaasa, 1995; Overbeek, et al., 2006). Some research discusses the causal sequence, whereas other research remains silent about it. Further research questions deal more with the impact of divorce on depression than with the role of depression or marital distress in marital dissolution. While a lot of research focuses on clinical populations, others research, mostly in epidemiology, uses nonclinical community samples. From this perspective, two approaches have been undertaken: a categorical view of depressive symptomatology versus a dimensional view that considers depression on a continuum of varying degree of complaints (Henne, et al., 2003; Ruscio and Ruscio, 2000). Numerous researchers seek to explain through which processes depression and divorce are related, focusing either on individual features or on relational dimensions.

Many studies involving distressed couples focus specifically on the couple's communication and conflict resolution. A "marital discord model" has been proposed with regard to depression (Gotlib and Hooley, 1988; Beach, et al., 1990). According to this model, in addition to individual vulnerability factors, marital discord decreases available support from the partner and marital distress aggravates major stressors in the relationship. Depressed patients are negative or deficient in communication, problem solving, and conflict resolution (Heim and Snyder, 1991; Christensen, and Shenk, 1991). In a longitudinal research, Merikangas (1984) found that divorce rates increases significantly when one, and to a larger extent both spouses, are depressed compared to the general population.

In addition to the relational factors of conjugal communication and adjustment, several dimensions can play a role on both the individual and the relational levels, as is the case for cognitive distortions or negative attribution style (Heene et al., 2003). Research on attribution styles stresses that, in the case of interpersonal or personal problems, depressed individuals display negative cognitions, blaming themselves for negative events (Finchman, et al., 1989, Heene et al., 2003). Attachment style is also a dimension that may potentially occur on both the individual and relational levels. Empirical findings claim that attachment style is an important mediator for relational functioning (Carnelley et al., 1994; Ceglian and Gardner, 1999) and that depression is related specifically to "fearful avoidance style," characterized by a negative self-image combined with distrust of others (Carnelley et al., 1994).

Other evidence reveals more generally that "insecure attachment style" is associated with depressive symptoms (Roberts, Gotlib, and Kassel, 1996). Focusing on personality traits, Zuroff and Fitzpatrick (1995) highlight the relationship between insecure attachment and depressive personality style as characterized by traits such as dependency or neuroticism.

On an individual level, personality research examines the links between personality traits and important life outcomes such as divorce (Roberts et al., 2007). Several prospective studies covering large time spans demonstrate that traits associated with neuroticism such as anxiety or sensitivity increase the probability of divorce (Kelley and Conley, 1987; Tucker et al., 1998; Roberts et al., 2007). Conversely, conscientious and agreeable individuals remain in their marriage longer (Kelly and Conley, 1987). As a matter of fact, personality traits shape the quality of long term relationships and, as emphasized by Karney and Bradbury (1995), neuroticism is one of the strongest and most consistent predictors of marital dissatisfaction, conflict, abuse, and, finally, dissolution.

To summarize, there is strong empirical evidence that marriage choices are constrained by individual social, cultural, and psychological characteristics. However, treating this well documented phenomenon as a stock control issue was highly provocative and triggered numerous public reactions.

We decided to take advantage of these criticisms and considered them in two respects in the present chapter. On one hand, they drove us to extend our initial model to cultural and psychological dimensions bound to the dynamic of the marriage market, namely the impact of religious affiliation and church attendance, as well as that of depression on marriage stability. On the other hand, these remarks prompted us to discuss our results on that matter in a way that plays down the provocative dimension of the article while broadening its scope and making it accessible to a broader audience. Therefore, the present chapter aims not only at estimating the social and individual benefits of a reduction in the likelihood of divorce through the reallocation of individuals in more optimal configuration, it also points out the potential advantages and pitfalls associated with interdisciplinary approaches in social sciences research.

3. Data and Parameters

We use data from the Swiss contemporary family survey conducted in 1999 (Widmer et al., 2003). It is a representative random sample of 1,534 couples, married or unmarried, aged from 18 to 75, residing in the three linguistic areas of Switzerland. A follow up of 1,074 of those couples was done in 2004 and examines how many couples separated between 1999 and 2004 (Widmer et al., 2006). Available data provide information for both partners on socio-demographic dimensions based on items measuring age, educational level, ethnicity, religious denomination and practices, and previous divorces. Individual characteristics such as depression also are recorded using a scale based on several items.

In order to determine the level of depression of each individual, a factor analysis is performed on a depression scale of six items (inspired by the CES-D scale, Radloff, 1977), measuring a lack of energy, anxiety, feeling of loneliness, depressive symptoms, aggressiveness, and somatic symptoms. Two factors emerge. The first factor measures somatic and physical symptoms and the second factor focuses on psychological symptoms. We retain this second factor that divides the population in two groups—the first gathering individuals showing a positive score for depression and the second consisting of people who score negatively on this factor, revealing no or scarcely no symptoms of depression, anxiety, or loneliness.

Then we use logistic regression analysis to estimate the specific influence of these variables on the break-up. The logistic regression model is usually used in social sciences to capture the qualitative nature of interdependencies in multivariate analysis (see Jaccard, 2001, for a more detailed explanation).

The aim of these models is to predict the probability that an individual will belong to a given group or category, knowing her/his personal characteristics. In our case the dependent variable represents the probability (or odds) of divorce.

The dependent variable is explained by a set of independent or predictor variables. Because of the nonlinearity of the logistic model, its coefficients are related to the impact of the predictor on the probability of divorce. Indeed, to have an idea of the quantitative effect of each predictor, we must compute the marginal effects for the average individual (or for any individual in the sample). Consequently, marginal effects measure the change in the probability of divorce if an independent variable increases by one unit, everything else being constant. Therefore, for each couple in the dataset, a set of variables used as predictors are constructed to measure homogamy in terms of difference of age (five categories), nationality as a proxy for cultural origin (six categories), level of education (four categories), and divorce from a previous partner (four categories) as a proxy for homogamy of family trajectories. Additionally, we consider dimensions such as spoken language (three categories), religious affiliation (four categories), church attendance (three categories), and depression (four categories), as declared by each member of each couple. Eventually, the parameter estimates produced by the logistic regression expressed as odds ratios are used to weight the criteria in the optimization model. A large weight associated with a given predictor indicates a strong statistical influence toward couple dissolution during the period of observation (Table 1).

Overall, the odds ratios follow the literature on the effects of homogamy on marital stability. Couples in which the wife is older than the man as well as those in which both partners have different family trajectories (especially when men have divorced) have greater odds of splitting. Conversely, when both partners are Christian, speak a Swiss national language, and/or are not depressed, the probability of divorce is significantly lower. However, some results balance the overall prediction of a positive effect of homogamy. For instance, the probability of a break-up is significantly higher when both partners have low levels of education (whereas odds are lower when partners are higher educated), do not attend religious services regularly, and/or declare depressive symptoms.

Table 1. Risk of couple dissolution (odds ratio) according to a set of categorical predictors

Criteria	Predictors	Odds ratio
Age difference	Wife is 5+ years older than husband	5.569**
	Wife is 4-2 years older than husband	2.455
	Wife is as old as husband (REF)	-
	Wife is 4-2 years younger than husband	0.995
	Wife is 5+ years younger than husband	1.144
Previous divorce	No previous divorce (REF)	-
	Wife has divorced previously	2.019
	Husband has divorced previously	4.184**
	Wife and husband have divorced previously	1.307
Difference in educational level	Wife and husband have a low educational level (REF)	-
	Wife has a higher educational level than husband	0.120*
	Wife has a lower educational level than husband	0.409*
	Wife and husband have a high educational level	0.400*
National heterogeneity	Wife and husband are Swiss citizens (REF)	-
	One is Swiss and the other from Western country	2.090
	Both from Western countries	2.970
	One is Swiss and the other from non-Western country	2.070
	Both from non-Western country	1.029
Religious heterogeneity	Both spouses have the same religion (REF)	-
	One spouse is Catholic the other Protestant	0.411*
	One spouse is Christian the other belongs to an other religion	6.258
	One spouse has a religion the other has no religion	1.669
Difference in religious practice	Both spouses practice religion the same way (REF)	-
	Both spouses do not practice religion	10.250**
	One spouse practices religion and the other does not	9.576
Difference in language	Both spouses speak the same language (REF)	-
	Spouses speak a different language	0.225*
Depression	Neither spouse feels bad or depressed (REF)	-
	Man feels bad or depressed	2.679*
	Woman feels bad or depressed	2.033
	Both spouses feel bad or depressed	5.678**

Global significance likelihood ratio test: Chi^2: 104.2415; df: 24; $p < .0001$.
* $p<.05$; ** $p<.01$.

4. MINIMIZING DIVORCE BY MEAN OF LINEAR ASSIGNMENT

The assignment problem is a category of optimization problems emanating from the academic discipline of operations research. Operations research is a field originally from military science with the objective of addressing logistical issues through mathematical models. After World War II, operations research has been applied in the industrial sector to deal with issues such as inventory and supply chain management. In this case, assignment problems deal with the matching of machines or workers to specific tasks in order to produce a given output at minimum cost.

As a matter of fact most academic developments of the assignment problems have been applied in the context of industrialized production. It is noteworthy that one of the rare but very well known uses of the assignment model outside industrial production is called the "stable marriage problem" (Gale and Shapley, 1962; Gusfield and Irving, 1989).

The assignment problem is a case of combinatorial optimization where the optimal solution is found out of a huge number of combinations. The algorithm, or the solution method, explores many of these combinations in an intelligent manner in order to find the optimal combination. To understand more intuitively the assignment problem, we present a production example.

Let us consider a workshop where four workers need to be assigned to each of four tasks. Each of the four workers can execute the four tasks. However, each worker will complete each task in different times according to its specific skills. Therefore, the goal is to assign each of the four workers to a single task to minimize the overall time of executing all tasks. In that particular case, the number of tasks is equal to the number of workers. It corresponds to the linear assignment problem.

We understand that it is a combinatorial problem since we need to try every possible combination leading to the lowest total completion time of all tasks. In this particular case, this is manageable since the number of combinations is 24 (i.e., 4! or 2*3*4).

When the number of matches is high, as is the case in real production problems, a computerized algorithm is necessary to obtain the optimal solution in a reasonable time. Many papers have been published on model applications and algorithm developments (for a general overview see Burkard et al., 2008; Lovász and Plummer, 1986; Schrijver, 2003).

In this chapter, we apply the linear assignment model to optimize spousal allocation in order to reduce the likelihood of divorce. In this perspective, women correspond to the workers and men to the tasks of the previous production example.

The optimization criterion is no longer the completion time of tasks, but a parameter reflecting the probability of divorce associated with each possible couple of men and women in the sample. Mathematically, the general form of the linear assignment problem applied to the marriage stability issue becomes a linear programming (LP) problem (Equation 1)[1]

We have a set of men and an equal number of women. The optimization process will lead to the optimal pairing of women and men in the sample until every man is paired with a woman. The linear assignement problem is presented under the form of a linear programming problem as follows: the first equation is minimized.

[1] A mathematical presentation of the method is available in our previous publication on that matter (Cao et al., 2010).

$$\min \sum_c \sum_w \sum_m p^c_{w,m} x_{w,m}$$
$$\text{s.t.} \sum_m x_{w,m} = 1, \forall w \in W$$
$$\sum_w x_{w,m} = 1, \forall m \in M$$

$$x_{wm} = \begin{Bmatrix} 1 \text{ if woman } w \in W \text{ is assigned to man } m \in M \\ 0 \text{ otherwise} \end{Bmatrix}$$

Equation 1. General form of the linear assignment problem applied to the marriage stability issue.

This is the objective function that is a multiple summation of the product of variable x (taking the values 1 or 0 to indicate whether woman w is paired with man m) with variable p which is the cost of divorce (the value of which corresponds to the odds ratios computed from the logistic regression presented above).

In the second part of the equation, "st" is an abbreviation that stands for "subject to." It is followed by the constraints of the assignment model that will ensure that a man will be paired exclusively with a single woman and vice versa. These constraints might seem obvious to the reader, but this needs to be spelled out for the algorithm implemented in the computer. This formulation has the advantage of being generic. Therefore, whatever the size of the set of men and women, it remains the same. In the present case, we use GAMS (Brooke et al, 1992; Rosenthal, 2007), a modeling langage, to generate an example of this problem based on our Swiss database and CPLEX (1992), a solver to obtain an optimal solution.

5. Implementation and Results

We implement the optimization model presented above into an integer programming (IP) model using the GAMS language. From the 1,074 couples surveyed, we eliminated 51 couples that presented missing values for at least one of the criteria considered. Then, the model had 1,023 couples, $1{,}023^2$ binary variables and 1,023! different solutions. We pre-compute the cost function for the $1{,}023^2$ possible couples and solve the model using CPLEX.

5.1. Global Results

The solution we obtained for 1,023 couples is optimal. In this solution, 99.41 percent of couples were reallocated. Figure 1 shows the variation of the objective function of all couples, computed as the difference between initial and final costs. Since the objective function improves in the final solution for approximately 75 percent of the couples, most of the points are above zero.

Figure 2 shows that for all criteria, the objective function in the final solution (dark columns) is lower than the objective function in the initial solution (white columns). In other words, no criterion was worsened to improve other criteria through the optimization process.

Figure 2 also reveals that with all criteria included, the total objective function improves by approximately 15 percent of its initial value.

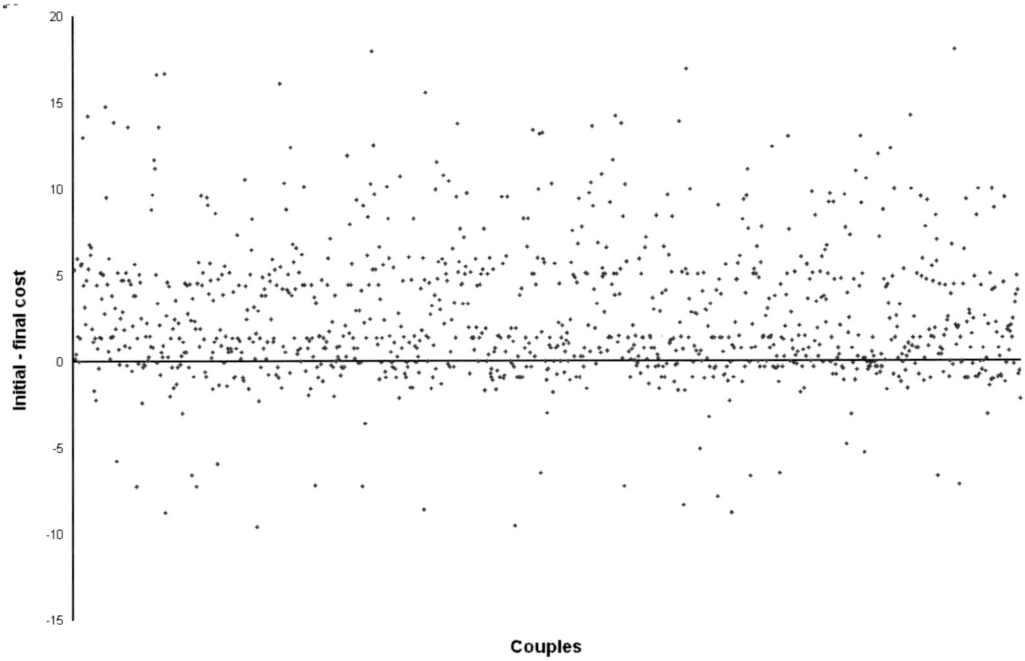

Figure 1. Improvement of the objective function between initial and final solutions for each couple in the sample (represented by one point on the figure).

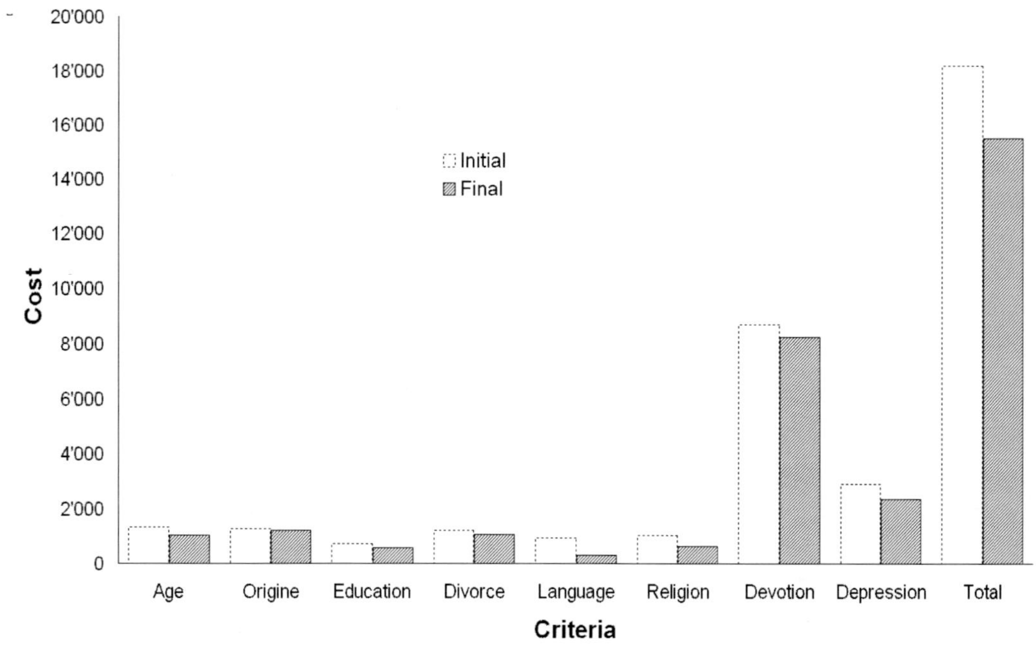

Figure 2. Improvement of the objective function between initial and final solutions.

Figures 3 and 4 show the number of couples in each category of the criteria selected in the initial solution (white columns) and in the final solution (dark columns).

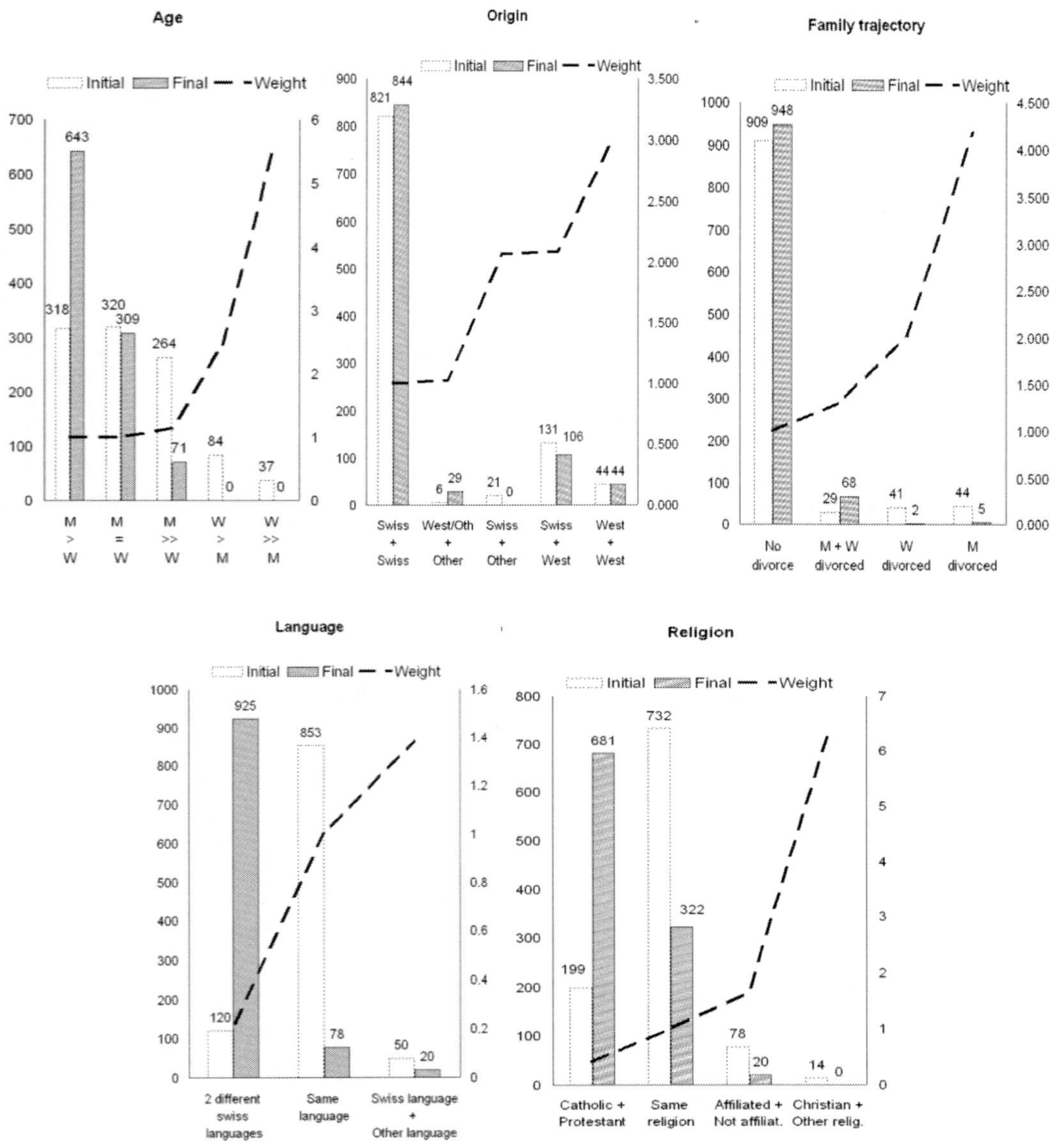

Figure 3. Dimensions for which high cost couples in initial solution are replaced by low cost couples in the final solution.

The cost function (dark broken line) reveals that low cost categories are grouped on the left and high cost categories are on the right. For five out of eight criteria (age, origin, family trajectory, language, and religion), white columns are lower than dark columns on the left (low cost categories) and white columns are higher than dark columns on the right (high cost categories). Therefore, in the final solution, high cost couples are replaced by low cost couples for these criteria (see Figure 3).

For the remaining criteria (education, devotion, and depression), in the final solution, the number of couples increases not only in configurations characterized by lower risk of break-up (the left part of the graphs) but also in more risky settings (right part of the graphs; see Figure 4).

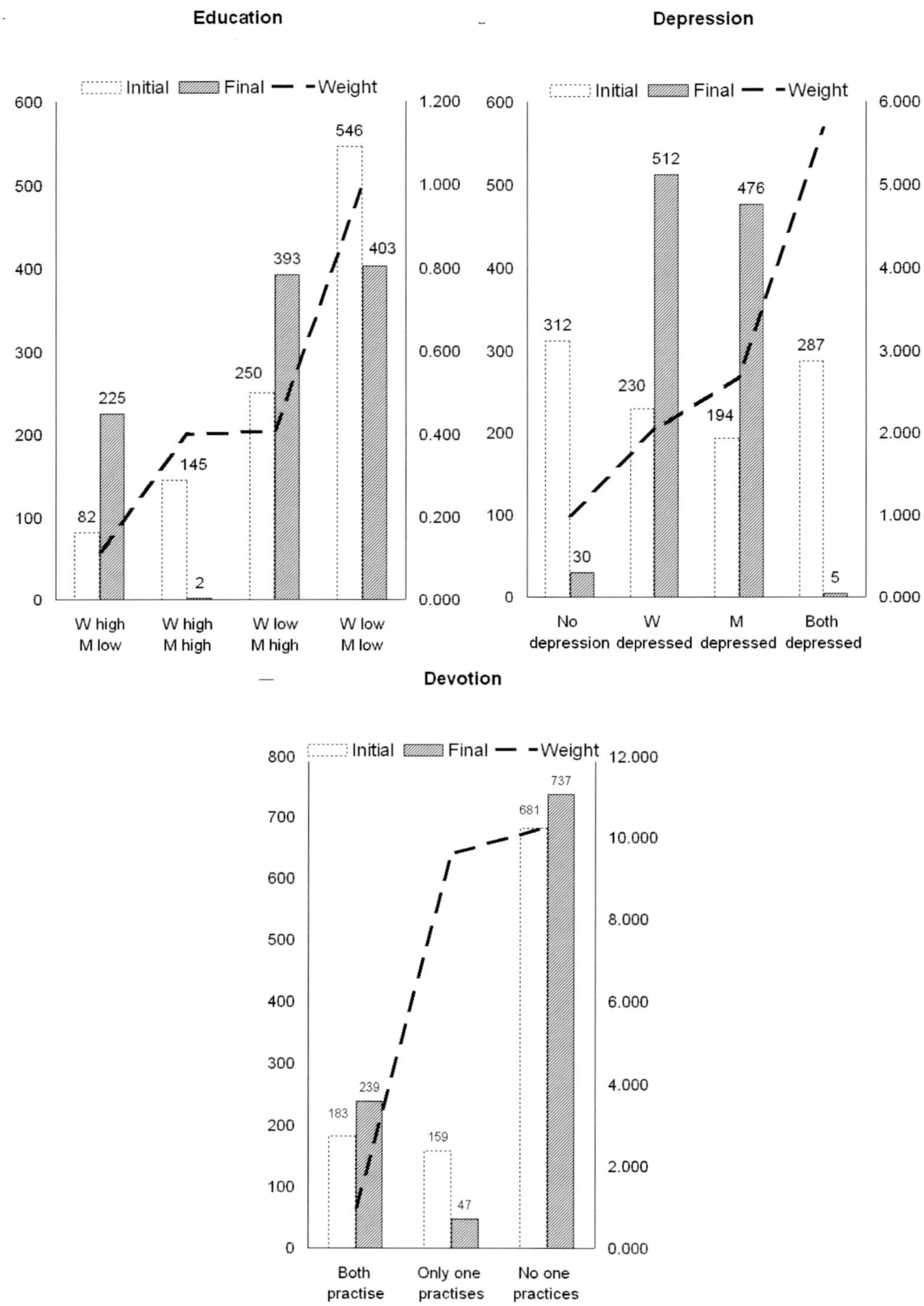

Figure 4. Dimensions for which the frequency of some high costs categories increase in the final solution.

However, as indicated in Figure 2, the total cost of these three criteria improves globally in the final solution. For the depression criterion, 282 homogamous couples in which both partners are depressed are combined with 282 "opposite" homogamous couples in which neither partner is depressed. This results in the formation of two sets of 282 heterogamous couples, one counting only depressive men the other only depressed women. Although in this case the costs of heterogamous couples (2.033 and 2.679) are higher than the cost of homogamous couples of non-depressive partners (1.000), they are much lower than the cost of homogamous couples in which both partners are depressed (5.678). Therefore, overall the objective function decreases by 282*(5.678 + 1 - 2.679 - 2.033) for this criterion. The same computation occurs for the educational criterion where two sets of 286 homogamous couples are combined (weighted 1 and 0.400) to form two sets of 286 corresponding heterogamous couples (weighted 0.120 and 0.409) that improve the final objective function. For the devotion criterion, the objective function is also improved with the transformation of 112 hetorogamous couples (weighted 9.576) into 56 homogamous couples (weighted 1) and 56 opposite homogamous couples (weighted 10.250). To summarize, in the final solution, the frequency of couples in some high cost categories may increase, but the objective function is improved overall for criteria concerning education, depression, and devotion. Overall, 67 percent of individuals have been attributed a partner in a different age category in the final solution; 51 percent for education, 17 percent for citizenship of origin, 9 percent for family trajectory, 84 percent for language, 61 percent for religion, 16 percent for devotion, and 59 percent for depression.

5.2. Profile Analysis

What is the profile of the couples in light of their propensity to divorce? Let us consider the groups of couples corresponding to the first and the tenth deciles of the weight distribution used for the optimization. The scores of the first group in the initial configuration range from 6.48 to 9.82, whereas for the same group in the optimized configuration, the range is [5.75 - 7.72]. On the other hand, for the tenth deciles the corresponding ranges are [22.14 - 31.89] and [18.15 – 21.08] for the initial and the optimized population respectively. This denotes the overall risk reduction brought about by the optimization for these contrasted groups not only on the total range of scores, but also on the difference between the first and last deciles of each group. Table 2 describes the profiles of the couples belonging to the four groups we described, by detailing the distribution of the items forming the eight criteria used for optimization.

Table 2 demonstrates that the optimization process tends to reduce the diversity of couple configurations as it increases the number of categories with no more than one percent of the sample, for example.

However, the remaining variability in all groups underlines the fact that there is no unique formula to pair individuals when considering the risk of divorce. However, by reducing the gap between higher and lower risk groups, the optimization process forms more homogeneous couples compared to the initial solutions. This result is confirmed by a lower standard deviation of the objective function in the final solution (3.95) compared to the initial solution (4.32). Figure 5 orders all couple profiles found in the initial and final solutions by their objective function. It shows clearly that cost profiles stemming from the final solution are concentrated on the left of the figure, while the original cost profiles are more widespread and more frequent among the highest scores. In other words, there are more low cost couples in the final solution than in the initial solution. Figure 5 also shows that some profiles associated with specific costs are overrepresented. The most frequent couple cost profiles provided by the objective function are 16.914 (n=67) and 16.323 (n=58).

Finally, Figure 6 confirms that there are more low cost profiles in the final solution than in the initial solution. For instance, if we only take into account the cost profiles that are lower than 18, the initial situation includes only 48 percent of such couples, whereas this proportion reaches 86 percent in the final solution.

Table 2. Profiles of higher and lower risk groups (first and last deciles of the cost distribution) in both the initial and final configurations, weighted, in percent (W=women; M=men)

Spouses characteristics	Initial High (1st decile)	Initial Low (10th decile)	Final High (1st decile)	Final Low (10th decile)
Age difference	%	%	%	%
W is 4-2 years older than M	2.8	18.4	0.0	0.0
W is 4-2 years younger than M	39.6	13.6	75.0	45.5
W is as old as M	28.3	16.5	21.3	45.5
W is 5+ years older than M	0.0	26.2	0.0	0.0
W is 5+ years younger than M	29.2	25.2	3.7	8.9
National heterogeneity				
Swiss + Swiss citizens	94.3	49.5	99.1	34.8
Swiss + West. country	3.8	33.0	0.9	32.1
Swiss + Other non West. country	0.9	5.8	0.0	0.0
West. + West. countries	0.9	9.7	0.0	26.8
West. + other/two other countries	0.0	1.9	0.0	6.3
Difference of educational level				
W low level + M low level	60.4	48.5	19.4	58.9
W high level + M low level	9.4	6.8	31.5	8.9
W low level + M high level	18.9	23.3	49.1	31.3
W high level + M high level	11.3	21.4	0.0	0.9
Previous divorce				
No divorce	99.1	63.1	100.0	77.7
W divorced	0.9	16.5	0.0	0.9
M divorced	0.0	18.4	0.0	0.0
M and W divorced	0.0	1.9	0.0	21.4
Difference of language				
Same language	89.6	70.9	0.9	29.5
Two different Swiss languages	10.4	14.6	99.1	64.3
Swiss + other language	0.0	14.6	0.0	6.3
Difference of religious affiliation				
Same religion	93.4	55.3	27.8	46.4
Catholic + Protestant	6.6	13.6	72.2	38.4
Christian + other	0.0	9.7	0.0	0.0
Affiliated + not affiliated	0.0	21.4	0.0	15.2
Difference of church attendance				
Both practice	100.0	0.0	100.0	0.0

Spouses characteristics	Initial High (1st decile)	Initial Low (10th decile)	Final High (1st decile)	Final Low (10th decile)
No practice	0.0	87.4	0.0	94.6
Only one practices	0.0	12.6	0.0	5.4
Depression				
No depression	46.2	1.0	8.3	0.0
M depressed	25.5	7.8	26.9	70.5
W depressed	28.3	10.7	64.8	26.8
Both depressed	0.0	80.6	0.0	2.7

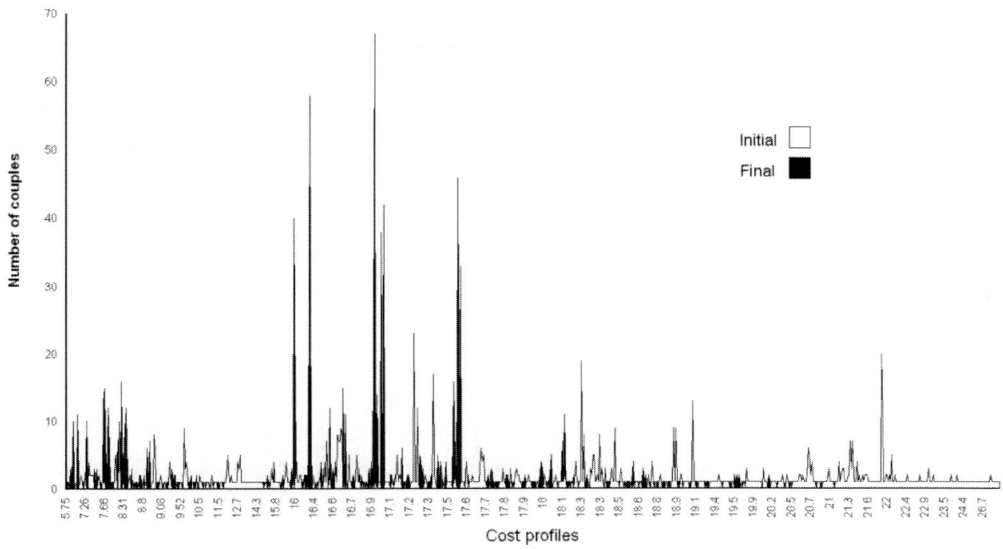

Figure 5. Couples' cost profiles distribution.

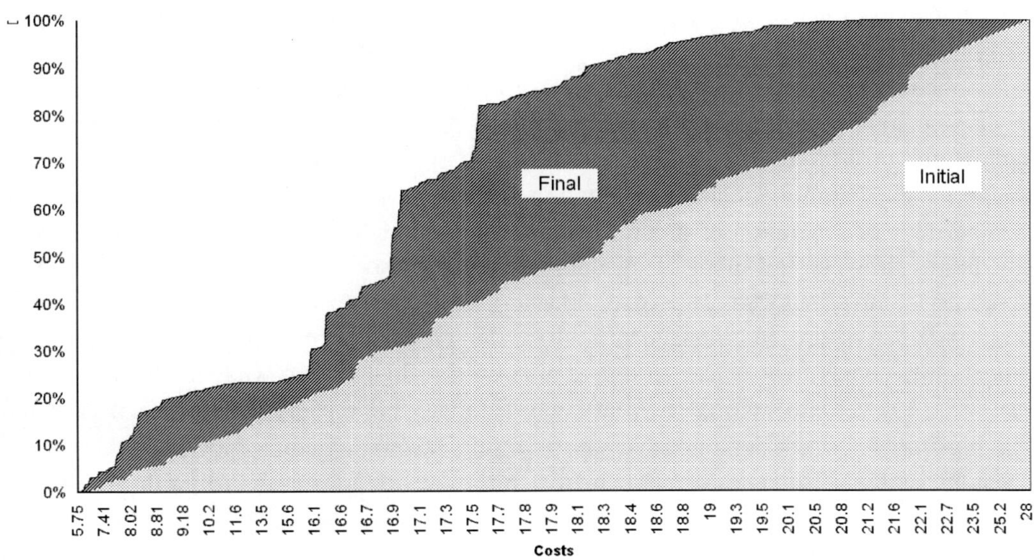

Figure 6. Cumulated proportion of couples in the initial and final solutions, ordered by cost profile.

CONCLUSION

This chapter proposes an innovative method for optimizing the allocation of partners in couples by applying an operation research model. In the optimization model we pair men and women in a way that minimizes the number of divorces for a given society. This allocation is done using empirical criteria obtained through straightforward statistical analyses such as logistic regression. We find that, within the set of demographic constraints characterizing the Swiss marriage market, three of four individuals can be reallocated to a couple with a higher chance of survival. This reallocation is associated with a 15 percent reduction of the objective function between the initial and the optimized configuration.

From this perspective, the current marriage market appears to be sub-optimally organized and therefore matching individuals according to a small number of quantitative criteria (e.g., age, education, cultural background, religious practice, and level of depression) following well-known algorithms of optimization may help reduce divorce and alleviate its economic, social, and psychological costs. The historical process of individualization in the Western world (Simmel, 1983 [1908]; Elias, 1991; Kohli, 1985) is characterized by a progressive shift from collective and consensual to diversified and privatized forms of social institutions, as, for instance, that of marriage (Goode, 1962). In many countries, marriages and divorces are now legally considered a private agreement. For some scholars, in late modernity the choice of a partner depends on the satisfaction associated with a pure relationship (Beck and Beck-Gernsheim, 1995; Giddens, 1992). The extent to which this corresponds to reality remains an open question since this claim is only poorly confirmed by empirical evidence. We state that the complexity of life trajectories in multiple spheres of social participation does not imply a complete de-institutionalization of social relationships (Sapin et al., 2007). This statement is supported by the growing success of online dating services that allow individualized bachelors performing highly customized, but institutionalized searches for a spouse or partner. The proposed methodology allows a better understanding of how structures of the marriage market affect conjugal mismatches. In this chapter, we extended our initial model (Cao, Fragnière, Gauthier, Sapin, and Widmer, 2010) with additional criteria such as religiosity and depression. It appears that some characteristics, although strongly associated with divorce, cannot lead to a large reallocation of partners because their distribution in the sample is highly skewed. This is the case with depressive symptoms and religious practice—although matches of individuals reporting high depression scores or absence of devotion have very high odds of separation or divorce, the number of individuals that can be reallocated is small due to the very low pool of available mates with adequate characteristics and good matches on other dimensions (i.e., age, education, and previous divorce). Moreover, when several parameters are interdependent (as in the case of birth cohorts and education), reallocation becomes tricky. Therefore, we also wish to integrate a dynamic structure in the model. These developments may help to better estimate the impact of mate selection within the highly complex set of demographic constraints characterizing current marriage markets.

Finally, is there a magic formula for matching potential partners in long-lasting happy couples? The answer to this rather provocative question is definitely a "no." Indeed, the purposes of this research have never been to look for such a formula because it would be at the same time useless and meaningless. Many reactions were triggered by the article published in the *European Journal of Operational Research* (Cao et al., 2010). Although a large majority of the comments posted on the Internet came from individuals who had not read the article itself but second hand summaries made by the international press, some of them raised interesting issues that should be taken seriously (see http://www.edwidmer.org/page-pub4-100).

We have been working in the field of family and life course research for years, and our research has never created such a buzz, leading us to go over the meaning of the reactions it triggered. One set of remarks concerns the limited set of explanatory variables included. The lack of inclusion of psychological factors was underlined with the point that love and personal inclination were not present in our line of reasoning. A similar critical point was made about cultural factors such as religion that were not included in the article published in the Journal of Operational Research. Another set of remarks focused on the ethical dimensions of the research—is it advisable to propose an optimization of the marriage market that assumes that mate selection should not be left to individuals but organized by the state or by another large scale specialized agency? A third set of reactions concerned some of the specific results of the research. The fact that marriages in which women were older than men were dismissed by the optimizing algorithm but those in which women had more educational credentials than men were not triggered a large series of reactions, some outraged and others amused, by the gender bias revealed by the results. Now that some time has passed, these reactions require some clarification on the intent as well as the limits of our research.

First, let us stress that the impact of age, religion, or educational differences on marriage are well known because they have been researched by sociologists for years. We underlined the importance of various sociological variables that influence the development of fulfilling conjugal relationships, as well as others. The gender bias structuring family relationships is well known—although it comes as a disappointment in the face of the public promotion of equality between men and women by public discourses and the mass media, it does not come as a surprise for scholars who study the family realm. Interestingly, our results triggered only limited media attention before we conceptualized them within the framework of optimization. This unexpected consequence of applying an econometric perspective on conjugal issues is interesting. It shows that classical results of sociological analysis gain more public relevance when they are framed within a normative model of change and their consequences for society are quantified rather than presented in a neutral way that fits more properly within the ethic of science. This leads us to clarify the conceptual status of the optimization principle in our research. Obviously, marriage will never be under the authority of an omniscient and powerful central agency in Western democracies, or, for that matter, in any other political regimes in the near future. As social scientists, we do not believe in social engineering of couples and families. This model is meant to be a theoretical model aimed at helping researchers to raise some interesting features of the organization of empirical marriages and other partnerships. In other words, the optimization procedure is not meant to impose a scientifically based approach to dealing practically with marriages on a large scale. Our attention while developing it was rather to stress the impact of the social structures on a large series of matters usually analyzed as stemming from personal choices and psychological characteristics. Indeed, much of the faith in marriage at the aggregate level of populations depends on the ways in which societies are organized. While optimizing marriage is impossible *per se*, critically considering the social structures that influence marriage and divorce, we believe, is a useful mission of the social sciences. The optimizing algorithm was developed as a way of stressing the large set of macrostructural constraints weighing over marriage (and other so-called personal decisions) in late modern societies. It does not negate the impact of psychological variables (which is added in this chapter) or of personal taste on mate selection and successful partnership. There are hundreds of studies on these influences and the data we had at hand were not detailed enough to make a sound contribution on those matters. Finally, the results the model produced are based on the dataset at hand, i.e., a sample of 1000 couples living in Switzerland. Although the international press took the data as context-free and considers its results as valid for countries worldwide, we wish to stress that they are bound to Switzerland. It may be that similar trends can be found in other Western countries, but further comparative research is needed before such a claim can be made. Overall, there is no magic formula upon which individuals can base their choice of the right spouse. However, there are social structures that can be reflected upon to make society more fair and family life more fulfilling.

REFERENCES

Amato, P.R., and Keith, B. (1991). Consequences of parental divorce for children's well-being: A meta-analysis. *Psychological Bulletin, 110,* 26-46.

Amato, P.R., (2000). The consequences of divorce for adults and children. *Journal of Marriage and the Family, 62,* 1269-1287.

Beach, S.R.H., Sandeen, E.E., and O'leary, K.D. (1990). *Depression in marriage.* New York: Gilford Press.

Beck, U., and Beck-Gernsheim, E. (1995). *The normal chaos of love.* Cambridge: Polity Press.

Becker, G. (1981). *A Treatise on the family.* Harvard University Press.

Berger, P., and Kellner, H. (1964). Marriage and the construction of reality: an exercise in the microsociology of knowledge. *Diogenes, 12*(46), 1-24.

Berscheid, E., and Reis, H.T. (1998). Attraction and close relationships. In Gilbert, D., Fiske, S., and Lindzey, G. (eds). *The Handbook of Social Psychology*, 4th ed., Vol. 2, 193-281, McGraw-Hill: New York.

Blackwell, D.L., and Lichter, D.T. (2004). Homogamy among dating, cohabiting and married couples. *The Sociological Quarterly,* 45: 719-737.

Blau, P.M., Blum, T.C., and Schwartz, J.E. (1982). Heterogeneity and intermarriage. *American Sociological Review*, 47: 45-62.

Blau, P.M., Schwartz, J.E. (1984). *Crosscutting social circles: Testing a macrostructural theory of intergroup relations.* Academic Press: Orlando, San Diego.

Bourdieu, P. (1979). *La distinction: critique sociale du jugement.* Paris: Ed. de Minuit.

Bourdieu, P. (1980). *Le sens pratique*. Editions de minuit: Paris.

Brooke, A., Kendrick, D., and Meeraus, A. (1992). *GAMS: General algebraic modeling system*. GAMS Development Corp.: Washington, DC.

Bumpass, L.L., Castro Martin, T.C., and Sweet, J.A. (1991). The impact of family background and early marital factors on marital disruption. *Journal of Family Issues, 12*, 22-42.

Bumpass, L.L., and Sweet, J.A. (1972). Differentials in marital instability: 1970. *American Sociological Review*, *37*, 754-766.

Burkard, R., Dell'Amico, M., and Martello, S. (2009). *Assignment problems.* Society for Industrial and Applied Mathematics (SIAM): Philadelphia.

Call, V.R.A., and Heaton, T.B. (1997). Religious influence on marital stability. *Journal for the Scientific Study of Religion*, *36*(3), 382-392.

Cao, N.V., Fragnière, E., Gauthier, J.-A., Sapin, M., and Widmer, E. (2010). Optimizing the marriage market through the reallocation of partners: An application of the linear assignment model. *European Journal of Operational Research*, 202, 547-553.

Carnelley, K., Pietromonaco, P. and Jaffe, K. (1994). Depression, working models of others, and relational functioning. *Journal of Personality and Social Psychology, 66,* 127-140.

Ceglian, C.P., and Gardner, S. (1999). Attachment style: A risk for multiple marriage? *Journal of Divorce and Remarriage, 31* (1/2), 125-139.

Cherlin, A.J., and Furstenberg, F.F. (1994). Stepfamilies in the U.S.: a reconsideration. *Annual Review of Sociology*, 359-381.

Cherlin, A.J., Chase-Lansdale, P.L., and McRae, C. (1998). Effect of parental divorce on mental health throughout the life course. *American Sociological Review*, 63: 239-249.

Christensen, A., and Shenk, J.L. (1991). Communication, conflict, and psychological distance in nondistressed, clinic, and divorcing couples. *Journal of Consulting and Clinical Psychology*, 59(3), 458-463.

Coleman, J.S. (1988). Social Capital in the Creation of Human Capital. *The American Journal of Sociology*, *94*, 95-120.

CPLEX Optimization Inc. (1992). *Using the CPLEX Callable Library and CPLEX Mixed Integer Library*. Incline Village, NV.

Durkheim, E. (2008 [1912]). *Les Formes Élémentaires De La Vie Religieuse: Le Système Totémique En Australie*. Paris: CNRS Editions.

Elias, N. (1991). *La société des individus*. Paris: Fayard.

Fay, B. (1996). *Contemporary philosophy of social science*. Wiley-Blackwell.

Felmlee, D., Sprecher, S., and Bassin, E. (1990). The dissolution of intimate relationships: A hazard model. Social Psychology Quarterly: 13-30.

Finchman, F.D., Beach, S.R., Bradbury, T.N. (1989). Marital distress, depression, and attributions: Is the marital distress-attribution an artifact of depression? *Journal of Consulting and Clinical Psychology, 57*(6), 768-771.

Gale, D., Shapley, L.S., (1962). College admissions and the stability of marriage. *American Mathematical Monthly,* 69, 9-15.

Giddens, A. (1992). *The Transformation of Intimacy*. Stanford: Stanford University Press.

Giddens, A. (2005). *Sociology* (4th edition). Cambridge: Polity Press.

Goode, W.J. (1962). Marital satisfaction and instability: A cross-cultural class analysis of divorce rates. *International Social Science Journal*, 14: 507-526.

Gotlib, I.H.; Hooley, J.M. (1988). Depression and marital distress: Current status and future directions. In S. Duck, D.F. Hay, S.E. Hobfoll, W. Ickes, and B.M, Montgomery (Eds), *Handbook of personal relationships: Theory, research and interventions.* (pp. 543-570). Oxford: John Wiley and Sons.

Gusfield, D., and Irving, R.W. (1989). *The Stable Marriage Problem, Structure and Algorithms.* The MIT Press: Cambridge Massachusetts.

Heim, S.C., and Snyder, D.K. (1991). Predicting depression from marital distress and attribution. *Journal of Marital and Family Therapy, 17*(1), 67-72.

Henne, E., Buysse, A., and Van Oost, P. (2003). A categorical and dimensional perspecive on depression within a nonclinical sample. *Family Process, 42*(1), 133-149.

Hohmann-Marriott, B.E. (2006). Shared Beliefs and the Union Stability of Married and Cohabiting Couples. *Journal of Marriage and Family*, 68: 1015-1028.

Jaccard, J. (2001). *Interaction Effects in Logistic Regression.* Thousand Oaks, CA: Sage Publications.

Jalovaara, M. (2001). Socio-economic status and divorce in first marriages in Finland 1991-93. *Population Studies, 55,* 119-133.

Janssen, J.P.G. (2002). *Do opposites attract divorce? Dimensions of mixed marriage and the risk of divorce in the Netherlands*, Dissertation, University of Nijmegen.

Kalmijn, M. (1994). Assortative mating by cultural and occupational status. *American Journal of Sociology*, 100: 422-452.

Kalmijn, M. (1998). Intermarriage and homogamy: Causes, patterns, trends. *Annual review of sociology*, 24: 349-421.

Karney, B.R., and Bradbury, T.N. (1995). The longitudinal course of marital quality and stability: A review of theory, methods and research. *Psychological Bulletin, 118*(1), 3-34.

Kelly, E.L., and Conley, J.J. (1987). Personality and compatibility: A prospective analysis of marital stability and marital satisfaction. *Journal of Personality and Social Psychology, 52*(1), 27-40.

Kohli, M. (1985). Die Institutionalisierung des Lebenslaufs. *Kölner Zeitschrift für Soziologie und Sozialpsychologie*, *37*, 1-29.

Lehrer, E.L., and Chiswick, C.U. (1993). Religion as a Determinant of Marital Stability. *Demography*, *30*(3), 385-404.

Lovász, L., and Plummer, M.D. (1986). *Matching theory*. Elsevier: Annals of discrete mathematics, Vol. 29.

Mastekaasa, A. (1995). Marital dissolution and subjective distress: Panel evidence. *European Sociological Review, 11*(2), 173-185.

Merikangas, K.R. (1984). Divorce and assortive mating among depressed patients. *American Journal of Psychiatry, 141*, 74-76.

Myers, S.M. (2006). Religious Homogamy and Marital Quality: Historical and Generational. *Journal of Marriage and Family*, *68*, 292-304.

Overbeek, G., Vollebergh, W., de Graaf, R., Scholte, R., de Kemp, R., and Engels, R. (2006). Longitudinal associations of marital quality and marital dissolution with the incidence of DSM-III-R disorders. *Journal of Family Psychology, 20*(2), 284-291.

Price-Brohnam, S, and Baslwich, J.O. (1980). The non-institutions: Divorce, desertion, and remarriage. *Journal of Marriage and the Family*, *42*, 959-972.

Radloff, L.S. (1977). The CES-D scale. *Applied Psychological measurement, 1*(3), 385-401.

Reiss, I.L. (1960). Toward a sociology of the hererosexual love relationship. *Marriage and Family Living, 22*(2), 139-145.

Roberts, B.W., Kuncel, N.R., Shiner, R., Caspi, A., and Goldberg, L.R. (2007). The power of personality. The comparative validity of personality traits, socioeconomic status, and cognitive ability for predicting important life outcomes. *Perspective on psychological science, 2*(4), 313-345.

Roberts, J.E., Gotlib, I.H., and Kassel, J.D. (1996). Adult attachment security and symptoms of depression. The mediating roles of dysfunctional attitudes and low self-esteem. *Journal of Personality and Social Psychology, 70,* 310-320.

Rosenthal, R.E. (2007). *GAMS—A User's Guide.* GAMS Development Corporation, Washington, DC, U.S.

Ruscio, J., and Ruscio, A.M. (2000) Informing the continuity controversy. *Journal of Abnormal Psychology, 109,* (3), 473-487.

Sapin, M., Spini, D., and Widmer, E.D. (2007). *Les parcours de vie: de l'adolescence au grand âge*. Presses Polytechniques et Universitaires Romandes, Lausanne.

Schrijver, A. (2003). *Combinatorial optimization. Polyhedra and efficiency*. Algorithms and Combinatorics, Vol. 24. : Berlin: Springer Verlag.

Simmel, G. (1983[1908]). *Soziologie - Untersuchungen Über Die Formen Der Vergesellschaftung*. Berlin: Dunker und Humbolt.

Swartz, D. (1996). Bridging the Study of Culture and Religion: Pierre Bourdieu's Political Economy of Symbolic Power. *Sociology of Religion*, *57*(1), 71-85.

Tschann, J.M., Johnson, J.R., and Wallerstein, J.S. (1989). Resources, stressors and attachments as predictors of adult adjustment after divorce: A longitudinal study. *Journal of Marriage and the Family, 4,* 1033-1046.

Tucker, J.S., Kressin, N.R., Spiro, A., and Ruscio, J. (1998). Intrapersonal characteristics and the timing of divorce: A prospective investigation. *Journal of Social and Personal Relationship, 15,* 211-225.

Tzeng, M.S. (1992). The effects of socioeconomic heterogamy and changes on marital dissolution for first marriages. *Journal of Marriage and the Family, 54,* 609-619.

Vaaler, M.L., Ellison, C.G., and Powers, D.A. (2009). Religious Influences on the Risk of Marital Dissolution. *Journal of Marriage and Family*, *71*(4), 917-934.

Voicu, M. (2009). Religion and Gender across Europe. *Social Compass*, *56*(2), 144-162.

Wagner, M. (1993). Sozial Bedingungen des Eherscheidingsrisikos aus der Perspektive des Lebensverlaufs. In Diekmann A., Weick S (eds), *Der Familienzyklus als sozialer Prozess*, Dunker and Humblot, Berlin, 372-393.

Whyte, M.K. (1990). *Dating, mating, and marriage*. Aldine Transaction: Piscataway, NJ.

Widmer, E.D., Kellerhals, J., and Levy, R. (2003). *Couples contemporains. Cohésion, régulation et conflits*. Zürich: Seismo.

Widmer, E.D., Kellerhals, J., and Levy, R. (2004). Quelle pluralisation des relations familiales? Conflits, styles d'interactions conjugales et milieu social. *Revue française de Sociologie*, 45, 1, 37-67.

Widmer, E.D., Kellerhals, J., and Levy, R. (2006). Types of conjugal interactions and conjugal conflict: a Longitudinal Assessment. *European sociological review*, 20: 63-77.

Yela, C., and Sangrador, J.L. (2001). Perception of physical attractiveness throughout loving relationships. *Current Research in Social Psychology*, 6(5), 57-75.

Zuroff, D.C., Fitzpatrick, D.K. (1995). Depressive personality style: Implications for adult attachment. *Personality and Individual Differences, 18*(2), 253-265.

In: HRM and Marketing Orientation in the New Era
Editor: Panagiotis Kyriazopoulos

ISBN: 978-1-62808-959-2

Chapter 6

TOWARDS A COMPETENCY ASSESSMENT MATURITY MODEL: A VIEW FROM SPANISH SOFTWARE INDUSTRY

Ricardo Colomo-Palacios[1*], Edmundo Tovar-Caro[1], Pedro Soto-Acosta[2] and Ángel García-Crespo[1]

[1]Universidad Carlos III de Madrid, Spain
Universidad Politécnica de Madrid, Spain
[2]Universidad de Murcia, Murcia, Spain

ABSTRACT

Human factors are critical for knowledge intensive tasks as software project success, so software managers need to know the individual capabilities of the staff to improve project performance and to guide practitioners through their professional careers. The difficulty on competencies assessment of professionals and the lack of reliable factors for competency certification, demonstrate the disadvantage of this profession compared to others. This paper proposes a model allowing organizations in general, and software project managers in particular, to identify and evaluate factors that compose, certify and make professional competencies, which are strategic for companies, in order to design proper tools to support the whole process. The described model is later applied to assess the competential assessment elements for Software Engineering in a European environment, such as the Spaniard.

Keywords: Software Engineering, Human Factors, Competencies, Competency Assessment, Human Capital

* E-mail: ricardo.colomo@uc3m.es

INTRODUCTION

In recent years, the IT field has expanded beyond traditional stove-pipe organizational systems to infiltrate companies and homes alike, and in this scenario, software has become crucial for everyday matters. Within software engineering research area, human factors are key issues.

Several authors have highlighet the importance of human capital in software engineering processes. Boehm points out that "After product size, people factors have the strongest influence in determining the amount of effort required to develop a software product "(Boehm, 1981), and "Personnel attributes and human resource activities provide by far the largest source of opportunity for improving software development productivity" (Boehm, Horowitz, Madachy, Reifer, Clark, Steece, Brown, Chulani, and Abts, 2000). In order to improve the capability of workforce, several initiatives as SEI's People-CMM (Curtis, Hefley and Miller, 2001) describe an evolutionary improvement path from ad hoc, inconsistently performed workforce practices, to a mature infrastructure of practices for continuously elevating workforce capability.

Defining staffing and competency requirements are part of many process areas in CMM-I (Software Engineering Institute, 2006) level 3. In particular, "Integrated Teaming", 11th process area, in the "Defined level", is all built up in the idea of finding people with competencies on which to base the integrated team's activities to sustain or achieve desired capability. More precisely, SP 1.3 "Assign Appropriate Team Members", describes that assigning proper team members means evaluating some relevant criteria including knowledge, skills, motivation, education and cultural background among other aspects. All of them are competency elements. Both People-CMM (Curtis, Hefley and Miller, 2001) and CMM-I (Software Engineering Institute, 2006) have adopted competency concept to characterize the level of knowledge, skills, and process abilities available for performing an organization's business activities.

The competence approach to human resources management has a long history. The early Romans already practiced a sort of competence profiling in attempts to detail the attributes of a "good Roman soldier" (Draganidis and Mentzas, 2006). More recently, early 20th century scientific management used the concept of competence (Taylor, 1911), and is well established in the field of human resources management since the middle of the seventies, due to the works by McClelland. McClelland (1973) defined competence as those characteristics that are found to consistently distinguish outstanding from typical performance in a given job or role. The concept of competence is associated with the analysis of professional activities and the inventory of what is necessary in order to accomplish the missions involved in these activities (Levy-Levoyer, 1996).

Competency assessment requires a previous classification of competences. Several authors (e.g. Levy-Levoyer, 1996; Martin and Staines, 1994) set up taxonomies in which particular or technical competences are established as those that are necessary to carry out a very specific task of a particular job position and include knowledge, abilities, and skills. On the other hand, universal or generic competences are those that, though not linked to a specific activity or function, do make possible the competent performance of the tasks related to the work position, inasmuch as they refer to characteristics or abilities of the individual's general behavior. These competences permit individuals to adapt to changes in a more efficient and rapid way (Levy-Levoyer, 1996). The use of these taxonomies allow to distinguish which competencies are transversal to different job positions, and therefore can be used for general evaluation methods, and which competencies are linked to a very specific job. The latter competencies need specific, tailored assessment methods.

Over the last several decades, business books and the trade press have flooded managers with workforce practices each demonstrated to produce benefits in at least some applications (Curtis, Hefley and Miller, 2001). These practices include competency-modelling, 360º performance reviews, knowledge management, competence based team-building, incentive based pay, mentoring, meeting management, and empowered work among others. Many of them are based on competency definition and assessment. People CMM bases also many of its practices in competency assessment. Competency assessments are used for promotion issues, assignment to specific positions, creating personal development plans, identifying relevant career options or evaluate the impact of workforce practices, among many others.

Project Human Resource Management (PMI) includes the processes required to make the most effective use of the people involved with the project (Project Management Institute, 2000). This PMI Knowledge Area includes topics as recruitment based on staffing skills, retention and performance evaluation. All these activities imply, or should imply, the use of a competence assessment system. For software project managers in particular, team competence issues are crucial to project success. Knowing who knows what and who can perform what can reduce the time it takes managers to build teams, can improve project productivity and can reduce inherent risks. Software Project managers need to know the software practitioners competence level in a reliable way in order to get the opportunity to improve productivity. The intrinsic difficulty of competency assessment is increased by the lack of maturity of the profession, due to the absence or weak reliability of different competency certifications. The lack of maturity of the profession's components, defined in (Ford and Gibbs, 1996), lead to a difficult implementation of the competency model in organizations, as the factors that could be competency certifications may not exist, be badly defined or not be applicable. So, knowing the implications of all factors in competency assessment will help software engineers performing management roles to assure project success by evaluating software engineers using reliable references. The objective of this paper is to establish a model, capable of diagnosing the maturity level of competency assessment in a specific scope. This model, valid for any profession, is described in section 2. As it has been pointed out previously, the model is especially interesting for its application in the scope of immature professions, so in Section 3 we apply the model in order to test the maturity of competency assessment in the field of Software Engineering in Spain.

COMPETENCY ASSESSMENT MATURITY MODEL NECESSITY

So far, success of competency assessment has been limited, in the sense that less assessments have been made than one could expect. Nevertheless, competencies are crucial when evaluating professional experience. Companies need efficient mechanisms to measure the output of their employees. However, the implementation of such a system depends on some aspects that need to be identified and evaluated, as both job positions and business outlook may modify characteristics of competency assessment systems. On one hand, the immaturity of some professions prevents to use components of a profession as competency generators or certifiers in a standardized manner, either because they do not exist, they lack definition or they are inapplicable. On the other hand, the lack of definition of professional profiles makes companies create job positions without any established guidance. At last, the very same condition of competency assessment, referring to access to tools and their usage, represents another factor to take into account when it comes to designing a company's system for competency assessment.

These considerations lead to the necessity to develop a model that, on one side, includes all aspects related to a company's assessment of professional competencies and, on the other side, measure the different factors evaluators should take into account when evaluating competencies. The objective of the proposed model is to represent and measure in a unique framework the different factors playing their role in the competency assessment of professionals within organizations. It is of vital importance to competency assessment in immature professions, for the different competency generators or certifiers here are not established or unknown. For Software Project Managers, is crucial to count on a model to ensure the competency assessment success is based on mature and stable elements in order to promote, assign, develop and train software engineers fairly.

DESCRIPTION OF THE FACTORS USED IN THE MODEL

The proposed model represents in a unique framework the different factors playing their role in competency assessment within organizations. The identified factors are represented in the figure 1.

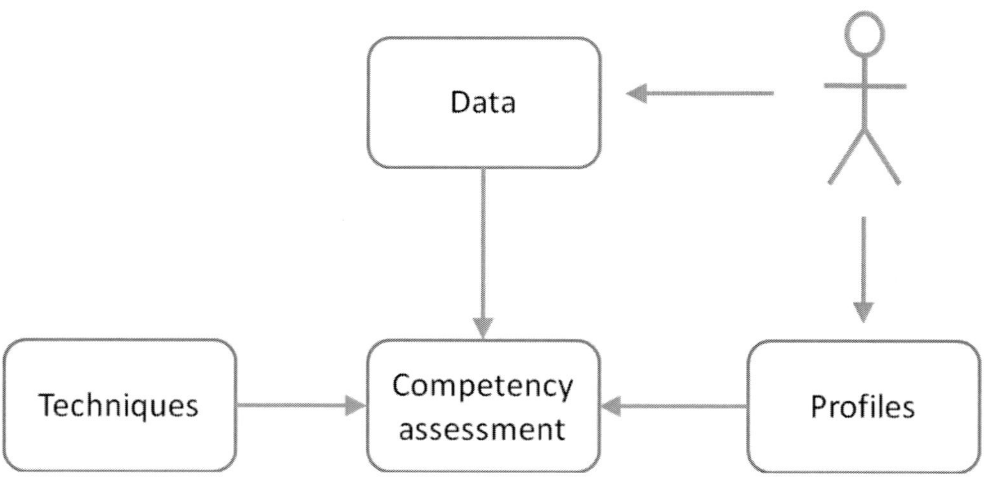

Figure 1. Factors in the model.

Competency assessment by organizations contains three fundamental factors: Competency Assessment Techniques, Data about employees' job performance and Professional Profiles which define the profession. In addition, Agents taking part in the model also need to be considered.

Techniques

Techniques used in competency assessment can be grouped in two main families: techniques related to the analysis of job positions and techniques related to individual competencies. The first, of which exist a great number, see (Pereda and Berrocal, 2003) for an introduction; allow making an inventory of the whole of competencies necessary for excellent or superior performance in the job position. Techniques for assessment of individual competencies are very well known and abundant, however, the amount and variety of methods may mislead the user. Instruments can be classified in three categories: Signs, Demonstrations and References. Signs are obtained through abstract tests, corresponding to psychological dimensions identified thanks to a great number of investigations and allowing measuring aptitudes and describing personalities (Levy-Leboyer, 1997).

Demonstrations are exercises simulating as close as possible a professional reality. They are developed in order to allow assessment of competencies put into practice on the tasks of the job position. References, as their name indicates, are testimonials using observation of previous behavior in similar situations where the required competencies were put into practice.

Data

Data ought to be understood as proof of the employee's performance and achievements. Data, also called "evidence portfolio components", are derived to a great extent from the profession models described earlier (Ford and Gibbs, 1996), as maturity of a profession acts positively upon validity and reliability of data used to evaluate professionals' competencies. The identified components are the following:

- Bachelor Degree (BA): university education, representing the professional's basic training.
- Post Graduation: master obtained after university degree.
- Unofficial training: courses with no officially recognized degree usually provided and financed by companies or administrations.
- Certification: unofficial, voluntary process to guarantee certain knowledge.
- License: obligatory and official process to guarantee certain knowledge.
- Affiliation: the act of taking membership to one of the professional associations.
- Accreditation: process aimed to assure quality of education programmes.

Professional Profile

When listing competencies needed for a certain job position, it is very important to count with an assessed list of professional profiles. As mentioned above, a great number of methods for analyzing job positions are available (Pereda and Berrocal, 2003). A guide enabling to award a certain competency level to a professional category will create better standardized job positions, contributing to the profession's maturity.

In addition to the three identified factors, there is another determining player in the model, who - if it may be external to the proper competency assessment -, does have an indirect influence. This factor is represented by Agents, unattached to the professional, but who do have an influence on his competencies. The identified agents are:

- Universities. Institutions for higher education composed of different faculties, each attributing the corresponding academic grades.
- Administrations. The whole of organisms charged with service management and execution of laws within a country.
- Labour conjuncture. Combination of factors and circumstances that occur in a nation's labour market. They affect the demand of labour force as well as the composition and quality of its competencies.
- Organizations. Charged with verification of its employees' competencies, as much during recruitment as during performance assessment. They are of – often indirect - influence to different aspects related to the professional model, such as Initial Education through Accreditation processes, License and Certification. In addition, they also affect career initiatives.
- Professional Associations. Groupings of professionals whose mission is to promote regulation and ethical codes of the profession.

Model Components Assessment

The objective of the proposed model is to determine maturity of competency assessment in a certain environment and for a specific profession, through obtained maturity of each of its components, for which we will describe a measuring method. As, Ford and Gibbs (1996), we have chosen to characterize the maturity of the infrastructure-level components of a profession in terms of four developmental or evolutionary stages:

0. Nonexistence: The component does not exist in any form.
1. Under Development: This component is been developed.
2. Specific: The component exists and is clearly identified with the given profession, but is not generally used.
3. Maturing. The component has existed for many years, is used and continually improved.

Application of the Maturity Model for Competency Assessment by Organizations on Software Engineering in Spain

Software Engineering Body of Knowledge, SWEBOK (Sobel and LeBlanc, 2004) defines Software Engineering as "The application of a systematic focus, disciplined and quantifiable in development, operation and maintenance of software. This is the application of Software Engineering."

Software Engineering is an ideal field to experiment with the model, as on one hand, there is a demand for establishment of Software Engineering as a mature profession, and on the other hand, its immaturity has been clearly shown (Ford and Gibbs, 1996), (Parnas, 1999), (Saiedian, Bagert and Mead, 2002), (McConnell, 2003), (Colomo-Palacios and Tovar, 2006), (Colomo-Palacios et al, 2010).

TECHNIQUES

Many recent works list the great number of methods to analyze the job position, however there is no existence of Spanish equivalents, probably because very little of the described instruments are available in a valid and adapted version (Levy-Leboyer, 1997). For assessment of individual competencies, methods are well known and abundant. However, the number and variety can be misleading to its user. Concerning implementation, data are not very optimistic. Systems for assessment of competencies and performances have been poorly exploited in Spain, due to the following reasons: badly defined objectives, lack of discernment during the assessment due to halo or average effect and absence of interviews with the employee or interviews being considered a formality (Pelegrin, 2003). Several authors (E.g. Colomo-Palacios et al., 2007; Acuña, Juristo and Moreno, 2006) have specific proposed techniques to assess software development teams' members.

The problems with evaluating results and competencies are common in Spaniard cultural environment and make that the true potential of these tools is not turned into account. It is therefore evident to say that techniques for competency assessment are correctly defined but badly implemented. Knowledge and competence management in the software engineering is often set up in large organizations, such as Daimler Chrysler, The NASA Software Engineering Laboratory (Becerra, 2000), Ericsson (Dingsoyr and Conradi, 2002), or Microsoft (Draganidis, Chamopoulou and Mentzas, 2006). In Spain, this kind of methods is used in various IT enterprises or departments, mainly in big firms … but it's only a small portion of the whole community of software developers (Colomo-Palacios and Tovar, 2006). We conclude that techniques for competence assessment of software engineers in Spain are specific.

DATA

The analysis of maturity of the data used for competency assessment of Software Engineers in Spain will be done separately for the different identified factors:

Bachelor Degree

Currently, Spain counts with three official titles in the field of IT (Information Technology): Technical Engineers in IT Management, in IT Systems and IT Engineers, but Bologna process is changing the higher education scenario, in which new Undergraduate degrees in which Software Engineering degrees are beginning to appear in higher education landscape. As much on national as on international level, there is a demand for the creation of a Bachelor Degree of Software Engineer, not sustained by the project, although international career recommendations (Sobel and LeBlanc, 2004) do regulate it. Although initial education is no guarantee to possess the technical and general competencies required for successful performance on a job position, heterogeneous degrees make that professionals enter on the labour market with very unequal competencies.

Post Graduation

The great novelty in Spain exists in the fact that Masters, which are nowadays being awarded by universities as their proper (unofficial) degree, or as a private degree by other institutions, will be converted into official degrees and will allow access to examination for the PDh Degree. Post Gradual degrees, except for MBA's which are required and accepted for different positions within Software Engineering, are not required by organizations, in spite of their acceptable implementation on national level. The component is therefore situated in the faze of "Specific".

Unofficial Training

Directly determined by companies. In the European Union, 62% of the companies provide their employees with training programmes, compared to 36% in Spain (Fernández, 2002). 63% of the training is offered during working hours, the percentage being higher in large and middle sized. The average duration of the training is of 26 hours. The component is situated in the face of "Specific".

Certification

Currently, certificates like "Certified Software Development Professional" (CSDP) or "European Certification of IT Professional" (EUCIP), are not known or asked for in Spain. At the same time, as a consequence of globalisation of some tools, facilities of apprenticeship and the emerged demand, manufacturers' certificates are being converted in alternative ways to enter the profession (Casanovas, Colom, Morlán, Pont, and Sancho, 2004). The importance of these certificates in the labour market is increasing, to the extent that 2, 16 % of all job offers require certification in any of Microsoft's ten currently existing certificates (Fernández, 2002). The component is placed in the face of "Specific".

License

Is of no application to Software Engineering in Spain, and thus belongs to the quadrant "Nonexistence".

Affiliation

Belongs to the quadrant "Specific". There are computer science associations (with specific chapters in Software Engineering) in Spain: ALI, ATI and AII. Nevertheless, they are not implanted in a generalized manner in the community.

Accreditation

Accreditation of degrees is currently being implemented in Spaniard universities and should not be taken into account for competency assessment. It is therefore situated in the quadrant "Under Development". Detailed analysis of the factors which compose Data for competency assessment, confirms the incidence of profession maturity as far as reliability of the data for competency assessment is concerned.

Professional Profiles

The old assumption of one single possible career in software development, programmers, analysts, project managers, directors, has been substituted by a new reality in which exists a large diversity of professional careers (Lee, Koh, Yen and Tang, 2002). In this business situation, profiles defined in career initiatives related to the IT field (Lee, Koh, Yen and Tang, 2002), or North American (O*Net, 2007), European (Office for National Statistics Occupational Information Unit, 2000) or Spaniard (Instituto Nacional de Estadística, 1994) occupational classifications, do not offer a valid explanation about professional careers, supporting the statements in (Lee, Koh, Yen and Tang, 2002). Therefore, software engineers find themselves undefined in the professional career they are confronted with. They also have to deal with undefined knowledge and skills necessary in each step of their career, adapting themselves to the company's needs which might or might not have been communicated during performance assessment appraisals, along with state of the art inquiries. This grade of lack of definition locates the component in the quadrant "Under Development".

SUMMARY

Our look at the current state of competency assessment by organizations on software engineering in Spain shows it to be quite immature. We can summarize our vision in the following table:

Table 1. Summary of elements for Software Engineering in Spain

Element	Factor	Value
Techniques		Specific
Data		
	Bachelor Degree	Under Development- Specific
	Post Graduation	Specific

Table 1. (Continued)

	Unofficial training	Specific
	Certification	Specific
	Licence	Nonexistence
	Affiliation	Specific
	Accreditation	Under Development
Professional Profiles		Under Development

Conclusion

The developed model allows to rate the maturity of competency assessment related to a profession in a stipulated context. Currently, and as it happens when the maturity of the profession is analyzed, one can state that no mechanism leading to the establishment of competency assessment for Software Engineers has been implemented or generalized in Spain, either due to a lack of maturity of the different factors of the profession, or to a poor exploitation of assessment systems or their inaccurate implementation by organizations.

Nevertheless, both the predictable maturity process of the profession and the interest paid by organizations to competency management, make us expect a clear change to the actual situation. Investigation on typology and levels of professionals' competencies and of education mechanisms and their certification becomes in these moments of change to educational environments of crucial importance. Therefore, an assessment is needed, not only on the mechanisms of competencies – such as education programmes or certifications – but also on their results, in shape of professionals who constitute labour markets and who show real competencies, giving them full scope in their job positions.

This article invites to a reflection on the situation and to take measures which will lead organizations to a better definition, a better distribution and a better implementation of the factors considered in this model.

References

Acuña, S.T., Juristo, N. and Moreno, A.M. (2006). Emphasizing Human Capabilities in Software Development. *IEEE Software, 23* (2), 94-101.

Becerra, I. (2000), Facilitating the Online Search of Experts at NASA using Expert Seeker People-Finder, *Proceedings of the Third International Conference on Practical Aspects of Knowledge Management*, Basel Suiza.

Boehm, B. W. (1981), *Software Engineering Economics*, Prentice Hall, Englewood Cliffs, New Jersey.

Boehm, B., Horowitz, E., Madachy, R., Reifer, D., Clark, B.K., Steece, B., Brown, A.W., Chulani, S. and Abts, C. (2000). *Software Cost Estimation with COCOMO II*, Prentice Hall, Upper Saddle River.

Bourque, P and Dupuis, R. (2004), *Guide to the Software Engineering Body of Knowledge*, IEEE Computer Society.

Casanovas, J., Colom, J.M., Morlán, I., Pont, A. and Sancho, M.R. (2004), *Libro Blanco sobre las titulaciones universitarias de informática en el nuevo espacio europeo de educación superior*, Proyecto Eice, ANECA, 2004.

Colomo-Palacios, R. and Tovar, E. (2006), Claves para comprender el grado de madurez en que se encuentra la profesión de la Ingeniería del Software en España, *Novatica*, 181, 41-46.

Colomo-Palacios, R., Ruano-Mayoral, M., Gómez Berbís, J.M. and García Crespo, A. (2007). Competency Assessment: Integrating COCOMO II and People-CMM for estimation improvement. *Clei Electronic Journal, 10*(2).

Colomo-Palacios, R., Tovar, E., García-Crespo, A. and Gómez-Berbís, J.M. (2010), Identifying Technical Competences of IT Professionals. The Case of Software Engineers, *International Journal of Human Capital and Information Technology Professionals*, 1(1), 31-43.

Curtis, B., Hefley, W. E., and Miller, S. A. (2001). *People Capability Maturity Model (P-CMM R) Version 2.0.* Technical report, Software Engineering Institute, Pittsburgh. Doc. Ref.: CMU/SEI-2001-MM-01.

Dingsoyr, T. and Conradi, R. (2002), A Survey of Case Studies of the Use of Knowledge Management in Software Engineering, *International Journal of Software Engineering and Knowledge Engineering*, 4(12) 391 - 414.

Draganidis, F., and Mentzas, G. (2006). Competency based management: a review of systems and approaches. *Information Management and Computer Security, 14*(1), 51-64.

Draganidis, F.; Chamopoulou, P. and Mentzas, G. (2006), An ontology based tool for competency management and learning paths. *6th International Conference on Knowledge Management* (I-KNOW 06), Graz.

Fernández, L. (2002), *Estudio de la oferta de empleo en Nuevas Tecnologías de la Información y de las Comunicaciones.* Requisitos para el empleo, Universidad Europea de Madrid.

Ford, G. and Gibbs, N.E. (1996), *A Mature Profession of Software Engineering*, Software Engineering Institute, Carnegie Mellon University, Pittsburgh, Pennsylvania, Technical CMU/SEI-96-TR-004.

Instituto Nacional de Estadística (1994), *Clasificación Nacional de Ocupaciones*, Instituto Nacional de Estadística, Madrid. Available online: http://www.ine.es.

Lee, S., Koh, S., Yen, D. and Tang, H.L. (2002), Perception gaps between IS academics and IS practitioners: an exploratory study, *Information and Management, 40*(1) 51-61.

Levy-Leboyer, C. (1997), *Gestión de las competencias*, Ediciones Gestión 2000, Barcelona.

Martin, G., and Staines, H. (1994). Managerial competences in small firms. *Journal of Management Development, 13*(7), 23-34.

McClelland, D. C. (1973). Testing for competence rather than for 'intelligence'. *American Psychologist, 28*, 1-14.

McConnell, S. (2003), *Professional Software Development,* Addison-Wesley, Boston.

O*Net (2007), *The Occupational Information Network*, U.S. Department of Labor, Bureau of Labor Statistics. Available OnLine: http://www.onetcenter.org/

Office for National Statistics Occupational Information Unit (2000), *Standard Occupational Classification 2000*, Available online, http://www.statistics.gov.uk/nsbase/methods_quality/ns_sec/soc2000.asp

Parnas, D.L. (1999), Software Engineering Programs Are Not Computer Science Programs, *IEEE Software, 16(6)* 19-30.

Pelegrín, C. (2003), Las evaluaciones del desempeño no se aprovechan, *Diario Expansión*, 11th October 2003.

Pereda, S. and Berrocal, F. (2001) *Técnicas de Gestión de Recursos Humanos por competencias*, Centro de Estudios Ramón Areces, Madrid.

Project Management Institute. (2000), *A guide to project management body of knowledge*, Project Management Institute, Pennsylvania.

Saiedian, H., Bagert, D.J. and Mead, N.R. (2000), Software Engineering Programs: Dispelling the Myths and Misconceptions, *IEEE Software,* 19(5) 35-41.

Sobel, A.K. and LeBlanc, R. (2004), *Software Engineering 2004*, The Joint Task Force on Computing Curricula IEEE Computer Society Association for Computing Machinery.

Software Engineering Institute. (2006), *CMMI® for Development*, Version 1.2, CMU/SEI-2006-TR-008.

Taylor, F. W. (1911). *The Principles of Scientific Management.* Harper and Brothers, New York.

In: HRM and Marketing Orientation in the New Era
Editor: Panagiotis Kyriazopoulos
ISBN: 978-1-62808-959-2

Chapter 7

EVALUATING IMPLEMENTATION MODEL OF AMT: A GRAPH THEORETIC APPROACH

Sanjeev Goyal*[*] *and Sandeep Grover
Department of Mechanical Engineering
YMCA University of Science and Technology, Faridabad, India

ABSTRACT

In present scenario, survival and success are the main objectives for any organisation. To achieve this, organisations are looking for more fundamental factors like flexibility, quality, reliability etc. Advance Manufacturing Technology (AMT) is such a technology which promises to attain these factors.

The organisations are reluctant to go for this technology, as it involves large cost and complex implementation process. Even the organisations which have not adopted AMT realize its potential for competitive advantage, but are unaware of the implementation strategies. Few researchers have modelled the implementation process but the authors have not come across of any mathematical modelling of implementation pertaining to AMT.

In the present work, endeavour has been made to enumerate relationships and interdependencies among different implementation factors in AMT. This has been used further to develop a mathematical model using graph theoretic approach.

This proposed model can be used for practitioners as guideline for finding the numerical index of their organisation.

Keywords: AMT, Implementation Process, Critical factors, Graph theoretic approach

1. INTRODUCTION AND LITERATURE SURVEY

With the quest of globalization, changing daily prices, increasing labour cost, increasingly sophisticated customer, a record number of companies are looking for advanced manufacturing systems so that they can become flexible, adaptive, responsive and innovative.

[*] Corresponding author: E-mail: goyal.sanjeev@hotmail.com.

Extensive literature available on AMT reveals the various facets of AMT covered by various authors and researchers across the globe.

1.1. Overview of AMT

Advanced manufacturing technology can be defined according its application and use. According to McDermott and Stock (1999), it is an automated production system of people, machines and tools for the planning and control of the production process, including the procurement of raw materials, parts, components and the shipment and service of finished products. In the same way, Small and Yasin (1997) described it as a group of computer-based technologies, including Computer-Aided Design (CAD), robotics, Flexible Manufacturing Systems (FMS), Automated Materials Handling Systems (AMHS), Computer Numerically Controlled (CNC) machine St. Pierre et al. (2004) feel that the pressure of quality, cost and delivery are the main hurdles for any company to remain competitive in today's scenario. Pagell et al. (2000) and Dangayach et al. (2004) find that advanced manufacturing technologies are looked as a tool for gaining competitive advantage for manufacturing industries. Advanced manufacturing technology provides the manufacturing company a competitive advantage at every level of the operation, if used in proper way. The benefits of advanced manufacturing technologies have been realised and classified into tangible and intangible [Kaplan, (1986); Choobineh, (1986)].The tangible benefits are reduced inventory, more return on equity, less cost per unit and intangible benefits are flexibility, competitive advantage, enhanced quality and improved delivery. Dangayach et al. (2006) conducted a survey on 120 companies and found that even, advanced manufacturing technologies are being touched by progressive firms in developing countries.

Advanced manufacturing technologies have enormous benefits but only few companies are able to fully utilize these benefits. According to beatty et al. (1992) only half of the companies adopting AMT are able to realise their goals. Godwin et al. (1996) feels that advanced manufacturing technologies often serve as a double edge sword for the organisations, imposing them challenges while providing competitive advantage. Momaya and Ajitabh, (2005) have classified the advanced manufacturing technology into three main components-hardware, software and brain ware. Hardware relates to the equipments, software to the knowledge of using them and brain ware to the reasons for using the technology in particular way.

Primrose (1991) and Small and Chen, (1995) have conducted studies in developed countries for AMS and find that with increasing globalization, companies are realizing the potential benefits of advanced manufacturing systems to remain in competition.

Thomas et al. (2007) conducted a survey on 300 SME's and classified them into three categories like large scale companies, which have already adopted AMS, medium sized companies, which have not adopted the AMS, but already realized its potential for competitive advantage, but don't know how to implement it and at the last, small scale industries which are reluctant to go for advanced manufacturing systems seeing its high cost and complexity.

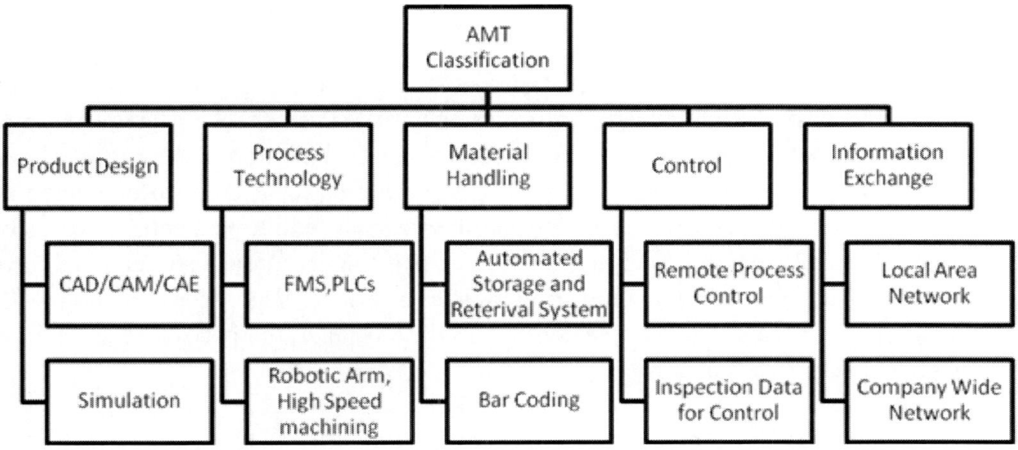

Figure 1. AMT Classification.

So, the work has to be carried out to make a standard implementation model for advanced manufacturing technology for medium sized industries. Already some researchers (Thomas et al. (2007); Badiru (1990); Schroder and Sohal (1999)) have developed different models for implementation of AMT. Although these models provide a helpful guideline for organisations implementing AMT, but the models involve many intangible steps and benefits which are difficult to quantify, many firms feel reluctant to go for implementation looking for higher cost involved. The authors, during literature survey have not come across evaluation of AMT Implementation issues by mathematical modelling leading to single numerical index. In the present work, it is proposed to accomplish the following

- Development of AMT Implementation model and use it as a system.
- Identify different subfactors and attributes thereof for implementation steps.
- Develop interdependencies/ relationships at system and subsystem level.
- Develop methodology by using Graph Theoretic Approach to evaluate proposed implementation model
- Use of proposed methodology for evaluation of single numerical index which can be used for comparison and ranking of different models.

2. AMT Implementation Strategy

Based on exhaustive literature survey and discussion with academicians and practitioner some critical steps have been identified and further broken into sub factors and later on their interdependency and overall numeric index is found with the graph theoretic approach. With a view to develop mathematical model, these steps and their sub factors are being discussed in brief.

2.1. Strategic Planning

The first and foremost factor of importance in strategic planning is the person or team responsible for the task. It is of utmost significance that related personnel have requisite skills and knowhow to define and develop the required planning platform. While developing strategic plans for the project financial risk need to be evaluated in order to determine the extent of financial exposure which provides the management with a parameter for decision making. The financial study involves various factors effecting the project structure and level of investment. The level of technology investment is also a major consideration while defining the strategic plans. The other factor that needs to be analyzed is government policies that may affect many decisions regarding the project.

Table 1. Literature review for identification of critical factors

Factors			Literature Survey
1.	Strategic Planning		
	(i)	Person Responsible	Beatty (1990), Jiménez et al. (1992), Shani et al. (1992), Slagmulder and Bruggeman (1992), Martínez Sánchez (1996), Sohal (1996), Udo and Ehie (1996), Boyer et al. (1997), Co et al. (1998), Burcher et al. (1999)
	(ii)	Financial Risk	Small et al.(1996),Thomas et al. (2007)
	(iii)	Level of Technology Investment	Dangayach et al. (2004)
	(iv)	Government Policies	Mital et al.(1999), Kunnathar (2000), Thomas et al. (2007)
2.	Concept Development		
	(i)	End User	Thomas et al.(2007)
	(ii)	Supplier Support	Jiménez et al. (1992), Martínez Sánchez (1996), Sohal (1996), Udo and Ehie (1996), Zhao and Co (1997), Co et al. (1998), Saberi et al. (2010)
	(iii)	Location	Thomas et al. (2007)
	(iv)	Feasibility Analysis	Jiménez et al. (1992), Slagmulder and Bruggeman (1992), Martínez Sánchez (1996), Small and Yasin (1997)
3.	Infrastructure		
	(i)	Size	Thomas et al. (2007)
	(ii)	Financial Position	Idris (2008)
	(iii)	Technology Competent Workers	Small and Yasin (1997), Yusuff et al. (2005)
	(iv)	Computerized Integration	Beatty (1992), Burcher et al. (1999), Ghani et al. (2000)

Factors			Literature Survey
4.	Performance Measurement		
	(i)	Flexibility	Marri et al. (2006), Small et al. (2002), Cost et al. (2008)
	(ii)	Quality	Small et al. (2003), Thomas et al. (2007), Gouvea da Costa et al. (2008)
	(iii)	Delivery	Reinsch et al. (2003),Thomas et al. (2007),
	(iv)	Cost	Thomas et al. (2007)
5.	Human Resource Practice		
	(i)	Recruitment	Macek (1982), Yusuff et al.(2005)
	(ii)	Employees' Training	Jiménez et al. (1992), Shani et al. (1992), Martínez Sánchez (1996), Sohal (1996), Udo and Ehie (1996), Boyer et al. (1997), Co et al. (1998), Burcher et al. (1999), Dangayach et al. (2004), Marri et al. (2006)
	(iii)	Employees' Motivation	Jiménez et al. (1992), Sambasivarao (1995), Martínez Sánchez (1996), Boyer et al. (1997), Barua (2008),Ghani et al.(2000)
	(iv)	Management Support	Jiménez et al. (1992), Nichols and Jones (1994), Martínez Sánchez (1996), Udo and Ehie (1996), Hottenstein et al. (1997), Zhao and Co (1997), Co et al. (1998), Thomas et al. (2007)
6.	Post Implement Evaluation		
	(i)	Customers' Feedback	Hon (2005), Thomas et al.(2007)
	(ii)	Production Rate	Zhao (1997), Yang (2006)
	(iii)	Competition	Thomas et al. (2007)
	(iv)	Quality of the Product	Thomas et al. (2007)

Ramamurthy, K. (1995) and Kumar et al (1996) find that failure of AMT is mainly because of the inadequate planning at the implementation stage. Planning majorly involves the assessment of the capabilities of the organisation to meet the requirements of the AMT. Management estimates the risk of implementing the AMT at the planning. Meredith (1987) lists some of the problems of implementing the AMT like expensive, complex systems, insufficient internal skills, incremental skill building: and the need for a different support infrastructure. The management should assess their organisation against these obstacles before choosing the path of advanced manufacturing system. The next important factor available for the planning an AMT is the technology available i.e. what advancements in the present technology are available in the market and how these new technologies can help organisation in competition.

2.2. Concept Development

Lewis et al. (1988) suggested that customers and suppliers should be involved in AMT implementation and they should be fully aware about the AMT implementation and its proper benefits. Personnel across functions especially from manufacturing should be involved at every stage in the technology implementation and the decision making should be decentralized to achieve the maximum benefits (Voss, 1995).

The workers should be consulted at every design and implementation stage and the companies should adopt bottom to top approach in order to ensure accrual of full benefits upon successful implementation.

One good example of such activities is that production supervisors should be made project leaders to ensure their active participation. The other major factor is thorough feasibility analysis that needs to be conducted and forms the basis of feedback to the decision making. Location also plays an important role as it determines access to customers and suppliers which largely influence the AMT implementation.

2.3. Infrastructural

Size of the company also decides what type of advance manufacturing technology can be implemented. The financial position of the company defines the level of expenditure that can be accrued to the project the capability of the company to bear the burden also in case of project extension/creep. The attitude of the owners and stake holders towards AMT plays an important in the successful implementation. Stake holders and owners should completely understand the AMT and its benefits. The level of technology awareness and acceptance in the organization and ease of computer/IT integration play important role in the successful implementation.

2.4. Performance Measurement

Mohanty et al. (1998) found that AMT can provide the benefit of flexibility to the organisation. The organisation should understand that competition is not only about cost and productivity but it also involves the flexibility, delivery on time and quality of the product. Organisation should estimate that how much flexibility is right for them, accordingly they can plan their AMT. Organisation should clearly understand the benefits and cost involved in implementation. Merely hearing the successes of the other companies about AMT does not guarantee any organisation to get the same benefit.

2.5. Human Resource Practice

The next step for the implementation process is development and implementation. This step involves workers training, workers motivation, finding technology competent workers and reviewing the management attitude. Sohal (1994) find that for getting the absolute benefits of technology implementation, the Pre training of workers is absolute necessary. Bessant (1993) find that the companies having higher basic skill levels, were able to exploit much of the innate flexibility in AMT achieve significantly higher productivity and other benefits So, to find technology competent workers is very much necessary. The motivation of workers is also important before implementing the AMT, as it helps in realizing the total benefits of the AMT. Management's positive attitude is also important, because it has to take many strong decisions before implementing the AMT. The decentralization of decision making is also important decision to be taken before implementing the AMT.

2.6. Post Implement Evaluation

The last step is to evaluate from time to time the AMT impact on various factors affecting the organisation. The main factors identified in this step are customer's feedback, production rate, quality of the product and competition. The customer's feedback is very important as this is the actual window from where the company can look the benefits of AMT implementation. Production rate, quality of the production should be continuously monitored, so that actual benefits of AMT can be realized. Competition is another factor that clearly helps to monitor and evaluate the benefits of AMT implementation.

3. Graph Theoretic Approach (GTA)

Graph theoretic and matrix model consists of digraph representation, matrix representation and permanent representation. It is a powerful technique that can be applied in various fields. Different researchers have applied this approach in various fields.

Table 2. Literature review of GTA

S.No.	Author/Authors	Field
1	Gandhi et al.(1996)	FMEA
2	Wani and Gandhi(1999)	development of the maintainability index of mechanical systems
3	Rao and Gandhi (2002)	failure cause analysis of machine tools
4	Huang et al.(2003)	for Capturing the Capability Envelope of a Machining Process
5	Grover *et al.* (2004)	to develop a mathematical model of the Total Quality Management (TQM)
6	Kulkarni (2005)	for performance evaluation of TQM in Indian industries
7	Faisal *et al.* (2006)	selection of a suitable supply chain strategy based on customer sensitivity and risk alleviation competency
8	Rao et al. (2006)	Selection, identification and comparison of industrial robots
9	Grover et al. (2006)	Role of human factors in TQM
10	Dou (2009)	to optimize single-product flow-line configurations of RMS

3.1. Main Objectives of the Graph Theoretic Approach

- It is a tool which is used to calculate the single numerical index of any issue
- It converts the intangible issues into tangible i.e it quantify the subjective issues.
- It also finds the interdependencies of the various subfactors in numerical way.
- It helps to compare the different organisations on the basis of the single numerical index.

3.2. Limitations of the Graph Theoretic Approach

Although, this mathematical approach has many advantages as discussed above but at the same time, it has some limitations, which are discussed below:

- If numbers of factors are too many, then to make the calculation possible, we have to group the factors. Although, factors are grouped according to the homogeneity among them, but still some subjectivity is involved, so different organisations can have different numerical index, but having the same factors.
- Factor selection depends upon the experience of the persons concerned and the extent to which resources are available, So, always chances of errors are there while selecting factors.

In this present work, the graph theoretic approach is being used to evaluate the earlier identified steps to calculate the overall implementation index. Also this technique has been used to find out the interdependencies of the various sub factors in numerical manner. The overall numerical index of the implementation model will help the different organisations to compare visually.

First of all digraph of each implementation step and their subfactors will be made. Then with the help of matrices these digraph will be converted into mathematical form and then a permanent function will be calculated which will represent the single numerical index for the implementation model.

4. AMT IMPLEMENTATION MODEL DIGRAPH

The AMT implementation model digraph is prepared to represent the modelling of the steps of implementation and their interdependencies. The Digraph consists of the set of nodes $N=\{n_i\}$, with i =1, 2, 3, 4...........K and a set of directed edges $A=\{a_{ij}\}$. A node n_i represents the ith implementation step and the edges represent the interdependencies between the implementation steps. The numbers of nodes are here equal to the no. of steps taken for the implementation model of AMT. If a node i has an importance over node j, then a directed arrow is drawn from 'i' node to 'j', while if the node 'j' has importance over the node 'i' then a similar directed arrow is drawn from 'j' to 'i'. The diagraph for the implementation model is shown in Figure 2.

Here the six nodes have been chosen depending upon the no. of steps in implementation model like Strategic Planning (F_1), Concept development (F_2), Infrastructural (F_3), Performance Measurement (F_4), Human Resource Practice (F_5) and Post Implement Evaluation (F_6).

As shown in Figure the directed edges are drawn according to the interdependencies of the implementation model steps. For example Strategy affect the concept development, infrastructural, human resource practice factors so directed edges have been drawn from the F_1 to F_2,F_3,F_5. Similarly with the literature survey and experts advice, other interdependencies have been prepared.

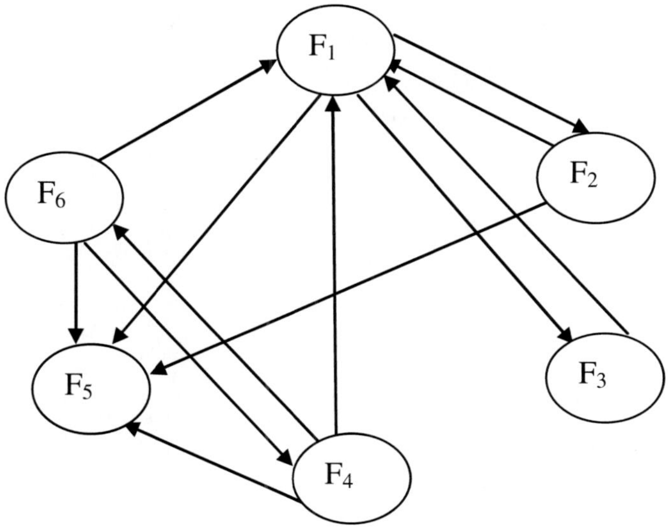

Figure 2. AMT Implementation model digraph.

4.1. AMT Implementation Model Matrix

The representation of the digraph becomes too complex if nodes are more so representation in matrix form makes it visually perfect. For matrix representation, consider a symmetric matrix A = [a_{ij}]. The value of a_{ij} represents the interaction of the ith factor with the jth factor.

a_{ij} = 1, if i is connected to j = 0, otherwise

Here a_{ii} = 0, as it is assumed here that there is no self loop. AMT Implementation model matrix is square and non-symmetric and is analogous to adjacency matrix in graph theory (Narsingh, 2000).The matrix representation of the digraph is shown in Figure 2.

Here, the off diagonal elements represent the interdependencies. Like 1 represents that element j is affected by i while 0 represents that no relationship exist between i and j. The diagonal elements are kept 0 here because their affect is not taken into consideration. For evaluating their effect, another matrix i.e. characteristic matrix has been made.

$$A = \begin{array}{c} \textit{Factors} \\ 1 \\ 2 \\ 3 \\ 4 \\ 5 \\ 6 \end{array} \begin{array}{c} \begin{array}{cccccc} 1 & 2 & 3 & 4 & 5 & 6 \end{array} \\ \begin{bmatrix} 0 & 1 & 1 & 0 & 1 & 0 \\ 1 & 0 & 0 & 0 & 1 & 0 \\ 1 & 0 & 0 & 0 & 0 & 0 \\ 1 & 0 & 0 & 0 & 1 & 1 \\ 0 & 0 & 0 & 0 & 0 & 0 \\ 1 & 0 & 0 & 1 & 1 & 0 \end{bmatrix} \end{array} \quad (1)$$

4.2. AMT Implementation Model Characteristic Matrix

This matrix is used to characterise the implementation model factors. Suppose I represent the identity matrix and F represents the implementation factors, then characteristic matrix can be written as C = [FI-A]

$$C = \begin{array}{c} Factors \\ 1 \\ 2 \\ 3 \\ 4 \\ 5 \\ 6 \end{array} \begin{array}{c} \begin{array}{cccccc} 1 & 2 & 3 & 4 & 5 & 6 \end{array} \\ \begin{bmatrix} F & -1 & -1 & 0 & -1 & 0 \\ -1 & F & 0 & 0 & -1 & 0 \\ -1 & 0 & F & 0 & 0 & 0 \\ -1 & 0 & 0 & F & -1 & -1 \\ 0 & 0 & 0 & 0 & F & 0 \\ -1 & 0 & 0 & -1 & -1 & F \end{bmatrix} \end{array} \quad (2)$$

Here all the implementation factors have been assigned equal value, which is not possible, so to see the effect of implementation factors and their interdependencies another AMT implementation model variable characteristic matrix (VCM) has been made.

4.3. AMT Implementation Model Variable Characteristic Matrix (VCM)

VCM has been constructed to characterize the AMT implementation factors and their effects. Consider a matrix D with off-diagonal elements a_{ij} representing interactions between implementation factors, i.e. instead of 1 (as in matrix 1).

Consider another matrix E with diagonal elements F_i, i = 1, 2, . . . 6, where F_i represent implementation factors of AMT, i.e. instead of F only (as in matrix 2). Considering matrices D and E, the VCM-F is written as

H = [E - D]

$$H = \begin{array}{c} Factors \\ 1 \\ 2 \\ 3 \\ 4 \\ 5 \\ 6 \end{array} \begin{array}{c} \begin{array}{cccccc} 1 & 2 & 3 & 4 & 5 & 6 \end{array} \\ \begin{bmatrix} F_1 & -a_{12} & -a_{13} & 0 & -a_{15} & 0 \\ -a_{21} & F_2 & 0 & 0 & -a_{25} & 0 \\ -a_{31} & 0 & F_3 & 0 & 0 & 0 \\ -a_{41} & 0 & 0 & F_4 & -a_{45} & -a_{46} \\ 0 & 0 & 0 & 0 & F_5 & 0 \\ -a_{61} & 0 & 0 & -a_{64} & -a_{65} & F_6 \end{bmatrix} \end{array} \quad (3)$$

Determinant of the matrix H provides characteristic of the system and represents the effect of the system consisting of factors and their interactions.

Determinant of matrix H carries positive and negative signs with some of its co-efficient. Hence, complete information will not be obtained as some will be lost due to addition and subtraction of numerical values of diagonal and off diagonal elements (i.e. F_i's and a_{ij}'s).

Thus, the determinant of matrix H does not provide complete information concerning the each factor's effect. For this, another matrix, AMT implementation variable permanent matrix (VPM-T) is introduced.

4.4. AMT Implementation Variable Permanent Matrix (VPM-T)

To see the total effect of implementation factors and their interactions, Variable permanent matrix has been made. Here T is taken as sum of D and E. Here E and D are the same matrices that were used for matrix H. The permanent of matrix equation 4 is multinomial and is called variable permanent function (VPF-T), also known as permanent of T (per T). It helps to analyse the intensity of factors affecting implementation of AMT from combinatorial considerations. This is evaluated by standard procedures and is same as determinant of matrix H but with all signs positive. The permanent for matrix equation 4 in general form is written as:

$$T = \begin{array}{c} \textit{Factors} \\ 1 \\ 2 \\ 3 \\ 4 \\ 5 \\ 6 \end{array} \begin{array}{c} \begin{array}{cccccc} 1 & 2 & 3 & 4 & 5 & 6 \end{array} \\ \begin{bmatrix} F_1 & a_{12} & a_{13} & 0 & a_{15} & 0 \\ a_{21} & F_2 & 0 & 0 & a_{25} & 0 \\ a_{31} & 0 & F_3 & 0 & 0 & 0 \\ a_{41} & 0 & 0 & F_4 & a_{45} & a_{46} \\ 0 & 0 & 0 & 0 & F_5 & 0 \\ a_{61} & 0 & 0 & a_{64} & a_{65} & F_6 \end{bmatrix} \end{array} \qquad (4)$$

$$\begin{aligned} VPF-T = per T = \prod_{i=1}^{6} F_i &+ \sum_i\sum_j\sum_k\sum_l\sum_m\sum_n (a_{ij}a_{ji})F_k F_l F_m F_n \\ &+ \sum_i\sum_j\sum_k\sum_l\sum_m\sum_n (a_{ij}a_{jk}a_{ki} + a_{ik}a_{kj}a_{ji})F_l F_m F_n \\ &+ [(\sum_i\sum_j\sum_k\sum_l\sum_m\sum_n (a_{ij}a_{ji})(a_{kl}a_{lk})F_m F_n \\ &+ \sum_i\sum_j\sum_k\sum_l\sum_m\sum_n (a_{ij}a_{jk}a_{kl}a_{li} + a_{il}a_{lk}a_{kj}a_{ji})F_m F_n)] \\ &+ [\sum_i\sum_j\sum_k\sum_l\sum_m\sum_n (a_{ij}a_{ji})(a_{kl}a_{lm}a_{mk} + a_{km}a_{ml}a_{lk})F_n \\ &+ \sum_i\sum_j\sum_k\sum_l\sum_m\sum_n (a_{ij}a_{jk}a_{kl}a_{lm}a_{mi} + a_{im}a_{ml}a_{lk}a_{kj}a_{ji})F_n] \\ &+ [\sum_i\sum_j\sum_k\sum_l\sum_m\sum_n (a_{ij}a_{ji})(a_{kl}a_{lm}a_{mn}a_{nk} + a_{kn}a_{nm}a_{ml}a_{lk}) \\ &+ \sum_i\sum_j\sum_k\sum_l\sum_m\sum_n (a_{ij}a_{jk}a_{kl})(a_{lm}a_{mn}a_{nl}) \\ &+ \sum_i\sum_j\sum_k\sum_l\sum_m\sum_n (a_{ij}a_{ji})(a_{kl}a_{lk})(a_{mn}a_{nm}) \\ &+ \sum_i\sum_j\sum_k\sum_l\sum_m\sum_n (a_{ij}a_{jk}a_{lm}a_{mn}a_{ni} + a_{in}a_{nm}a_{ml}a_{lk}a_{kj}a_{ji}] \end{aligned} \qquad (5)$$

In this total (n+1) 1.e (6+1) groupings have been made. These groups represent the measure of attributes and the relative importance. Here total 7 groups have been made and their importance is discussed below.

1. The first grouping represents the measures of inheritance level of implementation factors.
2. The second grouping is absent as there is no self loop in the digraph.
3. The third grouping contains interrelationships between the subfactors (i.e. a_{ij} a_{ji}) and measures of four remaining factors.
4. The fourth grouping represents a set of three factors relative importance loop and measure of three factors.
5. The fifth grouping contains two sub groups. The terms of the first subgroup represents the relative importance among the two factors and the measure of two implementation factors. The second subgroup contains the relative importance among the four factors and the measure of the two implementation factors.
6. The sixth grouping contains two sub groups. The first subgrouping is a set of 2 factor interdependence, i.e. $a_{ij}a_{ji}$, a set of 3 factor interdependence, i.e. $a_{kl}a_{lm}a_{mk}$ or its pair $a_{km}a_{ml}a_{lk}$ and measure of remaining implementation factor.The second sub-grouping is a set of five implementation factors interdependence, i.e. $a_{ij}a_{jk}a_{kl}a_{lm}a_{mi}$ or its pair $a_{im}a_{ml}a_{lk}a_{kj}a_{ji}$ and measure of remaining implementation factor.
7. Similarly seventh grouping analyses sub-grouping in terms of a set of two and four behavioural factor interdependence, 2 – three behavioural factor interdependence,3 – two behavioural factor interdependence and six implementation factors interdependence.

5. Application of Graph Theoretic Approach

Each factor is identified as a subsystem and graph theoretic approach is applied in each subsystem. Permanent characteristic matrix (similar to equation 5) is evaluated for permanent function considering various factors affecting the subsystem. The various factors affecting subsystems are identified in Figure 1. The dependencies of factors at subsystem level are visualized through digraphs. These digraphs lead to the inheritance of factors at system level through matrix and measures the corresponding variable permanent matrices are then derived for each subsystem and permanent function of each VPM is evaluated. The permanent functions of these matrices (similar to equation 5) will lead to inheritance of implementation factors. Thus, graph theoretic approach may be applied at every level. In order to avoid complexity, suitable scale may be used to assign value at subsystem level or sub subsystem. If all the factors are not equally important to an organization, suitable weights may be assigned. Table 2 suggests assignment of numerical values to factors. To get the complete value of multinomial (equation 5), the off diagonal elements in VPM-T (equation 4) are to be assigned numerical values.

As already discussed, these off diagonal elements represent interdependencies among implementation factors in AMT. However, this dependence among factors at system level (or subsystem level) cannot be measured directly and values can be assigned only after proper interpretation through a team of experts. It is suggested to use Table 3 for value of interdependencies.

Table 2. Quantification of AMT Implementation Factors

S.No.	Quantitative measure of Implementation Factors	Assigned values for factors
1	Exceptionally low	1
2	Very low	2
3	Low	3
4	Below average	4
5	Average	5
6	Above average	6
7	High	7
8	Very High	8
9	Exceptionally High	9

Table 3. Quantitative measure of interdependencies among Implementation Factors

S.No.	Quantitative measure of interdependencies	Assigned Values
1	Very Strong	5
2	Strong	4
3	Medium	3
4	Weak	2
5	Very Weak	1

6. IMPLEMENTATION MODEL INDEX

As already discussed, AMT implementation process is very complex and involves various steps. Total six steps were identified from the literature survey. From that a model has been prepared. As it involves various subjective terms, so it becomes necessary to quantify it for visualization. It becomes very useful to evaluate the intensity of the different factors affecting the implementation process. As the equation (5), contains measure of factors and their relative importance and is hence appropriate, and can be used for the evaluation of Implementation model Index So, any organisation willing to adopt AMT may just compare the implementation model index of different organisation. The permanent of VPM-T gives the overall Implementation model index.

T*= Permanent value of VPM-T

The numerical values of various factors and dependencies required for T* can be determined using the procedure already explained. The features of Implementation model index are highlighted below:

7. This index is a means to evaluate the content of implementation factors needed for an environment in an organization conducive to AMT.
8. Implementation factors affecting the AMT for an organization are represented by single numerical value. A higher value of index is an indicator of more conducive environment to AMT.

9. The value may be used for self-analysis of an organization and by this procedure. The permanent value can be increased by varying (increasing in particular) the implementation factors identified.

7. Methodology

To study the impact of factors and their interdependencies, graph theoretic approach has been used. The following step wise procedure has been adopted to calculate the single numerical index.

1. Identify various factors that affect implementation process of AMT.
2. Identify the sub factors affecting implementation factors in step (1).
3. Develop sub factor digraph considering attributes affecting each sub factor. The nodes in the digraph represent attributes identified in each sub factor. The interaction among attributes is represented by edges.
4. Develop sub factor matrix. This will be of size M X M, with diagonal elements representing attributes and the off diagonal elements representing interactions among them (equation 4).
5. At the sub subsystem level use Tables 2 and 3. This will provide numerical values for inheritance of attributes and their interactions.
6. Find the value of permanent function for sub factor (equation 5).
7. Repeat steps (3)-(6)for each sub factor.
8. Develop behavioural factor digraph and behavioural matrix at system level as explained in steps (3) and (4).
9. At system level, the permanent value of each sub factor (obtained in step 7) provides affect of each factor (i.e. diagonal elements in equation 4). The quantitative value of interactions among factors (i.e. off diagonal elements in equation 4) is obtained from Table 3 through proper interpretation by experts.
10. Find the value of permanent function for the system (equation 5). This is the value of the implementation model index. Based on the above-discussed methodology, the organization can evaluate the intensity of each factor for the implementation process of AMT.

8. Case Study

To demonstrate the proposed methodology to evaluate the intensity of critical factors affecting implementation process of AMT, a case study has been conducted in an organisation. This organisation is engaged in the manufacture of sheet metal components, having a turnover of US$1.3 million and employing 750 employees. This company manufactures 15–20 models of their products and change overtime of 60–90 min from one model to another has been reported. In this case, the permanent function value has been determined by substituting the values of factors (F_i) and interdependencies (a_{ij}) of AMT implementation. Numerical values are to be assigned to different categories of implementation factors (*i.e.*, F_1, F_2, F_3, F_4, F_5 and F_6) to measure each factor quantitatively.

For this purpose, a questionnaire was given in this organisation at the top, middle and lower management levels. After analysing the responses through this questionnaire, some experts were approached and the results were shared for their opinions. These experts were of the level of Deputy General Manager (DGM) and above. Each category is considered a subsystem and GTA is applied to each subsystem. Step by step methodology discussed in previous section is used to evaluate implementation model index in this case study.

First of all, digraph of each subsystem will be made. Then, variable permanent matrix of digraph for each subsystem is to be written as per equation 4. After that permanent function of the matrix is to be calculated as per equation 5. The digraph of the first subsystem (strategic planning) is shown below:

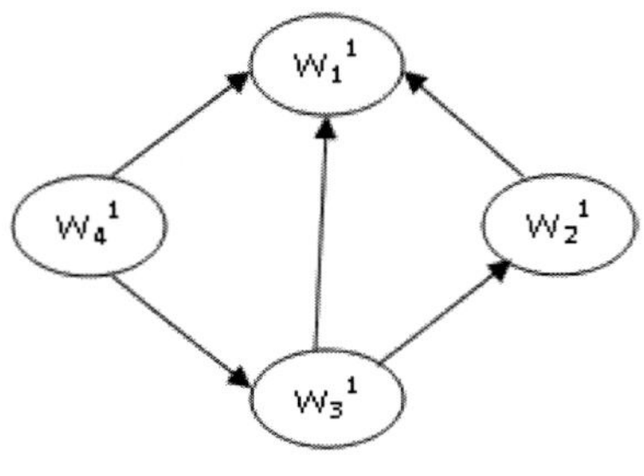

Figure 3. The digraph of the strategic planning subsystem Tss_1.

Here W_j^i represents jth sub factor of ith factor.

The general variable permanent matrix in general for the subsystem will be written as below.

$$T_{ss_1} = \begin{array}{c} Sub\,Factors \\ 1 \\ 2 \\ 3 \\ 4 \end{array} \begin{array}{c} \begin{array}{cccc} 1 & 2 & 3 & 4 \end{array} \\ \begin{bmatrix} W_1^1 & a_{12} & a_{13} & a_{14} \\ a_{21} & W_2^1 & a_{23} & a_{24} \\ a_{31} & a_{32} & W_3^1 & a_{34} \\ a_{41} & a_{42} & a_{43} & W_4^1 \end{bmatrix} \end{array} \quad (6)$$

In similar way the digraphs and permanent matrices of all six subsystems can be formed. The digraphs of the remaining five subsystems are shown below.

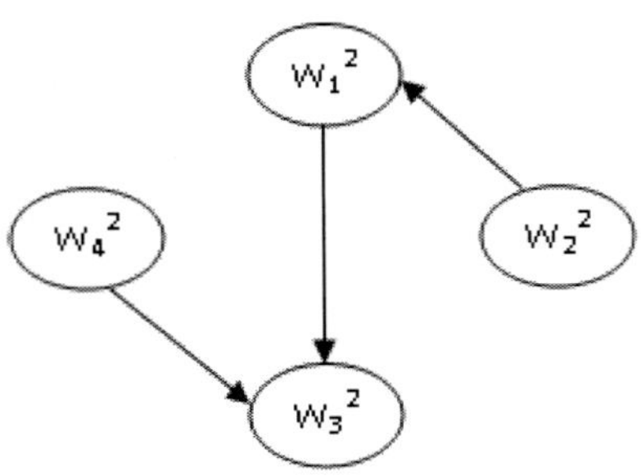

Figure 4. The Digraph of the second subsystem Tss_2.

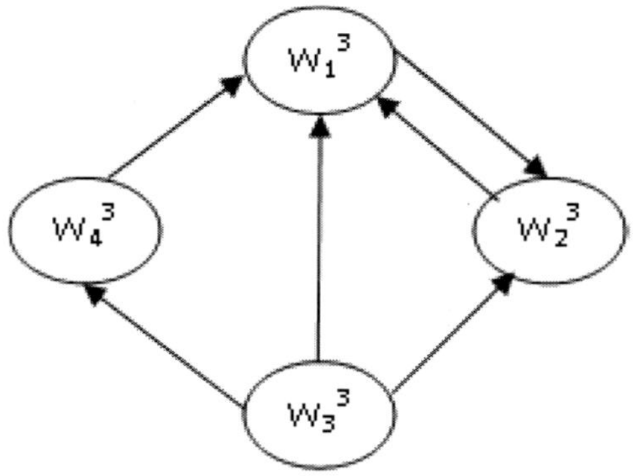

Figure 5. The Digraph of the second subsystem Tss_3.

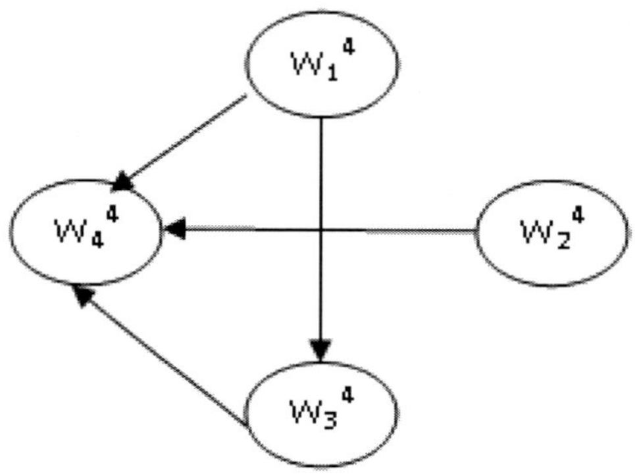

Figure 6. The Digraph of the fourth Subsystem Tss_4.

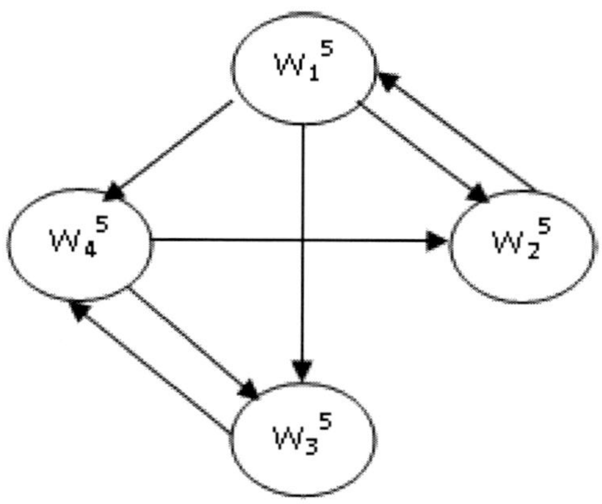

Figure 7. The Digraph of the fourth Subsystem Tss_5.

After making the digraph of all the subsystems, the next step is to put the values of inheritance of attributes and their relative importance from table 2 and table 3. The variable permanent matrices for different subsystems are shown below.

For the subsystem Tss_1 the values taken from table 2 are $W_1{}^1=7$, $W_2{}^1=5$, $W_3{}^1=6$, $W_4{}^1=4$ and from the table 3 are $a_{21}{}^1=3$, $a_{31}{}^1=4$, $a_{32}{}^1=2$, $a_{41}{}^1=3$, $a_{43}{}^1=3$

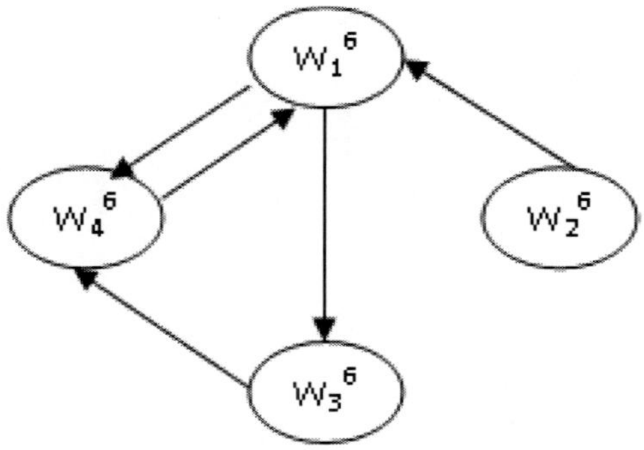

Figure 8. The Digraph of the fourth Subsystem Tss_6.

Substituting these values in equation 6 as follows:

$$T_{ss_1} = \begin{array}{c} \textit{Sub Factors} \\ 1 \\ 2 \\ 3 \\ 4 \end{array} \begin{array}{c} \begin{array}{cccc} 1 & 2 & 3 & 4 \end{array} \\ \begin{bmatrix} 7 & 0 & 0 & 0 \\ 3 & 5 & 0 & 0 \\ 4 & 2 & 6 & 0 \\ 3 & 0 & 3 & 4 \end{bmatrix} \end{array} \tag{7.1}$$

In similar way, the variable permanent matrices for other subsystems are written as:

$$T_{ss_2} = \begin{array}{c} \textit{Sub Factors} \\ 1 \\ 2 \\ 3 \\ 4 \end{array} \begin{array}{c} \begin{array}{cccc} 1 & 2 & 3 & 4 \end{array} \\ \begin{bmatrix} 8 & 0 & 4 & 0 \\ 2 & 6 & 0 & 0 \\ 0 & 0 & 7 & 3 \\ 0 & 0 & 0 & 5 \end{bmatrix} \end{array} \tag{7.2}$$

$$T_{ss_3} = \begin{array}{c} \textit{Sub Factors} \\ 1 \\ 2 \\ 3 \\ 4 \end{array} \begin{array}{c} \begin{array}{cccc} 1 & 2 & 3 & 4 \end{array} \\ \begin{bmatrix} 4 & 3 & 0 & 0 \\ 2 & 6 & 0 & 0 \\ 4 & 3 & 8 & 2 \\ 3 & 0 & 0 & 6 \end{bmatrix} \end{array} \tag{7.3}$$

$$T_{ss_4} = \begin{array}{c} \textit{Sub Factors} \\ 1 \\ 2 \\ 3 \\ 4 \end{array} \begin{array}{c} \begin{array}{cccc} 1 & 2 & 3 & 4 \end{array} \\ \begin{bmatrix} 8 & 0 & 3 & 4 \\ 0 & 8 & 0 & 4 \\ 0 & 0 & 8 & 3 \\ 0 & 0 & 0 & 9 \end{bmatrix} \end{array} \tag{7.4}$$

$$T_{ss_5} = \begin{array}{c c} \text{Sub Factors} & \begin{array}{cccc} 1 & 2 & 3 & 4 \end{array} \\ \begin{array}{c} 1 \\ 2 \\ 3 \\ 4 \end{array} & \begin{bmatrix} 7 & 3 & 4 & 2 \\ 3 & 7 & 0 & 0 \\ 0 & 0 & 6 & 3 \\ 0 & 4 & 3 & 6 \end{bmatrix} \end{array} \tag{7.5}$$

$$T_{ss_6} = \begin{array}{c c} \text{Sub Factors} & \begin{array}{cccc} 1 & 2 & 3 & 4 \end{array} \\ \begin{array}{c} 1 \\ 2 \\ 3 \\ 4 \end{array} & \begin{bmatrix} 7 & 0 & 4 & 3 \\ 3 & 7 & 0 & 0 \\ 0 & 0 & 8 & 4 \\ 4 & 0 & 0 & 9 \end{bmatrix} \end{array} \tag{7.6}$$

The permanent of matrix equation 6 – Per Tss_1, which will lead to inheritance of implementation factor 1, is evaluated on the lines of equation (5). The complete expression for the Per Tss_1 is given as:

$$\begin{aligned} Per\,Tss_1 = {} & W_1W_2W_3W_4 + [a_{12}a_{21}W_3W_4 + a_{13}a_{31}W_2W_4 + a_{23}a_{32}W_1W_4 + a_{24}a_{42}W_1W_3 + a_{34}a_{43}W_1W_2] \\ & + [(a_{12}a_{23}a_{31} + a_{13}a_{32}a_{21})W_4 + (a_{12}a_{24}a_{41} + a_{14}a_{42}a_{21})W_3 \\ & + (a_{13}a_{34}a_{41} + a_{14}a_{43}a_{31})W_2 + (a_{23}a_{34}a_{42} + a_{24}a_{43}a_{32})W_1] \\ & + [(a_{12}a_{21})(a_{34}a_{43}) + (a_{13}a_{31})(a_{24}a_{42}) + (a_{14}a_{41})(a_{23}a_{32})] \\ & + [(a_{12}a_{23}a_{34}a_{41} + a_{14}a_{43}a_{32}a_{21}) + (a_{13}a_{34}a_{42}a_{21} + a_{12}a_{24}a_{43}a_{31}) \\ & + (a_{14}a_{42}a_{23}a_{31} + a_{13}a_{32}a_{24}a_{41})] \end{aligned} \tag{8}$$

Substituting the values from equation (7.1)

Per Tss_1=840

Similarly, the permanent function of other subsystem can be determined.

Per Tss_2=1680

Per Tss_3=1344

Per Tss_4=4608

Per Tss_5=2898

Per Tss_6=4648

Implementation model critical factor digraph is shown in Figure 2 and Implementation model matrix at system level is developed through equations (1)-(4). Variable permanent matrix for this case study is written in symbolic form as:

$$VPM-T=\begin{array}{c} Factors \\ 1 \\ 2 \\ 3 \\ 4 \\ 5 \\ 6 \end{array}\begin{array}{c} \begin{array}{cccccc} 1 & 2 & 3 & 4 & 5 & 6 \end{array} \\ \begin{bmatrix} F_1 & a_{12} & a_{13} & 0 & a_{15} & 0 \\ a_{21} & F_2 & 0 & 0 & a_{25} & 0 \\ a_{31} & 0 & F_3 & 0 & 0 & 0 \\ a_{41} & 0 & 0 & F_4 & a_{45} & a_{46} \\ 0 & 0 & 0 & 0 & F_5 & 0 \\ a_{61} & 0 & 0 & a_{64} & a_{65} & F_6 \end{bmatrix} \end{array} \tag{9}$$

The value of the diagonal elements are taken from the permanent functions of the subsystem as F_1 = Per Tss_1, F_2= Per Tss_2, F_3 = Per Tss_3, F_4= Per Tss_4, F_5=Per Tss_5, F_6= Per Tss_6 and the values of the off diagonal elements are taken from the table 3.

To obtain variable permanent matrix for this example, values are substituted as discussed.

$$VPM-T=\begin{array}{c} Factors \\ 1 \\ 2 \\ 3 \\ 4 \\ 5 \\ 6 \end{array}\begin{array}{c} \begin{array}{cccccc} 1 & 2 & 3 & 4 & 5 & 6 \end{array} \\ \begin{bmatrix} 840 & 3 & 2 & 0 & 3 & 0 \\ 4 & 1680 & 0 & 0 & 3 & 0 \\ 4 & 0 & 1344 & 0 & 0 & 0 \\ 5 & 0 & 0 & 4608 & 3 & 2 \\ 0 & 0 & 0 & 0 & 2898 & 0 \\ 5 & 0 & 0 & 4 & 4 & 4648 \end{bmatrix} \end{array} \tag{10}$$

Value of permanent function for the system is evaluated as per equation (5). The value of permanent of above matrix (equation 10) is 1.177×10^{20}, which indicates intensity of critical factors affecting implementation model of AMT for the case considered. By carrying out similar analysis for different organizations numerical index can be obtained.

As suggested, this will help an organization to access AMT implementation and improve. For a particular period of time, similar organizations may be compared and rated. It is also suggested to find hypothetical best and hypothetical worst value of intensity of critical factors affecting implementation. Numerical index is at its best when the inheritance of all its factors is at its best. Since, inheritance of factors is evaluated considering sub factors and applying graph theoretic approach at the subsystem level, it is evident that numerical index is at its best when inheritance of sub factors is at its best. Since, Table 2 is used at subsystem level, maximum value of Per T_1 is obtained when inheritance of all the sub factors is maximum, i.e. value taken from Table 3 is 9. Thus, equation (7.1) may be rewritten for the maximum value of Per T_1 as

$$T_{ss_1}=\begin{array}{c} Sub\,Factors \\ 1 \\ 2 \\ 3 \\ 4 \end{array}\begin{array}{c} \begin{array}{cccc} 1 & 2 & 3 & 4 \end{array} \\ \begin{bmatrix} 9 & 0 & 0 & 0 \\ 3 & 9 & 0 & 0 \\ 4 & 2 & 9 & 0 \\ 3 & 0 & 3 & 9 \end{bmatrix} \end{array} \tag{11}$$

The value of the permanent of the above function is 6561, i.e. max. Per Tss_1 is 6561.

Similarly implementation index is at its worst when the inheritance of all its factors and sub factors is at its worst. This is the case when inheritance of all the sub factors is minimum, i.e. value taken from Table 3 is 1. Thus, equation (7.1) may be rewritten for the minimum value of Per T_1 as

$$T_{ss_1} = \begin{array}{c c} \textit{Sub Factors} & \begin{array}{cccc} 1 & 2 & 3 & 4 \end{array} \\ \begin{array}{c} 1 \\ 2 \\ 3 \\ 4 \end{array} & \begin{bmatrix} 1 & 0 & 0 & 0 \\ 3 & 1 & 0 & 0 \\ 4 & 2 & 1 & 0 \\ 3 & 0 & 3 & 1 \end{bmatrix} \end{array} \qquad (12)$$

The value of the permanent of the above function is 1, i.e. min. Per Tss_1 = 1. Similarly maximum and minimum values for each subsystem are evaluated and different values of permanent of subsystem matrices are summarized in Table IV. The value of per T indicates the value of intensity of critical factors affecting implementation index. Thus, the maximum and minimum value of numerical index indicates the range with in which it can vary. Experts can use this range to decide a threshold value for a given set of similar industries. Moreover, the values may be used for self-assessment of industry.

Table 4. Indicating the range of AMT implementation numerical index

System/ Subsystem	Current Value	Maximum Value	Minimum Value
Per T_1	840	6561	1
Per T_2	1680	6561	1
Per T_3	1344	7407	7
Per T_4	4608	6561	1
Per T_5	2898	8460	268
Per T_6	4648	8109	77
Per T	$1.177 \text{ X } 10^{20}$	$1.43 \text{ X } 10^{23}$	$2.25 \text{ X } 10^{6}$

9. Comparison of Different Organisations on the Basis of Graph Theoretic Approach

Using the proposed methodology, identification of an organization and its comparison with other organizations based on AMT implementation is carried out by considering their VPF. Two organizations are similar from the AMT viewpoint if their AMT digraphs are isomorphic. Two AMT digraphs are isomorphic if they have identical VPF. This means not only numbers of terms in each grouping/sub-grouping are the same but also the values are the same. Based on this a composite AMT identification set for an organization is written as:

$$\left[\left(J_1^T / J_2^T / J_3^T / J_4^T / J_{51}^T / J_{52}^T / J_{61}^T / J_{62}^T / ....\right)\left(V_1^T / V_2^T / V_3^T / V_4^T / V_{51}^T / V_{52}^T / V_{61}^T / V_{62}^T / ....\right)\right] \qquad (13)$$

where J_i^T represents the total number of terms in the ith grouping, J_{ij}^T T represents the total number of terms in J[th] subgrouping of the ith grouping. In case there is no subgrouping, the J_{ij} is the same as J_i^T; similarly V_i^T is the value of the ith grouping. V_{ij}^T is the numerical value of the jth subgrouping in the ith grouping. Numerical values of the T_i's and T_{ij}'s are substituted in the subgrouping or grouping to obtain V_{ij}^T. The subgroupings are arranged in decreasing order of size (i.e. number of characteristics in a loop).

In general, two organizations may not be isomorphic from the AMT viewpoint. Comparison is also carried out on the basis of the coefficient of similarity. The co-efficient is derived from the structure, i.e. the number of terms in different groupings and the permanent function, i.e. VPF and compares two organizations or a set of organizations on the basis of similarity or dissimilarity.

If the value of distinct terms in the jth subgrouping of the ith grouping of VPF of two organizations under consideration are denoted by V_{ij}^T and V'^T_{ij}, then criterion 1 of the coefficient of dissimilarity is given as:

$$C_{d-1}^T = \left[1/Y_1 \sum_i \sum_j \phi_{ij} \right] \tag{14}$$

where

$$Y_1 = \max \left[\sum_i \sum_j \left| V_{ij}^T \right| and \sum_i \sum_j \left| V'^T_{ij} \right| \right] \tag{15}$$

When subgroupings are absent $V_{ij}^T = V_i^T$ and $V'^T_{ij} = V'^T_i$

and $\phi_{ij} = \left| V_{ij}^T - V'^T_{ij} \right|$, when the subgrouping exists

and $\phi_{ij} = \left| V_i^T - V'^T_i \right|$, when the subgrouping are absent.

Criterion 2 of the coefficient of dissimilarity is given as

$$C_{d-2}^T = \left[1/Y_2 \sum_i \sum_j \phi_{ij}^2 \right]^{1/2}$$

where ϕ_{ij} is same as described above and

$$Y_2 = \max \left[\sum_i \sum_j \left(V_{ij}^T \right)^2 and \sum_i \sum_j \left(V'^T_{ij} \right)^2 \right]$$

When sub groupings are absent $V_{ij}^{T} = V_{i}^{T}$ and $V'^{T}_{ij} = V'^{T}_{i}$

Using equations 14 and 15, the coefficient of similarity is given as

$$C_{S-1}^{T} = 1 - C_{d-1}^{T}$$
$$C_{S-2}^{T} = 1 - C_{d-2}^{T}$$

where $C_{S-1}^{T}\, and\, C_{S-2}^{T}$ are the coefficient of similarity of two organizations under consideration based on criteria 1 and 2. It may be noted that the coefficient of similarity and dissimilarity lie in the range between 0 and 1. If two organizations are isomorphic or completely similar (in terms of the AMT environment), their coefficient of similarity is 1 and the coefficient of dissimilarity is 0. In a similar manner, if two organizations are completely dissimilar (in terms of the AMT environment), their coefficient of similarity is 0 and the coefficient of dissimilarity is 1.

9.1. Example for Comparison of Organisations

Similarity or dissimilarity among organizations in terms of the AMT implementation may be estimated using the methodology discussed in the previous section. An example is considered for demonstration of the methodology. Two organizations are considered whose AMT implementation is a function of three broad factors identified as strategic planning, concept development, infrastructural. These are designated by T_1, T_2, T_3 and T'_1, T'_2, T'_3 for organization 1 and organization 2,respectively. Although the factors identified are the same for both organizations, it is the inheritance and interaction of these factors that will lead to comparison. Based on the methodology discussed in Section 7 the variable permanent matrix (VPM) for organization 1 may be written as

$$\begin{array}{c c} Vertex & \begin{array}{ccc} 1 & 2 & 3 \end{array} \\ \begin{array}{c} 1 \\ 2 \\ 3 \end{array} & \begin{bmatrix} T_1 & T_{12} & T_{13} \\ T_{21} & T_2 & T_{23} \\ T_{31} & T_{32} & T_3 \end{bmatrix} \end{array} \tag{16}$$

Variable permanent function of equation 16 will lead to the permanent of the matrix per T_1^{*}

$$per\, T_1^{\times} = T_1T_2T_3 + T_{12}T_{21}T_3 + T_{13}T_{31}T_2 + T_{23}T_{32}T_1 + T_{12}T_{23}T_{31} + T_{13}T_{32}T_{21} \tag{17}$$

The expression for per T_1^{*} is arranged in N +1 i.e. four groups (the second group is absent as there are no self-loops) and contains N!, i.e. six terms. Similar to equations 16 and 17, VPM and the permanent function for organization 2 may be written down.

The values of inheritances and interactions, i.e. T_i's and T_{ij}'s are to be determined by experts. For the demonstration of the methodology these are taken from table 2 and table 3 as

$T_1=8, T_2=6, T_3= 7, T_{12}=5, T_{13}=3, T_{21}=3, T_{23}=2, T_{31}=4, T_{32}=2.$

$T'_1=7, T'_2=6, T'_3=5, T'_{12}=4, T'_{13}=3, T'_{21}=4, T'_{23}=3, T'_{31}=3, T'_{32}=1$

substituting the values, the permanent for organization 1 (equation 17) may be written as

per $T_1^*=336 + 105 + 72 + 32 + 40 +18= 603.$

Based on equation 13, equation 17 and the value of per T_1^*, the identification set for organization 1 may be written as

[1/0/3/2] [336/0/209/68]

On similar lines, the permanent for organization 2 may be written as

per $T_2^*= 210 + 80 + 54 + 21 + 36 + 12 = 413.$

The identification set for organization 2 may be written as

[1/0/3/2][210/0/155/48]

Whereas the identification sets help to visually analyse the effectiveness of various groups, equations 14 and 15 are used to compare similarities in organizations in terms of the AMT implementation.

Based on criterion 1 (equation 14), the coefficient of dissimilarity between the two organizations is 0.315. Thus the coefficient of similarity is 0.685. The comparison procedure helps organizations to compare different groups in identification sets, based on which they can analyse and improve the weak link in the AMT implementation.

Moreover, organizations can be compared or ranked in increasing or decreasing order of value of the coefficient of similarity or dissimilarity. Also organizations may be grouped in a given range of the value of the coefficient and the AMT implementation index may be compared for a given range.

10. Findings of the Research Paper

The paper endeavours to quantify the intensity of critical factors affecting implementation of AMT through systematic approach. The critical factors help an organization to assess their capability against AMT implementation. Also these factors help the organisation to implement the AMT in systematic way.

The proposed structural approach based on digraph and matrix method for the evaluation of intensity of critical factors affecting implementation of AMT identifies critical factors affecting AMT implementation. This section helps the managers to look into the factors which are more critical to the implementation to the AMT. It permits modelling of dependence among factors. Application of graph theoretic approach makes it convenient for visual analysis and computer processing. Visual analysis means, one gets the numerical score of the subjective factors and can compare their organisation with the peers. The intensity of critical factors affecting the implementation of AMT is indicated by a single numerical index, i.e. how one critical factor is affecting the implantation process as compared to other or in other words, how one factor is important to the other. It permits self-analysis and comparison of organizations. The method permits to consider different factors in alternative environment, i.e. one can simply change the factors according to the environment in which the organisation is working. Systematic methodology for conversion of qualitative factors to quantitative values and mathematical modelling gives an edge to the proposed technique over conventional methods. It provides single numerical index for comparing different implementation models. The methodology is useful for continuous improvement (Kaizen) as well as for breakthrough improvement. Sensitivity analysis to identify the critical elements is easily carried out. The method permits us to generate alternative environments. This is an effective tool for evaluation, comparison, ranking and selection of an optimum model. This approach is dynamic and can accommodate different factors according to the different environments.

11. Limitations

As with all implementation models, the present model has some limitations which are discussed below:

- Factor selection and comparison makes the input time large and difficult.
- It requires the user to have necessary experience although the graph theoretic analysis helps him.
- It requires the user is clear on his goals and objectives.

It may also be worthwhile to incorporate other multi attribute decision making methods to cross check the result of the graph theoretic method for implementation model.

References

Badiru, A.B. (1990) ‘Strategic Planning for Automated Manufacturing: Some Factors and Dimensions’, *Edited by Parasaci.et.al., elesevier. Science Publichers*, pp.17-39.

Barua, B., Islam, M.M.O. (2008) ‘Key Success Factors for Implementation of Advanced Manufacturing Technologies (AMTs)-Case Study Conducted on Selected Pharmaceutical Companies in Bangladesh’, *AIUB Bus Econ Working Paper Series,* No 2008-15.

Beatty, C. (1990) ‘Implementing advanced manufacturing technology’, *Business Quarterly*, Vol. 55, No. 2, pp. 46-50.

Bessant, J. (1993) 'The lessons of failure: Learning to manage new manufacturing technology’, *International Journal of Technology Management: Special Issue on*

Manufacturing Technology: *Diffusion, Implementation and Management*, Vol. 8, Nos. 2/3/4, pp. 197-215.

Boyer, K. K., Leong, G. K., Ward, P. T. and Krajewsky, L. J. (1997) 'Unlocking the potential of advanced manufacturing technologies' *Journal of Operations Management*, Vol.15, pp. 331–347.

Burcher, P., Lee, G. and Sohal, A. (1999) 'Lessons for Implementing AMT. Some case experiences with CNC in Australia, Britain and Canada', *International Journal of Operations and Production Management*, Vol. 19, pp. 515–526.

Choobineh, F. (1986) 'Justification of flexible manufacturing systems, in Flexible Manufacturing Systems: Current Issues and Models', edited by F. Choobineh and R.Suri, 2E Press, pp. 269-281.

Co, H. C., Patuwo, B. E. and Hu, M. Y. (1998) 'The human factor in advanced manufacturing technology adoption', *International Journal of Operations and Production Management*, Vol. 18, pp.87–106.

Dangayach, G.S., and Deshmukh, S. G. (2004) 'Advanced Manufacturing Technologies: Evidences from Indian Automobile Companies', *International Journal of Manufacturing Technology and Management*, Vol. 6, No.5, pp. 426-433.

Dangayach, G.S., Pathak, S.C., Sharma A.D. (2006) 'Advanced Manufacturing Technology: A way of Improving Technological Competitiveness', *International Journal of Global Business and Competitiveness*, Vol. 2, No. 1, pp. 1-8.

Dou, J., Dai, X., Meng, Z. (2009) 'Graph theory based approach to optimize single-product flow-line configurations of RMS', *International Journal of Advanced Manufacturing Technology*, Vol.41, pp.916-931.

Faisal, M.N., Banwet, D.K. and Shankar, R. (2006) 'Mapping supply chains on risk and customer sensitivity dimensions', *Industrial Management and Data Systems*, Vol. 106, No. 6, pp. 878–895.

Gandhi, O.P. and Agrawal, V.P. (1996) 'Failure cause analysis – a structural approach', *Transactions of ASME*, pp. 434-9.

Ghani, K.A., Jayabalan, V. (2000) 'Advanced manufacturing technology and planned organizational change', The Journal of High Technology Management, Vol.11, pp. 1-18.

Gouvea da Costa, S.E., Pinheiro de Lima,E. (2009) 'Advanced manufacturing technology adoption: an integrated approach', *Journal of Manufacturing Technology Management*, Vol. 20, pp.74-96

Godwin, J. U., Ehie, I. C. and Oluruniwo, F. (1995) 'Fulfilling the promises of advanced manufacturing systems', *Industrial Management*, Vol. 37, No. 5, pp. 23-28.

Grover, S., Agrawal, V.P. and Khan, I.A. (2004) 'A digraph approach to TQM evaluation of an industry', *International Journal of Production Research*, Vol. 42, No. 19, pp. 4031–4053.

Grover, S., Agrawal, V.P., and Khan, I.A. (2006) 'Role of human factors in TQM: A graph theoretic approach', *International Journal of Benchmarking*, Vol.13, pp.447-468.

Hon, K.K.B. (2005) 'Performance and Evaluation of Manufacturing Systems', *CIRP Annals-Manufacturing Technology*, Vol. 54, pp. 139-154.

Hottenstein, M. P., Casey, M. S., Dunn, S. C. (1997) 'Facilitation of advanced manufacturing technology: implementation and transfer', *Industrial Management*, Vol. 39, pp. 8–13.

Huang, Z. and Yip-Hoi, D. (2003) 'A graph based approach for capturing the capability envelop of a machining process', *International Journal of Manufacturing Science and Engineering*, Vol. 125, No.2, pp. 272-288.

Idris, F., Rejab, R., Ahmad, A. (2008) 'Relationships between Investments in Advanced Manufacturing Technology (AMT) and Performances: Some Empirical Evidences', *European Journal of Economics, Finance and Administrative Sciences*, Vol. 13, pp.67-77.

Jime'nez, J., Marti'nez, A., Navarro, L., Polo, Y. and Toma′ S, L. (1992) 'The process of implementing industrial robots in Spanish industry', *International Journal of Operations and Production Management*, Vol. 12, pp.43–56.

Kaplan, R.S. (1986) 'Must CIM be Justified by Faith Alone', *Harvard Business Review*, April, pp. 87-95

Kulkarni, S. (2005) 'Graph theory and matrix approach for performance evaluation of TQM in Indian industries', *International Journal of TQM Magazine*, Vol. 17, pp. 509-526.

Kunnathar, A., (2000) 'Factors Affecting the Adoption of Advanced Manufacturing Technology in Small Firms'. *Journal of Advanced Management.*

Kumar, V., Murphy, S. A. and Loo, S. C. K. (1996) 'An investment decision process: The case of advanced technologies in Canadian manufacturing firms', *International Journal of Production Research*, Vol. 34, No. 4. pp. 947-958.

Lewis, H. J., Towill, D. R. and Davies, A. (1988) 'The introduction of AMT - triumph or trauma', Towill, D. R. and Cherringlon. J. E. (ed.), *A Systems Approach to AMT Deployment, Springer-Verlag, London.*

McDermott, C.M. and G.N. Stock, (1999) 'Organizational culture and advanced manufacturing technology implementation'. *Journal of Operation Management* pp.521-533.

Marri, H.B., Irani, Z., Gunasekaran, A. (2006) ' A Framework of Justification Criteria for Advanced Manufacturing Technology Implementation in Small and Medium Enterprises', *European and Mediterranean Conference on Information Systems (EMCIS), Costa Blanca, Alicante, Spain.*

Macek, A.J. (1982) 'Human factors facilitating the implementation of automation', *Journal of Manufacturing Systems*, Vol.1, pp. 195-206.

Marti′nez Sa′ nchez, A. (1996) 'Adopting AMT: experience from Spain', *Journal of Manufacturing Systems*, Vol. 15, pp.133–140.

Meredith, J. R. (1987a) 'The Strategic advantages of new manufacturing technologies for small firms', *Strategic Management Journal*, Vol. 8, pp. 249-258.

Meredith. J. R. (1987b) 'Implementing the automated factory', *Journal of Manufacturing System*, Vol. 6, No. 1. pp. 1-3.

Meredith, J. R. (1987c) 'Implementing new manufacturing technologies: managerial lessons over the FMS life cycle', *Interfaces*, Vol. 17, pp. 51-62.

Mital, A., Pennathur, A., Huston, R.L., Thompson, D., Pittman, M., Markle, G., Kaber, D.B., Crumpton, L., Bishu, R.R., Rajurkar, K.P., Rajan, V., Fernandez, J.E., McMulkin, M., Deivanayagam, S., Ray, P.S., Sule, D. (1999) 'The need for worker training in advanced manufacturing technology (AMT) environments: A white paper', *International Journal of Industrial Ergonomics,* Vol. 24, pp. 173-184.

Mohanty R. P. and Deshmukh, S. G. (1998) 'Advanced manufacturing technology selection: A strategic model for learning and evaluation', *International Journal Production Economics*, Vol. 55, No.3, pp. 295-307.

Momaya, K. And Ajitabh, A. (2005) 'Technology Management and Competitiveness: Is There any Relationship', *International Journal of Technology Transfer and Commercialization*, Vol. 4, No. 4, pp. 518-524.

Narsingh, D. (2000), 'Graph Theory with Application to Engineering and Computer Science', *Prentice Hall of India Private Ltd, New Delhi.*

Nichols, W., Jones, O. (1994) 'The introduction of CIM: a strategic analysis', *International Journal of Operations and Production Management*, Vol. 60, 29–34.

Pagell, M., Handfield, R.D. and Barber, A.E. (2000) 'Effects of Operational Employee Skills on Advanced Manufacturing Technology Performance', *Production and Operations Management*, Vol. 9, No.3, pp. 222-238.

Primrose, P.L. (1991) 'Investment *in Manufacturing Technology'*, Chapman and Hall, London.

Ramamurthy, K. (1995) 'Influence of planning on implementation success of AMT', *IEEE Transactions on Engineering Management*, Vol. 42, No. 1, pp. 62-73.

Rao, R.V. and Gandhi, O.P. (2002) 'Digraph and matrix methods for the machinability evaluation of work materials', *International Journal of Machine Tools and Manufacture*, Vol. 42, pp.321–330.

Rao, V. And Padmanabhan, K.K., (2006) ' Selection, Identification and Comparison of Industrial Robots using Digraph and Matrix Methods', *International journal of Robotics and Computer Integrated Manufacturing*, Vol. 22, No.4, pp. 373-383.

Reinsch, S., Müsig, B., Schmidt.B., Tracht, K. (2003) 'Advanced manufacturing system for forging products', *Journal of Materials Processing Technology*, Vol. 138, pp.16-21.

Saberi, S., Yusuff, R.M., Zulkifli, N., Ahmad, M.M.H.M. (2010) 'Effective factors on advanced manufacturing technology implementation performance: A review'. *International Journal of Applied Science*, Vol. 10, pp.1229-1242.

Schroder, R. and Sohal, A.S. (1999) 'Organizational Characteristics Associated with AMT Adoption; Towards A Contingency Framework', *International Journal of Operations and Production Management*, Vol.19, No.12, pp. 1270-1291.

Shani, A. B, Grant, R. M., Krishnan, R. and Thompson, E., (1992) 'Advanced manufacturing systems and organizational choice: socio-technical system approach', *California Management Review*, Vol. 34, pp.91–111.

Slagmulder, R. and Bruggeman, W. (1992) 'Investment justification of flexible manufacturing technologies: inferences from field research', *International Journal of Operations and Production Management*, Vol. 12, pp.168–186.

Small, M.H. and Chen, I.J. (1995) 'Investment Justification Of Advanced Manufacturing Technology; An Empirical Analysis', *Journal Of Engineering and Technology Management,* Vol.12, No.1, pp. 27-55.

Small, M.H. and Yasin, M. M. (1997) 'Advanced manufacturing technology: implementation policy and performance', *Journal of Operations Management*, Vol. 15, pp. 349–370.

Small, M.H. and Yasin, M. M. (2003) 'Advanced manufacturing technology adoption and performance: the role of management information systems departments', *Integrated manufacturing systems*, Vol. 14, pp. 409-422.

Sohal, A. S. (1994) 'Investing in advanced manufacturing technology', *Benchmarking for Quality Management and Technology*, Vol. 1, No. 1, pp. 24-41.

Sohal, A. S. (1996) 'Assessing AMT implementations: an empirical field study', *Technovation*, Vol. 16, pp. 377–384.

St-Pierre, J. and Raymond, L. (2004) 'Short-term effects of benchmarking on the manufacturing practices and performance of SMEs', *International Journal of Productivity and Performance Management*, Vol. 53, No. 8, pp. 681-99.

Thomas, A.J., Barton, R., and John, E.G. (2007), 'Advanced manufacturing technology implementation, A review of benefits and a model for change', *International Journal of Productivity and Performance Management*, Vol. 57, No. 2, pp. 156-176.

Udo, G. J. and Ehie, I.C. (1996) 'Advanced manufacturing technologies–determinants of implementation success', *International Journal of Operations and Production Management*, Vol. 16, pp. 6–26.

Voss, C.A. (1995) 'Manufacturing strategy - the nature of the link between manufacturing strategy and organizational structure', *Chapman and Hall, London*.

Wani, M.F. and Gandhi, O.P. (1999) 'Development of maintainability index for mechanical systems', *Reliability Engineering and System Safety*, Vol. 65, pp.259–270.

Yang, S.Z., Wu, B., Li, B. (2003) 'Trends in the Development of Advanced Manufacturing Technology', *Frontiers of Mechanical Engineering in China*. Vol. 1, pp. 1-5.

Yusuff, R.M. (2005) 'Advanced Manufacturing Technologies in SMEs', *CACCI Journal*, Vol. 1, pp.23-29.

Zhao, H. and Co, H. C. (1997) 'Adoption and implementation of advanced manufacturing technology in Singapore', *International Journal of Production Economics*, Vol. 48, pp.7–19.

Biographical Notes

Sanjeev Goyal is working as a faculty in YMCA University of Science and Technology in Faridabad, India. He obtained B.Tech in Mechanical Engineering and M.Tech in Manufacturing and Automation. Presently, he is doing research in the area of Advance Manufacturing Technologies. He has published papers in National and International Conferences.

Dr Sandeep Grover has obtained bachelor's degree in Engineering, Master's degree in Technology, Master's degree in Business Administration and PhD in the field of Total Quality Management. He has authored about 60 papers in national and international journals and conferences. He guides research at postgraduate and doctorate levels and his research areas include Total Quality Management, Manufacturing Management, and Human Resource Management. With more than 20 years of teaching and research experience presently he is working as Professor and Chairman, Department of Mechanical Engineering at the YMCA University of Science and Technology in Faridabad, India.

In: HRM and Marketing Orientation in the New Era
Editor: Panagiotis Kyriazopoulos
ISBN: 978-1-62808-959-2

Chapter 8

WAITING TIME MANAGEMENT IN THE STUDENT AFFAIR / ADMISSIONS OFFICES: A CASE STUDY OF PAKISTANI UNIVERSITIES

Muhammad Imran Qureshi and Khalid Zaman*
Department of Management Sciences,
COMSATS Institute of Information Technology, Abbottabad, Pakistan

ABSTRACT

The objective of the study is to measuring the impact of longer waiting time on students' satisfaction at Student Affairs/ Admissions offices of Universities and Higher education institutions of Pakistan. As, increase in waiting time will lead to the dissatisfaction of the students and in some cases results in the reduced goodwill and increase in cost, so it is a point of concern in all universities that they reduce students / customers waiting time or try to minimize its impact on student 's satisfactions. The present study used observations method to find facts from five major universities of Khyber Pakhtonkhuwa (KPK) province of Pakistan. The result reveals that students have a major concern regarding long-queues and they feel unsatisfied with the implementations of waiting line management, as most of the universities have claimed before.

Keywords: Waiting Time Management, Student Affairs, Admission Office, Higher Education Institutes, Satisfaction, Pakistan

1. INTRODUCTION

Waiting is a complex phenomenon to which a consumer often reacts in an emotional way. Waiting is often psychologically painful, because it causes us to renounce more productive and rewarding ways of using our time and because it may increase the investment that we have to make to obtain a product or service. Waiting may also be costly in and of

* Corresponding author:, E-mail: khalidzaman@ciit.net.pk

itself as we become aware of the passage of time. In other words, there are both extrinsic disadvantages of waiting (e.g., profitable alternatives foregone) and intrinsic costs (Schwartz, 1975). Maister (1985) has proposed several situational effects on consumers' perception of waiting. Among others, he suggested the following four propositions: (1) Unoccupied time feels longer than occupied time; (2) preprocess waits feel longer than in-process waits; (3) uncertain waits are longer than known, finite waits; (4) unexplained waits are longer than explained waits.

The study of consumers' reactions while waiting for service (e.g., Baker and Cameron, 1996; Davis and Heineke, 1994; McDouglas and Levesque, 1999) has now become a major field of research. It is necessary to understand the variables that influence the perception of waiting time and the potential impact on service evaluations (Beqiri and Tadisina, 2002; Taylor, 1994). Previous research defined service evaluations as consumer satisfaction (Katz et al., 1991; Davis and Heineke, 1998; Pruyn and Smidts, 1998), service quality (Houston et al., 1998) and five service quality dimensions (Chebat et al., 1995). Hui and Tse (1996) found in an experimental setting that the acceptability of waiting had no significant direct effect on service evaluation, but had an indirect effect through affective response. Information about waiting duration increased the perceived waiting duration but influenced positively the service evaluation through a more positive affective response to the waiting experience.

Waiting for service is a pervasive and often unavoidable experience for customers and appears to be a strong determinant of overall satisfaction with the service and customer loyalty (see, Pruyn and Smidts, 1993; Taylor, 1994, 1995; Hui and Tse, 1996). Service marketers often attempt to counteract negative effects of waiting by shortening queues. Operations management techniques (see, Buffa and Sarin, 1987) are helpful in this respect. Mere reduction of objective waiting times, however, is not always feasible, because of the lack of control over the queuing situation (Taylor, 1994).or due to cost considerations.

As customers' satisfaction with the service will be affected by the perception of waiting time, an alternative approach to queuing is to find ways to make time pass as quickly and pleasantly as possible. One may thus reduce the negative effects of waiting even when objective waiting times cannot be shortened. Price at al (1995) indicate that the emotional responses to services have not been thoroughly researched in these patterns and, when they are, above all they lump together a large number of emotions in a single global dimension, or they distinguish satisfaction as a consequence of other globally considered emotional responses (Oliver, 1993, 1997). In any case, Weiner (2000) goes further in his reflections concerning emotional responses when he suggests that, in situations of negative service results where negligence is attributed to the provider in the productive process (control attributed to the causes of the failure), the emotional reaction will not be a simple dissatisfaction. Probably, anger, negative emotional reaction related with moral judgment (moral outrage) will be demonstrated due to attributing to the company the causal control of the negative result of the service. Consequently, the study of anger has a special interest as a central element of social behavior. Despite this, we have not come across any empirical research about service delay which examines the appearance of concepts, anger and satisfaction with service.

The above literature shows the strong relevance towards customer satisfaction and waiting line system. Therefore, the purpose of the stud is to what extent the waiting environment affects the overall satisfaction and how the waiting line affects the satisfaction with the service.

After introduction which is explained in Section 1 above, Section 2 describes theory of waiting lines. Methodological framework is explained in Section 3. Results are discussed in Section 4. Section 5 concludes the study.

2. Theory of Waiting Lines

Queuing systems or waiting lines exist throughout society and their adequacy has strong effect on quality of service and productivity. Queuing theory is concerned with mathematical study of queues or waiting lines, formulating mathematical models of queues and measuring performance using these models.

Waiting lines are formed whenever the current demand for a service exceeds the current capacity to provide that service. Because of difficulty in accurately predicting arrival pattern of customers for service and/or how much time is required to provide service to each customer, accurate decision regarding the capacity to be provided is made quite difficult. Excess service capacity involves excessive costs due to under utilization and insufficient capacity to meet peak loads causes waiting lines to become excessively long and customers may even quit the waiting lines.

The ultimate goal is to achieve an economic balance between the cost of service (i.e., cost of idle facility and employee) and costs associated with waiting for the service (i.e., social cost and cost of lost customers). Queuing theory does not directly solve this problem, but tries to provide vital information required for taking decisions.

2.1. Basic Concepts of Queuing Models

Input source (or source of arrivals or calling population) refers to the population from which arrivals to, waiting line come from. Size of input source is the total number of distinct potential customers. It could be finite (or exhaustible) or infinite (or inexhaustible).

Queue is characterized by the maximum permissible number of customers that it can contain. This also could be finite or infinite. In most of the practical situations, it is finite. Queue discipline refers to the order in which members of the queue are selected for service. The order is usually first-cum-first-served. However, priority-discipline models give priority to rush jobs and important customers over others and follow random selection, priority selection or last in first out (LIFO).

The service mechanism consists of one or more service facilities, each of which contains one or more parallel service channels or stations called Servers. Service Time (or Holding Time) is the time elapsed from the commencement of service to its completion for a customer at a service facility.

Interval Time is the time between consecutive arrivals of customers to waiting line. State of system is number of customers in queuing system and queue length refers to number of customers waiting for service. In other words, state of the system minus number of customers being served will give queue length.

The transient condition of the system refers to initial stage when the operation begins. The steady state condition is that condition when system becomes essentially independent of the initial state after lapse of some time.

The state dependent service rate and/or arrival rate assumes that the (mean) service rate is always a constant. But it may not be true in practice. Servers tend to work faster than they do when the backlog is small or nonexistent. The increased service rate may be due to compromise in quality or external assistance for certain phases of service.

The physical structure of waiting lines consists of:

a) One or more input sources with arrival distribution
b) None, one or more queue
c) One or more servers operating in series or parallel
d) Service discipline
e) Maximum number of customers allowed

The controllable aspects of queuing systems are:

a) Arrival rate
b) Number of servers
c) Service time
d) Maximum length of waiting line
e) Queue discipline or priority rules.

2.2. Important Assumptions of a Queuing Model

1. Each source has a well defined arrival pattern over time, i.e., inter-arrival or interval times are constant or randomly spaced over time with a known inter-arrival time probability distribution (poison distribution)
2. The service times at each channel (server) may be constant or random with a known service distribution (negative exponential distribution)
3. The potential arrivals may balk if the length of waiting line becomes excessive and decide not to join or arrivals may join the waiting line and subsequently renege, i.e., become impatient and leave before being served. They are lost by the service system.
4. In a steady state, the average rate of departure is equal to average rate of arrivals.

3. Methodological Framework

A questionnaire was used to gain the students feedback about their waiting experience during admissions process. Study involved the customers having two or more than two times waiting in the student affairs/ admissions office of universities in Khyber Pukhtoon Khawa province of Pakistan, namely, University of Peshawar, Hazara University, Mansehra, COMSATS Abbottabad, UET campus, Abbottabad and Fatima Women University, Peshawar, Pakistan. A convenience sampling was used to collect feedback from the students. An observations method was sued to determine the methods applied for waiting line management by the above mentioned universities. The study framework is shown in Figure 1.

3.1. Hypothesis of the Study

There are four main hypothesis of the study are:

H1: Waiting time can decrease students input in student affairs/ admissions office of the universities.

H2: Minimizing the waiting time can increase student satisfaction during admissions process.

H3: By reducing the delay in the service students can be satisfied.

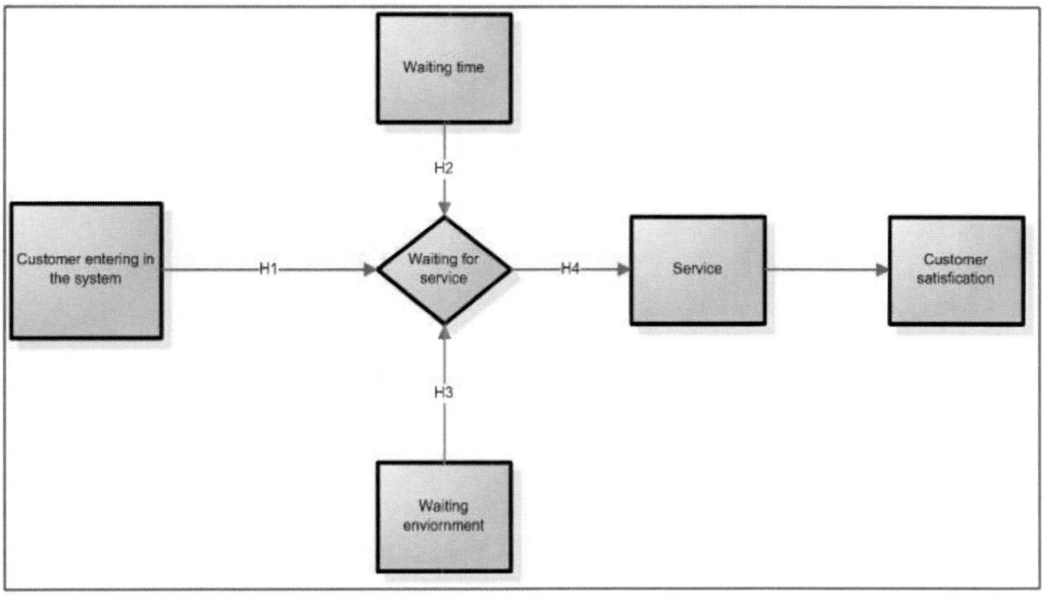

(

Source: Self constructed.

Figure 1. Theoretical Framework of the Study.

4. Results and Discussion

Feedback provided by the students showed that the customer's satisfaction decreases as the waiting time for the service increases. The data given in Table 1 shows the results from student feedback of question regarding waiting time and satisfaction.

Table 1. Student's Feedback

		Satisfied from service			
Waiting Time	No. of students	Yes	No	Yes %	No %
Less than10 minutes	50	40	10	80%	20%
Less than 20 minutes	50	27	23	54%	46%
Less than 30 minutes	45	18	27	40%	60%
Above 30 minutes	40	5	35	13%	88%

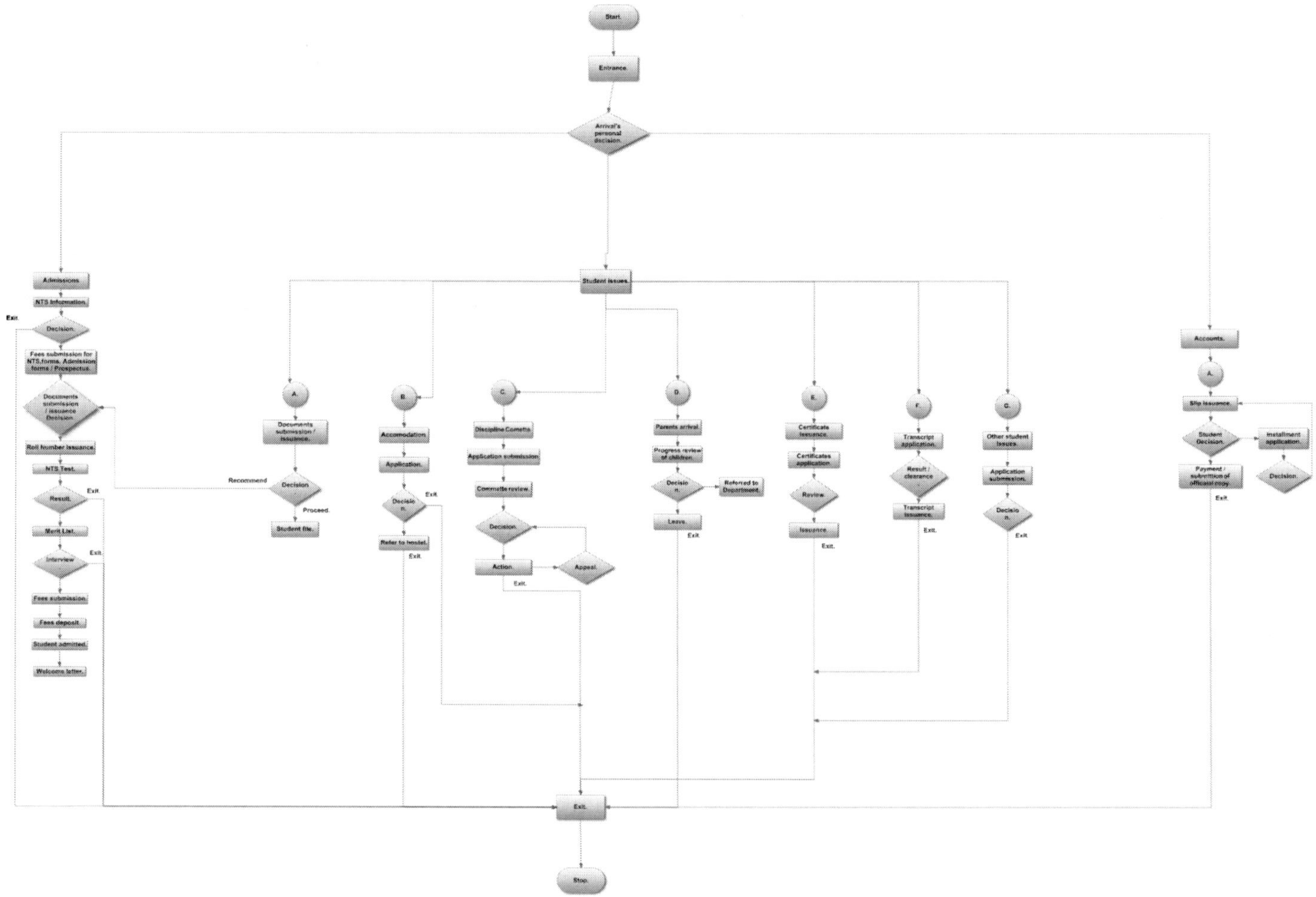

Figure 2. Existing flow chart of Student Affairs / Admissions.

4.1. Customer Arrivals / Population

An infinite population was considered. Observations showed that numbers of arrivals that visit the student affairs are in total 49. But visitors are classified according to their problems. Arrival rates of different problems are given as under?

$$\lambda = 17 / hour$$

Accounts

$$\lambda = 12 / hour$$

Information

$$\lambda = 20 / hour$$

Service rate: The service rate is calculated on the overall services that are provided to the arrivals which are 72 per hour and as the unit (student affairs) is categorized into the three servers so according to each server the observed service rate is;

Student related issues

$$\mu = 24 / hour$$

Accounts

$$\mu = 30 / hour$$

Admissions

$$\mu = 18 / hour$$

Table 2 shows the waiting line management pattern in different universities.

Table 2. Weighting line Management

	Popu-lation	Arrival Pattern	Arrival rate λ	Service Pattern	Service rate μ	Utili-zation	Exit
Accounts	Finite	Poisson	12	Exponential	30	40%	to population
Admissions	Infinite	Poisson	20	Exponential	18	111%	to population
Student Affairs	Finite	Poisson	17	Exponential	24	71%	to population

The model that can be used in this whole scenario of student affairs is the model1 which actually is;

$Lq = \lambda / \mu (\mu - \lambda)$ $Wq = Lq / \lambda$
$Ls = \lambda / \mu - \lambda$ $Ws = Ls / \lambda$

To apply the model and find the utilization of the three desks we proceed as following;

i) For Student Related Problems:

- *Average number in waiting line:*

To find average number in waiting line we can use the following formula
$Lq = \lambda / \mu (\mu - \lambda)$
$= 17^2 /24 (24-17)$
= 1.72 students

So we can say that approximately 2 students would be there is the waiting line.

- *Average number in system:*

Average waiting time can be calculated with the formula
$Ls = \lambda/ \mu - \lambda$
= 17/24-17
=2.4 students

- *Average waiting time in line*:

Average time in line is calculated as
$Wq= Lq/ \lambda$
=1.72/17
= 0.10 hour or 6 minutes

- *Average waiting time in system*:

This can be calculated as
$Ws = Ls/ \lambda$
= 2.4/17
= 0.14 hour or 8.4 minutes

ii) For Admissions:

- *Average number in waiting line:*

To find average number in waiting line we can use the following formula
$Lq = \lambda / \mu (\mu - \lambda)$
$= 20^2 /30 (30-20)$
= 1.33 students

- *Average number in system:*

Average waiting time can be calculated with the formula
$Ls = \lambda/ \mu - \lambda$
= 20/30-20
= 2 students

- *Average waiting time in line:*

Average time in line is calculated as
$W_q = L_q / \lambda$
$= 1.33/20$
= 0.06 hour or 3.99 minutes

- *Average waiting time in system*:

This can be calculated as
$W_s = L_s / \lambda$
$= 2/20$
= 0.1 hour or 6 minutes.

iii) For Accounts:

- *Average number in waiting line:*

To find average number in waiting line we can use the following formula
$L_q = \lambda / \mu\ (\mu - \lambda)$
$= 12^2 / 18\ (18-12)$
= 1.33 students

- *Average number in system:*

Average waiting time can be calculated with the formula
$L_s = \lambda / \mu - \lambda$
$= 12/18-12$
= 2 students

- *Average waiting time in line:*

Average time in line is calculated as
$W_q = L_q / \lambda$
$= 1.33/12$
= 0.11 hour or 6.65 minutes

- *Average waiting time in system:*

This can be calculated as
$W_s = L_s / \lambda$
$= 2/12$
= 0.16 hour or 9.6 minutes

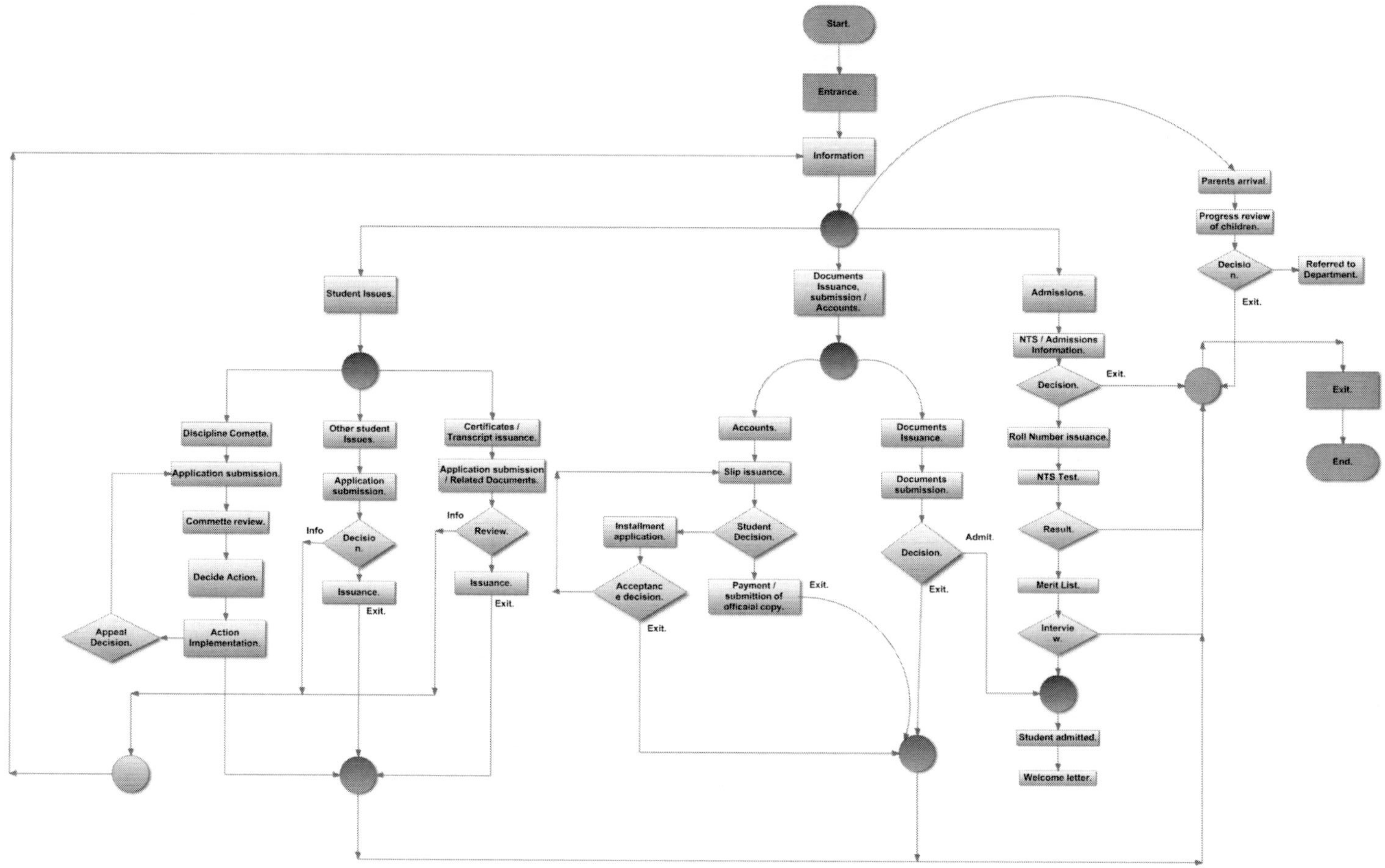

Figure 3. Recommended Flow Chart for Student Affairs.

CONCLUSION AND RECOMMENDATIONS

The present study examines the impact of waiting line management science to the waiting time of the customers at five major universities of the KPK province Pakistan. Feedback from customers/ students showed that increase in waiting time will increase dissatisfaction which results into lose of customers/ students as well as goodwill of the university. To reduce waiting time many organizations are using waiting line management tools and techniques to reduce customer waiting time. Implementations of these waiting line management strategies in higher education institutions can help these institutions in improving their service quality and customers / student satisfaction. A Recommended flow chart for student affairs/ Admission offices is given in Figure 3.

Recommended system can help admissions/ student affairs offices to reduce waiting time. Waiting time leads to the dissatisfactions of the customers so by reducing customers waiting time organizations can grab opportunity to provide customers satisfactions. In the current era higher education institutions are facing more competitive pressure, by implementing waiting line management science universities and higher education institutions can provide greater satisfactions to the customers/ students which will not only increase their goodwill among students but also provide better service to the customers/ students.

REFERENCES

Baker, J., Cameron, M. (1996), "The effects of the service environment on affect and consumer perception of waiting time: an integrative review and research propositions", *Journal of the Academy of Marketing Science* 24, 338–349.

Beqiri, M.S., Tadisina, S.T. (2002), "Perception of waiting time: effects of personality types, level of uncertainty, and criticality of service," *Decision Sciences Institute 2002 Annual Meetings Proceedings*.

Buffa, E.S., Sarin, R.K. (1987), *Modern Productions Operations Management*. Wiley, New York.

Chebat, J.C., Filiatrault, P., Gelinas-Chebat, C., Vaninski, A. (1995). "Impact of waiting attribution and consumer's mood on perceived quality." *Journal of Business Research,* vol. 34, no. 3, pp. 191-196.

Davis, M.M., Heineke, J. (1994). "Understanding the roles of the customer and the operation for better queue management." *International Journal of Operations and Production Management,* vol. 14, no.5, pp. 21-34.

Davis, M.M., Heineke, J. (1998). "How disconfirmation, perception and actual waiting times impact customer satisfaction." *International Journal of Service Industry Management,* vol. 9, no. 1, pp. 64-73.

Houston, M.B., Bettencourt, L.A., Wenger S. (1998). "The relationship between waiting in a service queue and evaluations of service quality: a field theory perspective." *Psychology and Marketing*, vol. 15, no. 8, pp. 735-753.

Hui, M.K., Tse, D.K. (1996). What to tell consumers in waits of different lengths: An integrative model of service evaluation. *Journal of Marketing* 60, 81–90.

Katz, K.L., Larson, B.M, Larson, R.C. (1991). "Prescription for the waiting-in-line blues: entertain, enlighten, and engage." *Sloan Management Review*, Winter, pp. 44-53.

Maister D. H. (1985). The Psychology of Waiting Lines, *The Service Encounter* (Cziepel J A, Solomon M R, SURPRENANT C F, eds.), Lexington Books, Lexington, 1985, pp. 113-123.

Maister, David. H. {1985), "The Psychology of Waiting Lines", in *The Service Encounter. Managing Employee/Customer Interaction in Service Businesses,* eds. John, A. Czepiel, Michael R. Solomon and Carol F. Surprenant, Lexington: Lexington Books, 113-' 23.

McDougall, G.H., Levesque, T.J. (1999). "Waiting for service: the effectiveness of recovery strategy." *International Journal of Contemporary Hospitality Management*, vol. 11, no. 1, pp.6-15.

Oliver, R.L (1989), "Processing of the satisfaction response in consumption: a suggested framework and research propositions", *Journal of Satisfaction, Dissatisfaction and Complaining Behavior*, Vol. 2 pp.1-16.

Oliver, R.L (1994), "Conceptual issues in the structural analysis of consumption emotion, satisfaction and quality: evidence in a service setting", *Advances in Consumer Research*, Vol. 21 pp.16-22.

Price, L, Arnould, E., Deibler, S (1995), "Consumer's emotional responses to service encounters. The influence of the service provider", *International Journal of Service Industry Management*, Vol. 6 No.3, pp.34-63.

Pruyn A, Smidts A (1998). Effects of Waiting on the Satisfaction with the Service: Beyond Objective Time Measures, *International Journal of Research in Marketing* 15 (1998), 321-334.

Pruyn, A.T.H., Smidts, A., 1993. Customers' evaluations of queues: Three exploratory studies. In: van Raaij, W.F., Bamossy, G. Eds.., *European Advances in Consumer Research,* Vol. 1. Association of Consumer Research, Provo, UT, pp. 371–382.

Schwartz, B. (1975), *Queuing and Waiting*, Chicago: University of Chicago Press.

Taylor, S (1994). Waiting for Service: The Relationship between Delays and Evaluation of Service, *Journal of Marketing* 58 (1994), 56-69.

Taylor, S, Claxton, J (1994), "Delays and the dynamics of service evaluations", *Journal of the Academy of Marketing Science*, Vol. 22 No.3, pp.254-64.

Taylor, S., (1995). The effects of filled waiting time and service provider control over the delay on evaluations of service. *Journal of the Academy of Marketing Science* 23, 38–48.

Taylor, S.A., Claxton, J.D. (1994). "Delays and the dynamics of service evaluations." *Journal of the Academy of Marketing Sciences*, vol. 22, no. 3, pp. 254-264.

Weiner, B (2000), "Attributional thoughts about consumer behavior", *Journal of Consumer Research*, Vol. 27 pp.382-7.

Yi, Y. (1990), "A critical review of consumer satisfaction", in Zeithaml, V (Eds),*Review of Marketing*, AMA, Chicago, IL, pp.68-123.

In: HRM and Marketing Orientation in the New Era
Editor: Panagiotis Kyriazopoulos
ISBN: 978-1-62808-959-2

Chapter 9

Designing for the Management of Indigenous Organizational Knowledge: A Case Study

Saqib Saeed[1], Rizwan Aamir[2] and Sohail Safdar[3]
[1]University of Siegen, Germany
[2]Bahria University Islamabad, Pakistan
[3]Universiti Teknologi Petronas, Malaysia

Abstract

Knowledge society paradigm advocates for equal access of knowledge but the digital divide is a major obstacle in realizing this concept. The systematic learning from day to day working knowledge can help organizations in coping with recurring problems. The lessons learned from this indigenous knowledge are important for growth, sustainability and process improvement in organizations. There have been several studies for knowledge management in organizational settings, but the organizational practices in geographical regions affected by digital divide are not much focused. In this paper we describe the case study of an educational institute in Pakistan where a software development project was carried out to manage indigenously produced organizational knowledge. Our paper highlights the problems and provides guidelines for newly established institutions on managing their knowledge in an effective way. We carry out a "SWOT" analysis of technology use to give an initial overview of the benefits and costs. Furthermore, we provide the design details of the system and discuss how the system helps in managing the knowledge produced in this organizational setting and on the basis of evaluation we establish a set of extended requirements for software system.

Keywords: Knowledge management, system design, case study, organizational knowledge, campus management system, computer supported cooperative work, management

1. Introduction

Recent shift of Knowledge society from information society focused on the knowledge management process (cf. Sharma et al, 2010; Lytras and Sicilia, 2005; Stehr, 2007). The knowledge society notion demands for equal knowledge accessibility for all sections of society. As a result, knowledge management paradigm has gained considerable importance from researchers recently. Different researchers have tried to setup models for transformation into knowledge societies (cf. Baqir and Kathawala, 2004; Chou, 2005; Sagasti, 2004; Soete, 2006). The evolution of knowledge management paradigm highlights the importance of knowledge and its creation, preservation and analysis processes. Developed countries thrived on this development and their enhanced focus on learning aspect of knowledge provided them a competitive advantage. In order to be competitive, organizations required well defined procedures for knowledge management and conservation. The optimization of processes requires considerable human and financial resources along with considerable time. In the newly established organizations, loose and evolving organizational structure, makes introduction of knowledge management procedures further complex. As a result ad-hoc organizational practices emerge to deal with problems locally. Therefore fragmented pieces of knowledge exist in different organizational sections, leaving other organizational sections unaware of its existence. As a result, indigenous knowledge is not uniformly present at the organizational level instead local instances of information are preserved at different levels, which could further make information exchange troublesome due to conflicting knowledge codification standards, formats etc. This situation can worsen if the organizations are geographically multi site. These deficiencies could be reduced to some extent by outsourcing or hiring the services of professional to channelize the knowledge management procedures. Organizations in developing economies are normally short on financial and human resources, so these short term knowledge import solutions for appropriation of organizational processes do not work. Furthermore, their work practices are differnt which require considerable thought and effort for a generic solution.

Information technology applications are an important tool for supporting knowledge management processes, as modern technological tools provide efficient ways to create, codify, store and extract knowledge. The embeddedness of IT tools in organizational processes is important and it is getting difficult for organizations to be competitive in the absence of efficient IT infrastructure.

The technology adoption speed is not uniform in entire world and this variation has resulted in digital divide. This digital divide also affects the knowledge management procedures as organizations from modern economies have better access to modern IT infrastructures whereas poor economies cannot afford these off the shelf applications. Another reason of limited adoption of 'off the shelf' components is adaptability of these applications according to local practices. It is vital to understand the social, organizational and cultural aspects to have a deeper insight in the practices and methodologies of organizations before IT deployment, as organizational processes and practices may vary from culture to culture. The negligence of these aspects mostly results in deployment of high end technology that is either not optimally used by people or is unable to satisfy organizational needs.

There has been considerable work on organizational knowledge management practices in computer supported collaborative work (CSCW) literature. Majority of this work is based on empirical studies of organizations geographically located in technologically advanced countries. It is interesting to analyze scientifically, how the organizations in countries confronted with digital divide manage their knowledge, but there is no huge body of knowledge focusing on this application area. As a result, we were interested in exploring the knowledge management processes in newly established organizations, but with a focus on their affiliation in poor economies. In order to get the empirical insight of knowledge management practices, we selected a higher education institution (HEI) in Pakistan.

The reason for selecting HEI as a case was twofold. Firstly, the indigenous data generated in such HEI is quite rich and secondly, HEIs seem to be more up-to-date technologically as compared to traditional medium sized business setups. Recently the higher education commission has encouraged setting up of new universities in Pakistan and as a result many public and private sector universities have emerged. Newly setup organizations are always confronted with ad-hoc and evolving organizational processes, so important indigenous data may get lost. This is an important case study for all organizations in similar situations to identify benefits of designing a knowledge management application.

Succeeding part of the paper is structured as follows. Section 2 highlights the related work in the area and points out what we contribute to the field. Section 3 describes the case details and research methods. Section 4 discusses the empirical details and section 5 presents SWOT analysis resulty. Section 6 describes the system design whereas section 7 provides the results of system evaluation which is followed by conclusion.

2. Related Work

The area of knowledge management has been explored extensively by the researcher in Human Computer Interaction/Computer Supported Cooperative Work discipline. Sveen et al. (2007) describe that new organizational forms originate new set of practices, so this highlights that a standard knowledge management methodology may not work in every organizational setting. This phenomenon highlights the need of understanding differnt organizational setups, with different cultural backgrounds to establish effective knowledge management methodologies in place. In the context of conventional organizations, Ackerman (1998) has empirically analyzed the usage of Answer Garden. Fitzpatrick (2003) has analyzed the knowledge sharing practices in a state department group.

Fagrell et al. (1999) have analyzed the knowledge sharing practices of mobile workers when they work outside of their office environments. Similarly, Fagrell and Ljungberg (2000) have looked at knowledge management issues in news journalists work environment. In the context of network organizations, knowledge management perspective has also been explored. Pipek et al (2003) looked into knowledge sharing practices of a network community of trainers and consultants. Reichling and Veith (2005) examined knowledge sharing practices in an industrial association.

Knowledge sharing practices in the context of less professional orgnizations has also been explored by some researchers. Smith and Lumba (2008) have outlined challenges for international networked NGOs in knowledge management. Saeed et al (2008) have described that expert recommending systems could help in networking different non governmental organizations (NGOs) and donor organizations so that the humanitarian projects could be better financed. Saeed et al (2010) have discussed nomadic knowledge sharing practices among social activists working in anti globalization movement.

All of the above mentioned studies have been done in technologically advanced countries but the body of knowledge discussing knowledge management practices in organizations located in areas affected by digital divide is very sparse. In this paper, we are focusing on an organization which is located at such place. This paper will help in understanding knowledge management perception and acceptability in less developed countries and will give us a better understanding of the problems associated with the knowledge sharing practices.

3. Case Description

The digital opportunity score of 0.29 ranks Pakistan at 127th position at digital opportunity index ranking system (WSIS, 2007). This gives the overall picture of technology density in the country. The organization which we focused has a campus in Islamabad, Karachi and two other affiliated institutes. The administrative staff at each of the location caries out different tasks like administering admission process, examination process, accounts management, course management and policy design. On the other hand, the staff at University head office looks after tasks of all the campuses and institutes. In order to get empirical data, different research methods were used. Most important were semi structured interviews of stakeholders and observations. Furthermore, the direct involvement of the authors in organizational issues ensured that they get first hand feedback from the stakeholders. At the stage of system design, participatory design methodology was applied.

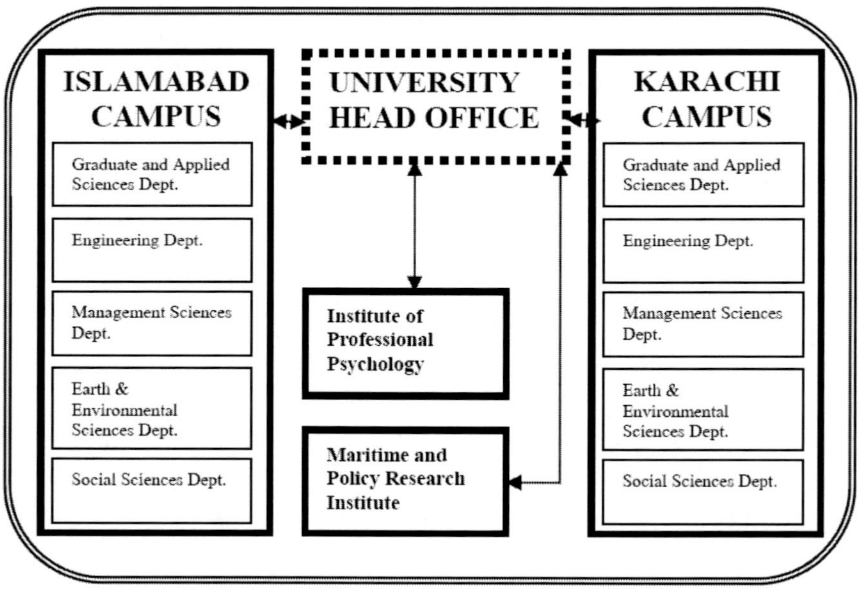

Figure 1. Organizational chart of HEI.

4. Empirical Findings

In this section we describe the empirical findings from our field work. In order to better understand the information flow, we have categorized the core functions of the employees in admissions, course registration, student's examination seating plan, result compilation, accounts, degree issuance and preparation of management reports.

I. Admission Process

The admission process is the main activity where every semester new students join the institution. The admission process consists of following three phases, prospectus/admission form selling, form submission and merit compilation. The practice was as follows that a hand-written manual register was used to keep record of sold and submitted application forms. Later this data was combined to make summaries based on daily progress, individual program admission status etc. Due to manual record keeping this could take enormous time and effort. Due to evolution of many new universities, there is a tough competition among institutions to attract good students. In order to analyze the success/failure of admission campaign early on helps to make amendments in decisions like extending the deadlines for form submission etc., but in manual system this kind of timely report formation was tedious to furnish. Furthermore, there was no way to identify the missing forms and hence there was no synchronization among forms selling and forms submission i.e. a form that was not sold could be submitted.

The merit compilation is a sensitive task where a single typographic mistake can lead to allowing admission to an ineligible candidate instead of the eligible one. The admission result compilation was done in MS Excel, where there was possibility of favouring a particular candidate.

II. Course Registration Process

In order to study, every student has to first register courses by filling a paper based form in triplicate, with his/her own personal information and courses information including course codes, titles, credit hours etc. After filling up the form, the students needed to get it verified from their respective course coordinators and then get it signed from respective head of department. The course coordinators had to verify the results of pre-requisite courses (if any) and check the maximum/minimum allowed number of credit hours etc.

Finally accounts section based on the number of courses had to generate a fee slip. It was difficult to check each and every pre-requisite course result for each student, so sometimes students were able to register courses without clearing the respective pre requisite courses. Furthermore, sometimes students register courses on two different forms to take more than allowed number of courses. Also it was difficult for accounts branch to track the status of the fee slips, if by accident two fee slips were generated for one student and if he/she submitted fee against one slip but remained a defaulter against other until he/she has brought the fee slip to accounts section to make this correction.

III. Establishing Seating Plan

The examinations were conducted in centralized way where an institution level date sheet was formulated. The seating plan was also developed manually for every student in each class irrespective of the fact that he had registered the course or not. A student name may appear in seating plan for a course that was not registered by him/her, so due to this every room may have some empty seats and as a result number of rooms and required examiners were increased which could have been reduced if a suitable seating plan could have been devised.

Furthermore, this setup encouraged students to easily change the seats in the examination rooms.

IV. Result Compilation Process

In order to compile the final examination result, data was entered in Microsoft Excel sheets leading to a lot of typographic mistakes. As a result, applications for correction in result were frequently received from teachers as well as students increasing administrative work. There were chances that a particular students' name may disappear from the list by mistake or a particular one is added without being registered for the respective course. Furthermore, grade calculation and other constraints were also difficult to manage as different departments had given different weight age to internal marks and final exam, so there were always chances of applying wrong marking distribution to a particular course result.

V. Fee Collection Process

The accounts department issued hand-written fee slips with the data regarding personal information and fee details. Every program/discipline had different fee structure and tuition fee was calculated based on credit hours registered. So, due to writing of each detail there might be possibility of writing incorrect value for a head and calculation of tuition fee based on credit hours registered. The summarized data required by management was also a big problem to compile and provide. Furthermore, tracking of defaulter students was also a troublesome process.

VI. Degree Issuance Process

Transcript compilation/generation process was also very complicated as each course record of student has to be entered into an excel sheet with the grades, credit hours, product etc. Based on this information, grading point average (GPA) and cumulative grading point average (CGPA) were calculated. This process was always vulnerable to wrong calculation of GPA/CGPA. In CGPA calculation another difficulty was to find repeated courses and to select one course with high grade to correctly calculate students result. Furthermore, cumulation of historical data was hard and error prone.

VII. Preparation of Management Reports

The summarized data could be of any type like students' information regarding their academic activities, admission details, personal information, fee information and faculty information asf. Preparation of summaries/cumulative reports required in decision making by higher management was very problematic. Either the summarized data was delayed or constituted incorrect data.

5. SWOT Analysis

In the presence of above mentioned problems the data collection/compilation from various departments/campuses at the head office was really a tough job, which used to take weeks and months resulting in excessive delays and considerable effort. So a SWOT analysis was carried out to analyze the situations and implementing IT systems in this organization.

Strengths of introducing technology could be highlighted as following:

- Transparency: All the activities could be monitored by summarized view and the whole information flow process can be tracked.
- Modernization: The automation will portray a positive image among stakeholders.
- Competitiveness: As most of the educational institutions have fierce competition to attract students, so better provision of services will increase the competitiveness.

While considering the opportunities of automating the organization the following points could be considered.

- Efficiency: The automated systems could improve the overall process efficiency and limited re-work will save the effort levels, which can be utilized to carry out other important work.
- Stakeholders' Satisfaction: Timely service provision will improve the interaction between stakeholders and will bring a positive image among stakeholders.
- Reduction of Operational Cost: Improved efficiency will lead to reduce in operational cost. Automation will decrease the cost and thus operational expenses are reduced and services can be offered at a competitive price, i.e. reduced fee for students.
- Education System Improvement: Automation of the system will also help in improving better education norms.
- Improvement in Employment Productivity: Automated systems can improve the productivity of employees, as instead of preparing regularly tedious reports and their verification will save enormous time and the time wasted on rectification of errors will also be used in productive tasks.

While counting on the weaknesses following points could be found.

- Investment: Setting up automated system will require extensive initial investment and continuous maintenance cost, which will include hiring IT professionals and the cost of licensed software.
- Lack of IT literacy among administrative staff: As most of the administrative staff lacked IT skills, a hindrance towards technological acceptability is foreseen.

Furthermore, following potential vital threats can also be foreseen.

- Chances of Misuse: As the system would be in the hands of technologically aware people and this system can be a target of misuse, where sensitive data maybe mishandled. On the other hand cyber attacks and viruses can also pollute the sensitive data.

- Dependency of Technology: There would be huge dependence on technology and in case of system failure, huge problems maybe experienced.

6. SYSTEM DESIGN

In order to realize software system, incremental design approach was followed. All the stakeholders were involved in design process, keeping in view the principles of participatory design. The back end technology was Oracle 9i/10g and front end applications were designed using developer 6i. Furthermore, some modules were realized using visual C#.Net and Asp.Net. The modules having web interace were developed in ASP.Net using C# because of its flexibility. The selection of oracle as a database was due to the growing size of organizational data.

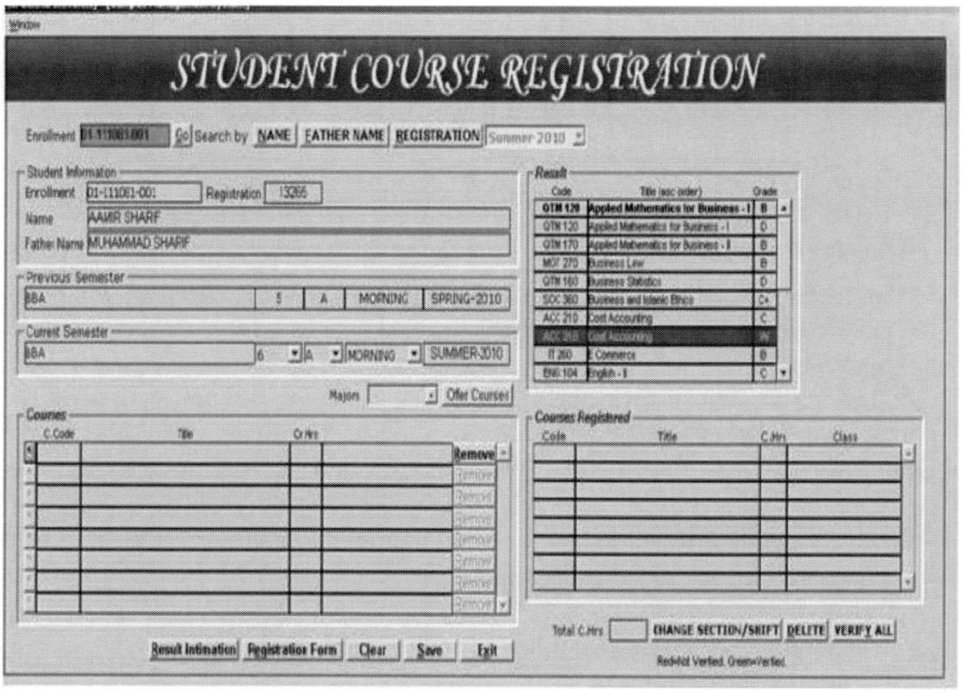

Figure 2. A snapshot of student registration form.

This campus management system (CMS) comprised of following modules:

- Admission System – to keep track of prospectus selling, form submission and merit list compilation.
- Student Registration System – to allocate enrolment numbers to new students after depositing the fee of first semester.
- Course Registration System - to register courses after going through automatic checks.

Table 1. Extended requirements set

Nr.	Problems	Solution	Technical requirements
1	Wrong admission form numbers for admission was entered frequently.	Valid admission form numbers should be entered by providing the list of valid form numbers.	Put a constraint on entering new admission form number by specifying a range of valid admission form numbers, so any new admission form number would fall in specified range.
2	Typographic mistakes while entering entry test marks lead to erroneous merit list.	Data entry of test marks by hand is ignored.	The data of entry test marks computed through optical mark reader (OMR) machine is directly plugged into the database against application numbers.
3	Sometimes admission form record is deleted by data entry operators (DEOs).	The access rights of data entry operators should be restricted while deletion of records.	Deletion of record facility is revoked from data entry operators and given to a single authorized person.
4	Ineligible admission form submission.	Application forms should be checked for eligibility criteria before submission.	Admission data entry/form submission of ineligible candidates is blocked by the system, and the eligibility criterion for all academic disciplines is initially set before start of admission process.
5	Fee slips issuance to applicants not eligible for admission.	Fees slip should only be issued to enrolled students.	Fee module is integrated with the admission module.
6	Typographic mistake while updating status of fee slips (paid/not paid).	Avoid re-entering of fee slip numbers to update its status.	Bar code is printed on fee slips to avoid wrong entry of fee slip numbers while updating its status.
7	Attendance of students was mistakenly marked for the past/future date.	Attendance must be marked on the current date.	Attendance of previous classes should be read only and advanced dates in calendar is de-activated to avoid marking wrong attendance of future days.
8	All summary reports were available only academic program-wise but not on university level.	There should be provision of showing aggregate information in all summary reports instead of only academic program based.	There should be possibility of customization of parameters before report generation to meet the needs of all stakeholders.
9	Locating specific information or grouping related information was not available.	There should be some clustering and grouping facilities available.	Data mining and visualization facilities based on customized parameters should be supported for trend analysis and strategy formulation.
10	Finding an expert on a specific topic was difficult to find by the management and in that cases they again have to rely on people based contacts.	There should be some kind of expertise recommendation mechanism.	In order to be a transparent expert finding system where profiles for every individual in the organization is created and expertise of every individual would be visible.
11	The tasks were handed to individuals in departments by the paper based registers and it was often troublesome to find who is taking care of a specific task.	A task monitoring option should be available to the system.	An automated task management module could be integrated where everyone could update the status of assigned task and it will enhance the awareness in the organization.

- Students' Attendance System – to mark daily attendance of students from classrooms.
- Fee System – to generate automated fee slips for students.
- Examination System – to manage students' exam marks and prepare consolidated results.
- Automated Exam Seating Plan System – to generate seating plan of students with the invigilation duty roaster for examination.
- Employee/Student ID card Generation System – to generate ID card for students and faculty members for security and identity purposes.
- Library System – to keep track of books, books issuance/return to/from students/faculty, due books, defaulter members etc.
- Payroll System – to generate pay slips of employees, bank statement, tax statements and other fund statements etc.
- Faculty Evaluation System – to manage students' feedback regarding faculty.

7. Evaluation

The introduction of IT artifacts in organizational boundaries has multiple effects (Attewell and Rule, 1984), so in order to measure the effectiveness of software system we carried out semi structured interviews. The findings were in conjunction with the improvisational change model (Orlikowski and Hoffman 1997). In the initial stage the employees were quite resistive to use the system as they were used to work with Microsoft Excel files and they feared that this new system might create problems for them. Once they were familiar with the system interface they started exchanging ideas on how to add different other features which can be helpful for them, thus paving the way for participatory design approach. If we look at the system design, we could analyze that the indigenous knowledge produced by the organization is structured by the introduction of the system. But in the literature of knowledge management, a shift is taking place from information towards knowledge (cf. Cohen and Pursak, 2001; Becks et al, 2004; Huysman and Wulf, 2004; Huysman and Wulf 2006; Reichling et al., 2007). In order to take advantages from these approaches there is need for developing suitable applications on top of this system. The potential of optimized methodologies in streamlining knowledge management process has been discussed (cf. Stehr, 2007; Joia, 2007; Brauch and Tzokas, 2008; Minocha and Stonehouse, 2008) In order to define the temporal and spatial aspects, there is need for proper data mining applications so that datasets could be generated based on different criteria and their comparison could yield meaningful information which is suitable for the future strategy making like introduction of new disciplines, etc. After evaluation we found the following extended requirements of the system.

Conclusion

Technology introduction in organizational boundaries is a complex task. In order to fill the digital divide and formulate a knowledge society, considerable policy directions are required (c.f. Zack, 1999; Samarajiva and Gamage, 2007; Sharma and Azura, 2005; Sharma,

2009). This paper gives an interesting case study of the problems faced by an institution and how these problems were removed by the introduction of technological system. This technological system helped to manage the indigenously produced knowledge and also to extract meaningful information instantly. Keeping in view the empirical problems, campus management system was designed and the problems mentioned in manual systems were removed. Now the students register their courses online by using the automated system in which all rules and regulations are implemented. Furthermore, now automated exam seating plan is fully liaison with the course registration.

The system also reduced the redundant work. Earlier there was a problem of delay in result compilation and announcement, as the list containing students' name, enrolment, program etc. has to be entered for each course's result. But now the exam data entry operator does not need to write names and other information, as all the data comes from course registration module itself. The ease of getting multiple reports has helped to better manage the institutional data. The features like trend of student's strength in last year's, admissions trend analysis, students' grading analysis, faculty information with their course workload and their feedback by students enable management to have an overall picture of proceedings in a quick and better way. Furthermore, we have carried out human centric evaluation of the system and generated a set of technical requirements which can further improve the working of the organization.

REFERENCES

[1] Ackerman, M.S. (1998). Augmenting Organizational Memory: A field study of answer garden, ACM Transactions on Information Systems 16(3): 203–224.

[2] Attewell, P., and Rule, J. (1984) Computing and Organizations: What We Know and What We Don't Know." *Communications of the ACM* 27, 1184-1192.

[3] Baqir, M. N., and Kathawala, Y. (2004) Ba for knowledge cities: A futuristic technology model.*Journal of Knowledge Management*, *8*(5), 83–95.

[4] Becks, A. Reichling, T. and Wulf, V. (2004) Expertise Finding: Approaches to Foster Social Capital, In *Huysman, M.and Wulf, V. Social Capital and Information Technology*, MIT-Press, Cambridge, MA, 333 – 354.

[5] Brauch, Y. and Tzokas, N. (2008) The translation of higher-level knowledge into different levels of managerial and creative competencies', I*nternational Journal of Learning and Intellectual Capital 2008 – 5(2), 223 – 240.*

[6] Chou, S.-W. (2005). Knowledge creation: absorptive capacity, organizational mechanisms, and knowledge storage/retrieval capabilities. *Journal of Information Science*, *31*(6), 453–465. doi:10.1177/0165551505057005

[7] Cohen, D. and Prusak, L. (2001). *In Good Company: How Social Capital makes Organizations Work*, Harvard Business School Press, Boston, USA.

[8] Fitzpatrick, G. (2003) Bootstrapping Expertise Sharing, in M. Ackerman, V. Pipek and V. Wulf (eds), *Sharing Expertise: Beyond Knowledge Management*, MIT Press, 81-110.

[9] Fagrell, H., Kristoffersen H., S. and Ljungberg F. (1999) Exploring Support for Knowledge Management in Mobile Work, In Proc. *ECSCW 1999*, Springer, 259-275.

[10] Fagrell, H. and F. Ljungberg (2000) A Field Study of News Journalism: Implications for Knowledge Management Systems In Proc. *PDC 2000.*

[11] Huysman, M.and Wulf, V. (2004) *Social Capital and Information Technology*, MIT-Press, Cambridge MA.

[12] Huysman, M. and Wulf, V. (2006) IT to Support Knowledge Sharing in Communities: Towards a Social Capital Analysis *Journal on Information Technology* (JIT), 21(1), 40-51.

[13] Joia, A. L. (2007) Knowledge management strategies: creating and testing a measurement scale', *International Journal of Learning and Intellectual Capital*, 4(3), 203-221.

[14] Lytras, M.D. and Sicilia, M.A. (2005) The Knowledge Society: a manifesto for knowledge and learning', *Int. J. Knowledge and Learning*, 1(1/2), 1-11.

[15] Minocha, S. and Stonehouse, G. (2008) Dimensions of KM: they know not its called knowledge… but they can manage it!, *International Journal of Teaching and Case Studies* 1(3), 253-265.

[16] Orlikowski, W., and Hoffman, D. (1997) An improvisational model for change management: The case of groupware technologies. *Sloan Management Rev.* 38 (2) 11–21.

[17] Pipek, V. Hinrichs, J. and Wulf, V. (2003)Sharing Expertise: Challenges for technical support in M. Ackerman, V. Pipek and V. Wulf (eds), *Sharing Expertise: Beyond Knowledge Management*, MIT Press, 111-136.

[18] Reichling, T., and Veith, M. (2005) Expertise sharing in a heterogeneous organizational environment, In *Proc. ECSCW 2005*, Springer, 325-345.

[19] Reichling, T.; Veith, M. and Wulf, V. (2007) Expert Recommender: Designing for a Network Organization, in: Computer Supported Cooperative Work: The Journal of Collaborative Computing (JCSCW), 16(4-5), 431 – 465.

[20] Saeed, S., Reichling, T. and Wulf, V. (2008) Applying Knowledge Management to Support Networking among NGOs and Donors in *Proc. IADIS international conference on E-Society*. April 9-12, 2008. Algarve, Portugal.

[21] Saeed, S., Pipek, V., Rohde, M., and Wulf, V. (2010) Managing nomadic knowledge: a case study of the European social forum. In *Proceedings of the 28th international Conference on Human Factors in Computing Systems* Atlanta, Georgia, USA, April 10 - 15, 2010.

[22] Sagasti, F. (2004). *Knowledge and Information for Development*. Northampton, MA: Edward Elgar.

[23] Samarajiva, R., and Gamage, S. (2007). Bridging the Divide: Building Asia-Pacific Capacity for Effective Reforms. *The Information Society*, *23*, 109–117. doi:10.1080/01972240701224200.

[24] Sharma, R. S., and Azura, I. M. (2005). Bridging the Digital Divide in Asia - Challenges and Solutions. *International Journal of Technology. Knowledge and Society*, *1*(3), 15–30.

[25] Sharma, R. S., (2009) A Policy Framework for developing knowledge societies (December 29, 2009). Journal of knowledge Management, Vol. 13, No. 5, pp. 373-386, 2009. Available at SSRN: http://ssrn.com/abstract=1529534.

[26] Sharma, R. S, Ng, E. W. J., Dharmawirya, M., and Samuel, E. M. (2010) a Policy Framework for developing knowledge Societies International Journal of Knowledge Society Research, 1(1), 22-45.

[27] Smith, J. G and Lumba, P. M. (2008) Knowledge Management Practices and Challenges in International Networked NGOs: The Case of One World International." *The Electronic Journal of Knowledge Management* 6(2), 167 – 176.

[28] Soete, W. D. (2006). *Understanding the Dynamics of a Knowledge Economy.* Cheltenham, UK: Edward Elgar.

[29] Stehr, N. (2007) 'Societal transformations, globalization and the knowledge society', *Int. J. Knowledge and Learning*, 3(2-3), 139-153.

[30] Sveen, F. O., Rich, E., Jager, M., (2007) Overcoming Organizational Challenges to Secure Knowledge Management, Information Systems Frontiers 9(5), 481-492

[31] WSIS (2007) *World Information Society Report 2007 Beyond WSIS* available http://www.itu.int/osg/spu/publications/worldinformationsociety/2007/WISR07_full-free.pdf, [Accessed 8.05.2010]

[32] Zack, M. H. (1999). Developing a Knowledge Strategy. *California Management Review*, *41*(3), 125–145.

BIOGRAPHICAL NOTES

Saqib Saeed is a Ph.D. student at University of Siegen, Germany. He is a certified software quality engineer and holds a Masters degree in software technology from Stuttgart University of Applied Sciences, Germany. He was working as lecturer at the department of Computer Sciences and Engineering at Bahria University Islamabad, Pakistan before coming to Siegen. His areas of interest are computer supported cooperative work and empirical software engineering.

Rizwan Aamir is currently working as Senior Lecturer/Manager in Information Systems department at Bahria University Islamabad. He holds Master degrees in computer engineering and computer science. His areas of interest are database design and system modeling.

Sohail Safdar was working as lecturer and program coordinator at the department of Computer Sciences and Engineering at Bahria University Islamabad, Pakistan. Currently, he is a PhD scholar at Universiti Teknologi Petronas Malaysia. His research interest lies in workflow systems

In: HRM and Marketing Orientation in the New Era
Editor: Panagiotis Kyriazopoulos
ISBN: 978-1-62808-959-2

Chapter 10

COMPARING THE FACTORS AFFECTING B2B E-RELATIONSHIPS VS TRADITIONAL

Irini Samanta[*]
Lecturer Graduate Technological Education Institute of Piraeus, Greece

ABSTRACT

Business to Business relationships in e-commerce has received widespread attention as one of the key drivers in sustaining an organization's competitive advantage, providing benefits such as the ability to carry out transactions around the world. In the world of e-commerce, success is defined by the firm's ability to build long-term customer relationships that bring value to the customers and stakeholders and sustain profitability to the organization. Companies can exploit relationships successfully worldwide by investing in a combination of innovative implementations of technology business process enhancements and organizational changes that are part of an overall e-marketing strategy. B2B internet usage is growing in popularity, ranging from cost savings to gaining benefits in the value chain most needed when assessing Business-to-Business relationships.

The present research investigates a sample of sixty Greek Business to Business firms and the factors that influence relationships in an internet environment comparing these factors to pre e-commerce period. The literature appears to be no investigation of this phenomenon within the context of Greek Business to Business Medium sized firms (MSF). Given this gap in the literature, the research problem investigated in this research is: How do relationships affect B2B firms in e-commerce?

Keywords: E-business, e-commerce, relationships, communication

---

[*] E-mail: isamanta@teipir.gr

Introduction

The ability of an organization to create and maintain profitable relationships with their most valuable customers are a durable basis of competitive advantage. The new eRa of business is built upon effective relationship management. Many B2B firms create what might be called a collaborative advantage by demonstrating special skills in managing relationships with key customers or by jointly developing innovative strategies with alliance partner. These firms have learned how to be good partners, and these superior relationship skills are a valuable asset (Kleindl, 2001).

A business marketer who wishes to find a preferred supplier list must be prepared to help the firm provide more value to its demanding customers. To this end, the marketer must provide exceptional performance in quality, delivery, and, over time, cost competitiveness (Mahadevan, 2003). Building and maintaining lasting customer relationships requires careful attention to detail, meeting promises, and swiftly responding to new requirements.

In an effort to anticipate, react and adapt to e-commerce, B2B firms are forced to move from the traditional management activity to a new relationship approach based upon new forms of exchange. This exchange is based on the joint efforts of the various buyers and sellers in the supply chain; it is characterized by collaboration by joint involvement of participants (Donaldson and O'Toole, 2007).

The rapid alterations of the business environment mainly influence B2B relationships and this research is an attempt to compare the firms' relationships to the time pre e-commerce to deal with these changes. Based on strategic issues this research identifies how firms operate in the new era in order to develop successful relationships.

The Importance of E-Business in B2B Firms

E-business influences all sectors and the all markets and is related with the total strategy and the operations of enterprise. It incorporates the total of operations that relates with the term e-commerce, by connecting these operations with networks that exceed the limits of enterprise.

Some profits that e-business offers in B2B transactions, are the increase of income that can be achieved via the technology, the alleviation of time and the cost of production of products or services, the improvement of service of customers as well as the possibility of increasing the share of market of enterprise. There are potential cost reductions in transaction costs, error reduction, and reduce lead time, which lead to lower costs of services and products and improved efficiency (Mahadevan, 2003).

According to Kalakota and Robinson (1999 p.243) "through e-business a firm can offer a fully integrated, tightly linked system, a searchable catalogue, improved ordering and delivery options, back office record keeping and billing, real-time inventory management, and constantly updated advertising and customer preference data gathering; often times a substantial cost reduction". Another huge advantage for companies conducting B2B e-business is the fact that interactions with the actors can be easily monitored and logged (Samanta, 2009, 2011). If this information is collected properly, it can provide a company with a wealth of marketing information (Fischer, 2002). B2B firms can also use e-business to differentiate their company from other similar companies. They can offer more customisation, premium customer service and lower price due to the cost savings (Fischer, 2002). Still the powerful relations that are developed in the enterprising partners allow the effective exploitation of knowledge and from the other hand allow the growth and import in the market of new products and services more rapidly, more economically and at extension more efficiently (Fischer, 2002).

B2B firms in e-commerce are involved in industrial transactions and communications trading with other businesses using the internet as the communication medium. The use of the internet for procurement and other industrial transactions greatly reduces the cost of doing business (Kleindl, 2001; Kyriazopoulos and Samanta, 2009).

Companies in order to retain a sustainable competitive advantage in relation to e-commerce according to (Porter, 2001) take into consideration five marketing strategies that can help them:

- Actively collaborating with supply chain partners
- Extending the company's reach up and down the supply chain
- Changing the supply chain flow path
- Growing revenue
- Transforming capabilities into new business.

The innovations of the electronic transactions underline a philosophy that refers to a total commitment of the industry and moreover maintaining that commitment on a constant basis. Investments in technological substructures, human potential, and co-operation with informatics industries, education and moulding of an organising culture comprise powerful commitments, which need clear strategic definition from the first steps of the involvement to electronic transactions (Yoffie, 1997; Eisenhardt and Brown (1998). Dann and Dann (2001) mention the need to answer the following questions prior to any attempt for operational activation at the internet:

- What does the industry try to achieve out of its activation at the electronic markets?
- Which is the focal point of the electronic activation?
- Which are the necessary additional substructures for its presence in the internet?
- How is the electronic expression completed by the actual operational activities?
- What kind of marketing outline is needed for the reassurance that the realization of the marketing programme won't be affected by the unstable electronic environment?

The effectiveness of the total planning and the marketing programs of an industry are related mostly to the degree of completion and cooperation that preserve the secondary marketing activities among them. This refers also to the need of connection of the electronic marketing activities to the ones that take place in natural markets (Honeycutt et al., 1998; Harridge and March, 2004).

Implementing Electronic Relationships in B2B Firms

The Internet has eliminated the barriers so that many firms can operate globally. B2B firms endeavour to improve the execution of business transactions by streamlining inter-organizational operations system (IOS) networks and applications. In order to face the influence of globalization, the intense competition and the new technologies in B2B electronic commerce, firms should redefine their strategy to increase customer satisfaction and to achieve better corporate decision-making, greater economic efficiency and more rapid exchange of information (McIvor and Humphreys, 2006). Furthermore, B2B firms should take into consideration some important factors, which are analyzed below, for the successful implementation of their activities in e-commerce.

Security

Security of transactions and information is a part of the successful conduct of e-business (Kehoe, 2001) and for e- commerce to be effectively conducted; it must be assured that the transaction environment is secure (Evans and Wurster, 1999). However, safeguard mechanisms such as the digital signature, encryption and firewalls provide sufficient security for e-commerce (Turner, 2000). Indeed, there is empirical evidence that on-line transactions are often safer than traditional transactions through phone, mail, or fax (Nelson and James, 1996) and the lack of security for internet transactions may be exaggerated (Broadbent, 1996). Nonetheless, businesses can take several steps to improve the security of on-line transactions, for example, by using a global public key infrastructure which is a spectrum of products that protects the integrity, confidentiality, and legitimacy of on-line transactions (Arden and Palmer, 1999).

Improved Communications

Hoffman and Novak (1996) proposed that communication on the web uses a many-to-many communication model because customers can interact with the medium, firms can provide content through it. Electronic interactions can result in faster communications and increased responsiveness.

The internet improves business communication through effective and efficient information search and exchange (Blankenhorn, 2001) as well as enhanced connectivity and interactivity (Dutta and Segev, 1999). That is, the internet facilitates effective and efficient access to information and allows firms to exchange information with their exchange partners (Fraser et al., 2000). Moreover, communication is improved at points along the value chain (Webster 2000). The internet enhances the communication aspects of the procurement process (Boyle and Alwitt, 1999).

Procurement

Procurement systems become networked through the internet, including activities ranging from information search on availability of other businesses to the supply of goods and services, through to delivery, contact management and invoicing, to payment (Blundon and Bonde, 1998). This e-procurement process reduces the formalisation of the communication between exchange partners, eliminating “the rules, paper work, hidden procedures and other obstacles” (Kalakota and Robinson, 1999, p. 243).

Improved Financial Performance

The next advantage relates to profitability - decreasing costs and increasing revenue. On the one hand, cost reduction is the most cited benefit of using internet-based technologies in B2B e-commerce (Evans and Wurster, 1999;Yoffie, 1997; Strader and Shaw, (1999).

As well, many firms benefit from using internet-based technologies in terms of savings on operational methods such as placing orders, receiving invoices, tracking shipments and processing payments and can achieve an electronic integration effect (DeJesus, 2000; Sraeel,1996; Straus and Frost, 1999). In addition to operational cost efficiency, marketing communication costs can also decrease directly by substituting the internet for other communication media (Rowley, 1996). For instance, online customer support documentation can dramatically cut the costs of printing and shipping paper-based technical support material (Mougayar, 1997). On the other hand, the internet can be used to generate revenue through a number of mechanisms such as increased speed to market, expanded global market, and decreased market entry barrier (Eid et al, 2006). Firms may distribute information using electronic mail or the web and ensure that it reaches its target as soon as the information is available. The internet also enables small firms to overcome entry barriers (Hoffman and Novak 1996), particularly to the global market (Ozarsky, 1999; Birch and Young 1997).

Improved Operational Efficiency and Supply Chain Management

B2B internet use improves operational efficiency through automated procurement, reduced errors and time in completing business transactions and increased flexibility and responsiveness. For example, as a result of implementing internet-based procurement, a New Zealand firm's accounts receivable staff received fewer calls asking for invoice or credit note reprints as customers were able to download these off the web site (Pavaloia, 2009).

Also, the web enables companies to effectively manage their supply chain in an integrated fashion by developing stronger relationships with their business partners, ultimately adding value to products and services sold to end customers (Kumar et al., 1994; Langford, 2000). Web-based electronic data interchange and electronic funds transfers enhance supply chain management, allowing swifter and more accurate transactions (Griffith and Palmer, 1999). For example, General Electric, in order to more effectively manage its sellers, has changed its business arena from a physical business community to an electronic one. Its Trading Process Network is an online business forum that allows the company to transact approximately US$1 billion worth of business with more than 1.400 sellers scattered around the globe. Its multi-tiered supply chain strategy is to promote the system to other sellers who would then promote the system to their sellers (Rayport and Sviokla, 1995).

Improved Customer Service

Internet-based customer service not only affects direct sales, but also improves customer relations that retain customers (Evans and Wurster, 1999). Using the internet as a medium can speed up service turn-around and enhance service delivery (Geiger and Martin,

1999). Customers can self-serve information, instead of waiting for sales representatives. Further, customer service is no longer limited by time. A business can take customer questions and/or service requests online and provide detailed answers within 24 hours (Stahl, 2002). The web also offers capabilities to improve customer service and decrease the cost of service delivery. For example, General Electric maintains an on-line searchable database with over 1,500 technical documents on its industrial products, reducing the cycle time for answering requests from 3 days to a matter of seconds (Arden and Palmer, 1999). Similarly, Federal Express offers their customers the ability to track their packages through their web site.

This on-line service enables the company's customers to track exactly where their packages are and when they will be (or have been) safely delivered (Pavaloia, 2009). Indeed, using the internet to support and improve customer service is part of the process of building customer relationships which takes the business relationship issues into the realm of cooperative relationships between exchange partners (Griffith and Palmer 1999; Webster, 2000).

Improved Partner Relationships and Collaboration

Relationships may facilitate in a long-term basis with intermediaries, through enabling shared databases and processes that contribute to closer customer relationships (Kalakota and Whinston 1997; Honeycutt et al., 1998). In addition to traditional modes of communication, e-mail, chartrooms and web-based video-conferencing allow exchange partners more opportunity to easily exchange documents and opinions, thus strengthening relationships (Boyle and Alwitt 1999).

Finally, the web strengthens B2B and B2C relationships by allowing firms to use multimedia information about products and services, such as sound and active pictures (Hicks, 2000). The information on the web site can be updated continuously and instantly, and is always available to consumers and business partners (Biland, 2000; Griffith and Palmer, 1999).

Research Methodology

Research Sample

This research examined the elements from the marketing point of view which influence B2B relationships in an electronic commerce. The research addressed to the population of 1.525 medium sized firms in the area of Attica to identify potential differences between the medium companies in a sample of 125 firms which operate their activities in e-commerce last five years.

The choice of sampling took place in a systematic method. Firstly, the firms are selected from the population which participated in the research as sellers and secondly, they recommended a firm participated in the research as a buyer in which they had a significant proportion of transactions. In total the sample is comprised of sixty (60) companies. The split amongst those is as follows: thirty of them make use of e-commerce (30-e-commerce) and the remaining 30 are their most important customers/buyers which make use of e-commerce (30).

The distribution of the personnel which responded in the questionnaire are marketing managers 26.7% sales managers 31.7% and logistics managers 21.7%. The number of employees (50% with more than 150 persons) suggests functional and complicated business circumstances. According to the business activities the total sample belongs to the manufacturing sector.

Questionnaire Design

The first step in questionnaire design was to determine the information needed to achieve the research objectives. In this research, the variables were a list of functions that are necessary in B2B firms operations and should be identified.

Communication (Heide, 1992; Arunkundram and Sundarajan, 1998). The variables used for the communication, co-operation, adaptation, delivery and flexibility performance are the followings:

Exchange of information in this relationship takes place frequently and informally, and not only according to a pre-specified agreement.

In this relationship, any information that might help the other party will be provided for them.

Both parties in the relationship will provide proprietary information if it can help the other party.

Both parties keep each other informed about events or changes that may affect the other party.

Delivery performance (Donaldson and O'Tool, 2000).

Speed of delivery relative to competitors. Percentage of orders delivered on-time.

Flexibility performance, volume flexibility, price, variety (product line) flexibility (Sawhney and Kaplan,1999a,1999b; Kaplan and Garicano, 2001)

Quality performance: Frequency of customer complaints. Adequacy of customer complaint tracking /feedback systems.

The questions, except those which were asking behavioral or demographic characteristics of the respondents, were in an ordinal type 5 points Likert scale.

Reliability was achieved because the instrument was pretested and modified before being administered. External validity concerns the generalizability of this research to a target population while internal validity concerns whether the relationship among the variables measured is genuine. Measurement validity is assessed theoretically and empirically in this research.

RESEARCH FINDINGS

The focus of this research is to ascertain how the companies' cooperation with each other changed (if at all) through the use of e-commerce as opposed to the time prior to them using e-commerce. As far as information exchange is concerned, most companies agree that working with e-commerce has helped improve communication and provide the appropriate information to their company (Table 1).

As far as security and privacy are concerned, though, improvement is less as we note a high frequency in the middle of the scale but 56% still report there are better and 20.5% much better.

Table 1. Communication and Information Exchange

	Much Worse	Worse	Neither Better nor Worse	Better	Much Better
More appropriate information is provided to our company	0	2	9	23	7
	0%	4.9%	22%	*56.1%*	17.1%
More reliable information is provided to our company	0	2	8	21	8
	0%	6.7%	20.5%	*53.8%*	20.5%
Better security and privacy is provided in distributing information	0	0	17	13	9
	0%	0%	*43.6%*	33.3%	23.1%
Both companies inform each other with regard to changes or events that might affect their counterpart	0	5	6	20	7
	0%	13.2%	15.8%	*52.6%*	18.4%
Both companies would provide specialised information if this could be helpful to their counterpart	0	1	6	23	8
	0%	2.6%	15.8%	*60.5%*	21.1%

We compare the response of the Buyers against those of the Sellers (Table 2). Using the X^2 test with a significant level of 0.05 only in: "*better security and privacy is provided in distributing information*" is there a significant difference.

Table 2. Communication and information exchange between "e-Buyers "e- Sellers"

Communication and Information Exchange	Pearson Chi-square	Approx. Sig.
More appropriate information is provided to our company	1.896	0.594
More reliable information is provided to our company	4.262	0.234
Better security and privacy is provided in distributing information	6.543	0.038
Both companies inform each other with regard to changes or events that might affect their counterpart	1.953	0.582
Both companies would provide specialised information if this could be helpful to their counterpart	1.487	0.685

THE IMPACT ON PRICES/COSTS

The following section refers to prices and costs and to what extent there have been changes (if any) once companies' cooperation is achieved through e-commerce. Apart from product price, that remains unchanged, and administration costs for logistics management are generally better. This means that those companies that use e-commerce believe that they make savings (in terms of having their costs reduced) as opposed to following the traditional methods of commerce and cooperation (Table 3).

Table 3. The impact on prices/costs

	Very Low	Low	Neither High nor Low	High	Very High
Impact on Product Prices	0	5	28	6	0
	0%	12.8%	*71.8%*	15.4%	0%
Costs relating to market research prior to each new order	0	4	15	18	2
	0%	10.3%	*38.5%*	46.2%	5.1%
Product/service order costs	0	7	8	15	4
	0%	17.9%	20.5%	*51.3%*	10.3%
Resulting cost of stocks	0	7	10	18	4
	0%	17.9%	25.6%	*46.2%*	10.3%
Communication costs between business and its supplier	0	5	9	17	8
	0%	12.8%	23.1%	*43.6%*	20.5%
Administrative costs for Logistics management	1	10	9	17	2
	2.6%	25.6%	23.1%	*43.6%*	5.1%

In the second level of analysis we wanted to ascertain whether there were any differentiations between the Buyers and the Sellers. The following (Table 4) demonstrates the values from the X^2 tests falls under 0.05 in any of the questions/statements so we come to the conclusion that all e-commerce companies respond in similar way.

Table 4. The impact on prices/costs among Buyers and the Sellers

	Pearson Chi-square	Approx. Sig.
How does the product price list compare between your physical sellers and those you transact with electronically (through e-commerce)	2.652	0.266
Costs relating to market research prior to each new order	7.301	0.063
Resulting cost of stocks	5.789	0.122
Communication costs between business and its supplier	6.839	0.077
Administrative costs for Logistics management	3.448	0.486

Most of the companies making use of e-commerce agree with the following statements (Table 5). The only exception is with regard to the last statement: "*if we were to ever lose our customer/supplier for this specific product then it would be hard for our company to replace them with a new customer/supplier*". This indicates that companies do not consider their customers/sellers irreplaceable.

Table 5. Switching barriers

	Strongly Disagree	Disagree	Neither Agree nor Disagree	Agree	Strongly Agree
Our company and its supplier depend on each other to a great extent in order to achieve their goals	0	4	1	30	7
	0%	9.5%	2.4%	*71.4%*	16.7%
Our business depends to a great extent on a customer with regard to achieving its goals	1	1	11	24	2
	2.6%	2.6%	28.2%	*61.5%*	5.1%
Changing our customer/supplier would be a significant setback for us	1	0	15	23	3
	2.4%		35.7%	*54.8%*	7.1%
If we were to ever lose our customer/supplier for this specific product then it would be hard for our company to replace them with a new customer/ supplier	6	12	13	8	2
	14.6%	29.3%	*31.7%*	19.5%	4.9%

Table 6. Switching barriers between "Buyers' vs. "Sellers"

	Pearson Chi-square	Approx. Sig.
Our company and its supplier depend on each other to a great extent in order to achieve their goals	9.545	0.023
Our business depends to a great extent on a customer with regard to achieving its goals	10.845	0.028
Changing our customer/supplier would be a significant setback for us	4.024	0.259
If we were to ever lose our customer/supplier for this specific product then it would be hard for our company to replace them with a new customer/supplier	4.497	0.343

Through comparing the responses from the Buyers with those received from the Sellers/Sellers we identify differences in both the first and second statements (Table 6). Most of the Buyers responding to the second statement neither agree nor disagree with it. Sellers/sellers agree with the second statement. That is expected as sellers traditionally rely on their customers more than the Buyers.

The next section refers to the product itself in relation to the time pre e-commerce. The variety and ease of research is better; also the ease in product process is much better (Table 7). Therefore, from the majority of companies engaged in e-commerce things are improving with the use of e-commerce in terms of product quality, the ease of research and product selection and ease in ordering process.

Table 7. Relation to the time pre e-commerce

	Much Worst	Worst	Neither Better nor Worst	Better	Much Better
Impact on Product Quality	0	6	15	18	2
	0%	14.6%	36.6%	*43.9%*	4.9%
Ease of research and product selection	2	4	7	17	11
	4.9%	9.8%	17.1%	*41.5%*	26.8%
Ease in ordering process	0	7	5	14	15
	0%	17.1%	12.2%	34.1%	*36.6%*

Table 8. Comparing the responses in relation to the time pre e-commerce

	Pearson Chi-square	Approx. Sig.
Product Quality	*10.582*	*0.014*
Ease of research and product selection	8.841	0.065
Ease in ordering process	4.636	0.201

Table 9. E-relationships improvement Just in Time (JiT)

	Much Worst	Worst	Neither Better nor Worst	Better	Much Better
Transaction and payment security	0	3	21	15	0
	0%	7.7%	*53.8%*	38.5%	0%
Qualitative consistency of delivery services	0	6	9	21	3
	0%	15.4%	23.1%	*53.8%*	7.7%
Jointly planning quality control systems	0	2	17	18	2
	0%	5.1%	43.6%	*46.2%*	5.1%
Improved implementation of JIT (Just-In-Time)	0	5	7	24	2
	0%	13.2%	18.4%	*63.2%*	5.3%
Economies of scale	0	5	12	18	3
	0%	13.2%	31.6%	*47.4%*	7.9%

Comparing the responses received from the Buyers and Sellers we only identify a difference in the first statement (Table 8). A large proportion of the Buyers believe that there is better variety whereas Sellers/Sellers believe that nothing has changed.

In reference to cooperation with the supplier, for all factors mentioned in this section (Table 9), the majority of the companies believe that there have been improvements through using e-commerce as opposed to transacting in the traditional manner. Only the transaction and payment security remains relatively unchanged.

The next stage in our analysis is to determine whether there are differences between Buyers and Sellers. In (Table 10) we demonstrate that all companies that use e-commerce have responded in the same way (with a 5% significant level).

Table 10. E-relationships improvement JiT "Buyer's vs. "Sellers"

	Pearson Chi-square	Approx. Sig.
Transaction and payment security	4.127	0.127
Qualitative consistency of delivery services	7.672	0.053
Jointly planning quality control systems	4.324	0.229
Improved implementation of JIT (Just-In-Time)	5.680	0.128
Economies of scale	5.800	0.122

RELATIONSHIPS WITH BUYERS/SELLERS

This section regards factors affecting company relationships. From semantic number factors (22) the answer frequencies of the 7 most important factors according to the statistic results are shown in (Table 11). The factors «Steady product quality in the long run» and «Consistency in product quality and specifications» affect intensively the relations with buyers/sellers. Following with high influence are «Forecast for shortening delivery times», «Timely product supply, as agreed», «Increased response the seller/buyer needs», «Improvement of the product's cost effectiveness» and «Lower prices when ordering higher quantities». We also note that influential of all factors is the company's fame. It is also the only factor which has a frequency (even though 2.5%) at the «no influence» code. It is worth mentioning that no factor is considered by the 40 companies to have no influence in their relations with Buyers/sellers.

For the seven most important factors X2 test are made between «E-commerce Buyers» and «E-commerce Sellers» (Table 12). All results are insignificant with the exception of the criterion *«The Fame of the business for the procedure of creating commercial relations»*. Therefore, the Buyers answer differently from the Sellers, given that both use e-commerce. Answers of e-commerce buyers and e-commerce sellers for the Buyers the fame of the business has some up to "high influence" in deciding to create business relations, while for the Sellers/Sellers it has high up to intense influence. Therefore, for the Sellers/Sellers it matters more compared to the Buyers.

Table 11. Factors affecting B2B relationships

	No influenc e	Minimal influence	Some influence	High influence	Intense influence
Forecast for shortening delivery times	0	1 (2.5%)	14 (35%)	21 (52.5%)	4 (10%)
Fame of the company for creating commercial relations	1 (2.5%)	0	*15 (37.5%)*	13 (32.5%)	11 (27.5%)
Steady product quality in the long run	0	0	3 (7.5%)	15 (37.5%)	*22 (55%)*
Timely product supply, as agreed	0	0	3 (7.5%)	*22 (55%)*	15 (37.5%)
Consistency in product quality and specifications.	0	0	3 (7.5%)	12 (30%)	*25 (62.5%)*
Increased response to the supplier/client needs.	0	1 (2.6%)	5 (12.8%)	19 (48.6%)	14 (35.9%)
Improved product cost effectiveness	0	1 (2.6%)	8 (20.5%)	18 (46.2%)	12 (30.8%)
Lower prices when ordering higher quantities	0	2 (5.1%)	5 (12.8%)	*17 (43.6%)*	15 (38.5%)

Table 12. Factors affecting B2B relationships between E-commerce –Buyers and e- commerce-Sellers

	Pearson Chi-square	Approx. Sig.
Forecast for shortening the anticipated delivery times	2.091	0.554
Company fame for the creation of commercial relations	*6.786*	*0.034*
Product quality steady in the future	2.619	0.270
Timely product supply, within the time-frame agreed	1.111	0.574
Consistency in quality and specifications of the products.	5.590	0.061
Increased response to the supplier/client needs.	1.143	0.767
Improvement to the effectiveness of the product cost	5.757	0.352
Lower prices when supplying larger quantities	2.318	0.314

CONCLUSION

The research showed the factors defining the suitability of activation in electronic markets for a company already active in physical markets. Thus the characteristics were set out of companies that can survive in the environment of the New Economy from which it emerges that the changes brought about by electronic business can hardly be characterized as revolutionary, as the factors do not especially differentiate in the electronic companies. E-commerce Buyers and Sellers indicated that they do share information amongst them in an effort to improve the services they offer to each other, introduce smoother transaction processes and also reduce transaction costs. This is an important finding as most of our sample businesses seem to enjoy the uniqueness of finding themselves in an advantageous position that other companies could possibly take some time to get themselves into. It appears in the research that through the development of electronic relations the exchange of information between buyers and sellers is improved, the cost of the supply chain reduced, as it works to improve management of warehouses and transport schedules. Communication and information exchange seems to play an active part in creating and maintaining active relations and interaction between the company and its clients. Communication practices are not limited to the time horizon of the user's visit to the company's electronic manifestation, but extend to regular updates via electronic or conventional means. Further benefits such as the volume of information that the supplier collects and manages contribute to the better regulation of production, and of the supply chain. Information completeness is something else situated between the supplier and the buyer and makes a decisive contribution to achieving successful relations.

The sellers of electronic markets are given the opportunity to directly manage the distribution of goods to their buyers by choosing the most efficient systems of physical distribution and reducing delivery times. The customization of information seems to help enterprises to gain control and that finding is confirmed by (Arunkundram and Sundarajan, 1998).

Therefore, the advantages from the development of electronic relationships according to the findings include better management of the supply chain both for the supplier and the buyer, quicker adaptation to the changes in the demands they have of each other, a drastic reduction in administrative costs, the attainment of lower prices in relation to physical markets, as Rayport and Sviokla (1995) revealed in their own research. Also, this ascertainment is confirmed by Sawhney and Kaplan (1999a 1999b) who state of the theory of reduced search cost which pushes down the prices of products in electronic markets. Kaplan and Garicano (2001) agree with the above view, pointing out that the most significant effect of electronic relations is the changes they make to the structure of transactions as regards the terms and cost elements that characterize them. The results of the present research confirm the findings of Strader and Shaw (1999) that the reduction in the costs of the supplier in physical and electronic markets is not the same for all companies active on the Internet.

The research showed that other cost factors participate in this philosophy and in this way it was adapted and completed by the results of the survey concerning the comparison of the supplier's costs in physical and electronic markets. Technology on its own does not constitute a competitive advantage; it must be leveraged with the rest of the company's cost data in order for it to more fully satisfy needs, a fact verified by Kleindl (2001).

The research showed the factors defining the suitability of activation in electronic markets for a company simultaneously active in physical markets. Thus the characteristics were set out of companies that can survive in the environment of the New Economy from which it emerges that the changes brought about by electronic business can hardly be characterized as revolutionary, but are probably the product of entrepreneurial growth as the factors do not especially differ between the pre-ecommerce period and the electronic one. Among the companies, it does not appear that there have been revolutionary changes in the companies active at the same time both in physical as well as in electronic commerce, as their behavior does not differ whether they are active in traditional commerce or in electronic commerce. E-commerce Buyers and Sellers indicated that they do share information amongst them in an effort to improve the services they offer to each other, introduce smoother transaction processes and also reduce transaction costs. This is an important finding as most of our sample businesses seem to enjoy the uniqueness of finding themselves in an advantageous position that other companies could possibly take some time to get themselves into.

Seller-buyer relationships characterized strategic partnerships as B2B firms operate in a strong demand, high growth, and highly competitive environment while their products characterized highly customized. Therefore the cooperation in development of tooling and manufacturing processes and coordination of JIT production and delivery between supplier and purchaser is compulsory. The marketing outline for the reassurance that the realization of the marketing programme won't be affected by the unstable electronic environment is the relational exchange, information sharing and communication. These factors are the key features to expand and increase the communication among seller –buyer and develop trust between them. As a result the information sharing increasing levels of trust reduce uncertainty and provide material incentives for co-operation. As a result relational exchange and communication consists the focal points of the electronic activation in order B2B firms achieve out their activation in electronic markets.

Managerial Implications

Firm leaders recognise the security and privacy of information as necessary prerequisite to develop the firm's effectiveness in e-commerce. This combined with the fame of the business for the procedure of creating commercial relations facilitate the presence of B2B in the new eRa environment with less possible damages. Then B2B firms will better coordinate and manage the relationships with their partners in a network committed to delivering superior value with better variety and product qquality.

FUTURE RESEARCH

A limitation is that the research sample didn't include the service sector. Another limitation may reside in the target of this study Greek medium sized firms. While enhancing the focus of this research, it may also limit the generalization of the results to some degree, at the same time creating the need for further studies in larger firms. Future research might explore, for example, how B2B firms learn about the features and services necessary to ensure success. It is hoped that by shedding light on the use of new information and communication technologies, this study will trigger further works to the improvement of B2B relationships theory and practices in a B2B e-context.

REFERENCES

Arden, M and Palmer, B 1999, 'Enabling secure applications with a public key infrastructure', *Security*, vol. 36, no. 5, pp. 81-2.

Arunkundram, R. and A. Sundararajan (1998), «An Economic Analysis of Electronic Secondary Markets: Installed Base, Technology, Durability and Firm Profitability,» *Decision Support Systems,* Vol.24, No. 1, pp. 3-16.

Birch, and Young, MA 1997, 'Financial service and the internet - What does cyberspace mean for the financial services industry?' *Internet Research: Electronic Networking Applications and Policy*, vol. 7, no. 2, pp. 120-8.

Broadbent, PE 1996, 'Transaction security: A «Net» non-issue', *DM News*, July 8, p. 17.

Blankenhorn, D 2001, 'Clued In: Quick course in the rules of wireless marketing', *B to B*, vol. 86, Oct 29, p. 15.

Boyle, BA and Alwitt, LF 1999, 'Internet use within the US plastics industry', *Industrial Marketing.*

Blundon, B. and A. Bonde (1998), «Beyond the Transaction,» *Information Week,* November 16, pp. 5ss-6ss.

Biland, AT 2000, 'A question of value -- e-commerce works best as an enabler of the personal.

Bensaou, Michael (1997). Interorganizational Cooperation: The Role of IT. Information Systems Research 8(2):107–124.

Dann, S. and S. Dann (2001), *«Strategic Internet Marketing,» John* Wiley and Sons Inc.

Donaldson Bill and Tom O' Toole (2000) Classifying relationship structures: relationship strength in industrial markets Journal of Business and Industrial Marketing volume 15 Number:7 pp: 491-506.

Donaldson Bill and Tom O' Toole (2007) Strategic Marketing Relationships John Wiley and Son Inc., NJ 07030 USA.

Dutta, S and Segev, A 1999, 'Business transformation on the Internet', *European Management Journal*, vol. 17, no. 5, pp. 466-76.

DeJesus, E 2000, 'Procurement: E-bound', *Healthcare Informatics*, vol. 17, no. 11, pp. 42-52.

Dwyer, FR, Schurr, PH and Oh, S 1987, 'Developing buyer-seller relationships', *Journal of Marketing*, vol. 51, no. 2, pp. 11-27.

Eisenhardt, K. M. and S.L. Brown (1998), «Time Pacing: Competing in Markets that Won't Stand Still,» *Harvard Business Review,* March-April, pp. 59-69.

Evans, P. and H. Wurster (1999), Blown to Bits: *How the New Technology of Information Transforms Strategy,* Harvard Business Press, Cambridge, MA.

Eid, R., Trueman, M. and Ahmed, A.M. (2006), "B2B international internet marketing: a benchmarking exercises", Benchmarking: An International Journal, Vol. 13 Nos 1/2, pp. 200-13.

Fischer, D. (2002). Textile Online: A Critical Overview. International Textile Bulletin. February, 22-26.

Fraser, J, Fraser, N and McDonald, F 2000, 'The strategic chanllenge of electronic commerce', *Supply Chain Management: An International Journal*, vol. 5, no. 1, pp. 359.

Griffith, DA and Palmer, JW 1999, 'Leveraging the Web for corporate success', *Business Horizons*, vol. 42, no. 1, pp. 3-11.

Geiger, S and Martin, S 1999, 'The internet as a relationship marketing tool - some evidence from Irish companies', *Irish Marketing Review*, vol. 12, no. 2, pp. 25-36.

Honeycutt, E, Flaherty, T and Benassi, K 1998, 'Marketing industrial products on the internet', *Industrial Marketing Management*, vol. 27, pp. 63-72.

Harridge-March, S. (2004), "Electronic marketing, the new kid on the block", Marketing Intelligence and Planning, Vol. 22 No. 3, pp. 297-309.

Hoffman, D.L. and T.P. Novak (1996), «Marketing in Hypermedia Computer-Mediated Environments: Conceptual Foundations,» *Journal of Marketing,* 60(July), 50-68.

Hicks, M 2000, 'Meeting the future - Virtual online conferencing can cut costs and boost collaboration', *PC Week*, Feb 21, p. 65.Hill, New York, pp. 19-33.

Heide, J 1994, 'Inter-organization governance in marketing channels', *Journal of Marketing*, vol. 58, no. 1, pp. 71-86.

Kalakota, R and Whinston, AB 1997, *Electronic Commerce: A Manager's Guide*, Addison-Wesley.

Kalakota, R, Robinson, M, 1999, e-business: Roadmap for Success, Addison Wesley Longman, London.

Kaplan, S. and M. Sawhney (2000), «E-Hubs: The New B2B Marketplaces,» *Harvard Business Review,* May-June, pp. 97-103.

Kleindl, B. (2001), *Strategic Electronic Marketing: Managing E-business,* South Western College Publishing, Cincinnati, OH.

Kyriazopoulos, P. and Samanta, I., (2009) *Managers' perceptions of using of e-marketing in B2B relationships* Journal SPOUDAI Publisher University of Piraeus.

Kehoe, L 2001, 'Focus shifts to security: Hackers, viruses, failing hubs - seldom have IT networks seemed so vulnerable', *Financial Times*, Oct 3, p. 15.

Kumar, N, Hibbard, J and Stern, L 1994, The nature and consequences of marketing channel intermediary commitment, MSI Working Paper.

Langford, B.E. and R. M. Cosenza (1998), «What Is Service/Good Analysis? » *Journal of Marketing Theory and Practice,* Vol. 6, No. 1, pp. 16-26.

Mahadevan, B. (2003). Making Sense of Emerging Market Structures in B2B E-commerce». California Management Review, (46), 1, 86-100.

McIvor, R. and Humphreys, P. (2006), "B2B commerce and its implications for the buyer-supplier interface", Supply Chain Management: An International Journal, Vol., Vol. 11 No. 2, pp. 131-9.

Mougayar, W. (1997), *Opening Digital Markets,* CyberManagement, Canada. Nagle, T. (1994), *The Strategy and Tactics of Pricing,* Prentice Hall.

Nelson, C. and R.James (1996), «Creative Strategy for Interactive Marketing/' in network context', *Journal of Marketing*, vol. 58, no. Oct., pp. 1-15.

Ozarsky, J. (1999), «Offline, on Message,» *Business 2.0,* August.pages?' *Australasian Marketing Journal*, vol. 7, no. 2, pp. 59-73.

O'Connor, J. and E. Galvin (2000), *Marketing in the Digital Age,* 2nd edition, Pearson Education Limited.

Pavaloia, V.D. (2009), "Web based application for SMEs economic and financial diagnose", Communications of IBIMA, Vol. 9 No. 4, pp. 24-30.

Porter, M, 2001, "Strategy and the Internet", Harvand Business Review, 62-78.

Rayport, J. F. and J.J. Sviokla (1995), «Managing in the Marketspace», *Harvard Business Review,* Nov-Dec, pp. 141-150.

Samanta, Irene, (2009) Can knowledge management assist firms to move from traditional to e-commerce: the case of Greek firms Chapter Book Social Web Evolution: Integrating Semantic Applications and Web 2.0 Technologies 13-digit ISBN: 978-1-60566-272-5 340 pages.

Samanta, Irene, (2011) *Influence B2B Relationships in Medium Sized Firms: Traditional vs. E-Commerce* - Journal of Marketing and Operations Management Research Journals Nova Science Publishers.

Sraeel, H 1996, 'Creating real value propositions with virtual banking', *Bank Systems and Technology*, vol. 33, no. 8, p. 6.

Strauss, J and Forest, R 1999, *Marketing on the Internet: Principles of Online Marketing*, Prentice Hall, New Jersey.

Stahl, B., 2002, From Product to performance: Creating business relationships, 18th IMP-Conference, Perth Urban, G.L., Sawhney, M. and S. Kaplan (1999a), «B2B E-commerce Hubs: Towards a Taxonomy of Business Models,» URL: http://gsbwww.uchicago.edu/ fac/ sLeven.kaplan/research/taxonomy.pdf.

Turner, C 2000, The information economy: business strategies *for competing in the digital age*, Kogan Page.

Webster, J 2000, 'An Alphabet Soup Of B2B Standards -- SOAP, ebXML, UDDI and others will slowly gain momentum in 2001', *Internetweek*, p. PG.45.

Yoffie, D.B. (1997), *Competing in the Age of Digital Convergence,* Boston: Harvard Business School Press.

Zineldin, 2000, 'Beyond relationship marketing: technological ship marketing', *Marketing Intelligence and Planning*, vol. 18, no. 1, pp. 9-23.

Biographical Notes

Irene Samanta obtained a degree (B.A.) in Business Administration from TEI of Piraeus (Greece), M.Sc. in International Marketing from University of Paisley (UK) and Ph.D. from the University of the West of Scotland (UK). Her Ph.D. research was on the modelling the relationships in B2B firms under e-marketing practices. Her main research interests are in the areas of e-relationships, e-marketing, international marketing and research methods.

She is working as a Lecturer in the above fields in the Department of Business Administration at TEI of Piraeus. She is author or co-author of several papers in various scientific journals, chapter-books, conference proceedings, and several articles in economic journals. She is co-author of three text books.

In: HRM and Marketing Orientation in the New Era
Editor: Panagiotis Kyriazopoulos
ISBN: 978-1-62808-959-2

Chapter 11

SUPPLY CHAIN NETWORK DESIGN OPTIMIZATION

Josefa Mula[1*], Julien Maheut[2] and Jose P. Garcia-Sabater[2]
[1]Research Centre on Production Management and Engineering (CIGIP),
Universidad Politécnica de Valencia, Spain
[2]Business Management Department,
Universidad Politécnica de Valencia, Spain

ABSTRACT

This chapter reviews several relevant works about mathematical modelling for supply chain network design problems. The purpose of this review is to identify current and future research in this field and to propose a taxonomy framework for optimization of supply chain configuration models. We are focused on optimization techniques and meta-heuristics algorithms in order to design and/or redesign a supply chain. The research objective is to provide readers with a starting point for optimization problems in supply chain network design aimed at mathematical modelling researchers. We identify the research aims and classify the works reviewed by providing the benefits and disadvantages of them. Then, the further research identified is highlighted.

1. INTRODUCTION

A supply chain is a network of facilities and distribution options that performs the functions of procurement of materials, transformation of these materials into intermediate and finished products, and the distribution of these finished products to customers. Supply chain management is a strategy through the integration of these different functions can be achieved (Shapiro, 2000). Supply chain network design is to provide an optimal platform for efficient and effective supply chain management. The design task involves the choice of facilities (plants and distribution centers) to be opened and the distribution network design to satisfy the customer demand with minimum cost. Since the multi-stage design problem is difficult to

* Corresponding author. Josefa Mula, Escuela Politécnica Superior de Alcoy, Edificio Ferrándiz y Carbonell, 2, 03801 Alcoy (Alicante), SPAIN. Tel.: + 34 96 652 84 23. Fax: + 34 96 652 85 85. E-mail addresses: fmula@cigip.upv.es, juma2@etsii.upv.es, jpgarcia@doe.upv.es.

solve optimally, researchers have utilized heuristic approaches to solve this problem. In this context, Farahani et al. (2010) provide a review on recent efforts and development in multi-criteria location problems in three categories including bi-objective, multi-objective and multi-attribute problems and their solution methods, i.e. heuristic and meta-heuristic techniques. Also, it provides an overview on various criteria used. Furthermore, Gunasekaran and Ngai (2009), considering the importance of build-to-order supply chain, present a review of the literature with the objectives of investigating the modeling and analysis of build-to-order supply chain and then developing a framework for modeling and analyzing it. One of the main findings of this research is that only limited analytical and simulation models are available to deal with the problems specific to build-to-order supply chain. Melo et al. (2009) provide a literature review of facility location models in the context of supply chain management. They concentrate their review on articles published in the last decade (including a few papers published in 2008) that go beyond location–allocation decisions (and thus, they exclude simple single facility location and pure resource allocation models). Moreover, they only consider discrete models. They list several important issues that enable a facility location model to become compatible with supply chain network design requirements, and survey the existing literature with respect to the following features: network structure and basis features, decision variables in supply chain network design, reverse logistics, other supply chain characteristics, supply chain optimization (performance measures and solution methodology) and applications.

In definitive, many approaches have been used to solve the problem of determining supply chain network design. These can be divided in five main categories: network optimization and/or mixed integer programming, stochastic optimization (Santoso et al. 2005) and robust optimization, heuristic methods, simulation (Stefanovic et al. 2009; Zhang and You, 2009) and hybrid methods, that is, methods that combine various of the above approaches. We are particularly interested in optimization, heuristic and/or hybrid methods as they are more suitable to describe concisely the problem, provide a closed group of solutions, get an optimal solution and evaluate the impact generated by changes in the inputs on the outputs measures. In this paper, an analysis of representative research on the topic is presented in an attempt to gain a better understanding of the optimization methods used in supply chain network configuration and provide a basis for future research. In general, we have selected papers based on the following main criteria to be included in this study: (i) supply chain configuration, (ii) optimization techniques and (iii) meta-heuristics algorithms. Product configuration works (Jiao and Zhang, 2005; Bin et al. 2006; Li and Chen, 2006; Li et al. 2008) have not been considered.

We analyze in detail each paper, but we do not describe or formulate the models that have been considered. This work neither intends to identify every bibliographic work nor to extend a review of them, but to provide the reader with a starting point to investigate the literature about the best methods for different supply chain network design problems. The objective of this paper is to (i) review and select representative literature; (ii) classify the selected literature based on the modeling approach, purpose, application, novelty and limitations; and (iii) identify future research directions.

The remainder of the paper consists of three other sections. The next section introduces the review methodology. Then Section 3 presents the taxonomy of the analyzed papers. Finally, the last section provides the conclusions and directions for future research.

2. Review Methodology

The search process was carried out with scientific-technical bibliographic databases which include publishing portals like Elsevier, Taylor and Francis, Wiley or Emerald. The following search criteria were applied: supply chain network design, supply chain configuration, network design, location combined with optimization and meta-heuristics techniques. Furthermore, the bibliographic references of the articles studied have served as a continuous search reference.

15 representative references were selected for the detailed study with a time frame of 5 years, in order to continue previous reviews already done. These references were obtained from journals, conferences and books. Table 1 shows the distribution of references according to the source.

Table 1. Distribution of references according to sources

Source	References
Advances in Engineering Software	1
Computers and Industrial Engineering,	3
Journal of Intelligent Manufacturing	1
Computers and Operations Research	1
European Journal of Operational Research	2
International Journal of Production Economics	2
International Journal of Advanced Manufacturing Technology	1
Proceedings of the international MultiConference of Engineers and Computer Scientists	2
Proceedings of the 37th International Conference on Computers and Industrial Engineering	1
Springer book chapter	1
TOTAL	15

3. Taxonomy

We propose five classification criteria: modeling approach, purpose, practical application, novelty and limitations. All of them are briefly described below:

Modeling approach: This approach consists in the type of representation, in this case, mathematics relationships, and the aspects to be considered in the supply chain.

Purpose: This/these is/are the objective/s defined in the mathematical model.

Practical application: This presents the application that each model considers in terms of supporting practical or case studies.

Novelty: Establish the authors' contribution in relation to the rest of the scientific literature.

Limitations: Identification of those characteristics which limit the model from being applied to certain environments.

3.1. Modelling Approach

The supply chain network design problem requires, mainly, discrete variables. Only, the reviewed work by Nagurney (2010) uses exclusively continuous variables. Also, optimization models based only on mixed-integer linear programming, multi-objective programming or network optimization are not the more representative in the scientific literature. In this context, the hybrid approaches combining mixed-integer linear programming with meta-heuristics followed by those that combine multi-objective integer linear programming with meta-heuristics are the more usually adopted by researchers. Works based on nonlinear programming are scarce. Likewise, heuristics and meta-heuristics algorithms are used as complementary techniques to solve the mathematical programming models. Resolution techniques based on tabu search, genetic algorithms, scatter search, harmony search, variable neighborhood search, rescaling search, simulated annealing, ant colony algorithms, iterated local search, hybrid taguchi-particle swarm optimization and memetic algorithms are adopted. Algorithms are, mainly, coded in C++ or Matlab. Frequently, the development and test of these algorithms are the main contribution of the research papers. Next, the details of each modeling approach used by the different reviewed works are provided.

Optimization Models

Mixed-Integer Linear Programming

Elmaraghy and Majety (2008) develop a supply chain design framework including linear/mixed integer multi-criteria optimization models for determining the identified supply chain design parameters. The selection of suppliers, determination of production quantities, inventory locations and sizes, selection of transportation method and transported quantities in a multi-stage, multi-level supply chain are investigated. Additional criteria including first-time quality and suppliers on-time delivery risk with and without allowing splitting of customer demand between suppliers are considered. LINGO is used for solving the formulated optimization problems.

Multi-Objective Programming

Afshari et al. (2010) present a multi-objective mixed integer programming formulation for location within network distribution problem to determine the volume of the inventory in both stocks and middle warehouses. The problem describes two location layers in a single-period. A weighting mechanism was used to unite all objective functions. The mix integer model is solved with LINGO software.

Network Optimization

Nagurney (2010) provides a system-optimization perspective that formulates both the supply chain design and redesign problems as variational inequalities that allows for the simultaneous determination of link capacities, through investments, and the product flows on various links, that is, the manufacturing, storage, distribution/shipment links, etc. The framework uses exclusively continuous variables and can handle linear, nonlinear and non-separable costs. The solution of their models (both design and redesign), which can handle congestion, yields the optimal supply chain network topology since those links with zero optimal capacities can, in effect, be eliminated. The models are implemented in FORTRAN.

Hybrid Models

Mixed-Integer Linear Programming with Meta-Heuristics

Altiparmak et al. (2009) propose a mixed integer programming formulation to the single-source, multi-product, multi-stage supply chain network design problem to determine the subsets of plants and distribution centers to be opened and to design the distribution network strategy that will satisfy all capacities and demand requirement for each product imposed by customers with minimum cost. The mixed integer linear programming model developed by Altiparmak et al. (2009) is solved by a heuristic approach based on a steady-state genetic algorithm for the single-source, multi-product, multi-stage supply chain network design problem. All algorithms are coded in C++ programming language.

Keskin and Üster (2007) present a mixed-integer problem formulation to solve a production distribution system design problem, which involves the determination of the best configuration, regarding location and size of the plants and distribution centers, their technology content, and product offerings and transportation decisions, for achieving a firm's long term goals. The authors consider a capacitated two-stage multi-commodity (multi-product) production distribution system design problem where: in the first stage, the products are transported from capacitated plants to capacitated distribution centers; and, in the second stage, they are shipped from distribution centers to retailer (customer) locations to satisfy the demands there for a variety of products. In their solution procedures, Keskin and Üster (2007) employ three alternative methods that include an exact method using CPLEX 9.0 (CPLEX is a trademark of ILOG, Inc.) and two heuristic approaches based on scatter search and tabu search meta-heuristics. The algorithms are implemented using C++.

Rahimi et al. (2010) present a mixed integer programming model to select the optimum numbers, locations and capacities of plants and warehouses to open so that all customer demand is satisfied at minimum total costs of the distribution network (including transportation and production costs). This study allows for multiple levels of capacities available to the warehouses and plants. Rahimi et al. (2010) use a heuristic procedure which contains two sub-procedures. They use harmony-search meta-heuristic as the main procedure and linear programming to solve a transshipment problem as a subroutine at any iteration of the main procedure. The problem has been coded using Matlab.

Rego and Sousa (2009) propose a mixed integer programming model to address the health care supply chain configuration problem that consists on deciding whether, when, and how to use an existing supply chain structure (e.g., deciding where to locate storage points, how to use those locations in the existing facilities, and how to move materials/people between those points). The model is a formulation of the multi-stage, multi-level, multi-product production-distribution system planning problem, based on a graph representation of the problem. The multi-period dimension of the problem is incorporated in the model through the replication of the supply chain with "inventory edges" connecting storage areas (i.e., at hospital distribution centers and point of care units) in subsequent periods. The authors develop two alternative approaches to solve the model: a tabu search algorithm and a hybrid algorithm based on tabu search and variable neighbourhood search). The algorithms were implemented in C++.

Ross and Jayaraman (2008) propose two mixed integer linear programming models, a strategic model and an executional model, for the location of cross-docks and distribution centers in supply chain network design. The model is characterized by multiple product families, a central manufacturing plant site, multiple cross-docking and distribution center sites, and retail outlets which demand multiple units of several commodities. The strategic model keeps track of the set of cross-docks and warehouses to open and operate as well as link the set of customer zones that are assigned to open cross-docks. The executional model takes the output from the strategic model as its input and solves the problem to identify the quantity of products to be shipped to open warehouses, the quantity to be shipped from open warehouses to open cross-docks and the quantity to be shipped from open cross-docks to customer demand zones. Then, two meta-heuristics based on simulated annealing were developed for computational testing, TABU-SA and RESCALE-SA. All algorithms are coded in C++ programming language. TABU-SA provides better quality solutions in less time, but RESCALE-SA provides a more exhaustive search. The authors recommend to integrate traditional simulated annealing with either a tabu search approach or re-scaling approach for the cross-docking problem.

Wang (2009) focuses on a multiple echelon defective (with losses of production) supply chain network design for choosing the appropriate corporations from a number of potential participators to become involved in the network, and to make optimal production–distribution planning decisions. The supply chain system contains several supply systems at various levels, and each supply system consists of many suppliers. When some suppliers encounter the production losses, the whole system will not meet the needs of customers. The mathematical model proposed is comprised of three modules or mixed integer linear programming models. Module 1 satisfies the quantity that customers need as the restrictions and pursue the minimum number of suppliers conforming to these restrictions to shrink the network framework and shorten the operation time. Module 2 will seek the combination of suppliers with the maximum yield rate from the feasible solutions satisfying Module 1, because the higher the yield rate is, the smaller the production losses of the supply chain are. Module 3 carries out distribution that must accord with the restrictions to the capacity of all the suppliers. Next, the author presents a novel two-phase mathematical approach called the 'two-phase ant colony algorithm' for defective supply chain network design, which is based on ant colony algorithms. To demonstrate the effectiveness and efficiency of the proposed method, the comparing of the numerical experiments with the results of the two-phase ant colony algorithm and the single-phase ant colony algorithm are performed by utilizing statistical method t-test of the mean values for the T-score.

Mixed-Integer Non Linear Programming with Meta-Heuristics

Courdeau et al. (2008) present a non linear integer programming formulation for the logistics network design problem, decisions must be made regarding: the selection of suppliers; the location of plants and warehouses; the assignment of raw materials to suppliers and of finished products to plants and warehouses (i.e., the activity mix of each facility); the flows of raw materials and finished products through the network. These decisions must be made in order to satisfy customer demand while minimizing the sum of fixed and variable costs associated with procurement, production, warehousing and transportation. Courdeau et al. (2008) introduce an iterated local search heuristic for the logistics network design problem variant arising when each raw material should be supplied by a unique supplier, and each finished product should be produced and distributed by a unique plant and a unique warehouse, respectively. The iterated local search heuristic exploits the combinatorial nature of the problem and relies on simple moves combined within a descent algorithm. Several perturbation operators are used to allow a broad exploration of the solution space.

Multi-Objective Programming with Meta-Heuristics

Altiparmak et al. (2006) proposes a multi-objective mixed-integer non-linear programming model to design the supply chain network for the product, i.e. select the suppliers, determine the subsets of plants and distribution centers to be opened and design the distribution network strategy that will satisfy all capacities and demand requirement for the product imposed by customers. The problem is a single-product, multi-stage supply chain network design problem. Altiparmak et al. (2006) develop a genetic algorithm to find the set of Pareto optimal solutions for solving the multi-objective mixed integer non-linear supply chain network design problem which was met on a producer of the plastic products in Turkey. All algorithms are coded in C++ programming language.

Bachlaus et al. (2008) develop a multi-objective mixed-integer linear programming model to design a multi-echelon supply chain network considering agility as a key design criterion. The design network conceived addresses a class of five echelons of supply chains including suppliers, plants, distribution centers, crossdocks and customer zones that aims to minimize the cost (fixed and variable) and maximizes the plant flexibility and volume flexibility. More specifically, the authors attempt to integrate the typical supply chain network by incorporating crossdocks sites at the intermediate level of distribution centers and customer zones. Bachlaus et al. (2008) propose a hybrid taguchi-particle swarm optimization algorithm to solve the agile supply chain optimization problem. The hybrid taguchi-particle swarm optimization meta-heuristic is a computational paradigm that draws its traits from the social and cognitive behavior of swarms. In contrast of genetic algorithms and other evolutionary strategies which exploit the competitive characteristics of biological evolution (e.g. survival of the fittest) particle swarm optimization exploits cooperative and social aspects.

Che and Chiang (2010) focus on performing the build-to-order supply chain network. The planning is designed to integrate supplier selection, product assembly, as well as the logistic distribution system of the supply chain in order to meet market demands. With multiple suppliers and multiple customer needs, the assembly model can be divided into several sub-assembly steps by applicable sequence. Considering three evaluation criteria, namely costs, delivery time, and quality, a multi-objective optimization mathematical model is established for the build-to-order supply chain planning in this study.

Che and Chiang (2010) apply a Pareto genetic algorithm to find solutions for the mathematical model. In addition, regarding build-to-order supply chain problems solving, the authors proposes a modified Pareto genetic algorithm to improve the solution quality through revision of crossover and mutation operations. After application and analysis of cases, the modified Pareto genetic algorithm is found to be superior to the traditional Pareto genetic algorithm in solution performance.

Moncayo and Zhang (2007) propose a multi-objective optimization approach to determine the supply chain design for a product comprising different subassemblies. There might be multiple suppliers that could supply the same components as well as many manufacturers that could assemble the product. Each of these options is differentiated by its lead time and cost. Given all the possible options the configuration problem is to select the options that minimise the total cost while keeping the total lead time within the orders' due date. Moncayo and Zhang (2007) introduce a Pareto ant colony optimization as an especially effective meta-heuristic for solving the problem of supply chain design. A number of ant colonies generate a Pareto optimal set of solutions of supply chain.

Table 2. Modeling approach codes

Modeling approach	Detail	Code
Linear Programming	Mixed Integer/Integer Linear Programming	ILP
Non Linear Programming	Mixed Integer/Integer Non Linear Programming	INLP
Multi-objective Programming	Multi-objective Integer Linear Programming Multi-objective Non Linear Integer Programming	MOILP MONLIP
Network Optimization	Network Optimization	NO
Heurístics and Meta-heuristics Algorithms	Heurístics and Meta-heurístics Algorithms	HEU

Table 3. Modeling approach of the reviewed works

Author	ILP	INLP	MOILP	MONLIP	NO	HEU
Afshari et al. (2010)			X			
Altiparmak et al. (2009)	X					X
Altiparmak et al.(2006)				X		X
Bachlaus et al. (2008)			X			X
Che and Chiang (2010)			X			X
Courdeau et al. (2008)		X				X
Elmaraghy and Majety (2008)	X					
Keskin and Üster (2007)	X					X
Moncayo and Zhang (2007)			X			X
Nagurney (2010)					X	
Pishvaee et al. (2010)			X	X		X
Rahimi et al. (2010)	X					X
Rego and Sousa (2009)	X					X
Ross and Jayaraman (2008)	X					X
Wang (2009)	X					X

Pishvaee et al. (2010) propose a model for integrated logistics network design to avoid the sub-optimality caused by a separate, sequential design of forward and reverse logistics networks. It addresses the issue of integrated multi-objective, multi-stage forward/reverse logistics network design including production, distribution, collection/inspection, recovery and disposal facilities with multiple capacity levels.

To design integrated forward/reverse logistics networks, a generalized multi-objective mixed integer non-linear programming formulation and a multi-objective mixed-integer linear programming variant model are developed. In order to find the set of non-dominated solutions, Pishvaee et al. (2010) develop an efficient multi-objective memetic algorithm. The proposed solution algorithm uses a new dynamic search strategy by employing three different local searches.

To evaluate the performance of the multi-objective memetic algorithm for integrated forward/reverse logistics network design problem, the multi-objective memetic algorithm is compared to the multi-objective genetic algorithm of Altiparmark et al. (2006). Both algorithms are coded in MATLAB 7.0. Numerical results show that the proposed multi-objective memetic algorithm outperformed the existing multi-objective genetic algorithm in terms of average ratio of Pareto-optimal solutions obtained. Also, the comparison between the multi-objective memetic algorithm and LINGO shows that the quality of solutions obtained by the multi-objective memetic algorithm on multiple capacity test problems is reasonable.

Table 2 provides the various types of modeling approach used in the works reviewed and Table 3 groups the reviewed works by the modeling approach they employ.

3.2. Purpose

These are considered quantitative aspects related to costs, customer service and supply chain operation. Regarding costs, the minimization of costs (MIC) and the maximization of gross yield rate (MAGYR) are contemplated, while the maximization of the service level (MASL), the minimization of delivery dates (MID), the maximization of the flexibility in volume distribution and delivery (MAF) and the maximization of the responsiveness of the network (MAR) are considered for customer services. The maximization of capacity utilization (MACU), the maximization of quality (MAQ) and the minimization of the number of partners (MINP) are also taken into account for supply chain operation. Table 4 classifies the works reviewed in terms of the purpose considered. The multi-objective model by Afshari et al. (2010) considers two objectives: (i) the minimization of transportation cost between central and regional warehouses, between regional warehouses and customers, and the minimization of installation cost for central warehouses and regional warehouses; and (ii) the maximization of the level of the customer satisfaction. Altiparmak et al. (2009) consider an objective function that minimizes the total cost of the supply chain. It consists of the fixed cost of operating and opening plants and distribution centers, the variable costs of production and distribution, costs of the transportation of raw materials from suppliers to plants, the transportation of the finished products from plants to distribution centers and from distribution centers to customers.

The mixed-integer non-linear programming model by Altiparmak et al. (2006) considers three objectives: minimization of the total cost of the supply chain (the fixed costs of operating and opening plants and distribution centers, the variable costs of transportation raw material from suppliers to plants and the transportation the product from plants to customers through distribution centers); maximization of customer services that can be rendered to customers in terms of acceptable delivery time (is the total customer demand, in %, that can be delivered within the stipulated access time); and maximization of capacity utilization balance for distribution centers (it is measured by the mean square error of capacity utilization ratios).

Table 4. Purpose of the reviewed works

	Costs		Customer				Operation		
Author	MIC	MAGYR	MASL	MID	MAF	MAR	MACU	MAQ	MINP
Afshari et al. (2010)	X								
Altiparmak et al. (2009)	X								
Altiparmak et al. (2006)	X		X				X		
Bachlaus et al. (2008)	X				X				
Che and Chiang (2010)	X			X				X	
Courdeau et al. (2008)	X								
Elmaraghy and Majety (2008)	X								
Keskin and Üster (2007)	X								
Moncayo and Zhang (2007)	X			X					
Nagurney (2010)	X			X					
Pishvaee et al. (2010)	X					X			
Rahimi et al. (2010)	X								
Rego and Sousa (2009)	X								
Ross and Jayaraman (2008)	X								
Wang (2009)	X	X							X

Bachlaus et al. (2008) formulate a multi-objective optimization model that aims to minimize the cost (fixed and variable) and maximizes the plant flexibility and volume flexibility. The total cost function minimizes the total fixed and variable costs, and is divided into four components: (i) the raw material purchase cost and transportation cost from suppliers to plants; (ii) the fixed and variable costs associated with plant operations; (iii) the variable cost of handling and inventory of products at distribution centers, and (iv) the transportation of products from plant to distribution centers, the transportation cost to ship product families from distribution centers to cross-docks and distribution costs to ship product families from cross-docks to customer zones. The flexibility objective conceived in this paper is divided into two types viz: distribution volume flexibility and delivery flexibility. Che and Chiang (2010) consider three objectives: obtain the minimum of the total cost including order cost, purchase cost, and transport cost; obtain the minimum delivery time of purchased parts transported to customers; and obtain the maximum part quality, which is calculated by yield/throughput in the production system of supplier. Courdeau et al. (2008) use an objective function to minimize the sum of all fixed and variable costs. Variable costs may include not only transportation expenses but also relevant acquisition, production and storage costs. Elmaraghy and Majety (2008) consider an objective function to minimize the cost of the total supply chain, which is the sum of production cost, inventory carrying cost, cost of on-time delivery and transportation cost in the complete supply chain.

In the objective function considered by Keskin and Üster (2007), the first term represents the fixed cost of locating the distribution centers, the second term is the total transportation costs from the distribution center to the customers, and the third term is the total transportation costs from the plants to the distribution centers.

The work by Moncayo and Zhang (2007) pursue to minimize two objectives: the total cost, which is the cost of obtaining components plus the cost of assembling plus the cost of delivering; and the time in which a manufacturing plant assemblies an assembly, which is the time of supplying the components plus the time of producing the assembly in a manufacturing plant.

The proposal by Nagurney (2010) seeks to determine the optimal levels of product processed on each supply chain network link coupled with the optimal levels of capacity investments in its supply chain network activities subject to the minimization of the total cost where the total cost includes the total cost of operating (production, storage and distribution activities) the various links and the total cost of capacity investments.

Pishvaee et al. (2010) consider a bi-objective model that pursues the minimization of total costs, which include both the tradeoff of fixed opening costs of facilities and variable transportation costs, and the maximization of the responsiveness of the network (forward and reverse responsiveness).

The model by Rahimi et al. (2010) minimizes total costs made of: the costs to serve the demands of customers from the warehouses, the costs of shipments from the plants to the warehouses, and the costs associated with opening and operating the warehouses and the plants.

Rego and Sousa (2009) consider an objective function that minimizes the sum of fixed administrative costs, fixed transportation costs and variable transportation costs, acquisition costs and inventory carrying costs.

Ross and Jayaraman (2008) use a strategic model and an executional model. The strategic model aims to minimize three types of costs. The first type of costs is fixed costs associated with operating open warehouses and cross-docks. The second are costs to transport multiple products from the warehouses to cross-docks. The third type are carrying costs (can also include holding costs and inventory costs) to supply multiple units of products from cross-docks to customer zones.

The executional model minimizes the transportation cost incurred by shipping product families to warehouses, the transshipment costs to ship product families from warehouses to cross-docks and the distribution costs to ship product families from cross-docks to customer zones.

Wang (2009) develops three modules or mixed integer linear programming models. Module 1 identifies the optimal minimum number of partners. Module 2 pursues the maximization of the gross yield rate. Module 3 pursues the minimization of T-score in terms of manufacturing and transportation costs having into account the reliability of partners.

As is illustrated in Table 4, the economy objectives are dominant followed by service-based objectives and operation-based objectives.

Table 5. Application of the reviewed works

Authors	Practical applications vs. illustrative examples
Afshari et al. (2010)	A practical case in an automotive part distribution corporation.
Altiparmak et al. (2009)	A total of 620 numerical examples are considered. Parameters of the problem are generated by a uniform distribution.
Altiparmak et al (2006)	A practical case with data obtained from a company which is one of the producers of plastic products in Turkey. The company has to import PVC from foreign suppliers. The company intends to establish new plants. Locations of distribution centers had been determined according to demand densities of 63 customer zones to be served and access time from distribution centers to customer zones.
Bachlaus et al. (2008)	The problem instances conceived in this paper corresponds to the dataset of a leading steel manufacturing company.
Chen and Chiang (2010)	An illustrative example involving a two-stage supply chain network is presented to demonstrate the effectiveness of the proposed approach.
Courdeau et al. (2008)	The performance of the algorithm is evaluated on randomly generated instances, and the solutions are compared with lower bounds computed by solving the linear programming relaxation of the problem.
Elmaraghy and Majety (2008)	A case study of typical automotive power train supply chain design and decision issues is used to illustrate the effect of various factors.
Keskin and Üster (2007)	They are constructed 10 random problems in each of the eight data sets using uniform distributions with the corresponding ranges of parameters
Moncayo and Zhang (2007)	An experimental example of a notebook supply chain is used to test the algorithm and show the benefits of utilizing two pheromones matrices and multiple ant colonies in supply chain optimization problems.
Nagurney (2010)	They illustrate the new framework with numerical examples that demonstrate the practicality and flexibility of the approach.
Pishvaee et al. (2010)	The algorithms are tested on seven test problems of different sizes selected in the range of test problems in the recent literature. Other parameters are generated randomly using uniform distribution.
Rahimi et al. (2010)	They use a simple numerical example.
Rego and Sousa (2009)	The approach has been tested on a group of problem instances based on real data and constructed with the support of hospital supply departments.
Ross and Jayaraman (2008)	Five problems were developed and solved five times. The setup for each problem is described by the number of warehouses, the number of cross-docks, the number of customer zones, the number of product families, and the operating cost structure that are used. The model implied more than 4000 decision variables and 5000 constraints.
Wang (2009)	The authors provide a real life example to illustrate the practicability as well as a comparison with the results of the single-phase ant colony optimization, in order to demonstrate the efficiency of their proposed model.

3.3. Practical Application

Table 5 describes the practical application, case studies or illustrative examples to validate the purposes of the works reviewed. Most of the analyzed models and algorithms are tested on artificial data sets.

Table 6. Novelty of the reviewed works

Authors	Novelty
Afshari et al. (2010)	The results showed to be practical and useful because of great similarities between the model and the studies case and ensured that this model can be applied for other cases.
Altiparmak et al. (2009)	The steady-state genetic algorithm can be used as an effective and efficient tool for designing the supply chain networks.
Altiparmak et al. (2006)	The genetic algorithm can be used as an acceptable tool for the multi-objective supply chain network problem.
Bachlaus et al. (2008)	The proposed solution methodology exhibits the global exploration capability to exploit the optimal or near optimal particles with faster convergence rate. Owing to the effective solutions obtained by the hybrid taguchi-particle swarm optimization algorithm, this approach seems to be an attractive way for a supply chain manager to determine location and distribution strategies under different experimental settings.
Che and Chiang (2010)	The proposed modified Pareto genetic algorithm is effective in solving integrated supplier selection, product assembly, and logistic distribution planning problems.
Courdeau et al. (2008)	The proposed heuristic is very stable. This heuristic is both easy to implement and fast. It is also flexible in the sense that it could be adapted to handle additional constraints such as single-sourcing constraints which require each customer to receive all products from the same warehouse. Computational experiments show that the heuristic clearly outperforms the branch-and-bound of CPLEX both in computation times and solution quality.
Elmaraghy and Majety (2008)	The developed framework allows customization to suit scenarios and considerations specific to a company at a given time. For example, the presented supply chain design framework assumes that each product unit requires one unit each of the individual components in the bill of materials. However, it can be easily extended to an expanded bill of materials with one-to-many relationships, which increase the problem size by adding more of the same cost items but the model structure would remain the same.
Keskin and Üster (2007)	Scatter search and tabu search algorithms that perform very well even on large size problems. The scatter search heuristic combined with the node-exchange heuristic and path relinking results in better optimality gaps and a high number of optimal solutions, thus, proving to be an effective method for solving the production distribution system design problem.
Moncayo and Zhang (2007)	There were tested two ways in which the quantity of pheromones in the pheromone matrix is incremented. In one way, this increment is a function of the two objectives, cost and time, while in the other the pheromone matrix is divided into two pheromones, one for the cost and another one for the time. It could be concluded that the number of solutions do not depend on if the pheromone is split or is a function of the two variables because both method explore the same solution space.
Nagurney (2010)	Unlike a classical system-optimization formulation, with origins in transportation science, the author explicitly considers capacities on the links as design variables of the proposed networks.
Pishvasee et al. (2010)	The main contribution consists of its ability to easily handle multiple capacity levels for the facilities within the forward/reverse logistics network and applying dynamic local search strategy.
Rahimi et al. (2010)	They present a unified model of the problem that includes the numbers, locations, and capacities of both warehouses and plants as decision variables of the model and develops at the same time the optimal distributing strategy from the plants to the warehouses and from the warehouses to the customers.
Rego and Sousa (2009)	This paper intends to contribute to the improvement of the logistic organization of health care services, through the development of an approach to support the formulation and implementation of their supply chain configuration strategies.
Ross and Jayaraman (2008)	They are focused in solving the cross-dock model, distribution center network design location problem.
Wang (2009)	They show that for this kind of large scale problem, the two-phase ant colony approach shows to be the better solution over that of the single-phase ant colony optimization.

3.4. Novelty

Table 6 describes the main novelty contributed by all the works reviewed.

3.5. Limitations

Table 7 summarizes the main limitations identified in all the works reviewed.

Table 7. Limitations of the reviewed works

Authors	Limitations
Afshari et al. (2010)	The model does not consider the multi-stage situation. There are two potential central warehouses that at least one of them should be located. There are not considered demand uncertainties.
Altiparmak et al. (2009)	The model does not consider the multi-source situation. There are not considered demand uncertainties.
Altiparmak et al. (2006)	The model does not consider the multi-source and multi-product situation. There are not considered demand and cost uncertainties. Computational efficiency could be improved.
Bachlaus et al. (2008)	Different search techniques should be developed that have the potential to search the optimal solution in minimum computational time. There are not considered demand uncertainties.
Che and Chiang (2010)	The demand is known and no shortages are considered. All evaluation criteria have equal weights. Parts assembly is under the assembly schemes. Assembly activity begins after all parts are received. Assembly and transportation losses are not considered. It considers a single-period planning.
Courdeau et al. (2008)	It considers a single-country environment and a single-period planning horizon. Additional considerations such as single-sourcing constraints and multiple transportation modes with different fixed and variable costs can be handled.
Elmaraghy and Majety (2008)	All criteria were weighted equally in the objective function. There are not considered demand uncertainties.
Keskin and Üster (2007)	The proposed model is thought for two-stage distribution center location decisions. There are not considered demand uncertainties.
Moncayo and Zhang (2007)	Although both methods proposed explore the same solution space, the Pareto optimal set of solutions generated by everyone is different. It means that depending on the preference parameters given by the planner a Pareto optimal set of solutions could be obtained. There are not considered demand uncertainties.
Nagurney (2010)	It considers a single product environment. Extensions could include risk and uncertainty, and environmental emissions, if sustainability is the goal, as well as to explicitly include the global dimensions with the addition of taxes, tariffs, exchange rates, etc.
Pishvaee et al. (2010)	It considers a single product environment. There are not considered demand uncertainties. It could be compared with other multi-objective meta-heuristics algorithms such as multi- objective tabu search or multi-objective scatter search.
Rahimi et al. (2010)	It considers a single product and at one time horizon.
Rego and Sousa (2009)	The experiments have been designed for illustrative purposes, and further work and additional algorithmic tuning are required.
Ross and Jayaraman (2008)	Focused on the strategic decision level, operational decisions as shipment and inventory control policies remain unresolved.
Wang (2009)	It considers a single product. Only one piece of order from customer at a time. Transportation losses are not considered. Re-processing orders of product are not considered

Conclusion

This work presents a representative selection of optimization models for supply chain network design. To study the analyzed works, a classification based on the analysis of five aspects has been proposed: modeling approach, purpose, practical application, novelty and limitations. The conclusions drawn from this work affirm that: (1) hybrid approaches combining classical optimization models such as mixed-integer linear programming and multi-objective mixed-integer linear programming with meta-heuristics are mainly adopted; (2) the minimization of costs by itself or combined, firstly, with other customer-based criteria and, secondly, with other operation-based criteria are the purposes dominant; (3) more proposed models validated by numerical examples are presented than case studies applied to real supply chains; (4) the main novelties of these works are related to the development of meta-heuristics algorithms rather than the modeling of supply chain network design problems; and (5) the main limitations identified are referred to the simple nature of the modeled problem (single-stage, single-source, single-product or single-period planning, among others) what is accord to the conclusion (3). Other limitations identified are the low computational efficiency and the lack of consideration of uncertainties in parameters such as demand.

After this work, we pointed out gaps in the literature with proposed future lines of research: (1) there is a need of improved supply chain network design models based on real-world supply chains, these models should be formulated according to the studied supply chain structure, the supply chain characteristics and its industry sector; (2) optimization models for supply chain network design should be tested with the most possible number of meta-heuristics algorithms in order to provide a good characterization of their usefulness for long range problems; (3) incorporate the meta-heuristics algorithms in a decision support system; (4) the incorporation of uncertainty in supply chain network design models could be achieved by using fuzzy mathematical programming; and (5) applying the supply chain network design models to real case studies in order to validate them is necessary. In this point, the collaboration with companies is crucial. Finally, this issue reflects the gap to be bridged between academic research and commercial applications. In an ideal world, academic research would address real world modeling needs not captured by commercial systems. For example, the fuzzy programming processing of demand and other uncertain factors, or, the integration of vehicle routing with a location analysis of distribution centers.

Acknowledgment

This work has been funded by the European Commission project entitled 'Resilient Multi-plant Networks (REMPLANET) (Ref. FP7-NMP2-SL-2009-229333)'.

References

Afshari, H., Amin-Nayeri, M., Jaafari, A.A. (2010). A multi-objective approach for multi-commodity location within distribution network design problem concurrent design of product modules structure and global supply chain configuration. *Proceedings of the international MultiConference of Engineers and Computer Scientists Vol III*, IMECS 2010, March 17-19,

Altiparmak, F., Gen, M., Lin, L., Paksoy, T. (2006). A genetic algorithm approach for multi-objective optimization of supply chain networks. *Computers and Industrial Engineering,* 51, 196-215.

Altiparmak, F., Gen, M., Lin, L., Karaoglan, I. (2009). A steady-state genetic algorithm for multi-product supply chain network design. *Computers and Industrial Engineering*, 56, 521-537.

Bachlaus, M., Kumar, M., Pandey, M.K., Mahajan, C., Shankar, R., Tiwari, M.K. (2008). Designing an integrated multi-echelon agile supply chain network: a hybrid taguchi-particle swarm optimization approach. *Journal of Intelligent Manufacturing*, 19, 747–761.

Bin, L., Liping, C., Zhendong, H., Yifang, Z. (2006). Product configuration optimization using a multiobjective genetic algorithm. *International Journal of Advanced Manufacturing Technology*, 30, 20–29.

Che, Z.H., Chiang, C.J. (2010). A modified Pareto genetic algorithm for multi-objective build-to-order supply chain planning with product assembly. *Advances in Engineering Software*. In press.

Cordeau, J.F., Laporte, G., Pasin, F. (2008). An iterated local search heuristic for the logistics network design problem with single assignment. *International Journal of Production Economics,* 113, 626-640.

ElMaraghy, H.A, Majety, R. (2008). Integrated supply chain design using multi-criteria optimization. *International Journal of Advanced Manufacturing Te*chnology, 37, 371–399.

Farahani, R.Z., SteadieSeifi, M., Asgari, N. (2010). Multiple criteria facility location problems: A survey. *Applied Mathematical Modelling*, 34, 1689–1709.

Gunasekaran, A., Ngai, E.W.T. (2009). Modeling and analysis of build-to-order supply chains. *European Journal of Operational Research*, 195, 319-334.

Jiao, J., Zhang, L., Prasanna, K. (2005). Process Variety Modeling for Process Configuration in Mass Customization: An Approach based on Object-Oriented Petri-Nets with Changeable Structures. *International Journal of Flexible Manufacturing Systems*, 16, (4), 335-361.

Keskin, B.B., Üster H. (2007). Meta-heuristic approaches with memory and evolution for a multi-product production/distribution system design problem. *European Journal of Operational Research*, 182, 663–682.

Li, L., Huang, G.Q., Newman, S.T. (2008). A cooperative coevolutionary algorithm for design of platform-based mass customized products. *Journal of Intelligent Manufacturing*, 19, 507–519.

Melo, M.T., Nickei, S., Saldanha-da-Gama, F. (2009). Facility location and supply chain management - A review. *European Journal of Operational Research*, 196, 401-412.

Moncayo-Martínez, L.A., Zhang D. (2007). Pareto ant colony optimisation: a meta-heuristic approach to supply chain design. *Proceedings of the 37th International Conference on Computers and Industrial Engineering,* Alexandria, Egypt, October 20-23.

Nagurney, A. (2010). Optimal supply chain network design and redesign at minimal total cost and with demand satisfaction. *International Journal of Production Economics*, 128, 200-208.

Pishvaee, M.S, Farahani, R.Z, Dullaert, W. (2010). A memetic algorithm for bi-objective integrated forward/reverse logistics network design. *Computers and Operations Research*, 37, 1100–1112.

Rahimi, M., Hemmati, A., Baygi, M.B., Mirpourian, S.M., Jaafari A.A. (2010). A Heuristic Procedure for Designing a Distribution Network in a Supply Chain System Using Harmony Search Meta-heuristic and Linear Programming. *Proceedings of the international MultiConference of Engineers and Computer Scientists* Vol III, Hong Kong, March 17-19.

Rego, N., de Sousa, J.P. (2009). Supporting the definition of strategies for the configuration of health care supply chains. S. Voß et al. (eds.). In: *Logistik Management: Systeme, Methoden, Integration*. Ein Physica Verlag Heidelberg Buch, Springer, pp. 435-456.

Ross, A., Jayaraman, V. (2008). An evaluation of new heuristics for the location of cross-docks distribution centers in supply chain network design. *Computers and Industrial Engineering,* 55, 64-79.

Santoso T., Ahmed S., Goetschalckx M., Shapiro A. (2005). A stochastic programming approach for supply chain network design under uncertainty. *European Journal of Operational Research*, 167, 96–115.

Shapiro, J.F. (2000). *Modeling the supply chain*. Pacific Grove: Duxbury Press.

Stefanovic, D., Stefanovic, N., Radenkovic, B. (2009). Simulation Modelling Practice and Theory. *Simulation Modelling Practice and Theory*, 17, 743–766.

Wang, H.S. (2009). A two-phase ant colony algorithm for multi-echelon defective supply chain network design. *European Journal of Operational Research*, 192, 243–252.

Zhang, L., You, X., Jiao, J., Helo, P. (2009). Supply chain configuration with co-ordinated product, process and logistics decisions: an approach based on Petri nets. *International Journal of Production Research,* 47, (23), 6681-6706.

In: HRM and Marketing Orientation in the New Era
Editor: Panagiotis Kyriazopoulos
ISBN: 978-1-62808-959-2

Chapter 12

School Accidents' Information Management: An Assessment of *SARIS* Pilot Implementation in the Greek Educational Sector

Athanassios Vozikis and Yannis A. Pollalis*
Departmant of Economics Science, University of Piraeus, Greece

Abstract

Accidental injuries are the leading cause of deaths among children in the western world. Research in various countries indicates that 10 to 25 percent of school-aged children injuries occur in (and around) school environment. However, this reality has not received the attention it deserves from the public educational and health community. Especially in Greece, as our research unveils, the absence of mechanisms for collecting, recording, reporting and analyzing school accidents' data is more than obvious. The main purpose of our research is to present the analysis and development of a *School Accidents Reporting Information System* (*SARIS*) and to evaluate its pilot implementation in the Greek educational sector. Moreover, our scope is to highlight *SARIS* importance in the achievement of injury prevention and health promotion objectives and to make propositions for its deployment and utilization in the context of public health and safety prevention policies.

Keywords: School accidents, information management, accident reporting systems, educational sector, implementation for information systems

1. Introduction

Accidents and premature deaths due to injuries rank high on the list of health burdens to society and individuals, globally and specifically in the E.U. (European Commission,

* Address for correspondence: Professor Yannis A. Pollalis; University of Piraeus; Department of Economic Science; 80, Karaoli and Dimitriou street,;18534 Piraeus , Greece; Tel: 210 4142353; Fax: 210 4142301; E-mail: yannis@unipi.gr.

2007). Injury is the leading cause of death for children in Europe (Graph 1) and, between the ages of 1 and 14 years, an injury death occurs at twice the rate of a death from cancer, or 8 times that of a respiratory-related death (Eurostat, 2006). (European Child Safety Alliance, 2007), (European Child Safety Alliance, 2001).

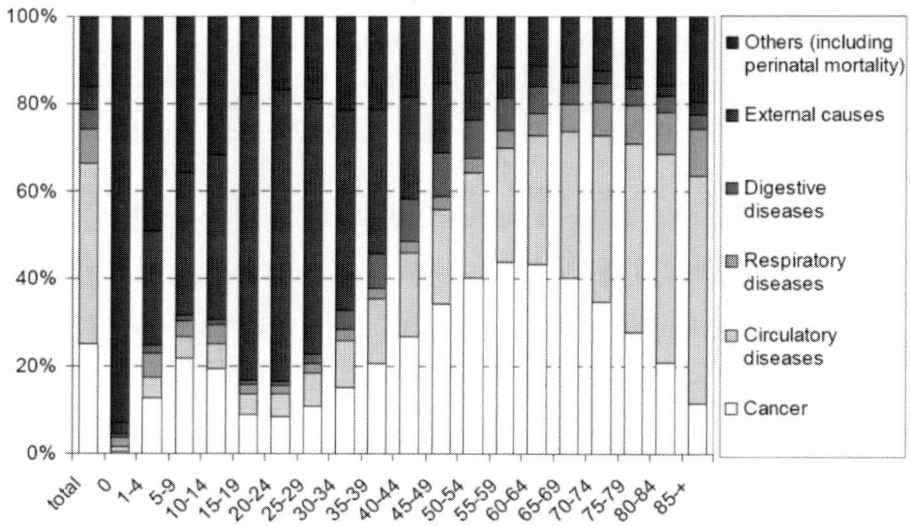

Source: EUROSTAT Causes of Death (COD), 2006.

Graph 1. Leading causes of death in the European Union by age group.

Despite the injury reductions and safety improvements over the last 20 to 30 years injury remains the leading cause of death for children and adolescents in every Member State in Europe, and more children and adolescents die of injuries than all other causes combined.

Of the 55,000 children under 20 years who die each year in the European Union, approximately 21% or a total of 13,000 deaths, are due to unintentional injuries (European Child Safety Alliance, 2007), (European Child Safety Alliance, 2001). There is great variability between the best performing countries compared to the injury rates that are 5 times higher in the countries with the poorer performance. Of the 18 countries that participated in the study, the highest injury rates are seen in Greece, Estonia and Belgium (Graph 2).

Injury is the leading cause of death in children and adolescents aged 0-19 years in Greece, as well. In 2005, 287 children and adolescents in this age group died as a result of injury. If the rate of injury death in Greece could be reduced to the level of the Netherlands, one of the safest countries in Europe, it is estimated that 140 or 49% of these lives could have been saved (European Child Safety Alliance, 2009).

Recent data from research in various countries indicates that 10 to 25 percent of school-aged children injuries occur in (and around) school environment (National Centre for Injury Prevention and Control, 2008), (WHO, 2008).

In this paper we present the conclusions of the pilot implementation of a Web- based School Accidents Reporting Information System (*SARIS*), developed to collect primary data of school accidents and consequently to facilitate the detection of their main causes, from a sample of schools in the Greek Secondary Education. For accomplishing our research, the creation and participation of a school network was assured, with different characteristics (building, region, number of students, school hours etc), so that comparisons to be made possible and results to be drawn. Finally, we make propositions for the deployment and utilization of *SARIS* in the context of public health and safety prevention policies.

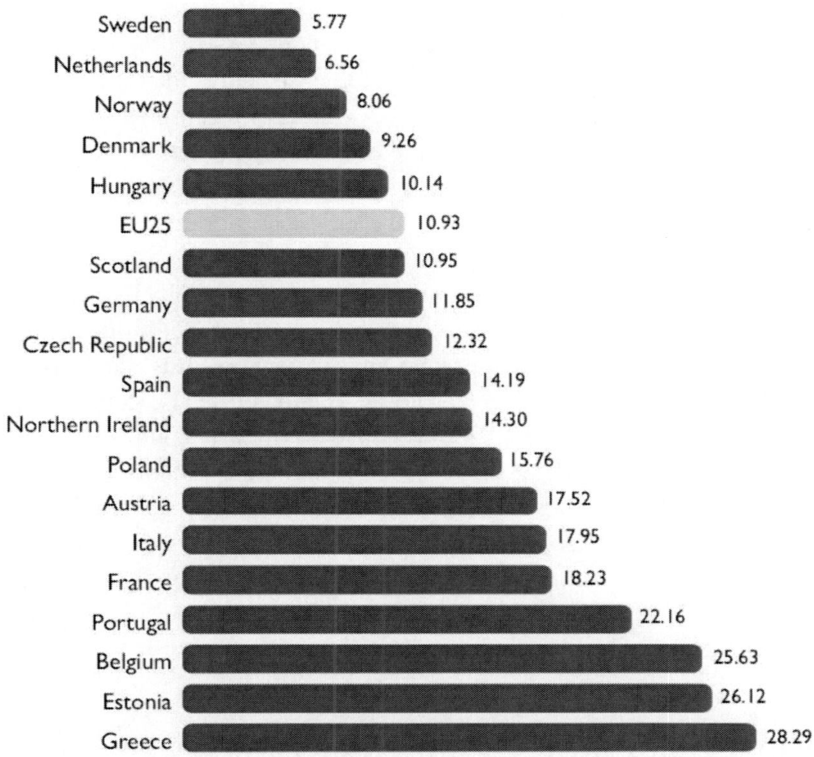

Source: WHO Mortality database (as averages for 5 years for 1998-2003 or most recent five years of data).

Graph 2. Unintentional injury deaths in children and adolescents. (rate per 100 000 population 0-19 years in 18 CSAP countries and EU25).

2. School Accidents - Theoretical Background

Children spend a majority of their time in schools. Children's physical, psychological and behavioural characteristics make them particularly inclined in accidents. The school environment contains a wide variety of potential hazards. Risks vary considerably as students move through the school day. Students begin in supervised, structured classroom environments; move to science labs and perform art activities; take lunch periods; participate in physical and at times aggressive activity in gymnasiums, on playing fields, and during recess; and finish by walking, riding bicycles, or taking the school bus home (Children's Safety Network at Education Development Center, 1997) The research literature indicates that an estimated 10 to 25 percent of all injuries to children and adolescents occur on school property, either unintentionally or through violence (U.S. Congress, 1995), with the unintentional injuries to account for more than 90 percent of all injuries occurring at school (Posner, 2000).

School accidents in Greece are estimate to account for about 30 percent of all injuries to school aged children, the highest rate among the 18 countries that participated in the study of the European Child Safety Alliance, (2007). Yet serious injuries that happen on school grounds and result in hospitalization have not been well studied in Greece.

School accidents have an important social and economic impact on health care costs, lost school time, lost work time for parents, rehabilitation costs and some times deaths (European Commission, 2005), (Polinder S., Meerdin W.J., Mulder S., Petridou E., Beecka E.v. and EUROCOST Reference Group, 2007), (Institute of Medicine, 1999). Since injury prevention in a centralized location such as a school may be relatively economical, research into the number and types of injuries occurring in the schools, and during school-related activities, could have practical benefits (Vorko and Jovic, 2000).

School-accident data are usually acquired at regional levels by schools, hospitals, community health offices, ambulance services and education authorities. These data are collected primarily to provide site, service and patient records, and to satisfy legal requirements (Association of State and Territorial Health Officials, 2002), (Association of State and Territorial Health Officials, 2005). There is often a complex procedure behind accident recording and reporting that may, for example, relate to the school environment in the primary sector and secondary schools (National Research Council and Institute of Medicine, 2007). This has a result many schools to under-report accidents (Stark, Wright, Shiroyama and Lee, 1997). Most relevant research in the medical and public health literature (Latif, Williams and Sibert, 2002) focuses on the underreporting of school injuries and the poor quality of data collected, rather than possible prevention measures.

3. Current School Accidents Reporting in Greece

By National law, it is the responsibility of every school principal, to record in the school daily register any incident in the educational facility. So any accident in the school environment has to be recorded in this official book. But there is no obligation for school accidents to be reported on any authority, in the educational or health sector. Of course, the school principal has to take all the necessary prevention measures and in the case of any accident to evaluate its severity and either to call the appropriate staff (gym instructor, nurse) to take care of the student and to communicate with student's family, or to call the accident and emergency centre (EKAB), the local health centre or hospital. Only, in case of severe accidents, the principal has to inform the local education authority.

Currently, no comprehensive guidelines are available for school administrators and other health and education professionals interested in addressing the problem of injuries in the school environment. Thus, schools need to start by assessing the causes of injuries within individual schools in order to identify the leading causes of injury and to prevent them.

Also, health care providers are not responsible for reporting school accidents data. Although many hospitals may have information systems where much of the accidents data resides, these resources have not been organized to support data sharing between providers, educational and health agencies. The public health community has long recognized that reporting of school accidents is incomplete, which greatly hampers successful public prevention interventions. Various researches estimate that only about 10% of the school accidents are actually recorded in the daily paper-based school registry (Georgiakodis and Vozikis, 2004), (Center for Research and Prevention of Injuries, 2003). is also, thus significantly reducing its value. The current reporting system is very labor intensive, it often requires multiple steps of data entry and the information exists in a form that exceeds the point of optimal use.

Studies undertaken in accident and emergency (A&E) departments (Center for Research and Prevention of Injuries, 2005), or in secondary schools in Greece (Georgiakodis and Vozikis, 2004; Pollalis and Vozikis, 2007) have provided some information on the spectrum of school injuries, but research findings never fed back to the authorities or to the relevant schools. The potential for using accident data to improve the school safety is complicated, by the number of agencies involved and remains unrealized in Greece. Patterns and causes of school injuries are poorly understood, and resources to help public health and education professionals address injuries are scarce. Schools usually respond to injuries on an ad hoc basis -after the damage is done (Towner, Jarvis, Walsh, Aynsley-Green, 1994; Pollalis and Vozikis, 2007). Injury events are not consistently tracked and it is often difficult to identify who has responsibility for preventing a recurrence (Petridou E., 2003).

4. Research Scope and Methodology

The primary goals of the pilot implementation of SARIS is to develop a production-capable information system, which if successful could be rolled out nationwide, and to create an initial architecture that could be leveraged across other reporting systems in the educational or health care sector. Moreover, our scope is to highlight *SARIS* importance in the achievement of injury prevention and health promotion objectives and to make propositions for its deployment and utilization in the context of public health and safety prevention policies.

Our research started on 2005 and completed at the end of 2008. The main steps for the SARIS Project included:

- The bibliographical research,
- The creation and participation of a secondary school network with educational units of various characteristics (building, region, number of students, school hours etc),
- The participation of local public health departments and accident and emergency (A&E) departments
- The description of the existing (if any) school accidents reporting system
- The definition of the required minimum data set, for the formation of the *SARIS* data base
- The demonstration of the feasibility of Internet architecture for school accidents reporting.
- The evaluation of the pilot's acceptance by school personnel and local health departments and other involved.
- The evaluation of production readiness of the pilot.
- The operational experience to assist in production planning.
- The evaluation of the different modes of data input used. Which input modes were preferred, how well did they work, should they all be used in a production mode?
- The Identification and documentation of system acceptance issues.
- The assessment of the training and support level of pilot needs

- The identification of operational difficulties, especially as they might impact transition to production.
- The collect of metrics based on the evaluation criteria.
- The evaluation of effectiveness during and after the pilot.

To provide comprehensive feedback on the *SARIS*, only school staff and local public health departments participated in the pilot. So, we selected randomly 32 public secondary school units from the Attica region and make the proposition to participate in our research project. Only 12 school units accepted to participate, taking in consideration their infrastructure, organizational readiness, staff availability and willingness to address the issue of school accidents. We also discussed possible pilot participation with the Ministry of Health and Welfare and there were proposed that the system in its production should ideally be supported by Regional Health Administrations, hospitals' A&E Depts, EKAB and a number of physicians or nurses. These participants in the full production phase of SARIS, should be able to provide a reasonable number of accidents primary and follow-up data and reports that would then be evaluated for timeliness, usefulness, and ease of use by the appropriate administrator of SARIS and by the participating Ministries. So, in our network was added a local General Hospital's A&E Dept, the EKAB and school staff (nurses and physicians).

The implementation of SARIS pilot was performed for a full educational period (September to June), and school accidents data were recorded to the system during that period.

Although the SARIS pilot focuses only on school accidents reporting, representatives from other educational and health care surveillance areas needed to participate in the requirements and design phase to ensure the pilot provided sufficient flexibility to incorporate their needs (Meaney, Williamson, Perry, 2007).

A pilot such as SARIS required considerable ongoing dialog and support. Without strong support from the participants, the pilot would not have succeeded and would not be able to adequately determine the viability of using the Internet to report school accidents.

5. SARIS General and High-Level Requirements

While each information system in the Greek Schools' Network (GSN-www.sch.gr) has its own specific system requirements unique to its user community, *SARIS* adopts the general requirements for a Web-based reporting system that can apply across GSN environment:

- *The privacy of a student's medical record is protected.* Privacy involved technical, physical, and administrative controls. From a technical perspective, data must be protected from unauthorized users when in transmission, when in use, and when in storage (National Research Council, 2009).
- SARIS support school accidents reporting based on a common architecture framework across GSN applications. A common architecture supported the sharing of hardware and software resources, and increased the staff efficiency in managing these resources.

- The architecture supporting SARIS is reliable. The architecture defines the necessary network infrastructure to allow reliable connections between all entities involved in the reporting and use of reported data, and defined the necessary working components to allow reliable access to the data. For school accidents reporting, reliability was key to user acceptance both from the perspective of those who reported the data and those who analyzed the data.
- The architecture supporting SARIS is scalable. The architecture scaled to support adding new modules as they converted to the Web-based methodology, and to provide acceptable performance.
- *The architecture supporting* SARIS *is flexible.* Flexibility was needed to allow the system to easily incorporate changing needs and expanding functionality, changes in technology, and changes in law or policy.
- The SARIS architecture is compliant with National E-Government technology architecture requirements. The E-Government requirements are in progress.
- *The* SARIS *reporting system is user friendly.* Ease of use was critical for user acceptance.
- *The* SARIS *reporting system is able to co-exist with other reporting methods currently in use.* Switching from existing reporting methods to a Web solution was evolutionary versus revolutionary. The Web solution was able to integrate into the current reporting structures.
- SARIS rely on mainstream technology and uses open standards products. This requirement supports the National E-Government technology architecture requirements, as well as the GSN requirements.

Below is a diagram showing the elements of the common architecture and information flows of SARIS (Graph 3):

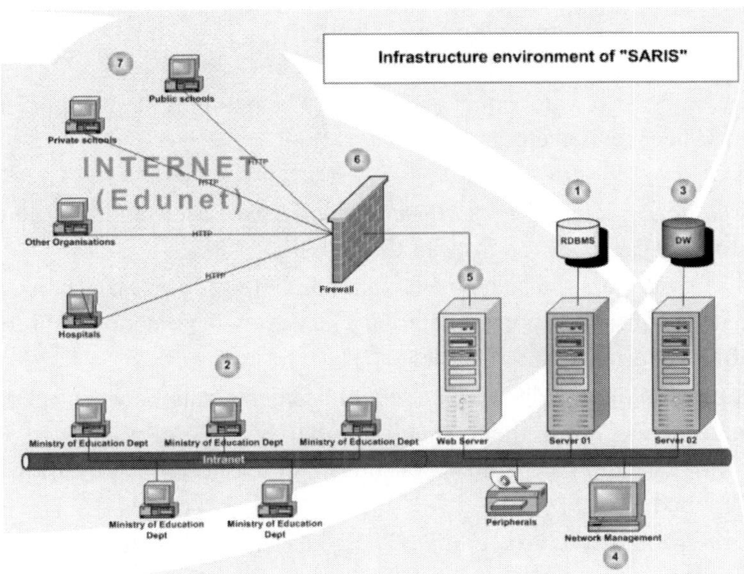

Graph 3. Architecture and information flows of SARIS.

SARIS resources and information management is analyzed in the seven following units:

- Unit 1 – Data base
- Unit 2 – Application
- Unit 3 – Data Warehouse

A graphical presentation of information management is shown in Graph 4:

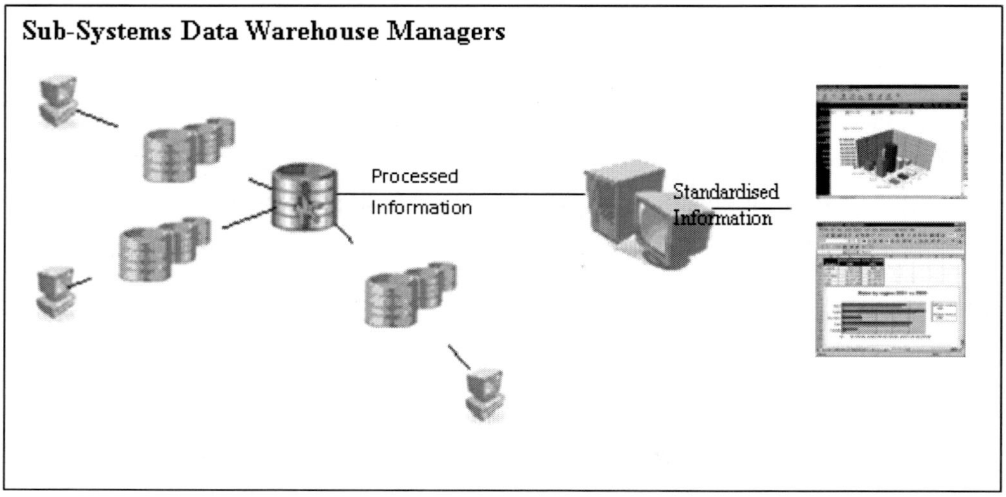

Graph 4. Information process to Data Warehouse.

- Unit 4 – System Administration
- Unit 5 – Web Server
- Unit 6 – Firewall
- Unit 7 – Safety Interaction with SARIS system

Additionally, interviews were conducted with participating schools, in order to determine user requirements. The requirements are listed below:

- *SARIS supports various modes of user input.* Ease of use should be viewed as a strong motivator for system use. (European Commission, 2003).
- SARIS provide case management functions for educational units. Schools were required to confirm reported accidents. Case management refers to tracking the status of a reported school accident.
- SARIS provide quality delivery of school accidents data between schools and health care units. This requirement specified that SARIS pilot needed to work with participating health care units to ensure that data necessary to allow case follow-up is supplied.
- *SARIS controlle access to the data.* The goal was to provide controlled mechanisms for accessing data to support efficient workflow processes. At any point in time, only those authorized and with a need to know had access to the data.

- *SARIS provide security and data protection.* As mentioned in the general requirements, it was an absolute necessity to protect the privacy and confidentiality of students' personal health data. National organizations are addressing privacy and data security. SARIS pilot complied with National E-Government Technical Architecture guidelines and E.U. guidelines.
- SARIS support capture of high quality data. Elimination of duplicate data entry aided in improving data quality as well as automatic data validation at the point of data entry (Mulder S., 2000). Data validation also included checking that all required data has been entered. SARIS pilot needed to identify the business rules for data validation.
- SARIS provide feedback to the participating Ministries. Feedback included defined queries and reports as well as ad hoc query and report capability. SARIS production deployment will need to address specifically what feedback is needed.
- *SARIS assist in identifying duplicated reports.* There were several ways that reports might get duplicated. One way is that the school accident data were recorded directly via a Web-based form and at the same time manually from the faxed report. Another way was that for the same school accident, a student went to multiple health care units.
- *SARIS satisfy national, regional and school unit specific school accidents reporting requirements.* Ministries must regulate which school accidents must be reported. Having the reporting requirements easily accessible online could enhance the usefulness of the system (Consumer Safety Institute, 2005), (Center for Research and Prevention of Injuries, 2003), (European Child Safety Alliance, 2003)

6. Assessing SARIS Pilot Implementation

The pilot implementation of *SARIS* demonstrated an acceptable and well-received Internet approach for providing GSN services, for easily extend any additional applications. Additionally, the selected architecture fitted in with GSN longer-term Internet strategies, including compliance with National E-Government strategies.

During the 10 months of *SARIS* pilot implementation, 166 school accidents were reported from the 12 participating school units. Ten school units reported the school accidents through *SARIS* system, while only one reported the accidents by e-mail and one reported no accident. The total population in the 12 school units was 4.506 students, that makes an *Overall Incident Rate* of 3,7 per 100 students, significantly higher of that reported (or estimated) by various studies (Sosnowska and Kostka, 2003), (Brook and Heim, 1997), (Williams., Latif and Cater, 2003), (Currie, Williams, Wrigh, Beattie and Harel, 1996), (Laflamme, Menckel, 1999). Through *SARIS*, various characteristics of school accidents were recorded (as unique student record number, age of student, sex of student, date and time of injury, treatment and follow-up, place of occurrence, mechanism of injury, activity when injured, object/substance producing injury, type of injury, part of the body injured, etc). All recorded data in this pilot phase were reviewed and minor corrections and modifications were performed, showing the great acceptance of the system, its friendly interface and comprehensive content. Finally a number of comprehensive reports were produced and sophisticated techniques of data mining were applied.

The success of the SARIS pilot implementation depends heavily on identifying the social welfare earned for each entity involved. Participating entities believe that they succeeded a synergistic relationship across all levels -National level, school level, health care unit level and students. Consequently, the social welfare is not specifically identified with a particular report level, but provides benefit at all crucial parameters:

- *Reporting of school accidents data was identified as a strategic goal for both educational and health care sectors.* Quality recording and reporting with SARIS provides the health care sector with a global view of reported accidents and alerts local educational entities.
- *Data accuracy and quality.* Data accuracy and quality ensured by the classification of school accidents data, avoiding re-keying of data and by applying business rules at the time of data entry.
- *Number of school accidents cases reported.* As noted before, it is generally accepted that there is significant under-reporting of school accidents. All the participating school units stated that they reported all the school accidents identified.
- *A Web-based system of mainstream technology.* The *SARIS* pilot was based on an architectural framework where school accidents data collected at the centralized hub, interfaced directly with other Public Health information Systems, which currently processes data electronically transmitted to the state using alternative methods.
- *Training.* It was the people who made the pilot system successful and it was very important to plan for the needs of the pilot participants, both those who directly use the pilot system and those who are in the management chain responsible for it. The training program developed for the system, addressed security strategy and security policies. On-site staff available to guide new users through their initial experiences with the system must also supplement the training. This will provide an added benefit of allowing pilot staff to observe the product system in use and access its usability.
- *Technical Service/Help Desk.* The pilot phase provided a help desk function to users with rapid, timely resolution of questions and concerns as they were raised during the pilot. *SARIS* pilot implementation required considerable ongoing dialog and support. Without buy-in and strong support from the participants, *SARIS* would have not succeeded and would not have been able adequately to determine the viability of using the Internet to report school accidents. At several points during the operational period, staff spent additional on-site evaluation time.

Discussions with school unit managers and staff defined some constraints on their participation. The rules that govern administration processes within the educational sector are complex and time consuming. There are many unfilled openings in the IT area in the educational sector caused by organizational inefficiencies (Pollalis and Dimitriou, 2008; Pollalis and Macris, 2009). With recent budget cuts, staff head count is also below the level for sustainable operations. In addition to a very tight staffing situation, any change produces very strong resistance. We believe that school staff participation is essential, based on *SARIS* goal for leveraging the pilot across other school units and our valid concern regarding ongoing production operation after the pilot.

Discussion - Proposals for Students' Injury Prevention and Health Promotion Policies

Nowadays, schools are assuming to play an increasingly important role in health promotion, disease prevention and injury prevention. Public health professionals are important partners for educators and other school personnel, bringing expertise and resources that can strengthen efforts to prevent injuries and violence in schools (Williams., Latif and Sibert, 2002).

As *SARIS* pilot was considered successful, a strategy must be developed to reward school staff involvement. If additional support can be provided to school staff, they could be freed up to implement the deployment. Or alternatively, the method of contracting-out could be used with the requirement of knowledge transfer. This deployment plan is necessary for the long lead-time it takes to obtain budget and staffing within the school unit (Pollalis, 1996). In addition, strong political and management support will be needed if redirection of resources is required.

Finally, there are some supplementary interventions, along with *SARIS* full productive operation in a nationwide deployment, that can promote and strengthen public policies in health and injury prevention:

- In cooperation with school officials, review and apply injury prevention guidelines, such as those being developed by the Center for Disease Control and Prevention (CDC) (2001) and the American Academy of Pediatrics/National Association of School Nurses (2005).
- Provide information and technical assistance to schools interested in developing and evaluating the impact of school-based injury prevention activities.
- Assist state and local education agencies to assess and track the causes of injuries within individual schools systems in order to develop strategies to address these injuries.
- Mandate reporting of school injuries and assist the central source (department of education or department of health) with accessing, tabulating/analyzing and reporting on injuries (Children's Safety Network, 2002), (American Academy of Pediatrics; American Public Health Association; and the National Resource Center for Health and Safety in Child Care, 2002).
- Disseminate findings broadly (officials, staff, students and communities) and use these for developing and evaluating interventions.
- Collaborate with school administration, education and health officials, students, and families in community-wide injury and violence prevention efforts.

References

American Academy of Pediatrics, (2005), *Health, Mental Health, and Safety in Schools Guidelines,* American Academy of Pediatrics and National Association of School Nurses, ISBN 13: 978-1-58110-167-6.

American Academy of Pediatrics; American Public Health Association; and the National Resource Center for Health and Safety in Child Care, (2002). *Caring for our children:*

National health and safety standards: Guidelines for out-of-home child care, 2nd ed. Elk Grove Village, IL: American Academy of Paediatrics.

Association of State and Territorial Health Officials (2002) *Making the Connection: Health and Student Achievement*; The Society of State Directors of Health, Physical Education, and Recreation, Washington, DC.

Association of State and Territorial Health Officials (2005), Issue Brief: Data Collection in Schools, Washington, DC.

Brook U. and Heim M. (1997). Accidents among high school students in Israel: A recurrent disease?, *Patient Education and Counseling*, 31: 237-242.

Center for Disease Control and Prevention (CDC) Division of Adolescent and School Health (DASH), (2001) *School Health Guidelines to Prevent Unintentional Injuries and Violence, Morbidity and Mortality Weekly Report*, December 7, 2001 / 50(RR22);1-46

Center for Research and Prevention of Injuries (CEREPRI) (2003) European Home and Leisure Accident Surveillance, *Annual EHLASS Report: Greece 2002.*

Center for Research and Prevention of Injuries (CEREPRI) (2005) *Injury Statistics Portal* http://www.euroipn.org/stats_portal.

Children's Safety Network (1997) Injuries in the School Environment: A Resource Guide (Second Edition), Newton, MA: Education Development Center, Inc.

Childrens' Safety Network, (2002). Integrating Injury and Violence Prevention into Child Care Settings, Maternal and Child Health Bureau, Consumer Safety Institute (2005). THE INJURY DATABASE (IDB) CODING MANUAL, DATA DICTIONARY VERSION 1.1 – European Commission, Directorate General for Health and Consumer Protection, The Netherlands.

Currie CE, Williams JM, Wright P, Beattie T, Harel Y (1996). Incidence and distribution of injury among schoolchildren aged 1 1-15, *Injury Prevention*; 2: 21-25.

European Commission (E.C.) (2003), "Implementation of the Minimum Data Sets on Injuries (MDS-Is)", *European Commission / Health and Consumer Protection* (DG Sanco), Vienna.

European Commission (E.C.) (2005), "*Burden of Fatal Injuries in the European Union*", *Report of the Task Force on Burden of Injuries, Working Party on Injuries and Accidents*European Commission / Health and Consumer Protection (DG Sanco), Athens.

European Commission (E.C.) (2007), "Injuries in the European Union: Summary 2003-2005", European Commission / Health and Consumer Protection (DG Sanco), Vienna

European Child Safety Alliance (ECSA), (2001), *Priorities for Child Safety in the European Union: Agenda for Action*, Amsterdam, The Netherlands.

European Child Safety Alliance (ECSA), (2003), *A Guide to Child Safety Regulations and Standards in Europe*, Amsterdam, The Netherlands.

European Child Safety Alliance (ECSA), Eurosafe (2007), "*Child Safety Summary Report Card for 18 Countries*", Amsterdam, The Netherlands.

European Child Safety Alliance (ECSA), Eurosafe (2009), "*Child Safety Report Card for Greece*", Amsterdam.

Georgiakodis F., Vozikis A., (2004) The epidemiology of school accidents in Greece: Research findings from Secondary schools, *Proceedings of the 17th Greek Statistical Conference*, p. 83-92.

Institute of Medicine (Committee on Injury Prevention and Control, Division of Health Promotion and Disease Prevention) (1999), *Reducing the Burden of Injury: Advancing*

Prevention and Treatment. Bonnie RJ, Fulco CE, and Liverman CT (eds). National Academy Press: Washington, DC.

Laflamme L, Menckel E. (1999). Injuries in Swedish schools during recesses: distribution and patterns, *Safety Science* 33: 89-101.

Latif AHA, Williams WR, Sibert J. (2002), Primary school accident reporting in one education authority. *Arch Dis Child*; 86:91-4.

Meaney S., Williamson E., Perry I. J. (2007). Pilot Implementation of the European Injury Database (IDB), National Suicide Research Foundation, Department of Epidemiology and Public Health, Ireland.

Mulder S., (2000) European Home and Leisure Accident Surveillance System: Evaluation of the classification and reportings system, Consumer Safety Institute, Amsterdam, The Netherlands.

National Center for Injury Prevention and Control (NCIPC), Centers for Disease Control and Prevention (2008), The CDC Childhood Injury Report: Patterns of Unintentional Injuries among 0-19 Year Olds in the United States, 2000-2006, Atlanta GA.

National Research Council and Institute of Medicine. (2007). *Challenges in Adolescent Health Care: Workshop Report.* Committee on Adolescent Health Care Services and Models of Care for Treatment, Prevention, and Healthy Development. Board on Children, Youth, and Families, Division of Behavioral and Social Sciences and Education. Washington, DC: The National Academies Press.

National Research Council (2009). *Protecting Student Records and Facilitating Education Research: A Workshop Summary.* Margaret Hilton, Rapporteur. Committee on National Statistics and Center for Education, Division of Behavioral and Social Sciences and Education. Washington, DC: The National Academies Press.

Petridou E., (2003). From injury research to injury prevention: facilitating the connection, *Injury Control and Safety Promotion*, Vol. 10, No. 3, pp.

Pollalis, Y. A. and Macris, A., (2009) "Strategic Planning for Information Resources: Enhancing Managers' Participation through Ontology-based Modeling", *International Journal of Technology Management*, Vol. 44, No. 4.

Pollalis, Y.A. and Dimitriou, N.K., "Strategic Management of Knowledge in Virtual Enterprises: A Systemic Multi-methodology toward Competitive Advantage", *International Journal of Information Management*, Vol. 28, No. 4, pages 305-321, August 2008.

Pollalis, Y.A. and Vozikis, A., "Insurance and the Internet: evaluating the e-business context of insurance companies in Greece", *Quarterly Review of Economics and Business (SPOUDAI)*, Volume 57 (1), 2007.

Pollalis H., Yannis A., "A Systemic Approach for Re-engineering: Integrating IS Planning, BPR, and TQM Efforts", *Information Systems Management*, Vol.13, No.2, January 1996.

Polinder S., Meerdin W.J., Mulder S., Petridou E., Beecka Ed van and EUROCOST Reference Group (2007), Assessing the burden of injury in six European countries, Bulletin of the World Health Organization 2007;85:27-34.

Posner, M. (2000). Preventing school injuries: A comprehensive guide for school administrators, teachers, and staff. New Brunswick, NJ: Rutgers University Press.

Sosnowska S. and Kostka T. (2003). Epidemiology of school accidents during a six school-year period in one region in Poland, *European Journal of Epidemiology* 18: 977–982.

Stark C, Wright J, Shiroyama C, Lee J. (1997) School injuries in the west of Scotland: estimate of incidence and health service costs. *Health Bulletin*; 55:44—8.

Towner EML, Jarvis S N, Walsh S S M, Aynsley-Green A (1994) Measuring exposure to injury risk in schoolchildren aged 11-14, BMJ 1994; 308:449-52.

U.S. Congress, Office of Technology Assessment (1995). *Risks to Students in School.* Washington DC: U.S. Government Printing Office.

Vorko A., Jovic F. (2000), Multiple attribute entropy classification of school-age injuries, *Accident Analysis and Prevention* 32 (2000) 445–454.

Williams W.R., Latif A.H.A. and Cater L. (2003). Accidents in the school environment: perspectives of staff concerned with data collection and reporting procedures, *Public Health* 117 (2003) 180–186.

Williams W.R., Latif A.H.A. and Sibert J (2002).Secondary school accident reporting in one education authority, *Child:Care, Health and Development,* 28,1,101–108.

World Health Organization (WHO) (2008), *World report on child injury prevention*, Geneva.

In: HRM and Marketing Orientation in the New Era
Editor: Panagiotis Kyriazopoulos
ISBN: 978-1-62808-959-2

Chapter 13

ANALYSING AND EVALUATING THE ROLE OF E-COMMERCE

Irene Samanta*
Graduate Technological Education Institute of Piraeus,
Department of Business Administration, Piraeus, Greece

ABSTRACT

The increased competition, along with the globalisation effect, have undoubtedly set new grounds for conducting business. This situation actually urges corporations and organisations throughout the world to acquire and maintain competitive edges and core competencies that will eventually provide the basis for success. Around the globe companies are striving for profitability; a fact that logically tests and underlines the necessity for cost-cutting, innovative solutions and higher margins or returns to be achieved. Markets are expanding and constantly developing, creating new needs and opportunities for revenues. The present study investigates and identifies the general principles that apply to the electronic commerce on a more wide range and analyzes the factors that have contributed to the emergence and expansion of e-commerce. Also, the latest trends on a general world-wide basis are explored as well as the basic risks that are associated to commercialising on the internet are identified. In a rapidly changing environment, where the most prominent business solutions are basically found within the boundaries set by the great technological advancements and the globalization in effect, corporations throughout the world are striving for success.

Keywords: E-commerce, internet, internet marketing, electronic consumer

1. INTRODUCTION

The Internet (Net) is a network of computers reaching worldwide. A way to understand the Internet is to examine the technology which supports it. Even if technology details are very complex for common people, its concept is characterised by simplicity. Nevertheless,

* E-mail: isamanta@teipir.gr.

very often there is confusion between the terms of Internet and World Wide Web: even if they are used in day to day speech without distinction, they have major differences: Internet is a worldwide data communications system, providing connection between computers, with hardware and software infrastructure, whereas the Web is one of the services communicated via the Internet.

Internet's basic applications and guidelines exist for almost a decade, the network had been popular to public, very recently, in the early 1990s. Its growth, during this decade, was impressive, since it was estimated that the Internet grew by 100% per year, especially in 1996 and 1997.

A good reasoning about this, is the lack of central administration, allowing organic growth of the network, preventing any company from over controlling the network. Because of communications development, new findings had been presented by graduate students, across North America, during the 1960s, 1970s and 1980s, since they considered Internet as their opportunity of free communication as well as a tool of expression liberation.

The complex communications infrastructure of the Internet, is consisting of its hardware components and a system of software layers that control various aspects of the architecture. While the hardware can often be used to support other software systems, it is the design and the rigorous standardisation process of the software architecture that characterises the Internet. Nevertheless, Internet's use of Unicode had been developed a lot the last decade, due to high technology's evolution.

Because the Internet is a distributed network comprising many voluntarily interconnected networks, it has no governing body. During November 2005, the World Summit on the Information Society, established the Internet Governance Forum (IGF), in order to discuss Internet-related issues (Vlachopoulou M., 1999).

The Internet is a worldwide system of interconnected computer networks, which is consisting of millions of private and public, academic, business, and government networks of local to global scope, which are linked with various types of technologies. It carries a lot of information and services, such as electronic mail, online chat, file transfer and file sharing, online gaming, and the inter-linked hypertext documents and other resources of the World Wide Web (WWW).

It's most common uses deal with e-mail, a method of sending electronic text messages between people, equivalent to the traditional way of sending letters.

Another very important element deals with the fact that the Internet, allows computer users to connect to other computers very easily, no matter where they are. This can be done, with no security, authentication or encryption technologies, depending on the situation. (Strauss and Frost, 1999).

The overall objective of this research is to critically analyse and evaluate the role of e-commerce in the market. companies use e-commerce and measure consumers reactions to this new way of business. For this reason, there will be an analysis which will concern the advantages and disadvantages of e-commerce, as well as the expansion of e-commerce in the world market. The most important part will be the identification of the trends and risks of consumers towards e-commerce, and there will be a discussion over the ways of overcoming any existing obstacles.

The current study fundamentally aims at exploring and providing a thorough analysis and overview of the potentials and the risks attached to E-commerce both for consumers and businesses. In addition, the research will go further, by investigating the latest trends as far as the electronic commerce is concerned, as well as the threats that are been set by this relatively new mode of selling and trade.

2. Theoretical Framework

2.1. Internet's Usage

Liebermann and Stashevsky (2002) argue that in the knowledge age the Internet has managed to revolutionise marketing and trade as it clearly constitutes a global mode that facilitates the worldwide marketplace and has emerged to a significant marketing tool.

The rapid growth of internet applications and usage has been well accredited to the ease of access and the convenience of the individuals. This issue combined with the globalisation effect that urges for a wider marketplace, has evidently caught the attention of corporations around the world in an attempt to reach international consumers and buyers and expand their shares of the global markets (Javalgi and Ramsey, 2001). Today, people can find virtually all product categories and lines through the web and explore alternative choices within minimum time required; this situation has led to a significant reduction of time spend at the respective "search of alternatives" stage in the overall consumer buying behaviour, which in turn has further promoted the use of internet as a mode of purchase activities (McCrohan, 2003). This has fairly contributed to the development of the E-commerce. "The Internet provides affordable, accessible technology to bring together buyers and sellers, large and small, right across the globe" (Subba Rao, 2000, p. 54).

The Internet allows greater flexibility during working time and eliminates the location distance, due to high-speed connections and Web applications.

Nowadays, every user can be connected via Internet undertaking that there is a cellular network, which can support this kind of device's technology. So Internet can be viewed on various mobile devices, such as datacards, mobile phones, cellular routers and handheld game consoles. Another reason, facilitating Internet frequent use deals with small screen pocket-sized devices; therefore, all Internet services, including email and web browsing, can be available. Internet can be used as a tool to create a competitive advantage because it can create new product opportunities, it can have cost savings through online communications, online support, since it s very useful to inter-firm collaboration, especially for RandD, the use of internet as an information search, the establishment of the company Web site for marketing and sales promotion, the transmission of data, as a tool to improve customer relations.

The number of people using the internet on a global basis is constantly increasing with a rapid rate of growth. As of 2000 approximately 150 million individuals were estimated to use the web as a primary source of information retrieval and as a secondary source of consumption habits (Subba Rao, 2000). Nowadays, these figures are basically expected to have increased by almost 20%; a fact that signifies a rather radical change in the way corporations are doing business and buyers are processing their purchases (Polymenakou and Tsironis, 2003).

Therefore, the internet can be regarded as a new market (Ricciuti, 1995) connecting the supply side producers, sellers to demand side, that is consumers. It is important to note that internet promotes consumption and ultimately helps firms to grow resulting ultimately in national economic growth (Kabundi, 2004, p. 12).

The main communication language for the Internet is English. Except for English, the most popular languages, are Chinese with 17%, Spanish 9%, Japanese 7%, French 5% and German 5%.

As far as region is concerned, 40% of the world's Internet users are based in Asia, 26% in Europe, 17% in North America, 10% in Latin America and the Caribbean, 4% in Africa, 3% in the Middle East and 1% in Australia.

The most recent data, according to Internet World Stats, state that as of June 30, 2008, 1.463 billion people use the Internet, in a worldwide basis.

Internet use expands rapidly. More than 20% of internet users in several countries buy products and services on line (Taylor Nelson Sofres, 2002), while particularly in the USA this percentage is 50% (Forrester Research, 2003). It is also estimated that the number of users by the year 2000 worldwide was 500 million with an annual growth rate of 10%. Internet use started in the early 1970s in the US Defence Department. Public use however exploded in the early 1990s, the cultural barrier was short lived and marketing on the internet become soon generally accepted (Donaton, 1994; Krol, 1992). According to the (DO Site, 2008) for the year 2007 the total number of the internet user population in 2007 was 965.2 millions, distributed in various regions in millions as follows: America (276.5), Europe (269.6), Asia (368.4), Oceania (17.9) and Africa (32.8).

The access to computers measured as a percentage of households has increased in 2006 a lot and mainly in the northern European countries. More specifically, according to the latest data of Eurostat (2006) in the access range of (80% - 100%) fall in decreasing order the countries: Denmark, Iceland, Sweden and Netherlands. In the range of (70% - 79%) fall similarly Germany, Luxembourg, Norway, Finland, and UK. In the range of (60% - 69%) is Austria and Malta. In the range of (50% - 59%) are Ireland, Belgium, Spain, France and Cyprus. In the range of (40% - 49%) fall Italy and Portugal. In the range of (30% - 39%) is World. As for the post communist countries, Slovenia falls in the range of (60% - 69%), followed by Estonia, Hungary and Slovakia (50% - 59%), then come Poland, Latvia and Lithuania (40% - 49%), Czech Republic (39%) and Romania, Bulgaria (under 30%). Besides, there is an additional way to measure the degree of computer access. This way refers to the percentage of the individuals (population) that used the computer last year (as shown in table 2 in the appendix). More precisely, according to the latest data (year 2007) of Eurostat, northern European countries have the highest access, while post communist countries do not exceed 70%. Thus, in the access range of (90% - 100%) fall in decreasing order Iceland and Norway. In the range of (80% - 89%) fall similarly Sweden, Netherlands, Denmark, Finland, Luxembourg, UK and Germany. In the range of (70% - 79%) are Austria, Belgium and France. In the range of (60% - 69%) fall Ireland and Spain. In the range (50% - 59%) is Malta. Finally, in the range (40% - 49%) are Cyprus, Portugal, Italy and World. Regarding the post communist countries the highest percentage is in Slovakia (68%) and the lowest in Bulgaria (37%).

2.2. The Web as an Important Part of the Economy and E-Commerce

Internet makes market more efficient than the conventional markets (Hoffman and Novak, 1996, p.9). However, the realisation of the above mentioned efficiency relies on the provision of a secure system for the adoption of electronic commercial transactions. Security problem is regarded as a barrier. Besides, consumers should be helped to search easily in web sites (Hoffman and Novak, 1995).

Cronin (1996) asserts that internet can improve business performance, since competitive advantages are available from internet connectivity as follows. First, cost savings (using the internet as a communication channel), performance improvements (by the widespread use of internet to information collection), facilitates distributed decision making and helps organisational flexibility, helps market penetration (through the external connectivity with the customers), product transformation (including the development of the internet-based products and services).

Global sales promotion can be done now easily on the web. A lot of companies have their own web sites, where they advertise their products and encourage customer interaction. For SMEs this is a very low cost method of sales promotion. According to Ellsworth and Ellsworth (1996) a good site for sales promotion has to include the following main characteristics: information rich and regularly updated; clear navigation paths; integration of the site with other marketing channels used by the company.

Web helps distribution of products especially for publishing firms (Jones, 1994). Furthermore, Web makes the ordering on line and saves time (Michalski, 1995). Thus, business transactions become faster and easier. Firms can reach remote geographical areas and make new market segments (Sharples, 1995) and increase sales. According to Fisher (2008) the revenues for music publishers through internet distribution increased by 4%, and for recording artists by 12%.

The cost of information becomes cheaper due to the Internet, not only because of the savings from research but also because of lower transformation cost.(Strauss et al., 1999, p.15). For Steven R. Lerman from the MIT, internet is the new economy which has major differences from the old one, since it spreads worldwide, it promotes ideas, concepts, information rather than tangible things and it is interactive, selling intelligent products, because clients are able to fulfil their needs. Generally, the old economy with the new one has a lot of differences, since new economy states that the company in order to be successful, must take into account the external environment of the economy. It is also oriented to clients customisation, by giving all its attention to the personal characteristics and is in favour of standardisation, whereas it defines that in order to develop a competitive advantage, it will have to exploit all the resources, in order to be the leader. Another very important characteristic of the new economy is the need for corporate strategies, rather than business strategies, since the new marketing concept states that the company must be independent from the consumer, by trying to make a liaison with the client. On the other hand, old economy focuses only in the company, with scarce resources to develop products, whereas it rejects standardization and value chain is been considered as rigid. Internet had been developed as a very important business for many companies, since many of the most important ones are advertising and commerce through the Internet, because it is cheaper than the traditional way of transaction. This is known as e-commerce and it is been characterised by speed, since it can transmit information to a vast number of people, at the same time. Other Internet activities, is the e-shopping, based on which, a person can order a product online and receive it by mail in a very short period of time, or even downloaded, e.g. an article. Also, the Internet developed personalised marketing, by allowing a company to target a specific person or a specific group of people, more efficiently than the traditional ways of advertising.

Electronic commerce (e-commerce) is "*the description applied to a wide range of technologies used to streamline business interactions*" (Jobber, 2004). It involves the use of computers, the Internet and shared software that send and receive information. Such information includes, for instance, product specification, purchase orders and invoices, or any other type of data that need to be transmitted to customers, suppliers or the public.

According to Keegan (2001), e-commerce is "*when trading goods and services over the Internet, both business-to-consumer and business-to-business. The latter is sometimes also referred to as e-business*". Krajewski (2002) mentions that "*electronic commerce is the application of information and communication technology anywhere along the entire supply chain of business processes. It encompasses business-to-business as well as business-to-consumer and consumer-to-business transactions*" (Krajewski et al, 2002). E-commerce has to do with all forms of economic activities that are performed through electronic connections (Wigand, 1997, cited in Delfmann et al, 2002).

E-commerce provides a very effective and efficient way of selling. As the business environment keeps changing, companies need to use more effective tools of conducting business. More specifically, "*the growing interpenetration of economies, the globalisation of markets and the increased interdependence of economic agents are reshaping the national and international competitive environments*" (Ghobadian and Gallear, 1996, cited in Rao et al, 2003), require the differentiation from the traditional ways of conducting sales.

By implementing a web site which supports electronic commerce, a company can achieve the promotion and selling of its products more easily and more successfully than the traditional way. According to Wymbs (2000), e-commerce can eliminate the boundaries between countries, it can offer strategic innovation, and it cuts the cost of interaction and the transaction costs. Furthermore, electronic commerce enables companies to be more flexible in their internal operations and to be more responsive to the expectations and the needs of their customers. Therefore, both companies and customers can gain several benefits by using this tool.

2.3. Internet Marketing and Business

On line marketing is the basis of the relationship marketing, since it gives the opportunity to bring buyers and sellers together (Kandampully J., 2003, p.444).

Web became a commercial medium, for it creates the computer-mediated environment (CME), which allows for "machine-interaction" and "person-interaction" (Hoffman and Novak, 1996). Since web creates a new environment for marketing activities, which is different from the traditional media, then, conventional marketing activities are under transformation in order to face the new environment. Companies seek to attract the online customers. Constantinides (2004) supports that the Web experience contains searching, browsing, finding, selecting, comparing and evaluating, interacting and transacting with the online firm. A well-constructed site affects positively online consumer behaviour. This is proved in reality, for based on the collection of online and either in-store of US retailers in 2002 Nielsen Net Ratings (2003) found that compared to average internet users, customers visiting well designed web sites are ten times more likely to visit the brick-and-mortar stores. Experience has shown that design in the Web affects online consumers by 46,1%, followed by information (25,1%) (Fogg et al., 2002).

Small or big business can benefit from having a website, by practicing on line marketing. For businesses whose customers are spread in different places worldwide, there will probably be very difficult to find another way of attracting customers, apart from online marketing use, without the low expenses costs Web presence offer, through the reasonably low costs and its worldwide reach

Especially for home businesses, the Internet offers the opportunity to grow, due to low cost for starting a business and maintain its web presence. Since most home businesses have a "virtual" location, the website, provides low cost mediums in order to let its customers to get information about the company and its products. Nevertheless, Internet Marketing should be a very important part of business plan and marketing strategy.

Internet encourages a new way of collaboration and information shared in many industries. Collaboration between employers can be very prosperous, because of low cost and sharing of ideas, knowledge, and abilities, since people can communicate to each other and at the same time they can collaborate with low cost. The ideas derived from this on line collaboration can be applied to all target groups, even in niche markets. Also, Internet "chat", allows people to stay in touch while working, since messages can be sent and be read quickly, through Internet and e-mail. Internet collaboration allows managers and project teams to share data and information, in a wide variety of sectors, such as scientific research, software development, business or marketing planning. Internet is not a fashion but a new way of living (Vlahopoulou, 1999, p.254).

Due to globalisation and to intense competition, today there is a need for business network, which managed to introduce a new concept of trade and compete.

Based on Wilkinson (2001), the concept of trade includes a lot of different types of networks which were used for exchanging goods or services.

Today's business network had introduced a new way of competition, dealing not with competition between firms, but between networks. Therefore, the competitive advantage deals with which firm has the better network and through "competitive collaboration" (Hamel *et al.,* 1989), each member contributes to the value chain by benefit at the same time from it (Kothandaraman and Wilson, 2001). So, the competitive advantage, derived from this cooperation, is not only mutual benefits, but also the strong relationships with the stakeholders, in a worldwide basis (Kandampully J., 2003, p.445). More and more companies are using Internet, in order to meet customers' demands and needs with speed and to be effective at lower cost. IT evolution made possible what is been described as "the second economic revolution" (Essig and Arnold, 2001). Businesses are trying to built their relationships with their stakeholders, including customers, suppliers, retailers, brokers, co-producers, employees, and shareholders. Nowadays, many businesses have managed to do e-business, with great success, like amazon.com, the world's largest online retailer, which started in 1995 and by 2007,it reached annual sales of US $15 billion. Therefore, Internet becomes useful, since it replaced the traditional distribution channels of wholesalers, brokers, and retailers. Nevertheless, Internet should improve itself, by inventing new and efficient ways in order to built and maintain the relationships between businessmen, employers and partners.

2.3.1. Companies Reconstruct their Marketing

Web became a commercial medium, for it creates the computer-mediated environment (CME), which allows for "machine-interaction" and "person-interaction" (Hoffman and

Novak, 1996). Since web creates a new environment for marketing activities, which is different from the traditional media, then, conventional marketing activities are under transformation in order to face the new environment. Companies seek to attract the online customers. Constantinides (2004) supports that the Web experience contains searching, browsing, finding, selecting, comparing and evaluating, interacting and transacting with the online firm. A well-constructed site affects positively online consumer behaviour. This is proved in reality, for based on the collection of online and either in-store of US retailers in 2002 Nielsen Net Ratings (2003) found that compared to average internet users, customers visiting well designed web sites are ten times more likely to visit the brick-and-mortar stores. Experience has shown that design in the Web affects online consumers by 46,1%, followed by information (25,1%) (Fogg et *al.,* 2002).

2.4. Electronic Consumer

According to Lee (2002) and Liebermann and Stashevsky (2002), the difference between the traditional and online buying behaviour is the step of building trust and confidence. There are two types of factors that determine consumer behaviour: the controllable factors and the uncontrollable factors. According to the study of Cheung et al. (2003) the uncontrollable factors in consumer behaviour are consumer characteristics and environmental influences.

According to Constantinides (2004) the controllable elements discussed in the literature influencing the online consumer behaviour are broadly classified under the following three categories: functionality factors, psychological factors and content factors. Functionality factors include usability (convenience, site navigation, ordering/payment process, search facilities, accessibility) and interactivity (customer service after sales, interaction with company personnel, customisation and network effects). “Usability” is regarded as an important quality criterion of information systems (Preece et *al.*, 1994) and Web sites (Osterbauer et *al.*, 1999). Usability of Web sites has been constantly improving during the years (Internet Confidence Index, Yahoo/AC Nielsen, 2002). Today, according to Nielsen (2008) usability is much helped by the search engines. Technological progress has also helped usability. “Site speed” is important for the convenience of the online consumer, since the average time spent by the online customer per page is low and steadily declining (Cockburn and McKenzie, 2001).

Psychological factors include transaction security, customer data misuse, customer data safety, uncertainty reducing elements as well as guarantees/return policies. Content factors include aesthetics (design, presentation quality, style) and marketing mix (communication, product, fulfilment, price, promotion and characteristics). Cheung et al. (2003) claim that the controllable factors are product (or service) characteristics, medium characteristics and the merchant (or intermediary) characteristics. Similar opinion is shared by Kossecki and Kaczor (2006) who put emphasis on trust and they claim that trust is the most important factor determining consumer behaviour in ecommerce (Kyriazopoulos and Samanta, 2009). Trust includes no risk regarding transactions, security in payments, quality of product and loyalty. “Technological elements and online trust” are very important, for according to Harris Interactive (2001) 70% of the US Web users are seriously concerned about their internet safety, and personal data (see also section 1.3 on barriers, mentioned above).

Reputation and long lasting relationship with customers depends on trust. The positive impact of internet on the consumer depends on accessibility of the consumers to use internet as a channel of distribution (Doherty et al., 1999). Further, according to (Doherty et al., 1999), internet offers direct communications possibilities as well as cost saving.

2.4.1. Electronic Consumer Profile

Electronic retailers (companies that do not have any physical stores and market directly to the consumers through the internet) are able to offer their product at lower prices than their store-based competitors (Kotzab and Madlberger, 2000). In the European area, according to Kotzab and Madlberger (2000), e-tailing (as an innovative retail format) can be regarded as an extension of retailing. According to (Kotzab and Madlberger, 2000) Europe is the largest retail market in the world, with one-third of the five million commercial businesses.

The market volume of electronic commerce is large but the actual size varies across various empirical studies (Kotzab and Madlberger, 2000). Sanders and Temkin (2000) predict US on line sales volume for 2004 to be US$3.2 trillion. Bricks-and-mortar companies (that is companies which have physical assets mainly in stores and distribution facilities) dominate western European online retail, especially in the UK. The online expenses are higher in Northern Europe than in the Western Europe. According to the findings of (Kotzab and Madlberger, 2000), in the year 1998 the average online expenses were €25 (Sweden) followed by €23 (Finland), €22 (Denmark), €13 (Western Europe). These levels are expected to increase during 2001-2002 (Jørgensen, 2000). Based on the study of Mintel Oxygen Reports - E-commerce (2008) in which it is examined the internet retailing in the UK, Germany, France, Italy and Spain, it is found that UK online sales were the largest in Europe worth 18.5 €billion (2007), followed by 13 €billion in Germany (2007), France (7 €billion), Italy (1.1 €billion) and Spain (1 €billion). According to Mintel Oxygen Reports - E-commerce (2008) European ecommerce has shown a remarkable growth and that UK is the most developed online market in Europe. Besides, according to the forecasts of Mintel Oxygen Reports - E-commerce (2008) the growth prospects in European ecommerce are very good and more specifically: Spain will see the largest growth, with sales growing from just 1 billion Euros last year to 4,2 €billion by 2012, France is expected to reach 21.4 €billion by 2012, UK is expected to reach 56 €billion by 2012. Finally, Germany, although the largest European country is expected to have the slowest growth rate, but the volume of this trade is considerable. In the next pages, in order to measure the percentage of population that buys over the internet (online penetration), section 1.5.2 will be divided in the following subsections: 1.5.2.a (examining the total online penetration across countries), 1.5.2.b (examining online penetration by types of products bought across countries), 1.5.2.c (analyzing online penetration by age structure across countries), 1.5.2.d (examining online penetration by education level across countries) and finally 1.5.2.e (online penetration by gender between various countries). According to the findings of (Kotzab and Madlberger, 2000), the internet as a distribution channel in Europe is still different than that of the United States. In the USA 10% of the households use the internet for shopping. In Europe, however, the picture differs among countries. Thus, the internet shopping in Europe has as follows:

- Early adopters (eg. Sweden) have a high online penetration, but a small market size
- Awakening giants (UK and Germany) have medium online penetration but high market volume

- middleweights (France and Italy)
- There are small countries (The Netherlands, Austria, Denmark) which have a moderate retail penetration but rapid growth rates.
- World was not examined in this study

Based on Reitsma (2000, p. 13) the percentage of the online shoppers of total population in Europe ranges from 2% (France) to 12% (Sweden). In year 2007 however, this percentage in Europe and many other countries has increased considerably (as shown in table 7 in the appendix). The northern European countries have the highest percentage, while the post communist countries have the lowest. More specifically, according to the latest data (2007) of Eurostat, Norway comes first with (48%) followed by UK (44%), Denmark and Netherlands (43%), Germany (41%), Sweden (39%), Luxembourg (37%), Finland and Iceland (32%), Ireland, Austria and France (26%), Malta (16%), Belgium (15%), Spain (13%), Cyprus (8%), Italy (7%), Portugal (6%) and World (5%). The post communist countries, apart from Poland (11%) and Slovakia (10%), have percentages lower than 10%.

2.4.2. Product Type

In Europe the most preferred products in online shopping are books, CDs, software, hardware and gifts (Reitsma, 2000). According to the latest data of Eurostat for the year 2007 however, the structure of types of products bought over the internet has changed. In table 5 of the appendix is shown the percentage of all individuals who ordered 8 types of products for the year 2007 in each country. The codes of these types of products are analysed in table 6 of the appendix. The main conclusion is that in all types of products in the Northern European countries have the highest internet penetration, and that product "travel and holiday accommodation" has the highest penetration among all types of products examined, followed by books, magazines, films and music. More precisely:

For product type 1 (food/groceries): UK is in the range (10% - 19%), while all the rest (including the post communist countries) are below 10%.

For product type 2 (household goods (e.g. furniture, toys, etc.)): In the range (20% - 29%) are Germany and UK. In the range (10% - 19%) are Finland, France, Netherlands and Norway. All the rest (including the post communist countries) are below 10%.

For product type 3 (films/music): In the range (20% - 29%) are Norway and UK. In the range (10% - 19%) are Denmark, Germany, Iceland, Luxembourg and Sweden. All the rest (including the post communist countries) are below 10%.

For product type 4 (books/magazines/e-learning material): In the range (20% - 29%) are Germany, Iceland, Luxembourg and Norway. In the range (10% - 19%) are Austria, Denmark, Finland, France, Netherlands, Sweden and UK. All the rest (including the post communist countries) are below 10%.

For product type 5 (cloths, sports goods): In the range (20% - 29%) fall Denmark, Germany, Norway and UK. In the range (10% - 19%) are Austria, Finland, France, Iceland, Luxembourg, Netherlands and Sweden. All the rest (including the post communist countries) are below 10%.

For product type 6 (computer software (incl. video games)): In the range (10% - 19%) are Denmark, Germany, Iceland, Luxembourg, Netherlands, Norway and UK. All the rest (including the post communist countries) are below 10%.

For product type 7 (shares/financial services/insurance): In the range (10% - 19%) are Iceland, Norway and Sweden. All the rest (including the post communist countries) are below 10%.

For product type 8 (travel and holiday accommodation): In the range (40% - 49%) fall Iceland and Norway. In the range (30% - 39%) there is none. In the range (20% - 29%) fall Denmark, Finland, Germany, Iceland, Luxembourg, Netherlands, Sweden and UK. In the range (10% - 19%) are France and Spain. All the rest (including the post communist countries) are below 10%.

2.4.3. Age

In Europe, according to (Reitsma, 2000) the online consumer profile has the following characteristics regarding age: the average age ranges from 36 (Germany) to 44 (UK). In the year 2007 however, according to Eurostat, the percentage of the individuals who use computer within the last year (at various age ranges) has shown that in all age ranges both capitalistic and post communist countries show a high percentage, and that capitalistic countries come first (especially the northern countries). Further, from the age range (45 – 54) and up the distance of the post communist countries from the capitalistic countries increases. It should be also noted, that the age range from 16 years to 54 years has the highest penetration rate among all age ranges. The above conclusions are based on table 3 of the appendix, and a summary of findings follows.

In the age range (up to 15) there are not enough data apart from Portugal (94%) and Italy (64%). In the age range (16 - 24): (90% – 100%) penetration have Denmark, Iceland, Netherlands, Sweden, Austria, Belgium, Luxembourg, Norway and Spain. (80% - 89%) penetration show Cyprus, World, Ireland and Malta. (70% - 79%) penetration has Italy. Regarding the post communist countries: (90% – 100%) penetration have Hungary, Latvia, Lithuania, Poland, Slovakia and Slovenia. The remaining three countries of the table (Bulgaria, Romania and Serbia) have penetration rate within the range (70% - 79%).

In the age range (25 – 34): leaders with a penetration rate (90% - 100%) are Austria, Denmark, Finland, France, Iceland, Luxembourg, Netherlands, Norway and Sweden. (80% - 89%) have Belgium, Denmark, Ireland and Spain. (70% - 79%) has Portugal. Finally, (60% - 69%) show Cyprus, World, Italy and Malta. Regarding post communist countries, they have all penetration rates lower than 90%.

In the age range (35 – 44): leaders with a penetration rate (90% - 100%) are Denmark, Finland, Germany, Iceland, Netherlands, Norway and Sweden. (80% - 89%) have Austria, Belgium, France and Luxembourg. (70% - 79%) has Ireland. Finally, (60% - 69%) shows Malta. Regarding post communist countries, they have all penetration rates lower than 79%.

In the age range (45 – 54): leaders with a penetration rate (90% - 100%) are Denmark, Finland, Iceland, Netherlands, Norway and Sweden. (80% - 89%) have Germany and Luxembourg. (70% - 79%) show Austria, Belgium and France. In the range (60% - 69%) there is no country. In the range (50% - 59%) are Ireland and Spain. Italy falls within (40% - 49%) and in the range (30% - 39%) are Cyprus, World and Portugal. As for the post communist countries they have all penetration rates lower than 79%.

In the age range (55 – 64): leaders are Iceland, Sweden and Norway (80% - 89%), followed by Denmark and Netherlands (70% - 79%), Finland and Luxembourg (60% - 69%) and finally Austria, Belgium and France (50% - 59%). Spain and World have a percentage lower than 29%. Regarding the post communist countries they have all penetration rates below 39%.

In the age range (65 – 74): leaders are Denmark, Iceland, Netherlands, Norway and Sweden (50% - 59%). Regarding the post communist countries they have all penetration rates below 20%.

In the age range (75 and over) there are not enough data available, but the striking thing is that Norway has a penetration rate 42%.

2.4.4. Education

In Europe, according to (Reitsma, 2000) the online consumer profile regarding education has the following characteristics: the percentage of users with higher education ranges from 53% (Sweden) to 73% (France). According to recent data of the year 2007, according to Eurostat, the internet penetration is positively affected by education level in all countries (capitalistic as well as post communist). Besides, in all levels of education the capitalistic countries (especially the northern ones) have higher internet penetration than the post communist countries.

Regarding the case "individuals with no or low formal education", in the range of internet penetration (30% - 39%) fall Denmark and Norway. In the range (20% - 29%) are Finland, Germany, Iceland, Luxembourg, Netherlands and Sweden. In the range (10% - 19%) fall Austria, France and UK. All the remaining countries, including the post communist ones, have an internet penetration rate below 10%.

Regarding the case "individuals with medium formal education", in the range of internet penetration (40% - 49%) fall Denmark, Germany, Luxembourg, Netherlands, Norway and UK. In the range (30% - 39%) are Finland, France, Iceland, Malta and Sweden. Austria and Ireland fall in the range (20% - 29%), while below 19% are all the rest including the post communist countries.

Regarding the case "individuals with high formal education", in the range (60% - 69%) fall Denmark, Netherlands, Norway and UK. In the range (50% - 59%) are Germany, Ireland, Luxembourg, Netherlands, Norway and Sweden. In the range of (40% - 49%) fall Austria, Finland, Iceland and Malta. All the remaining countries (including the post communist ones) show an internet penetration lower than 29%.

2.4.5. Gender

According to Eurostat (2007), shown in tables 8 and 9, we observe that the internet penetration between males (16 – 74 years old) is generally higher than that of the females (16 – 74 years old), and that the northern European countries show the highest internet penetration, while the post communist countries have the lowest internet penetration rates. A brief description hasas follows.

For the males: In the range of internet penetration (50% - 59%) falls Norway. In the range (40% - 49%) fall UK, Denmark, Netherlands, Germany, Luxembourg and Sweden. In the range (30% - 39%) fall Iceland, Finland and Austria. In the range of (21% - 29%) are Ireland, France and Malta. Below the internet penetration 20% fall all the rest countries as well as the post communist countries.

For the females: In the range of internet penetration (50% - 59%) there is no country. In the range (40% - 49%) fall Norway and UK. In the range (30% - 39%) fall Denmark, Netherlands, Germany, Sweden, Finland and Iceland. In the range of (21% - 29%) are

Luxembourg, France, Ireland and Austria. Below the internet penetration 20% fall all the rest countries as well as the post communist countries.

2.4.6. Estimations for Future Trends

The prospects for the e-commerce sector are very prominent for the next few years, with some forecast predict 70% growth of people shopping online. (Staunton, 2008)

By 2013, almost 50% of European citizens are going to shop online. This is a major increase compared to 21% from 2006. The major growth will be expected to be presented in Southern Europe, even though the penetration of broadband internet and shopping online still remain very low. (Staunton, 2008).

As far as North-Western Europe is concerned, France is been predicted to present growth in internet shopping, since recent broadband connections have not been replaced by higher levels of online shopping. One of main reasons justifying the relatively slow evolution of e-commerce in France, is Minitel system existence, which is a network like internet, with few e-commerce facilities. This network is dated from 1983 and it is estimated that almost 32% of the population still use this technology.

As far as the Nordic region, it is expected to have a major growth until 2013, as far as e-commerce sector is concerned: it is estimated that more than three-quarters of adults are going to shop online in Denmark, as well as 60% of Swedish consumers, until then. Also, the Netherlands are about to double the e commerce use, over the next six years. This market growth is attributed to several factors, such as an almost perfect telecoms infrastructure, an urbanized society and a technology-expert population. (Staunton, 2008).

For the next five years, the number of Europeans citizens who are about to shop online, will grow from 100 million to 174 million, with an average yearly net retail spending expected to be from around €1,000 to €1,500. In total, this estimation will cause European e Commerce a total spending of €263 billion in 2011, with the most popular sectors for online shopping to be travel, clothes, groceries, and consumer electronics all above the €10 billion per year (Favier, 2006).

CONCLUSION

During the last decades, the use of Internet has been expanding greatly throughout the world, since a substantial part of world trade is been conducted electronically. The Internet connects easily and simply millions of users, consumers and retailers.

Therefore, Internet revolution had influenced e-commerce evolution, which had caused radical changes as far as the traditional commerce is concerned. That is the reason why e-commerce will become the major force for the evolution of the international information society, since, all the trade world, consumers, businessman, and governments of different countries will have to take action in the information society. In order to achieve a successful entrance into the new electronic markets of Internet will be the creation of communicative strategies as well as the developmental tactics of e-commerce. For some companies, e-commerce has already been a way of making business. Therefore, e-commerce would be a very important part of trading. In order to be effective, it has to create, a complete supply chain, which will give choices for transportation, warehousing, distribution channels, information about consumers, suppliers, products as well as the market.

On the other hand, special measures should be taken for consumers as well, since their confidence has to be won, in order for businesses and markets to be developed.

Develop private investments in e-commerce, in order to make the stock exchange and the contribution of the venture capitals to advance, leading to the exploitation of the stock market.

Finally, educate small businesses should in order to understand the possible benefits of e-commerce, concerning saving of money, creation of new markets and the prevision of new opportunities for the new products and services.

REFERENCES

Cohen, L., Manion, L. and Morrison, K., 2001, "*Research Methods in Education*", 5th Edition, Routledge Falmer Taylor and Francis group.

Collis, J. and Hussey, R., 2003, "*Business Research*", 2nd Edition, Palgrave Macmillan.

Constantinides, E. (2004), "*Influencing the online consumer's behaviour: The web experience*", Vol. 14, No.2, pp.111-126.

Cronin, M. J. (1996), "*The Internet Strategy Handbook: Lessons from the new frontier of business",* Harvard Business School Press, Boston MA.

Delfmann, W., Albers, S., Gehring, M., 2002, "*The impact of electronic commerce on logistics service providers*", International Journal of Physical Distribution and Logistics Management Volume 32 Number 3, pp. 203-222.

Denscombe, M., 2002, "*Ground Rules for Good research*", 1st Edition, Open University Press, McGraw-Hill House.

Donaton, S. (1994), "OK To put ads on the internet, but mind your netiquette", *Advertising Age,* Vol. 65, N0. 18, pp. 3-62.

Doherty, N., Ellis Chadwick, F. and Hart, C. (1999), "Cyber retailing in the UK: the potential of the internet as a retail channel", *International Journal of Retailing and Distribution Management,* Vol. 27, No.1. pp.22-36.

Farier J. (2006),"*Europe's e-Commerce, Forecast 2006to 2011"*, available at: http://www.forrester.com.

Easterby Smith, M., Thorpe, R., Lowe, A., 2002, "*Management Research: an introduction*", 2nd Edition, Sage Publications Ltd, London.

Ellsworth, J. H. and Ellsworth M. V., (1996), *Marketing on the Internet – Multimedia Strategies for the WWW,* John Wiley, New York, NY.

Eurostat available at: <http://epp.eurostat.ec.europa.eu/portal/page?_pageid=1996,45323734and_dad=portaland_schema=PORTALandscreen=welcomerefandopen=/science/isoc/isoc_ecandlanguage=enandproduct=EU_science_technology_innovationandroot=EU_science_technology_innovationandscrollto=96>, 15/09/010.

Fogg, B.G., Soohoo, C., Danielson, D., Marable, L., Stanford, J. and Tauber, E. (2002), "How do people evaluate a Web site's credibility? Results from a large study", *Persuasive Technology Lab, Stanford University*, available at: www.consumerwebwatch.org/news/report3_credibilityresearch/stanfordPTL_TOC.htm.

Forrester Research (2003), "*Forrester Research projects US ecommerce to hit nearly $320 billion"*, press release, available at: *technographics: the online consumer 1998 to 2003"*, available at: www.forrester.com/ER/Press/Release/0,1769,823,00.html>.

Ghose, A. and A. Sundararajan (2005a), "Pricing security software: theory and evidence", *Proceedings of the 2005 Workshop on Economics of Information Security.*

Ghose, A. K. Huang and A. Sundararajan (2005b), "Versions, successive generations and pricing strategies in software markets: Theory and Evidence". *Mimeo*, NYU.

Ghosey, A., and Sundararajanz, A., (2006), "Evaluating Pricing Strategy Using eCommerce Data: Evidence and Estimation Challenges", *Leonard Stern School of Business, New York University.*

Glazer, Rashi (1991), "Marketing in the Information-Intensive Environment: Strategic Implications of Knowledge as an Asset", *Journal of Marketing,* 55 (October) 1-19.

Grabner-Kräuter, S. and Kaluscha, A. E. (2003), "Empirical research in online trust: a review and critical assessment", *International Journal of Human-Computer Studies*, Vol. 58, No. 6, pp. 783-812.

Green, D. (1999), "How will the traditional retailer compete with-commerce retailers evolving in today's marketplace: the supply chain perspective", *presentation at the Annual Conference of the Council of Logistics Management,* 18 October, Toronto.

Grewal, D., Iyer, G.R. and Levy, M. (2002), "Internet retailing: enablers, limiters and market consequences", *Journal of Business Research*

Hoffman, D. L. and Novak, T. P., (1995), "*Marketing in Hypermedia Computer-Mediated Environments: Conceptual Foundations*", *Project 2000 working paper no. 1, Owen Graduate School of Management,* Vanderbilt University.

Hoffman, D. and Novak, T. P., (1996), "*A New Marketing Paradigm for Electronic Commerce"*, The Information Society. February, 19. Available at: http://sloan.ucr.edu/blog/uploads/papers/A%20New%20Marketing%20Paradigm%20for%20Electronic%20Commerce%20%5BHoffman,%20Novak%20-%20Feb%201996%5D.pdf.

Hoffman, D. L., Novak, T. P. and Peralta, M.A. (1999), "*Building consumer trust online"*, Communications of the ACM, Vol. 42, No. 4, pp. 80-85.

Hoffman, D. L. Novak, T. P. and Chatterjee, P. (2006) "*Commercial Scenarios for the Web: Opportunities and Challenges"*. Available at: ≤http://sloan.ucr.edu/blog/uploads/papers/hoffman,%20novak,%20and%20chatterjee%20(1995)%20JCMC.pdf≥

Internet Confidence Index, Yahoo/AC Nielsen (2002), available at: <http://www.emeraldinsight.com/Insight/viewReferences.do;jsessionid=4A1A7A7EE2B98871F43EEA34D36B902C?contentId=1509308andrefType=Ref>

Jones, R. (1994), "*Digital's World-Wide Web server: A case study*", Computer Networks and ISDN Systems, 27-2, November, 297- 306.

Kabundi, A., (2004), "*Estimation of Economic Growth in France Using Business Survey Data"*, IMF Working Paper No.04/69, International Monetary Fund, April. Available at: www.ssrn.com, as id878892.pdf.

Kandampully J.(2003),"*B2B relationships and networks in the Internet age*", Management Decision, pp.443-451.

Keegan, W. J. and Schlegelmilch, B. B., 2001, "*Global Marketing Management: a European Perspective*", 6th Edition, Prentice Hall.

Kossecki, P, and Kaczor, U., (2006), "*No Trust, No Transaction –The Implications For The Internet Suppliers*", Available at: www.ssrn.com as id944358.pdf.

Kossecki, P., (2006), "*Trust and Sustainable Development of the eCommerce*". Available at: www.ssrn.com as ssrn-id625983.pdf.

Krajewski, L. J. and Ritzman, L. P., 2002, "*Operations Management*", 6th Edition, Pearson Education, Inc.

Kyriazopoulos, P. and Samanta, I., (2009) Managers' perceptions of using of e-marketing in B2B relationships Journal SPOUDAI Publisher University of Piraeus

Livanis E.and Tourtoglou L.(2001),"*An analysis of the effectiveness and necessity for growth of the e-commerce. Evidence from Consumers industries*", Paper.

Mintel Oxygen Reports - *E-commerce (2008),* Available at: <http://www.mintel.com/press_releases/331159.htm>

Michalski, J. (1995), "People are the killer app", *Forbes ASAP*, June 5, 120-122.

Porter, M. E. and Miller (1985), "*How Information gives you competitive advantage*", Harvard Business Review, July-August.

Reitsma, (2000), *eCommerce Enters Europe,* Presentation of Forrester Research Inc.

Ricciuti, M. (1995) "*Database vendors hawk wares on Internet*", Infoworld, 17-2. Jan. 9, 10

Saunders, M., Lewis, P., Thornhill, A., 2007, "*Research Methods for Business Students*", 4th Edition, Pearson Education Limited, Prentice Hall.

Sekaran, U., 2003, "*Research methods for Business: a skill building approach*", 4th Edition, John Wiley and Sons.

Stanton C.(2008),"*E-Commerce across Europe*", Progress Reports, Vision.

Strauss J.and Frost R.(1999),"*On the Marketing Internet*", Prentice Hall.

Strategic International - Kataras SA (2001) *"E-Commerce in World. From Fiction to Reality"*, available at: http://www.strategic.gr/

Van Maanen, J., 1983, "*Qualitative Methodology*", Sage Publications, Inc., London.

Vlachopouou m.(1999),"E-Marketing",Rosili.

Wallace, D. J. (1995), "*Shopping online: A sticky business*", Advertising Age, April 10, 20.

In: HRM and Marketing Orientation in the New Era
Editor: Panagiotis Kyriazopoulos
ISBN: 978-1-62808-959-2

Chapter 14

SHOPPING VALUE, SATISFACTION AND ITS BEHAVIORAL OUTCOMES IN THE PURCHASE OF PRIVATE LABEL BRANDED PRODUCTS: A THEORETICAL FRAMEWORK

Anubhav Anand Mishra[1]* and Manish Kumar Srivastava[2]
[1]The ICFAI University Dehradun, Rajawala Road, Selaqui
Dehradun, Uttarakhand, India
[2]Faculty of Management Studies,
The ICFAI University Dehradun, Rajawala Road, Selaqui
Dehradun, Uttarakhand, India

ABSTRACT

The current study proposes a framework to understand the effect of consumer shopping value (i.e., utilitarian and hedonic) derived from the experience of purchasing PLB products on consumer satisfaction and its behavioural outcomes (i.e., loyalty and word of mouth communication). It is also proposed that various demographic variables like gender, age, and income and different product categories (food and grocery, apparel and consumer durables) will have statistically significant moderating impact on the relationship between utilitarian and hedonic values with consumer satisfaction. Although theory is not sufficient for addressing such a relationship directly, it is meaningful to investigate the above mentioned constructs. Therefore, the current study is raising a few broad research questions and research propositions.

Keywords: Consumer shopping value, hedonic and utilitarian values, consumer satisfaction, loyalty, word-of-mouth

* Phone: +91-9358290801 Email: anubhavmishras@gmail.com.

INTRODUCTION

The retail industry has been at the helm of India's growth strategy. The retail sector has progressed dramatically from traditional village fairs and street hawkers to impressive malls and plush retail outlets. According to Joseph *et al.* (2008), India is the seventh-largest retail market in the world, and is expected to grow at a Compound Annual Growth Rate (CAGR) of over 13% till 2012. Furthermore, it is estimated to grow from US$427 billion in 2010 to US$637 billion in 2015. Organised retail sector has been growing at a faster pace than traditional outlets. A report by investment bank, Northbridge Capital, 'Indian Retail Research 2009' estimates that although, organised retail accounts for just 14%, or US$63 billion, yet this sector is expected to grow 40% faster than the overall market to reach US$90 billion in 2010. Higher disposable incomes, alterations in people's lifestyle, easy availability of credit cards, high exposure of brands through media, and increasing number of malls and branded outlets have enabled this transition of sales from traditional outlets to organised retail. The Indian government in 2005 allowed foreign direct investment (FDI) in single brand retail up to 51 percent. This has opened up a lot of opportunities in the organised retail sector.

An ever increasing competitive marketplace has led the retailers to seek strategies to insulate themselves and increase their profit. Along with this, consumers have an increasing number of shopping venues available to them (i.e. brick and mortar stores, catalogues, television, and internet), and therefore, deciding where to shop has become a key decision (Kirkup and Rafig 1999). Moreover, large-format, modern retail chains in India have established themselves by reaching critical volumes, and hence, the next step of the classical retail story has begun with the introduction of private label branded (PLBs) products (Ailawadi 2001; Corstjens and Lal 2000). In turn, these strategies would enable them to build a competitive advantage. PLBs are the brands that are owned, controlled and sold exclusively by a retailer (Baltas 1997). Furthermore, Fitzell (1992) has suggested that exclusivity is the key word as competitors in the same market do not carry the same PLBs. In this light, PLBs are also known as store brands, retailer brands, own brands, wholesaler brands or distributor own brands. The present scenario is such that, PLBs have proliferated in a number of product categories and have garnered large market share. When compared with national label brands (also known as manufacturer's brands), PLBs offer a large plethora of value. It can be seen that apart from other benefits, PLBs offer retailers a means to differentiate their stores, achieve consumer loyalty, as well as increase their profitability.

From the point of view of consumers, a PLB is a guarantee of consistency, quality and value. The ways in which PLBs add value are by offering choice at the same price, filling price gaps and by launching innovative products which may not have sustainable volumes nationally. The third is the best way for private labels to create value and build a brand for themselves. A thorough review of existing literature has lead to the conclusion that only a few studies (Corstjens and Lal 2000) have directly dealt with PLBs by addressing consumer loyalty. The 'store-as-the-brand' strategy has become one of the most important means of developing consumer loyalty among speciality store retailers (Smith 2000). According to a study by 'New Merchandising' in 1999, "By creating a retail store as a brand, the retailer is better able to deliver a perception of selling higher-quality, fashion-forward merchandise." In turn, this type of branding strategy enables the retailer to establish a market-based relational asset that endows a source of competitive advantage.

Traditionally, consumer buying behaviour has been depicted as a rational and goal oriented framework (e.g. Howard and Sheth 1969). This goal seeking and task related behaviour has been the predominant theory for many years. However, in more recent years consumer behaviour literature has shifted its focus upon the role of emotions and pleasure (Adaval 2001; Bagozzi and Gopinath 1999). This school of thought has deliberated upon consumer shopping orientation in terms of 'economic' versus 'recreational' orientation (e.g. Bellenger and Korgaonkar 1980) or 'hedonic' versus 'utilitarian' orientation (e.g. Babin *et al.* 1994; Hirschman and Holbrook 1982). The basis of consumer shopping orientation/value has extended from the acquisition of a product or service (Grewal *et al.* 1998) to its consumption (i.e., its use or appreciation) (Hirschman 1984) and finally, to the enjoyment of the entire shopping experience (Babin *et al.* 1994). Babin *et al.* (1994) have confirmed in their study that the two aspects of goal-seeking (i.e., utilitarian value) and pleasure-oriented (i.e., hedonic value) behaviour are complementary and intertwined, and therefore, they need to be taken together into account to achieve a richer understanding of the consumer buying process.

Researchers have continuously sought to investigate the utilitarian and hedonic aspects of shopping value in several disciplines including sociology, psychology, and economics, although the terminology was not used consistently (Batra and Ahtola 1990; Hamilton 1987). Hamilton (1987: 1541), an economist, has stated that, "We use goods in two ways. We use goods as symbols of status and simultaneously as instruments to achieve some end-in-view." This view point has clearly combined both facets of utilitarian as well as hedonic consumption. This multidisciplinary recognition of the utilitarian and hedonic elements of consumption has mirrored a parallel theoretical development in the field of consumer research as well.

Literature Review

Perceived Shopping Value

The value concept has been used in a wide range of diverse disciplines, such as economics, accounting, finance, strategy, production, management, and marketing. In the field of economics, value finds a place within the context of exchange, that is, a goods' value to a consumer is represented by the price that the consumer is willing to pay and the relationship between that price and the utilities or satisfaction the goods provides (Richins 1994). In the field of marketing, value is also researched mostly in the exchange context, but more from the point of view of consumers' perceptions of value when faced with choices of products or services to purchase (Richins 1994). According to Rokeach (1973: 5), value is, "...an enduring belief that a specific mode of conduct or end-state of existence is personally or socially preferable to an opposite or converse mode conduct or end-state of existence." Further elaborating, values are the fundamental determinants for the selection and maintenance of the goals or ends toward which individuals strive, while at the same time regulating the manner in which the strive takes place (Vinson *et al.* 1977). In turn, these values have been found to affect various aspects of consumption behaviour and attitudes (Donthu and Cherian 1992).

This value conceptualization has been linked to consumer's perceptions towards market transactions. Payne and Holt (2001) proposed that simply viewing value as part of an individual transaction process is not viable but value is created and changed over time as a result of an ongoing series of transactions. Woodruff (1997) consolidated on the several concepts of value to define consumer value as a "consumer's perceived preference for and evaluation of those product attributes, attribute performances, and consequences arising from use that facilitate achieving the consumer's goals and purposes in use situations." Woodruff (1997) concluded that perceived value occurred at various stages of the purchase process, and therefore, perceptions of value can be generated before the product or service acquisition and its use.

In the marketing literature, the role of consumer value on consumer's behaviour has been revised and re-examined at length (Zeithaml 1988). A thorough review of the extant literature on the conceptualisation of value reveals its multifaceted and highly fragmented nature. There are many conflicting points of view and consequently, there is no widely accepted way of putting all the views together (Woodruff 1997). The definition of value varies with a wide range of usages in accordance with research contexts and researchers (Zeithaml 1988). In most of the cases, the concept of value is related to an individual's enduring beliefs.

Shopping can provide both task related (product acquisition) or hedonic value through responses evoked during the experience (Babin *et al.* 1994: 645). Value of a product or service is dependent on its role in creating a favourable consumption experience. To create and maintain lasting relationships with one's consumers, marketers need to go beyond the price and quality mix to provide experience-based value. To be more specific, value involves an interaction between a subject (such as a consumer) and some object (such as a product or service). Value is considered to be relativistic as it is comparative (based on ranking of objects), personal (differing among people), and situational (dependent on the context in which an evaluation is made) (Holbrook 1986). Value necessitates a preference which implies a certain degree of relative affective response.

Utilitarian and Hedonic Shopping Value

Utilitarian and hedonic dimensions of consumption have been well recognized by consumer behaviour researchers. Batra and Ahtola (1990) developed a scale to measure the consumers' attitude towards brands and the resultant behaviours, and confirmed that attitude towards brands and consumption behaviour has at least two distinct dimensions, namely, hedonic and utilitarian. According to the authors, the hedonic value is related to sensory attributes and focuses on consummatory affective gratification, while, the utilitarian value is related to functional and non-sensory attributes and focuses on instrumental expectation. In addition to Batra and Ahtola's study (1990), Spangenberg *et al.* (1997) have also developed a scale for measuring the utilitarian and hedonic components of attitudes. Both the group of researchers chose specific product categories and specific brands within each of those categories in order to examine the utilitarian and hedonic dimensions of products and services. Both the scales appeared to be somewhat reliable in measuring the attitudes of the consumers with respect to those specific product categories and classes (i.e., potato chips, cooking oil, dish washing detergent, personal computers, and vacation resorts). The major limitation of these scales was that they could not be transferred across various product categories and classes. Crowley *et al.* (1992) have provided further evidence of the existence of hedonic and utilitarian elements in attitudes towards product categories.

Babin *et al.* (1994) conducted a study to develop a scale specific to the measurement of utilitarian and hedonic value. The study was based on accepted methods for scale development in consumer research. The authors made use of focus group interviews to assist in establishing the contents of each dimension and thus, were able to validate the scale psychometrically and theoretically. Confirmatory factor analysis was employed to finalise a fifteen item scale. The scale exhibited reliability and construct validity across different samples as well as situations.

Babin *et al.* (2005) did a study in the service industry (restaurant) to extend the notions of utilitarian and hedonic value to account for outcomes of consumer service encounters. The research focused on presenting a model that incorporated service quality, consumer affect, and perceived shopping value and these were related to consumer satisfaction and intention to engage in word-of-mouth activity. The model was then tested on a sample of South Korean consumers based on an actual restaurant experience. They confirmed the ability of the consumer service value scale to account for utilitarian and hedonic value, the role of functional and affective service environment components in shaping consumer satisfaction and future patronage intentions and the relative diagnosticity of positive affect.

Carpenter *et al.* (2005) conducted an empirical research to examine whether consumers value the in-store experience that retailers provided as part of the store as a brand concept. They used a self-administered questionnaire to survey a sample of young adult consumers (n = 188). Statistical techniques such as MANOVA with post hoc tests were used to evaluate the data. The findings from the statistical models revealed that consumers expected both hedonic as well as utilitarian value to be present when shopping in the store as a brand context.

According to a study conducted by Rintamaki *et al.* (2006), the perceived consumer shopping value can be disintegrated into tripartite conceptualizations namely, hedonic, utilitarian and social dimensions. The third dimension identified, i.e., the social dimension is a new addition in their findings. The authors have concluded that retailers can add hedonic and social values in the design of stores, and their marketing programs in order to increase consumer patronage. They further stressed that successful retailers should understand that consumer value encompasses concrete and abstract aspects of the shopping experiences starting right from the entrance to check out, and from making buying decisions to consuming and experiencing the product.

Utilitarian and hedonic consumption attitudes not only influence the purchase of a product, but they also influence the post purchase intention. Park and Mowen (2007) conducted a study to find whether hedonic and utilitarian motives also influence individual's inclination to exchange the old product model with the newly introduced and upgraded model if any exchange offer is being provided. The conclusions of their study showed that if an exchange offer is introduced then the buyer will be willing to exchange the product provided that he purchased the product for hedonic purposes and not for utilitarian purposes.

Fiore and Kim (2007) conducted a study to reflect the integrative (experiential and utilitarian) nature of shopping experience. They proposed a theoretical framework to help researchers develop empirical studies blurring experiential and utilitarian approaches to shopping experience.

Nguyen *et al.* (2007) conducted an empirical study to explore the impact of hedonic shopping motivations and supermarket attributes on shopper loyalty. They made use of a sample of 608 supermarket shoppers in Ho Chi Minh City, Vietnam to test the model. Structural equation modelling was employed to analyze the data. The study concluded that supermarket attributes and hedonic shopping motivations had positive effects on shopper loyalty. The authors also found that the impact of hedonic motivations on shopper loyalty was different between the younger and older, as well as lower and higher income groups of customers. However, the study did not find such difference between female and male shoppers.

Consumer Satisfaction

On the surface, consumer satisfaction seems to be an uncomplicated concept. However, its definition is not a static one, but rather it has evolved over time. In the words of Oliver (1981: 27), consumer satisfaction is, "the summary psychological state resulting when the emotion surrounding disconfirmed expectations is coupled with the consumer's prior feelings about the consumption experience." Engel and Blackwell (1982: 501) have opined it to be, "an evaluation that the chosen alternative is consistent with prior beliefs with respect to that alternative."

It is obvious from the above definitions, that numerous researchers have defined the construct of satisfaction differently. It can surely be ascertained that all the above definitions indicate an overwhelming effect on consumer satisfaction management. By summarising the above definitions it is quite apparent that consumer satisfaction is:

1. Some type of emotional (affective), cognitive, and/or an impulse (conative) response.
2. Established on an assessment of product-related standards, product consumption experiences, and or purchase-related attributes (e.g., salesperson).
3. Articulated before choice, after choice, after consumption, after extended experience, or just about any other time a researcher may enquire consumer about the product or product related attributes.

Even though, multiple definitions and conceptualisations of the consumer satisfaction construct are present in the existing literature, yet it can be said that research stream is quite robust. However, the research has increased with the linking of consumer satisfaction with the overall performance of the firm (Anderson *et al.* 1994). It is also worthwhile to note that a majority of the studies have been focused on the product level, although research at other levels like brand, store, salespersons etc. has also been undertaken but is remarkably less developed conceptually and empirically.

One of the most popular streams of research involves the development of measures for the consumer satisfaction construct. Wirtz and Lee's (2003) empirical study on the quality and context-specific applicability of consumer satisfaction measures is quite important to the context of the present study. They tested nine of the most commonly used consumer satisfaction measures for their cognitive (utilitarian) and affective (hedonic) content. They concluded that all the nine measures showed the ability to capture both the dimensions of the construct. Sivadas and Baker-Prewitt (2000) concluded in their empirical study that consumer satisfaction does have an influence on relative attitude, word of mouth communication and repurchase intentions but had no direct effect on store loyalty. Yet, the study also put forward that the presence of favourable relative attitude and consumer recommendations was the key to the development of loyalty. Reynolds and Beatty (1999) put forward that the consumer's perception of benefits does have a positive effect on the consumer's satisfaction with the salesperson. It is also positively associated to the loyalty towards the salesperson, salesperson word of mouth communication and share of purchase. The authors also concluded that the effects related to satisfaction with the salesperson, loyalty, and word of mouth communication had a spill over effect on the satisfaction with the company, and loyalty and positive word of mouth communication towards the company as a whole. Carpenter and Fairhurst (2005) examined the effect of utilitarian and hedonic shopping benefits on consumer satisfaction, loyalty, and word of mouth recommendation in a retail store branded context. The authors concluded the presence of positive relationships between utilitarian and hedonic shopping benefits, consumer satisfaction, consumer loyalty, and word of mouth communication. Their study was unique due to the relative newness of the context (i.e., retail branded products) in which the study was conducted. Researchers (Chandon *et al.* 2000) have concluded that the relative appeal of hedonic value when compared with utilitarian value is dependent on the nature (hedonic or utilitarian) of the product or service. This indicates that the role and relative importance of utilitarian characteristics versus hedonic aspects may vary across different products or services.

Based on these evidences, the present study proposes that:

- P_1: The consumer's perception of utilitarian shopping value will be positively associated with the consumer's satisfaction with PLB product's purchase experience.
- P_2: The consumer's perception of hedonic shopping value will be positively associated with the consumer's satisfaction with PLB product's purchase experience.

Consumer Loyalty

The conceptualisation of the loyalty construct has evolved over the last century. The first academic exploration in the field of brand loyalty can be ascribed to Copeland (1923). However, Copeland's (1923) work lacked well-underlying conceptual and methodological bases. The major developments in this domain started in the late 1960s and the 1970s. Early researchers focussed on loyalty towards tangible goods brands (Cunningham 1956; Day 1969; Tucker 1964). Cunningham (1956) defined brand loyalty in very simple terms as, "the proportion of purchases of a household devoted to the brand it purchased most often." However, Cunningham (1961) broadened the spectrum of analysis by assessing consumers' loyalty towards the store rather than on brands.

An extensive review of past literature indicated that a majority of the initial research laid emphasis on the behavioural dimension of loyalty. This is epitomised by Tucker (1964: 32) who opined that, "no consideration should be given to what the subject thinks nor what goes on in his central nervous system, his behaviour is the full statement of what brand loyalty is." Jacoby (1971) has confirmed that previous studies had focussed primarily on the behavioural outcomes and as a consequence these studies completely ignored consideration of what went on in consumer's minds. It was always measured in terms of its outcome characteristics (Jacoby and Chestnut 1978). To further explain, the measures were primarily directed to determine the sequence of purchase or buying patterns (Tucker 1964), proportion of purchase devoted to a given brand or in other words share of total purchases (Cunningham 1956: 118; Farley 1964: 9) and probability of purchase (Maffei 1960). Day (1969) was the pioneer researcher who introduced the two-dimensional concept of brand loyalty and stated that loyalty should be evaluated with both the behavioural (i.e., repeat purchase) as well as attitudinal (i.e., affective aspect) criteria. In a review of 53 operational definitions, Jacoby and Chestnut (1978) concluded that a central theme that runs through all the definitions is that loyalty is related to the proportion of expenditure dedicated to a specific brand or store. Jacoby and Chestnut (1978) were the first authors who provided a conceptually clear and precise definition of brand loyalty. They expressed that brand loyalty is composed of six necessary and collective conditions and defined brand loyalty as, "(1) the biased (i.e., non-random) (2) behavioural response (i.e., purchase) (3) expressed over time (4) by some decision-making unit (i.e., a person or group of persons) (5) with respect to one or more alternative brands (i.e., out of a set of such brands) and (6) is a function of psychological (decision-making, evaluative) processes."

Notwithstanding these determining works, there is still no universal agreement on the definition of loyalty (Jacoby and Chestnut 1978; Uncles *et al.* 2003). Majumdar (2005) has stated that, "customer loyalty is a complex, multidimensional concept." The complexity of consumer loyalty is reflected in the wide range of definitions available within the literature. According to Uncles *et al.* (2003), three popular conceptualizations of consumer loyalty exist. Firstly, consumer loyalty is an attitude that leads to a relationship with the brand. Secondly, consumer loyalty is expressed primarily in terms of revealed behaviour. Thirdly, buying is moderated by the individual consumer's characteristics, circumstances, and/or the purchase situation. Oliver (1997) has defined loyalty as, "a deeply held commitment to re-buy or re-patronize a preferred product or service consistently in the future, thereby causing repetitive same-brand or same brand-set purchasing, despite situational influences and marketing efforts that have the potential to cause switching behaviour." Past data have confirmed that a vast majority of consumers are polygamous in their purchase decisions and tend to offer their loyalty to a portfolio of brands within a product category (Uncles *et al.* 2003). This consumer phenomenon has led to another definition of customer loyalty, "an ongoing propensity to buy the brand, usually as one of several" (Uncles *et al.* 2003). Specifically, loyalty can be defined as a consumer's intention or predisposition to purchase from the same firm again (Edvardsson *et al.* 2000) and it is a result of the conviction that the value received from one seller is greater than the value available from other alternatives. Sirdeshmukh *et al.* (2002: 20) have defined consumer loyalty as, "an intention to perform a diverse set of behaviours that signal a motivation to maintain a relationship with the focal firm, including allocating a higher share of the category wallet to the specific service provider, engaging in positive word of mouth (WOM), and repeat purchasing."

It is proposed that:

- P_3: The consumer's satisfaction with the PLB product's purchase experience will be positively associated with the consumer's attitudinal loyalty to the PLB products.
- P_4: A significant and positive effect will exist between consumer's loyalty (attitudinal) and word of mouth communication (behavioral loyalty) in the purchase of PLB products.

Word of Mouth Communication

The importance of WOM has been long recognized by diffusion of innovation researchers (e.g. Ryan and Gross 1943), and has been acknowledged as the most important communication source between consumers (Derbaix and Vanhamme 2003). WOM is a social process of personal influence, in which the interpersonal communications between a sender and a receiver can vary the receiver's behaviour or attitudes. This interpersonal communication plays a major role in influencing the opinions and has also long been recognized by sociologists and psychologists, who in turn, identified the importance of "opinion leaders" in this process (Katz and Lazarsfeld 1955). This highly regarded ability of individuals to influence other people's opinions is of prime interest to organizations that are seeking to market their products and services, and especially for those organisations whose market offerings cannot be easily trialled prior to purchase (Rogers 1995). According to Arndt (1967), "informal communication is probably the oldest mechanism by which opinions on products and brands are developed, expressed, and spread."

The WOM network of consumers is a subset of a larger social network and is functionally dependent on it. A few examples of WOM networks are neighbourhoods, social organisations, and places of business, e-mail exchanges, chat rooms, web sites and other forms of internet communications. Generally these networks operate independently as small clusters. Within these networks some consumers are regarded as opinion leaders as they have a high influencing power on the decisions of other members of the network.

Heckman (1999: 2) has defined WOM communication as, "...when people convey genuine enthusiasm for a product or service to others." In the marketing context, Westbrook (1987: 261) has defined WOM communications as, "informal communications directed at other consumers about the ownership, usage, or characteristics of particular goods and services and/or their sellers." In general, WOM can be defined as an informal type of communication between private parties with reference to the evaluation of goods and services (Dichter 1966) and it has been considered to be one of the most powerful forces in the market place (Bansal and Voyer 2000) and the formation of consumers' attitudes (Bone 1995). WOM communication strategies are engaging because they combine the prospect of overcoming consumer resistance with considerably lower costs and fast delivery, especially through technology, such as the Internet.

Ennew *et al.* (2000) have put forward the view that suggests that the value of WOM cannot be the same across product, market and organisational contexts. For instance, the influence of WOM is greater for products that have a predominance of experience and credence qualities or for products whose purchase is highly associated with perceived risk. In this light, it is imperative to bring to the notice that, WOM communications offer consumers the ability to make more informed choices and consequently the consumers can benefit from reduced perceived risk of a certain buying behaviour.

Roselius (1971) cited that risk averse consumers found WOM to be a very useful strategy in reducing most types of risk including functional, time, financial, psychological and social. Perceived risk is inherent in a majority of purchase situations, which explains why consumers like to undertake a pre-purchase trial. A study by McKinsey and Company found that 67% of the sales of consumer goods were based on WOM (Taylor 2003).

According to Rosen (2000) the most elemental motivation behind WOM communication is that people talk because they are programmed to talk. It is in the inherent nature of individuals to share their experiences and to rely on others as sources of information instead of relying on formal and organizational sources such as advertising campaigns (Bansal and Voyer 2000). Without a doubt, WOM communication is exceedingly effective because of the fact that the source of the information has nothing to gain from the consumer's subsequent actions (Schiffman and Kanuk 1997). To simply state, consumers appreciate WOM communication for the reason that it is seen as a more reliable and trustworthy medium than any other information sources (Day 1971).

Herr *et al.* (1991) conducted a study to ascertain the connection between WOM information and product evaluation. They concluded that negative WOM communication decreases the product familiarity. Their research primarily concentrated on the method via which the communication took place (i.e., vividly vs. pallidly) and the type of communication exchanged (i.e., anecdotal vs. attributed related).

Giese and Spangenberg (1997) conducted a study to examine the effects of WOM behaviour on the evaluation of products and found similar results to those of Herr *et al.* (1991). The authors made use of an experimental method to demonstrate that negative WOM communication is influential in reducing the product familiarity. On the other hand, the study concluded that positive WOM communication does not enhance the familiarity with a product.

- P_5: The consumer's satisfaction with the PLB product's purchase experience will be positively associated with the consumer's word of mouth communication behavior about the PLB products.

Private Label Brands

The earliest studies on PLBs go all the way back to the 1960's. These studies were primarily focused on describing the PLB prone consumers for segmentation purposes (Burger and Schott 1972; Rao 1969). The demographic, psycho graphic and behavioral characteristics of PLB consumers revealed that educated households, large families, and older female heads were more likely to use PLBs. However, the absolute magnitudes of the effects were small and this lead Frank and Boyd (1965) to conclude that there were no socio-economic differences between national brands and PLB buyers.

Not long time back, PLBs were considered to be cheap imitations of poor quality bought only by less affluent customers (Veloutsou *et al.* 2004), but now they have become innovators and are quick to offer consumer products that match with the latest trends in the markets (for instance, organic farming, fair trade, exoticism, gourmet dishes and so on). Bellizzi *et al* (1981) conducted a survey to obtain the perceptions of national, private label, and generic brands through a series of Likert-type scales. The respondents rated private label brands below the national brands on attributes related to quality, appearance, and attractiveness. In the same way, Cunningham *et al.* (1982) concluded that consumers rated national brands as being superior to private label and generic brands in terms of taste, appearance, labeling, and variety of choice.

Livesey and Lennon (1978) concluded that some shoppers exhibited an aversion to buying store brands regardless of the amount of savings associated with their purchase. Invariably, all studies indicate that private label brands suffer from a low-quality image compared with national brands. In other words, to be successful, PLBs need to have a combination of low price and high quality (Stambaugh 1993: 69). It is also worthwhile to note that a major focus on quality as opposed to price would help in producing favorable perceptions of PLBs and increase consumers' loyalty toward these products. Rao (1969) conducted a study to describe the PLB prone consumer in terms of store loyalty. The author defined store loyalty as a repurchase rate, or the proportionate number of times a housewife visited the same store consecutively. The study concluded that the proportion of PLB coffee purchases was significantly related to the calculated store loyalty index. The study also found that some consumers may be less likely to differentiate among PLBs from different retail chains. The author attributed this consumer characteristic to consumer price sensitivity as PLBs were cheaper than national brands. This interaction of the value for money and the quality argument is an important facet of a modern day retailer's PLB marketing strategy.

Richardson *et al.* (1994) conducted a study to investigate the correlation of price sensitivity (i.e., value for money) with greater PLB purchases. Quite opposite to the popular notion, the authors found that perceived quality was a better indicator of purchase than consumer's perceived value. This was a path breaking finding as PLB marketing strategies focus primarily on either price or quality. These findings indicated that a strategy focused on improving the quality would be more beneficial to retailers. Burton and colleagues (1998) developed a scale to measure consumers' attitudes towards PLBs. They employed a multi-item scale to and found that consumers' attitudes toward PLBs were negatively correlated with brand loyalty, price-quality perceptions and impulsiveness.

In particular, Baltas (1997) conducted a study to examine consumer characteristics that drive consumers to have a positive attitude towards PLB products. The study concluded by finding four basic variables, namely, purchase behaviour, reasons for preference, attitudes toward PLB products, and involvement. The study also suggested that, due to this reason, consumers may actually prefer buying PLB products from a familiar retailer who offers them a guarantee for the purchase of a low-priced product, instead of buying an unknown brand that has a level of uncertainty and financial risk. Corstjens and Lal (2000) employed game theoretic analysis to study the role of PLB in building store loyalty. The researchers found that quality PLBs can be utilized by the retailers to differentiate them. Furthermore, quality PLBs can be an instrument for retailers to generate store loyalty and store profitability. Conceivably, the most important finding of the study was the complimentary nature of national brands and PLBs.

Ailawadi *et al.* (2001) conducted a study to identify the demographic and psychographic variables that have an impact on the consumer's usage of PLBs and national brand promotions by considering the economic benefits, hedonic benefits, and costs of partaking in these behaviors. The authors employed structural equation model to study the relationship of these attributes with the use of PLBs, in-store promotions for national brands and out-of-store promotions for national brands. They concluded that consumer demographics (i.e., income, employment status, children in the household, type of residence, age, sex, and education) indirectly affect the usage of PLBs and national brand promotions, but they do affect psychographic characteristics (i.e., product quality, savings, entertainment, exploration, and self-expression). In turn, these psychographic variables have a direct effect on the usage of PLBs and national brand promotions. Furthermore, the authors also identified various psychographic variables that lead to consumer's usage of PLBs and concluded that economic benefits and costs (i.e., price and quality) are correlated to the use of PLBs. Additionally, the use of out of store promotions was positively correlated with utilitarian and hedonic benefits.

The study also identified a typology of consumers based on their usage of PLBs, national brands, and promotions.

The study identified four well defined and distinct consumer segments. The first segment identified was deal-focused consumers who were categorized as heavy users of promotions regardless of the product type (PLBs or national brand). The second segment was termed as store brand focused who used PLBs most frequently. Furthermore, the third segment consisted of users of both deal and store brands. The last segment consisted of non-users of both deals and store brands.

MODERATING EFFECT OF DEMOGRAPHIC VARIABLES AND PRODUCT CATEGORY

It is also proposed that various demographic variables like gender, age, and income as well as different product categories (food and grocery, apparel and consumer durables) will have statistically significant moderating impact on the relationship between utilitarian and hedonic values and consumer satisfaction.

- P_6: Demographic factors (age, income, and gender) will significantly moderate the relationship between utilitarian value and consumer satisfaction.
- P_{6a}: The relationship between utilitarian value and consumer satisfaction will be significantly moderated by the age of the consumers, such that it will be positive for higher age consumers and vice versa.
- P_{6b}: The relationship between utilitarian value and consumer satisfaction will be significantly moderated by the income level of consumers, such that it will be positive for low and mid level income consumers and vice versa.
- P_{6c}: The relationship between utilitarian value and consumer satisfaction will be significantly moderated by the gender of consumers, such that it will be positive for males and vice versa.
- P_7: Demographic factors (age, income, and gender) will significantly moderate the relationship between hedonic value and consumer satisfaction.
- P_{7a}: The relationship between hedonic value and consumer satisfaction will be significantly moderated by the age of the consumers, such that it will be positive for lower age consumers and vice versa.
- P_{7b}: The relationship between hedonic value and consumer satisfaction will be significantly moderated by the income level of consumers, such that it will be positive for higher level income consumers and vice versa.
- P_{7c}: The relationship between hedonic value and consumer satisfaction will be significantly moderated by the gender of consumers, such that it will be positive for females and vice versa.
- P_8: The category of product (food and grocery, apparel and consumer durables) will significantly moderate the relationship between utilitarian value and consumer satisfaction.

- P_9: The category of product (food and grocery, apparel and consumer durables) will significantly moderate the relationship between hedonic value and consumer satisfaction.

Theoretical Model

Based on the review of previous research, the following model is proposed. Fundamentally, the proposed model (Figure 1) shows the structural dimension of the effect of consumer shopping value (i.e., utilitarian and hedonic) on consumer satisfaction and its behavioural outcomes (i.e., loyalty and word of mouth communication). In other words, the proposed model focuses on the development of PLB satisfaction and loyalty based on the consumers' perceived shopping value derived from the purchase experience. The consumers' perceived shopping value (i.e., utilitarian and hedonic) derived from the purchase experience of PLBs lead to the development of feelings and attitudes (i.e., satisfaction) towards the PLBs. In turn, PLB satisfaction affects attitudinal and behavioural loyalty toward the PLB. The model also lays emphasis on the moderating effect of various demographic variables like gender, age, and income and different product categories (food and grocery, apparel and consumer durables) will have on the relationship between utilitarian and hedonic values with consumer satisfaction.

This model is suggestive of structural relationships among the variables that can be tested by the help of a structural equation modelling procedure. Moreover, it reflects the theoretical and structural dimensions showing the path structure that considers all co-variances.

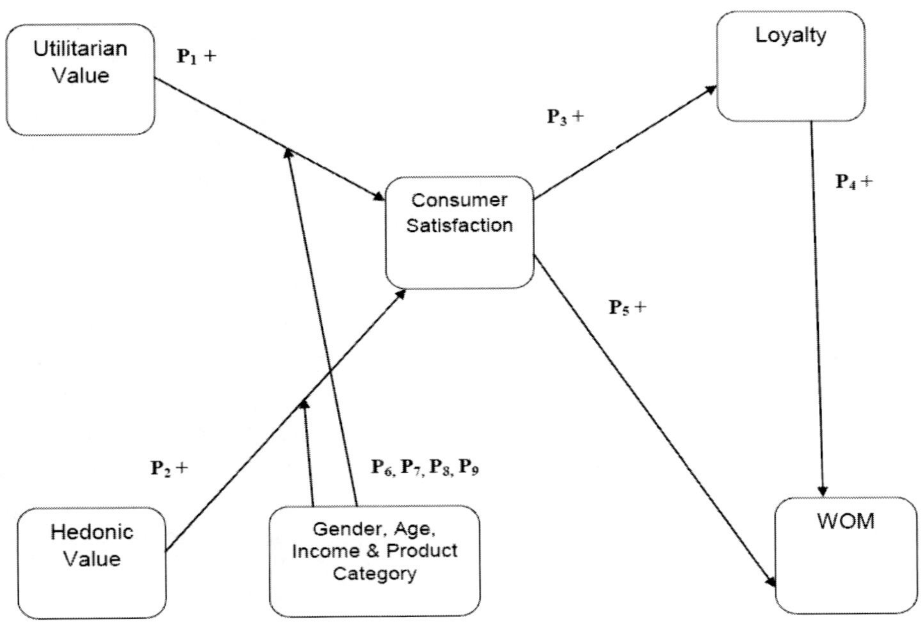

Figure 1. The Theoretical Model.

RESEARCH QUESTIONS

The current study proposes a framework to understand the effect of consumer shopping value (i.e., utilitarian and hedonic) derived from the experience of purchasing PLB products on consumer satisfaction and its behavioural outcomes (i.e., loyalty and word of mouth communication). Although theory is not sufficient for addressing such a relationship directly, it is meaningful to investigate the above mentioned constructs. It is also proposed that various demographic variables like gender, age, and income and different product categories (food and grocery, apparel and consumer durables) will have statistically significant moderating impact on the relationship between utilitarian and hedonic values and consumer satisfaction. Therefore, the current study is raising the following broad research questions:

- How is consumer's shopping value (i.e. utilitarian and hedonic) derived from the experience of purchasing PLB products related to consumer satisfaction?
- How is consumer's shopping value (i.e. utilitarian and hedonic) derived from the experience of purchasing PLB products linked to consumer satisfaction, consumer loyalty and word of mouth communication?
- Is the linkage of above mentioned constructs significantly different for the different types of PLB product categories (i.e., food and grocery, apparel and consumer durables)?
- Is the above relationship significantly different with regards to demographic characteristics (gender, age, and income)?

POTENTIAL CONTRIBUTIONS

The proposed framework has the potential to make insightful theoretical and managerial contributions. Theoretically, the proposed framework will significantly contribute to two major literature streams. Firstly, the PLB literature will be enhanced insofar as this is the first effort (Indian context) aimed at proposing to investigate the impact of PLB on consumer shopping value, satisfaction, and its resultant consumer behavior.

Secondly, the present research will also contribute to the satisfaction literature. Scholars in this area have traditionally viewed satisfaction to be a cognitive response to the comparison of the actual consumption experience with some comparison standard (confirmation/ disconfirmation paradigm). This paradigm firmly dominates the satisfaction literature. Recently, there has been increasing calls for satisfaction measures to capture not just how the consumer thinks the product has performed relative to the comparison standard, but also the resulting consumer emotion (Woodruff and Gardial 1996). The argument is that the higher the level of emotions generated by products and services (both positive and negative), the more motivating consumer satisfaction is in terms of future behaviours such as loyalty or word of mouth communication (Woodruff and Gardial 1996). The present paper adds to the satisfaction stream of research by providing a framework to find an evidence of an affective route, in addition to the cognitive route, to consumer satisfaction.

As a result, this proposition will help researchers in making consulting recommendations to PLB retailers of the three different product categories (vis-a-vis food and grocery; apparel;

consumer durables) in developing and implementing more efficient strategies for increasing their consumer's satisfaction and thus, winning over their loyalty.

REFERENCES

Adaval, R. (2001), "Sometimes it just feels right: The differential weighting of affect-consistent and affect-inconsistent product information", *Journal of Consumer Research* 28, pp. 1-17.

Ailawadi, K.L. (2001), "The retail power-performance conundrum: What have we learned?" *Journal of Retailing* 77, pp. 299-318.

Ailawadi, K.L., Neslin, S. and Gedenk, K. (2001), "Pursuing the value-conscious consumer: Store brands versus national brand promotions", *Journal of Marketing* 65 (1), pp. 71-89.

Anderson, E.W., Fornell, C. and Lehmann, D.R. (1994), "Consumer satisfaction, market share, and profitability: Findings from Sweden", *Journal of Marketing* 58, pp. 53-66.

Arndt, J. (1967), "Role of product-related conversations in the diffusion of a new product", *Journal of Marketing Research* 4, pp. 291-95.

Babin, B.J., Darden, W.R. and Griffin, M. (1994), "Work and/or fun: Measuring hedonic and utilitarian shopping value", *Journal of Consumer Research* 20, pp. 644-56.

Babin, B.J., Lee, Y-K., Kim, E-J. and Griffin, M. (2005), "Modeling consumer satisfaction and word-of-mouth: Restaurant patronage in Korea", *Journal of Services Marketing* 19 (3), pp. 133-9.

Bagozzi, R.P. and Gopinath, M. (1999), "The role of emotions in marketing", *Academy of Marketing Science Journal* 27, pp. 184-206.

Baltas, G. (1997), "Determinants of store brand choice: A behavioural analysis", *Journal of Product and Brand Management* 6, pp. 315-24.

Bansal, H.S. and Voyers, P.A. (2000), "Word-of-mouth processes within a service purchase decision context", *Journal of Service Research* 3, pp. 166-77.

Batra, R. and Ahtola, O. (1990), "Measuring the hedonic and utilitarian sources of consumer attitudes", *Marketing Letters* 2, pp. 159-70.

Bellenger, D.N. and Korgaonkar, P.K. (1980), "Profiling recreational shopper", *Journal of Retailing* 56, pp. 77-91.

Bellizzi, J.A., Hamilton, J.R., Krueckeberg, H.F. and Manin, W.S. (1981), "Consumer perceptions of national, private and generic brands", *Journal of Retailing* 57, pp. 56-70.

Bone, P.A. (1995), "Word-of-mouth effects on short-term and long-term product judgments", *Journal of Business Research* 32, pp. 213-23.

Burger, P.C. and Schott, B. (1972), "Can private brand buyers be identified?" *Journal of Marketing Research* 9, pp. 219-22.

Burton, S., Lichtenstein, D.R., Netemeyer, R.G. and Garretson, J.A. (1998), "A scale for measuring attitude toward private label products and an examination of its psychological and behavioral correlates", *Journal of the Academy of Marketing Science* 26, pp. 293-306.

Carpenter, J.M. and Fairhurst, A. (2005), "Consumer shopping value, satisfaction, and loyalty for retail apparel brands", *Journal of Fashion Marketing Management* 9, pp. 256-69.

Carpenter, J.M., Moore, M. and Fairhurst, A. (2005), "Consumer shopping value for retail brands", *Journal of Fashion Marketing Management* 9, pp. 43-53.

Chandon, P., Wansink, B. and Laurent, G. (2000), "A benefit congruency framework of sales promotion effectiveness", *Journal of Marketing* 64, pp. 65-81.

Copeland, M.T. (1924), "Principles of Merchandising", A.W. Shaw Company, Chicago and New York.

Corstjens, M. and Lal, R. (2000), "Building store loyalty through store brands", *Journal of Marketing Research* 37, pp. 281-91.

Crowley, A.E., Spangenberg, E. and Hughes, K.R. (1992), "Measuring the hedonic and utilitarian dimensions of attitudes toward product categories", *Marketing Letters* 3, pp. 239-49.

Cunningham, R.M. (1956), "Brand loyalty-what, where, how much?" *Harvard Business Review* 34, pp. 116-28.

Cunningham, R.M. (1961), "Customer loyalty to store and brand", *Harvard Business Review* 39, pp. 127-39.

Cunningham, I.C.M., Hardy, A.P. and Imperia, G. (1982), "Generic brands versus national brands and store brands", *Journal of Advertising Research* 22 pp. 25-32.

Day, G.S. (1969), "A two-dimensional concept of brand loyalty", *Journal of Advertising Research* 9, pp. 29-35.

Day, G.S. (1971), "Attitude change, media and word of mouth", *Journal of Advertising Research* 11, pp. 31-40.

Derbaix, C.M. and Vanhamme, J. (2003), "Inducing word-of-mouth by eliciting surprise-A pilot investigation", *Journal of Economic Psychology* 24, pp. 99-116.

Dichter, E. (1966), "How word-of-mouth advertising works", *Harvard Business Review* 44, pp. 147-57.

Donthu, N. and Cherian, J. (1992), "Hispanic coupon usage: The impact of strong and weak ethnic identification", *Psychology and Marketing* 9, pp. 501-10.

Edvardsson, B., Johnson, M.D., Gustafsson, A. and Strandvik, T. (2000), "The effects of satisfaction and loyalty on profits and growth: Products versus services", *Total Quality Management* 11, pp. 917-27.

Engle, J.F. and Blackwell, R.D. (1982), "Consumer Behavior", Dryden Press, Chicago.

Ennew, C.T., Banerjee, A.K. and Li, D. (2000), "Managing word of mouth communication: Empirical evidence from India", *International Journal Bank Marketing* 18, pp. 75-83.

Farley, J.U. (1964), "Why does "brand loyalty" vary over products*?"* *Journal of Marketing Research* 1, pp. 9-14.

Fiore, A.M. and Kim, J. (2007), "An integrative framework capturing experiential and utilitarian shopping experience", *International Journal of Retail and Distribution Management* 35, pp. 421-42.

Fitzell, P.B. (1992), "Private Label Marketing in the 1990s", *Global Book Productions*, New York.

Frank, R.E. and Boyd Jr., H.W. (1965), "Are private-brand-prone grocery customers really different?" *Journal of Advertising Research* 5, pp. 27-35.

Giese, J.L. and Spangenberg, E.R. (1997), "Effects of product specific word of mouth communication on product category involvement", *Marketing Letters* 7, pp. 187-9.

Grewal, D., Monroe, K.B. and Krishnan, R. (1998), "The effects of price-comparison advertising on buyers' perceptions of acquisition value, transaction value, and behavioral intentions", *Journal of Marketing* 62, pp. 46-59.

Hamilton, D.B. (1987), "Institutional economics and consumption", *Journal of Economic Issues* 21, pp. 1531-53.

Herr, P.M., Kardes, F.R. and Kim, J. (1991), "Effects of word-of-mouth and product attributes information on persuasion: An accessibility-diagnosticity perspective", *Journal of Consumer Research* 17, pp. 454-62.

Hirschman, E.C. and Holbrook, M.B. (1982), "Hedonic consumption: Emerging concepts, methods and propositions", *Journal of Marketing* 46, pp. 92-101.

Hirschman, E.C. (1984), "Experience seeking: A subjectivist perspective of consumption", *Journal of Business Research* 12, pp. 115-36.

Holbrook, M.B. (1986). "Emotion in the Consumption Experience: Toward a New Model of the Human Consumer". In: The Role of Affect in Consumer Behavior: Emerging Theories and Applications, Peterson, R.A., Hoyer, W.D. and Wilson, W.R. (Eds.), Heath, Lexington, MA, pp. 17-52.

Howard, J.A. and Sheth, J.N. (1969), "The Theory of Buyer Behavior", John Wiley and Sons, New York.

Jacoby, J. (1971), "A model of multi-brand loyalty", *Journal of Advertising Research* 11, pp. 25-30.

Jacoby, J. and Chestnut, R.W. (1978), "Brand Loyalty Measurement and Management", John Wiley and Sons, New York.

Joseph, M., Soundararajan, N., Gupta, M. and Sahu, S. (2008), "Impact of organized retailing on the unorganized sector", *Indian Council for Research on International Economic Relations*.

Katz, E. and Lazarsfeld, P.F. (1955), "Personal Influence", Free Press, Glencoe, IL.

Kirkup, M. and Rafig, M. (1999), "Marketing shopping centres: Challenges in the UK context", Journal of Marketing Practice: *Applied Marketing Science* 5, pp. 119-33.

Livesey, F. and Lennon, P. (1978), "Factors affecting consumers' choice between manufacturer brands and retailer own brands", *European Journal of Marketing* 12, pp. 158-70.

Maffei, R.B. (1960), "Brand preferences and simple Markov processes", *Operations Research* 8, pp. 210-18.

Majumdar, A. (2005), "A model for customer loyalty for retail stores inside shopping malls– An Indian perspective", *Journal of Services Research–Special Issue,* pp. 47-64.

Nguyen, T.T.M., Nguyen, T.D. and Barrett, N.J. (2007), "Hedonic shopping motivations, supermarket attributes, and shopper loyalty in transitional markets: Evidence from Vietnam", *Asia Pacific Journal of Marketing and Logistics* 19, pp. 227-39.

Oliver, R.L. (1981), "Measurement and evaluation of satisfaction process in retail setting", *Journal of Retailing* 57 (Fall), pp. 25-48.

Oliver, R.L. (1997), "Satisfaction: A Behavioral Perspective on the Consumer", Irwin/McGraw-Hill, New York.

Park, S. and Mowen, J.C. (2007), "Replacement purchase decisions: on the effects of trade-ins, hedonic versus utilitarian usage goal, and tightwadism", J*ournal of Consumer Behaviour* 6, pp. 123-31.

Payne, A. and Holt, S. (2001), "Diagnosing customer value: Integrating the value process and relationship marketing", *British Journal of Management* 12, pp. 159-82.

Rao, T.R. (1969), "Are some consumers more prone to purchase private brands?" *Journal of Marketing Research* 6, pp. 447-50.

Reynolds, K. and Beatty, S. (1999), "Customer benefits and company consequences of customer-salesperson relationships in retailing", *Journal of Retailing* 75, pp. 11-32.

Richardson, P.S., Dick, A.S. and Jain, A.K. (1994), "Extrinsic and intrinsic cue effects on perceptions of store brand quality", *Journal of Marketing* 58, pp. 28-36.

Richins, M.L. (1994), "Valuing things: The public and private meanings of possessions", *Journal of Consumer Research* 21, pp. 504-21.

Rintamäki, T., Kanto, A., Kuusela, H. and Spence, M.T. (2006), "Decomposing the value of department store shopping into utilitarian, hedonic and social dimensions: Evidence from Finland", *International Journal of Retail and Distribution Management* 34, pp. 6-24.

Rogers, E.M. (1995), "Diffusion of Innovations", *Free Press,* New York.

Rokeach, M. (1973), "The Nature of Human Values", *Free Press,* New York.

Roselius, T. (1971), "Consumer rankings of risk reduction methods", *Journal of Marketing 35, pp. 56-61.*

Rosen, E. (2000), "The Anatomy of Buzz: How to Create Word-Of-Mouth Marketing", Doubleday, New York.

Ryan, B. and Gross, N.C. (1943), "The diffusion of hybrid seed corn in two Iowa communities", *Rural Sociology* 8, pp. 15-24.

Schiffman, L.G. and Kanuk, L.L. (1997), "Consumer Behavior", Prentice Hall, Englewood Cliffs.

Sirdeshmukh, D., Singh, J. and Sabol, B. (2002), "Consumer trust, value, and loyalty in relational exchanges", *Journal of Marketing* 66, pp. 15-37.

Sivadas, E. and Baker-Prewitt, J. (2000), "An examination of the relationship between service quality, customer satisfaction, and store loyalty*", International Journal of Retail and Distribution Management* 28, pp. 73-82.

Smith, B. (2000), "The store as a brand", *DSN Retailing Today* 39, pp. 19-20.

Stambaugh, S. (1993), "To store brand or not to store", *Aftermarket Business* 103 (6).

Taylor, J. (2003), "Word of mouth is where it's at", *Brandweek* 2, pp. 26.

Tucker, W.T. (1964), "The development of brand loyalty", *Journal of Marketing Research* 1, pp. 32-35.

Uncles, M.D., Dowling, G.R. and Hammond, K. (2003), "Customer loyalty and customer loyalty programs", *Journal of Consumer Marketing* 20, pp. 294-316.

Veloutsou, C., Gioulistanis, E. and Moutinho, L. (2004), "Own labels choice criteria and perceived characteristics in Greece and Scotland: Factors influencing the willingness to buy", *Journal of Product and Brand Management* 13, pp. 228-41.

Vinson, D.E., Scott, J.E. and Lamont, C.M. (1977), "The role of personal values in marketing and consumer behavior", *Journal of Marketing* 41, pp. 44-50.

Westbrook, R.A. (1987), "Product/consumption-based affective responses and postpurchase process", *Journal of Marketing Research* 24, pp. 258-70.

Woodruff, R.B. (1997), "Customer value: The next source for competitive advantage", *Journal of the Academy of Marketing Science* 25, pp. 139-53.

Woodruff, R.B. and Gardial, S.F. (1996), "Know Your Customer: New Approaches To Understand Customer Value And Satisfaction", John Wiley and Sons.

Writz, J. and Lee, M.C. (2003), "An examination of the quality and context-specific applicability of commonly used customer satisfaction measures", *Journal of Service Research* 5, pp. 345-55.

Zeithaml, V.A. (1988), "Consumer perceptions of price, quality, and value: A means-end model and synthesis of evidence", *Journal of Marketing* 52, pp. 2-22.

In: HRM and Marketing Orientation in the New Era
Editor: Panagiotis Kyriazopoulos
ISBN: 978-1-62808-959-2

Chapter 15

How to Make Profit Through Micro Blogging? The Case of Dell on Twitter

Charleen Karunaratna and Kevin Lü*
Brunel University, Uxbridge, UK

Abstract

The growth of social interactivity and user engagement via the Internet is revolutionising the business environment by slowly blurring the lines between companies and their target audiences. In recent times, social networking has attracted vast attention from the business community. Through social networking, a new breed of virtual customers is emerging who are more powerful, able to create content and actively voice opinions about brands and products. Online platforms such as Twitter are fast becoming trusted sources of information and businesses are now seeing enormous potential for building relationships with customers. This study investigates the current trend of social media and to ascertain whether it can be effectively used by organisations for Customer Relationship Management using Dell on Twitter as a case study. The findings depict that online social network, such as Twitter, can be an important ingredient for building closer relationships with customers.

Keywords: Marketing, Customer Relationship Management and Social CRM

1. Introduction

Online social media is changing the way business performed by providing companies with new opportunities for communication, marketing and customer relationship management. These platforms are essentially user-driven where the power lies with the technologically savvy consumers. This transition is rapidly revolutionising the relationship between buyer and seller (Lanz, Fischhof and Lee, 2010). Furthermore, due to the recent economic downturn, companies are cutting back on their marketing budgets and turning to social networking platforms like Twitter which are cost- effective way of reaching

* E-mail: kevin.lu@brunel.ac.uk.

customers (Langley, 2008). Micro-blogging allows users to publish quick and short messages without going through the hassle of writing long blogs or e-mail messages. Furthermore, social networks are creating new platforms for businesses to engage and connect with their customers bringing about an innovative concept called social CRM (Greenburg, 2010). This allows companies to cost-effectively utilise social networking platforms such as Twitter to directly converse and build relationships with stakeholders, improve customer service and for market research purposes (Postman, 2009). If properly implemented, platforms like Twitter can be ideal environments for building long-term relationships with customers and can offer financial rewards as evident in the case of Dell.

The company Dell was founded in 1984 by Michael Dell with the idea of selling build- to-order computers directly to customers without the need for retail intermediaries (Dell Inc, 2010). Dell is now the number one PC provider in the US and ranked second in the world (Datamonitor, 2009). In the current social media era, Dell is a prime example of an early adopter company that has gone passed experimenting and actually made a $6 million profit from its activities on Twitter (Morrissey, 2010). After negative publicity from Jeff Jarvis in 2005, Dell heavily invested in social media initiatives to listen, better understand and directly engaging with its customers (Jarvis, 2007; Morrissey, 2010). Dell now employs a cross-platform of social networking sites (Facebook, Twitter and LinkedIn), blogs and communities to communicate with customers (Kaplan and Haenlein, 2010). Hence, Dell became one of the top ten social media brands of 2009 (Morrissey, 2010). Dell is an interesting case because it has successfully managed to integrate social media into its communications and corporate way of life making it an important benchmark for other companies thinking of doing the same. With increasing attention paid to social media technologies nowadays, there is a growing need to explore its use and effectiveness within the corporate world. From an academic perspective, social networking is a relatively new area of research that has not been examined at great length thus this study aims to make a contribution to the literature gap. Taking this into consideration, this study aims to contribute by investigating the use of social networking i.e. Twitter for CRM through focusing on Dell as a case study. Conducting a semi-structured interview with a senior member of staff of Digital Communications at Dell (SSDell) provided vital industry information regarding the social media practices at Dell and undertaking a questionnaire further enhances the results by evaluating the topic from a consumer perspective. It is intended that results of this study will benefit marketers who are interested in utilising online social networking for CRM and considering to integrate social media into their business practices. The structure of this paper is as follows, section 2 provides literature review, section 3 discusses Dell's success over Twitter, and section 4 presents the conclusion.

2. Related Work

There are a number of areas related to this study, CRM, online social media and social media practices at Dell. A brief review on these aspects is presented in this section.

2.1. Customer Relationship Management (CRM)

Overall, CRM can be considered as a strategic approach that efficiently utilises key corporate resources and technologies to build closer relationships with current (potential) customers so as to increase customer satisfaction and improve shareholder value (Finnegan and Currie, 2010).

Technology in business has not only improved working practices i.e. productivity, increase economies of scale, and enhanced delivery channels but has also created a demand for outstanding customer service (Kincaid 2003; Kalakota and Robinson, 2001; Wu and Hung, 2009). The consolidation of company CRM strategies with modern technology, such Internet, brought about 'Electronic Customer Relationship Management' (eCRM) (Kennedy, 2006; Finnegan and Currie, 2010), which employs techniques such as Web technology, data warehousing, contact management and customisation to build closer customer relationships (Kennedy, 2006; Wu and Hung, 2009; Turban et al, 2006). eCRM initiatives also enhances one-to-one relationships with customers through improving communication channels and enhances customer service, enabling greater segmentation and more precise targeting of customers (Chen and Chen, 2003).

Social network technologies are redefining how companies communicate and interact with customers. Social platforms such as Twitter are dynamic customer- driven channels that put the customer in control (Petouhoff, 2010). As the corporate use of social netwrok begins to grow, companies need to revaluate their CRM strategies to make the most of these opportunities (Chen Bocheng and Liang Bing,

2006). This is where social CRM comes in. Social CRM is a newly emerging concept and the new buzzword for marketers today. Greenburg (2010) defines social CRM as "a philosophy and a business strategy, supported by a technology platform, business rules, processes and social characteristics, designed to engage the customer in a collaborative conversation in order to provide mutually beneficial value in a trusted and transparent business environment". Social CRM can be seen as a business strategy that is designed to bring the business closer to its customers through social network interactions. More emphasis is now being placed on conversations and customer relationships and thus social CRM can be seen as an evolved form of traditional CRM.

While social CRM initiatives come with huge resource undertakings and company cultural shifts, successful implementation can transform the company as a whole and offer great rewards i.e. customer loyalty and financial rewards (Modiglioani, 2010). Better understanding of customer needs and efficient use of social CRM can allow companies to build relationships with customers, improve customer satisfaction, encourage brand trust and help bridge the gap between businesses and customers in the long run. (Kalakota and Robinson, 2001; Modiglioani, 2010).

2.2. Dell and Social Media

Dell is one of the early adopters who have successfully utilised social media to connect and engage with customers resulting in tangible returns in the form of sales leads, product development input and financial rewards. Dell is predominantly an Internet retailer therefore it was perfectly natural for them to move into the social media arena.

In 2005, Jeff Jarvis unleashed a blogging upheaval, now known as 'Dell hell' after being frustrated by the level of service he received from Dell (Jarvis, 2007). He turned to blogging to vent his frustration and made a great number of unhappy customers following suit (Morrissey, 2010; Jarvis, 2007). This brought Dell's attention to the power of social media and in 2006, Dell launched its own blog – Direct2Dell aimed at the blogging public (Dell Inc, 2010). It then followed this with Ideastorm.com, a forum that allowed customers to offer advice and suggestions on new product ideas. Over the years, Dell developed a cross-platform community by having a presence on social network sites such as Facebook and Twitter (Long Hog, 2008). Dell has been most successful on Twitter making $6 million through its activities on its DellOutlet site and connects with around 3.5 million customers through various social media platforms (Morrissey, 2010).

Dell achieved first mover advantage by adapting social media into their business strategy before their competitors. In terms of Twitter, Dell segmented users demographically i.e. Dell UK and Dell Canada and adopted the 'Think Global, Act Local' strategy by tailoring twitter accounts to suit each country e.g. through language. Dell has managed to build up a loyal brand following on Twitter by using tactics such as exclusive discount offerings i.e. product vouchers through the DellOutlet account to offer something of value to users, crowdsourcing to personalise product offerings and generate new ideas as well as providing customer care through the Dell Cares account (Morrissey, 2010). The most successful and popular Dell account on Twitter is the DellOutlet (Morrissey, 2010).

Dell also has a number of other social media initiatives, include:

- Direct2Dell – Company blog that provides news about the workings of Dell thus making them transparent to their customers.
- IdeaStorm – This platform allows Dell to crowdsource by inviting customers to contribute to new product ideas and in turn enables Dell to listen and learn from its customers thus creating a beneficial market research initiative. By brainstorming ideas with customers, Dell is better able to tailor products and fix any company mishaps accordingly.
- Support Forums – Dell offers interactive forums that allows users to communicate, share ideas and seek technical support through videos and podcasts thus creating an online support network.
- Networking sites – Dell has a presence on various social network sites such as Facebook, LinkedIn and Twitter creating a community of followers, to interact and engage with users in two-way dialog. This is effectively used as not only a marketing tool but also to build closer relationships with customers on their terms.

3. Case Study: Social Media at Dell

In order to understand the success of Dell, in this study, a semi-structured interview with a senior member of staff of Digital Communications at Dell (SSDell) has been conducted which is aimed to provide vital industry information regarding the social media practices at Dell. Additionally, a questionnaire survey used to further enhances the results by evaluating the topic from a consumer perspective has been undertaken. The questions in the questionnaire are targeted on the issues identified in the interview. There are two hundred and two hundred and fifty-two respondents completed questionnaire who are the users Dell on Twitter. Instead to present the findings of the interview and the questionnaire survey separately, this section they are presented together under related issues with discussion and analysis.

One of the objectives for this research is to investigate reasons for the social media success of Dell. SSDell depicts that Dell has achieved success over the years by "*building direct relationships with customer*" and therefore the emergence of social media platforms such as Twitter provided a perfect opportunity to extend their direct relationships onto these social platforms.

According to SSDell, one reason why social media has become so popular is because "...we (everyday people like you and me) as a culture have over time become less and less trusting in government officials and companies and the technology has allowed us to have conversations with people online who are like ourselves." This is in support of Wirtz, Schilke and Ullirch (2010) who state that social media platforms are now trusted information sources with more emphasis being placed on word-of-mouth recommendations rather than on what companies are saying.

When asked if a presence on Twitter can enable a company to build closer relationships with customers, (70%) of respondents strongly agreed and agreed, (20%) neither agreed nor disagreed while the remaining (10%) disagreed and strongly disagreed (See Figure 1).

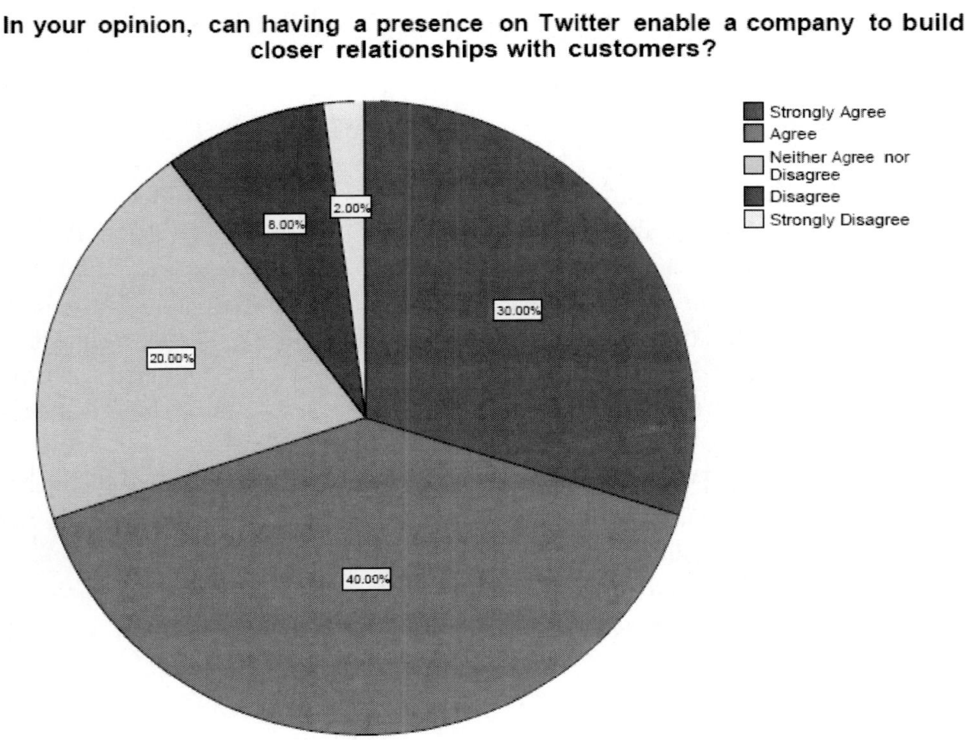

Figure 1. Question 4 – Results.

Interview findings show that Dell is effectively utilising social media technologies to crowdsource ideas from customers (Ideastorm), to provide customers with something of value i.e. exclusive discounts (Twitter) and to offer technical support while providing customers with rich and informative content (blogs and newsfeeds). For the DellOutlet on Twitter, when asked if the newsfeeds were informative and up-to- date, survey (questionnaire) results revealed (60%) agreed, (8%) strongly agreed, (26%) neither agreed nor disagreed and (6%) disagreed which suggests that Dell is catering to customer needs. In return, customers are providing feedback and having an input in product development. This supports the social exchange theory which denotes that network relationships are based on mutual benefits (Antheunis, Valkenburg and Peter, 2010). Additionally, SSDell points out that the importance of having a presence on more than one platform allows a business to follow its audience. Questionnaire findings suggest that apart from Twitter, people tend to use other platforms: (62%) use Facebook, (14%) LinkedIn, (12%) Delicious, (10%) Bebo and (2%) MySpace. Therefore it can be beneficial for a company to have a social presence on a variety of social platforms as evident with Dell.

Findings further suggest that Dell's social media programmes are supported by its various business areas such as legal, customer support, public sector and corporate hence social media activities are not restricted to one department but involve every part of the company. Furthermore, it was found that Dell uses a hub and spoke structure where, according to SSDell, "...you have a central team who provides the strategy...within teams you will have a leader who follows that central strategy and feeds back into that central team...Social Media has very much developed from that one team that owned it and controlled it all to being actually a piece of many, many people's work." This shows that for social media strategies to work, they need to be implemented as company-wide initiatives involving all employees and departments, consistent with suggestion by Hart, Hogg and Banerjee (2004) and Kalakota and Robinson (2001).

Interview findings also portray social network channels as effective feedback mechanisms which alert companies like Dell to real-time customer issues. This allows them to take corrective steps or change any unpopular strategies where necessary. Furthermore, this was acknowledged in research by Gartner Inc. (2009) when outlining the business application of Twitter. Questionnaire findings support this fact when asked if Dell listens and responds quickly to tweets posted on the DellOutlet, a majority (14%) strongly agreed and (58%) agreed with (22%) neither agreeing nor disagreeing and (6%) disagree and strongly disagree.

According to SSDell, Dell is not perfect by any means but being an early adopter and not being afraid to experiment has led to its social media success. She goes on to say: "...in general, having that guiding goal of using social media to build relationships with customers, to understand what customers want and to use that information to help inform our business strategy and in turn helps us be a stronger company - I think this is beneficial for any company."

These findings suggest that Dell is primarily focused on the needs of its customers and through monitoring customer conversations it can better cater to customer needs and making improvements to business practices as required. When respondents were asked whether the DellOutlet is more focused on sales rather than customer needs, (40%) disagreed, (30%) neither agreed nor disagreed and (22%) agreed with (2%) strongly agreeing and (6%) strongly disagreeing showing that customers are still suspicious of marketing activities on these sites and resistant to Twitter being used as a sales tool (See Figure 2 below). Holden (2008) confirms this stating that on these social sites, customers are not interested in sales talk. Therefore businesses have to be transparent and authentic when interacting with customers on these social sites.

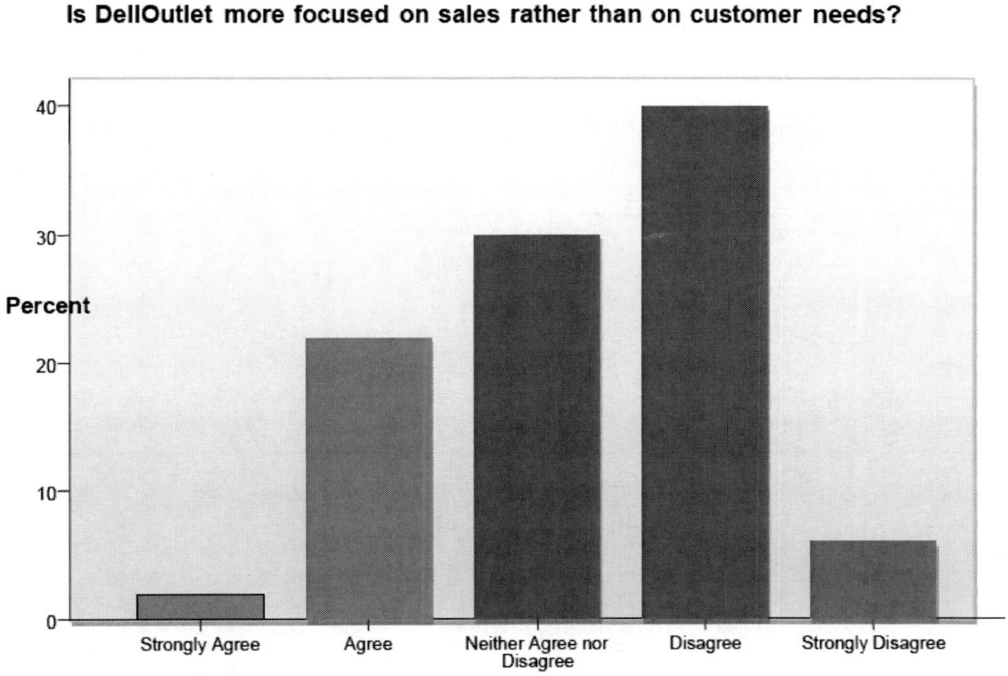

Figure 2. Question 11 – Results.

SSDell points out prior to implementing social media, a listening audit needs to be conducted whereby customer objectives are matched to company objectives and the overlap is where social media strategies fit in. Additionally SSDell suggests to "*...Take your time, get used to it, properly resource what you need to do so you don't get surprised*" and moreover, to ensure that all employees follow ethical guidelines and recommends to: *"...always represent your company...From Dell's perspective, you are transparent, you always have to be very customer friendly and supportive of whatever is happening or whatever issues customers might face."* Being open and transparent is vital to creating trusting relationships with customers on these sites. When asked if respondents could trust what a Dell representative tweeted about, (42%) agreed, (30%) neither agreed nor disagreed (16%) strongly agreed and (8%) Disagreed and (4%) strongly disagreed suggesting that employee are a trusted source on Twitter (See Table 1).

Another objective of this study is to evaluate whether social platforms such as Twitter can be effective for building relationships with customers. This is discussed according to the three social CRM elements: customer engagement, company listening and Trust building.

Questionnaire findings (Figure 3) analysed the uses of Twitter and found that (36%) mostly use it for entertainment; (28%) communication (20%) customer service and only (10%) for discount searching with (4%) newsfeeds and (2%) follow / tweet companies. This shows that Twitter is mainly used for entertainment purposes and communications, which isconsistent with Postman (2009) calling it a communications tool. Therefore to be successful on these sites, businesses need to entertain customers with rich content and use platforms like Twitter to converse with them. Furthermore, when asked on average how many hours they spend on Twitter each week, a majority (44%) spent 6 – 10 followed by (38%) 0 – 5 hours; (14%) 11 –15 hours and (4%) 16 – 20 hours.

Table 1. Question 14 – Results

Can you trust what a Dell employee tweets about?

	Frequency	Percent	Valid Percent	Cumulative Percent
Valid Strongly Agree	40	16.0	16.0	16.0
Agree	106	42.0	42.0	58.0
Neither Agree nor Disagree	75	30.0	30.0	88.0
Disagree				
Strongly Disagree	20	8.0	8.0	96.0
Total	11	4.0	4.0	100.0

What do you mostly use Twitter for?

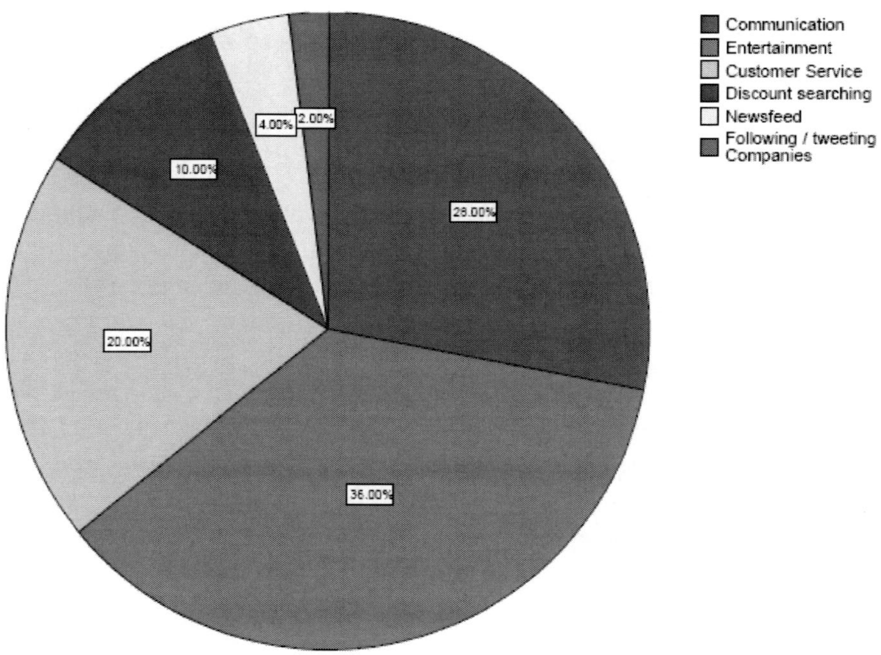

Figure 3. Question 1 – Results.

On Twitter, interview findings rank employee involvement as the most influential factor for trust building. Trust is essentially needed when building online relationships due to the lack of a physical presence. By Dell employees appearing open and transparent, trusting relationships can be formed as proposed by Elg (2002). SSDell states that being "*transparent*" is vitally important to build relationships with customers on social platforms. Employee spokespeople with personalised Twitter accounts such as KerryatDell and RichardatDell are engaging with various audiences and personalising relationships through sharing ideas and experiences, offering advice and having discussions with customers about topics of interest.

In this way, Dell shows that it is open and transparent with customers and as such is able to build direct personal relationships. Cook (2008) and Jacob (2009) agree denoting that employee spokespeople give companies human personalities, which according to Gremler and Gwinner (2000) is preferred by customers. KerryatDell uses her account to share insights from social media events that she attends or speaks at thus creating interesting and informative content which according to Garety (2010) is useful for building trusting relationships. (50%) of questionnaire respondents agreed that Dell representatives on DellOutlet humanise the company, (26%) strongly agreed with (16%) neither agreeing nor disagreeing and (8%) disagreeing (See Figure 4. below).

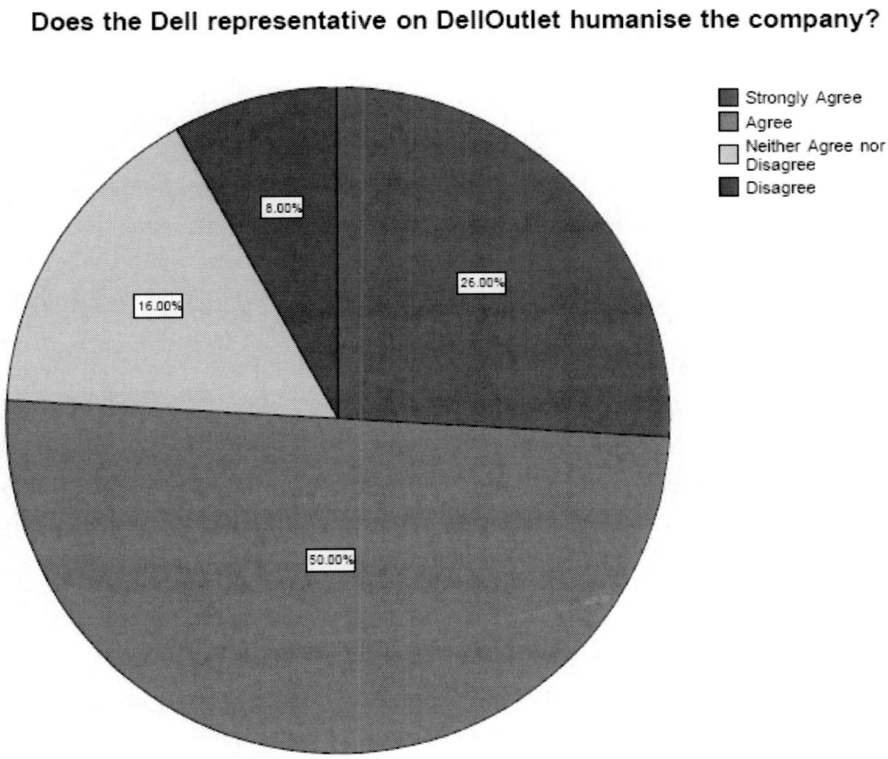

Figure 4. Question 13 – Results.

Conclusion

In this study, Dell was chosen as a case study and used to undertake primary research on why Dell has been successful at using social media. Primary research findings revealed that Dell is using social media to communicate with customers, crowdsource ideas from the public and offer exclusive discounts and customer support via Twitter. Consistent with the theory of social exchange, Dell in turn receives increase sales, customer feedback and customers suggestions for product ideas. Furthermore, results establish that Dell has reorganised its various business departments to make social media a company-wide initiate involving everyone in the organisation. Dell has achieved success mainly because it listens and focuses on building direct relationships with customers through these social platforms.

This study also evaluated the effectiveness of Twitter as a platform for building customer relationships through Social CRM. Furthermore, in terms of listening, it was found that Twitter offers an effective way to provide customer support and its real- time nature acts as an efficient early warning beacon used to collate customer issues faster than traditional means i.e. call centres. Thus corrective steps can be taken and unpopular strategies changed to increase customer satisfaction in the long run. This can be effectively achieved through social platforms such as Twitter and since these platforms put customers in charge, listening is crucially important.

Based on the study results, the following recommendations are put forward for marketers who wish to utilise social media:

- Having a presence on more than one network is recommended since research suggests that customers are not restricted to one platform and as such businesses need to follow suit.
- Marketers need to conduct a listening audit by comparing company objectives with customer objectives and apply social media strategies to the overlap. Furthermore, marketers need to properly resource and understand how social networking platforms such as Twitter work before jumping on the bandwagon.
- Following the example of Dell, companies need to ensure that social media strategies are implemented as companywide initiatives involving all employees and every department in order to achieve success.
- When using social networking platforms such as Twitter, listening and engaging customers on their own terms is crucially important. Customer conversations should be based on relationship building and encouraging trust in the brand and not used as sales pitches.
- Platforms such as Twitter operate in real-time environments therefore having a constant presence on these sites is vital to monitor brand conversations and to stay connected with customers.
- When using these social networking sites, it is important to be open and transparent with customers. Employee spokespeople can help to humanise the brand and thus create loyal followings.
- Finally, successful social media practices as in the case of Dell need to be benchmarked for advice on best practices and to mimic their success.

There are several areas related to social media marketing that require further research. Further studies should examine cases in other forms and applications of social media, one case we are currently working on is Starbucks(coffee company) on Facebook, to ascertain the common factors between these two cases, therefore to form better understanding on related issues. In the context of social CRM, a systematic solution is required to answer the challenges faced when social media is increasingly adopted as platform for interacting with customers. Finally, cross- disciplinary research is required to analyse how customer groups are formed, merged, split, or influenced, for example, social networking theory (Freeman, Linton C. (2004) has been established long before the merge of online social media, useful findings could be generated through a cross-disciplinary approach that combining the marketing perspective with a social networking influence perspective to ultimately provide a effective and efficient social marketing strategies.

* The interview transcript and the full data analysis report on questionnaires will be available upon requests.

REFERENCES

Antheunis, M.L, Valkenburg, P. M and Peter, J (2010) 'Getting acquainted through social network sites: Testing a model of online uncertainty reduction and social attraction'. Computers in Human Behaviour, 26 (1) pp. 100 – 109.

Chen Bocheng, W.H.I and Liang Bing, H. C. W. L. (2006) 'A Functional Framework for Integrating eCRM with Workflow Management Based on Customer Value'.*Tsinghua Science and Technology*, 11 (1), pp. 65 – 73.

Chen, Q and Chen, H (2003) 'Exploring the success factors of eCRM strategies in practice'. *Database Marketing and Customer Strategy Management*, 11 (4) pp. 333 –343.

Cook, N (2008) '*Enterprise 2.0: How Social Software Will Change the Future of Work*'. Surrey and Burlington: Gower Publishing Company.

Datamonitor (2009) 'Dell Inc: Company Profile'. [Online] Available at:www.datamonitor.com (Accessed: 20 July 2010).

Dell Inc. (2010) 'History: Company Timeline'. [Online] Available at:http://www.dell.com/content/topics/global.aspx/about_dell/company/history(Accessed: 25 July 2010).

Elg, U (2002) 'Inter-firm Market Orientation: Its Significance and Antecedents in Distribution Networks'. *Journal of Marketing Management*, 18 (7/8) pp. 663 – 656.

Finnegan, D. J. and Currie, W. L. (2010) 'A multi-layered approach to CRM implementation: An integration perspective'. *European Management Journal*, 28 (2) pp. 153 – 167.

Freeman, Linton C. (2004) '*The Development of Social Network Analysis: A Study in the Sociology of Science'*. Vancouver: Empirical Press.

Garety, P (2010) 'How to build trust in Social Networking Sites', Enzine articles [Online] available at: http://ezinearticles.com/?How-to-Build-Trust-in-Social- Networking-Sitesandid=4701265 (Accessed: 01 September 2010).

Gartner, Inc. (2009) 'Gartner Highlights Four Ways in Which Enterprises Are Using Twitter', Press release [Online] 26 March Available at: http://www.gartner.com/it/page.jsp?id=920813 (Accessed: 02 August 2010).

Greenburg, P. (2010) '*CRM at the Speed of Light: Social CRM Strategies, Tools andTechniques for Engaging Your Customer'*, 4th edn. USA: McGraw Hill Company.

Gremler, D, D. and Gwinner, K. P (2000) 'Customer-employee rapport in service relationships'. *Journal of Service Research* 3 (1) pp. 82 – 104.

Hart, S., Hogg, G. and Banerjee, M. (2004) 'Does the level of experience have an effect on CRM programs? Exploratory research findings'. *Industrial Marketing Management*, 33 (6) pp. 549 – 560.

Holden, P. R (2008) '*Virtually Free Marketing: Harnessing the power of the Web for your small busines*s'. London: A and C Black Publishers Ltd.

Jacobs, I. (2009) 'Lessons of the Magic Curry Kart'. *CRM Magazine*, 13 (9) p. 10.

Jarvis, J (2007) Dell Learns to Listen, Bloomberg Business Week, 17 October [Online] Available at: http://www.businessweek.com/bwdaily/dnflash/content/oct2007/db20071017_277576.htm?chan=top+news_top+news+index_top+story (Accessed: 20 July 2010).

Kalakota, R and Robinson, M (2001) '*e-Business: Roadmap for success'*. Canada: Addison Wesley Longman, Inc.

Kaplan, A. M. and Haenlein, M. (2010) 'Users of the world, unite! The challenges and opportunities of Social Media'. *Business Horizons*, 53 (1) pp. 59 – 68.

Kennedy, A. (2006) 'Electronic Customer Relationship Management (eCRM): Opportunities and challenges in the digital world'. Irish Marketing Review, 18 (1/2) pp. 58 – 68.

Kincaid J.W. (2003) '*Customer relationship management: getting it right!'*. New Jersey: Prentice-Hall Inc.

Langley, N (2008) *'Web 2.0: the vision and the reality'. Computer Weekly,* pp. 26 –28.

Lanz, L. H, Fischhof, B and Lee, R (2010) '*How Hotels are Embracing Social Media in 2010?'*. 4Hoteliers [Online] Available at: http://www.4hoteliers.com/4hots_fshw.php?mwi=4854 (Accessed: 01 March 2010).

Long Hog (2008) 'Social Media Marketing at Dell: Strategies for Success'. [Online] Available at: http://www.longhop.net/social-media-marketing-dell-strategies-success/ (Accesses: 20 August 2010).

Modiglioani, P. (2010) 'Defense Acquisition Enterprise 2.0'. *Defense ATandL*, 39 (2) pp.56 – 60.

Morrissey, B. (2010) 'Does Social Sell?'. *Adweek*, 51 (7) pp. 8 – 9.

Petouhoff, N (2010) 'The Social Customer Economy: How to use Twitter for customer service interactions'. *Customer Relationship Management*, 14 (3) pp.14.

Postman, J. (2009) *SocialCorp: Social Media Goes Corporate*, USA: New Riders Wirtz, B, W, Schilke, O and Ullrich, S (2010) 'Strategic Development of Business Models: Implications of the Web 2.0 for Creating Value on the Internet' Long Range Planning, 43 (2/3) pp. 272 – 290.

Wu, I. L and Hung, C. Y (2009) 'A strategy-based process for effectively determining system requirements in eCRM development' *Information and Software Technology*,51 (9) pp. 1308 – 1318.

In: HRM and Marketing Orientation in the New Era
Editor: Panagiotis Kyriazopoulos
ISBN: 978-1-62808-959-2

Chapter 16

THE EFFECT OF SERVICE QUALITY ON CUSTOMER RETENTION: THE CASE OF WIND, A MOBILE PROVIDER

Panagiotis G. Kyriazopoulos*
Graduate Technological Education Institute of Piraeus,
Department of Business Administration, Piraeus, Greece

ABSTRACT

This research examines service quality and its effect on customer retention in the mobile phone industry. The research investigates how customers' perceptions are configured and measure service quality. The case of the WIND mobile phone provider is analysed and the results achieved through this research are based on WIND subscribers. For the purpose of the research, quantitative analysis, correlation analysis and hierarchical regression analysis were used. The results reveal the high level of importance of service quality in influencing customer retention and its subsequent influence on the overall performance of the company.

Keywords: TQM, Customer Retention, Marketing

1. INTRODUCTION

Quality, nowadays, appears to be one of the most critical aspects for the strategic management of service firms. Customer satisfaction and loyalty are crucial and essential for long-term survival and success (Johnston, 1995).

Because of its importance, researchers have devoted a great deal of attention to service quality, but there are still some issues that need to be addressed. Those issues refer to the conceptualization and measurement of service quality. A majority of studies have shown that

* E-mail: pkyriaz@teipir.gr.

quality, customer retention and the identification of what constitutes value to customers are identified by many companies as either important or very important (Zeithaml et al., 1996).

In the following research, the factors that influence customer perceptions in selecting service providers are examined for mobile companies with the point of reference case being one company in particular, WIND. It was deemed valuable in relation to all the concepts of service quality to be studied, as well as for examining service quality as an important factor for retaining customers.

The overall objective of the following research study is to identify the way in which mobile companies and particularly WIND use service quality in order to retain their customers and how the latter perceive the service quality provided. A number of more specific sub-objectives can be illustrated as follows: to clarify the factors (criteria) that influence customers' perceptions in selecting service providers; to examine service quality as an important factor for retaining customers; to identify the pros and cons of the WIND company; and finally to investigate customers' perceptions of WIND's service quality.

2. Literature Review

2.1. Service Quality Theories

Service quality is a topic that has been frequently studied in the service marketing literature. Efforts to understand and identify service quality have been undertaken in the last three decades.

Before that, the idea of managing for quality was quite narrow and specific. Quality was perceived as synonymous with just meeting a set of technical specifications for products and services. It was through that notion, however, that the connection was gradually made to every process and person in the organization (Samanta, 2008).

The meaning of service quality can be inferred from the following quotation: "Service quality differs from quality of goods, in that services are intangible. This presents a challenge to marketers; services cannot easily be communicated to customers, and quality may be difficult to assess. Services are characterized as being intangible, perishable, produced and consumed simultaneously and heterogeneous" (Zeithaml et al., 1996).

One of the most widely used models in the service management literature is the SERVQUAL model, which is based on the concept of service quality gaps (Parasuraman et al., 1985).

Service quality is defined as a function of the gap between customers' expectations of a service and their perceptions of the actual service delivered. The strategic process of quality improvement is determined by SERVQUAL gaps. It has been demonstrated that higher quality results in higher corporate performance (Buzzell and Gale, 1987).

The SERVQUAL model identifies specific criteria by which customers evaluate service quality. These criteria are classed in five major dimensions (Parasuraman et al., 1985):

1. Tangibles: the appearance of physical facilities, equipment, personnel and communication materials.
2. Reliability: the ability to perform the promised service dependably and accurately.
3. Responsiveness: the willingness to help customers and provide a prompt service.

4. Assurance: the competence of the system and its credibility in providing a courteous and secure service.
5. Empathy: the approachability, ease of access and effort taken to understand customers' needs.

2.2. Service Quality Measurement

Quality for a company that operates in a service industry is a measure of the extent to which the service provided meets the customers' expectations. The perception of quality is influenced not only by the service outcome but also by the entire procedure for the service provision (Ghobadian et al., 1994).

The researcher argues that prior expectations are compared with the service delivery process and defines "prior expectations" as the a priori image of what will be received when the customer purchases a service. Several factors could influence the a priori image, such as the marketing communication mix, word of mouth and price.

On the other hand, the actual quality is the real level of service quality provided and that is determined not only by the service provider but also by the customers' perceptions. Perceived quality is the customer's feeling for the quality of the service provided. The three key possible quality outcomes, according to Ghobadian et al. (1994, p. 50), are:

1. Satisfactory quality, where the customer's expectations are exactly met.
2. Ideal quality, where the perceived quality is higher than the customer's expectations.
3. Unacceptable quality, where the perceived quality is lower than the customer's expectations.

The provider should take into consideration that either condition (1) or condition (2) needs to be attained in order to fulfil customers' expectations. To reach these targets the provider should have a clear thesis and opinion about the customer's expected service quality and set higher levels of satisfactory quality than those of competitors.

2.3. Customer Retention in the Mobile Phone Sector

In general, customer retention is defined as the future propensity of a customer to stay with the service provider. Customer retention has often been regarded as an aspect of the customer relationship management construction, including customer loyalty and retention (Zeithaml et al., 1996; Grigoroudis et al., 2005). For any company aiming to retain its customers, it is necessary to:

1. Respond directly to their needs by constantly improving the service quality offered (Haywood-Farmer, 1988; Kettinger and Lee, 1994).
2. Win customers' trust towards the company (Morgan and Hunt, 1994).
3. Increase the switching cost for changing to other service providers, making it a comparatively unattractive choice, and expand its application (Fornell, 1992).

As Leisen and Vance (2001) remark, "in telecommunication services it is frequently pointed out that once customers have been acquired and connected to the telecommunication network of a particular operator, their long-term relations with the focal operator are of greater importance to the success of the company in competitive markets than they are in other industry sectors".

2.4. The Mobile Phone Sector in Greece

The mobile telephony sector has been one of the fastest growing in Greece during the last decade. This rapid growth and development of the telecommunication industry have occurred since the adoption of several technological advancements. The mobile industry has been widely spread in Greece since the first year of mobile companies' operations.

The telecommunications industry has the highest growth in Greece and that is because companies have invested a lot of money in technological equipment and in the information technology infrastructure in general. Mobile telephony in Greece could be regarded as a highly competitive market and that is attributed to the high quality of services provided by the telecommunication companies in order to satisfy their customers. The network coverage in Greece is 95%–100% and that is a numerical reference that bears witness to the potentiality of the mobile market. Another point, from a technological perspective, that gives evidence about how dynamic this market is considered to be is the development of the 3D generation telephony, including video calls and generally high-speed data exchanges. The development of the UMTS (3G) network is in the vanguard of the technological advances in the mobile phone industry. For the adoption of the 3G technology, which is far more complex than the 2G network, quite heavy investments of money were required in order for companies to have at their disposal all the resources and capabilities for designing and implementing this system (http://www.WIND.com.gr).

Today, WIND Hellas is one of the major companies in Greece, with 4 million customers or 40% of the total population. WIND Hellas was established in 1992 and launched its operations in Greece in June 1993, placing the first call made from a mobile phone in this country. In 18 years, the company has become established as a technology pioneer and has offered innovative products that have changed consumers' way of communication. To date, WIND has invested more than €2 billion in infrastructure and new technologies.

In 2007, WIND acquired and merged with the fixed and broadband operator Tellas, incorporating its infrastructures, operations and services. This was one of the biggest technology projects in Europe; it was delivered in 2010 and established WIND as the only telecommunications provider in Greece, offering mobile, fixed telephony and Internet services.

In December 2010, a new era began for WIND after its successful acquisition by foreign investors. The company's new shareholders, six of the largest worldwide investment funds, manage more than 80 billion dollars in total. Following the acquisition, they secured the future prospects of the company by offering €420 million, one of the largest private investments in Greece during the past 2 years.

In June 2011, WIND started the modernization and upgrading of its national radio network in cooperation with Huawei. It is a major project that will be concluded in 3 years and will result in the leading and fastest-performing network in Greece with speeds of up to

42 Mbps, offering its customers a real mobile broadband experience. Meanwhile, in December 2011, the company proceeded with the renewal of the usage rights in the 900 MHz band by paying the total sum of €93.2 million, another large investment in the Greek economy.

WIND Hellas has developed a nationwide state-of-the-art technical network, thus providing population coverage that approaches 100%. Each year, it invests more than €150 million in its mobile and fixed infrastructure to ensure the maximum service quality. In this way, all WIND subscribers – even those living in the most remote regions of Greece – enjoy full network coverage.

Today, WIND Hellas is the only integrated telecom operator in Greece offering mobile, fixed and Internet services from a single point of sale and service under a single bill.

Having developed the "Responsible Corporate Citizen" profile, WIND Hellas is distinguishing itself for its social contribution. From the beginning of its operation, the business activities of WIND have focused on the strategy of corporate social responsibility "In Action"; this includes a multi-sided action plan of social contribution placing particular emphasis on the axes involving responsible business activities, environment and society.

3. Research Methods

For the purposes of this research project quantitative research took place from September to November 2011. The questionnaire created was distributed to 100 WIND subscribers. Of these 100 WIND subscribers, we obtained a response from 92 and 1 of those was unreachable, so the active response rate was 92.9% (active response rate=92/100-1=0.929=92. 9%).

Through this questionnaire, in which the simple random method was used, information was obtained about some demographic elements of the respondents, such as age, gender, job occupation and educational background, as well as information about consumer attitudes and feedback regarding the technology and the services they may use in the mobile phone sector. This procedure involved questioning the respondents regarding the "what, when, how and where" of their behaviour, in order to gather empirical information and to provide the quantifiable data for the research.

The method used for the statistical analysis is the correlation analysis to measure how the variables or rank orders are related and the stepwise multiple regression model to examine the pros and cons of the WIND company and their effect on customer retention.

H1 = The relation between satisfaction and customer service is positive.
H2 = The relation between high charges and satisfaction is positive.
H3 = The effect of service quality on customer retention is positive.

4. Research Analysis

4.1. Demographic Results

In the first part of the research analysis, it was regarded as meaningful to take a closer look at some basic demographic characteristics. The research findings show that 51.09% of the respondents were women and 48.91% were men.

We notice that 52.17% fall into the age group 26–32, 19.57% fall into the group 33- 40, 16.30% belong to the age group 19–25 and the smallest percentage, which is 11.96%, consists of persons who are more than 40 years old.

4.2. Consumers' General Attitudes in the Mobile Sector

4.2.1. Satisfaction with the Services Provided Generally

The specific question results that are depicted show that quite a large percentage, 61.96%, of the respondents are satisfied with the provided services by the mobile phone carriers. That means that the subscribers have realized that Greek mobile phone companies offer them technology-driven services and generally provide them with a good level of service quality. The factors that influence subscribers' satisfaction and of course the extent to which this happens will become clearer and more specific in the analysis that will follow. Also, 22.83% of the respondents fall into the category of those who are very satisfied, 10.87% appear to be neutral and only a small number, 4.35%, seem to be satisfied little.

4.2.2. Criteria when Choosing a Mobile Phone Network

The specific questions' results indicate that customers consider coverage as their main criterion when choosing a mobile phone network. They are interested in being provided with a high level of coverage and immediately after that they require low charges and generally cheap tariff plans. We can notice that they appear to be relatively neutral regarding after-sales services and free terminals, while they seem to pay more attention to the company's brand name, because subscribers' perceived quality can easily be determined by several marketing communication means such as adverts, word of mouth and sales promotional tools with the result of having created in their mind a prior brand image for a specific telecommunication company.

4.2. Descriptive Analysis

The descriptive analysis conducted led us to very important results. Firstly, the satisfaction parameter should be taken into account as it is obvious that most of the subscribers are satisfied with the services WIND provides. The analysis shows that one of the strong points of the WIND company, registered by the respondents and of course the subscribers, is customer service. The second strong advantage of the company, according to the analysis, appears to be its innovative services. WIND has recently launched an especially advanced service that actually improved the company's brand image a great deal.

As far as the disadvantages are concerned, low coverage seems to be the first if we set an order of priority and then follows the lack of loyalty programmes.

WIND subscribers consider their company to be a reliable one, since the factor of reliability reaches 60%. The descriptive analysis shows that high service quality plays an extremely important role in retaining subscribers in a mobile service carrier. Of the respondents, 96% do consider high service quality to influence customer retention and if we take into consideration this exceedingly high percentage we reach the conclusion that service quality has a great impact on customer retention.

4.3. Correlation Analysis

Correlations measure how variables or rank orders are related. Through the current correlation analysis we draw very important conclusions. There is a positive correlation between satisfaction and customer service. The better the customer service, the more satisfied the customer is.

That means that if WIND is to keep its customers satisfied, it should focus on high levels of specialization of its staff and on its technological infrastructure. When the employees have a complete knowledge of the customer profile the company will respond successfully to its customers' needs.

Another important hypothesis that can be drawn from the analysis is that there is a positive relationship between reliability and switching barriers, meaning that the more reliable the company is, the more difficult it is for the subscriber to switch to another network. So, from this hypothesis could be drawn the conclusion that reliability has an impact on customer retention. It would be especially profitable for the company to provide high service-quality levels in order to retain its customers rather than attracting new ones, which would be considerably more costly.

Further, there is a negative correlation between high charges and satisfaction. High charges influence satisfaction, meaning that when the company sets high prices, customers feel less satisfied. It is of great importance for WIND to examine all these relationships and to work out the impact that each factor has on satisfaction and further on customer retention.

4.4. WIND's Advantages and Their Impact on Satisfaction

4.4.1. Stepwise Multiple Regression Model

Through this statistical model, the company's strongest advantages are examined along with their effect on customer satisfaction and consequently on customer retention.

In table 1, the standardized beta value for good customer service is 0.31, for high coverage it appears to be 0.35, for innovative services it is 0.24 and finally for competitive prices it is 0.18.

We reach the conclusion that the better the customer service is, the more satisfied the subscriber is. The second hypothesis is that the better coverage the subscriber has, the more satisfied he is.

The third hypothesis is that the more innovative services the carrier offers, the more satisfied the customer is, and finally the more competitive the prices are, the more satisfied the customer is.

All these conclusions, achieved by statistical analysis and cited in table 1, lead the WIND company to realize how important it appears to be for its long-term survival to provide innovative services by focusing on and investing in advanced technology. Only then will the company keep its customers loyal and satisfied.

Table 1.

Variables	Multiple R	B	Std	error	Beta b	Sign.t
Good customer service	0.55	0.40	0.10	0.31	3.80	0.000
High coverage	0.66	0.35	0.08	0.35	4.52	0.000
Innovative services	0.72	0.29	0.09	0.24	2.95	0.004
Competitive prices	0.73	0.24	0.10	0.18	2.16	0.033

4.4.2. WIND's Disadvantages and their Impact on Satisfaction

Stepwise Multiple Regression Model

In this part of the analysis, which examines WIND's disadvantages, the above model was used with the purpose of making clear the weak points of the company and how these affect subscribers' perceptions.

Table 2 shows that the standardized beta values are -0.43 for low coverage, -0.26 for lack of loyalty programmes and -0.23 for bad customer service.

That means that high levels of those three variables that appear to be the three more powerful disadvantages of the WIND company lead to poor levels of satisfaction. If the company is to keep its customers loyal, it should emphasize, firstly, its technological infrastructure because from the above results it is obvious that the disadvantage that appears to have the strongest impact on customer satisfaction and consequently on customer retention is low coverage.

Also, the company should strengthen its loyalty programs, for example by making stronger offers. Finally, bad customer service in this part does not seem to have such a strong impact since it comes third and it was presented previously as one of the company's advantages.

Table 2.

Variables	Multiple R	B	Std	error	Beta b	Sign.t
Low coverage	0.53	-0.38	0.072	-0.43	-5.25	0.000
Lack of loyalty programmes	0.62	-0.30	0.10	-0.26	-3.040	0.003
Bad customer service	0.65	-0.23	0.08	-0.23	-2.60	0.011

4.5. Factors Related to Service Quality that Influence Customer Retention

4.5.1. Stepwise Multiple Regression Model

In this part, which is the last one from the research analysis conducted, the determinants of service quality that have the strongest impact on customer retention are investigated.

Table 3 depicts that the beta value for reliability is 0.33, for marketing communication it is 0.25 and for accuracy it is 0.26.

The final conclusion of this segment of the analysis is that the three variables, which also constitute three of the factors that determine service quality, have the strongest impact on customer retention.

The stronger these factors are, the more possible it is for the customer to remain in WIND's network.

This statistical relationship becomes obvious, more concisely, in table 3. WIND, as a company, should take into consideration the weight and the seriousness of those three variables and concentrate on taking measures that will reinforce its reliance, image (adverts, packaging, advanced promotional tools) and precision to maintain a high service-quality level and therefore retain its customers.

Table 3.

Variables	Multiple R	B	Std.	Error b	Beta t	Sign. t
Reliability	0.54	0.29	0.08	0.33	3.53	0.001
Marketing communication	0.61	0.17	0.06	0.25	2.93	0.004
Accuracy	0.65	0.20	0.07	0.26	2.80	0.006

5. Implications and Conclusion

5.1. Managerial Implications

Our findings show implications relevant to the importance of building trust with customers, and clearly demonstrate the value of trust in customer retention. The stronger the trust in the relationship between a mobile provider and a customer, the more probable it is for the customer to continue using its services in the long run. Such strategies that build up trust include improving the quality of communication with customers and eradicating any potential short-term profit-driven actions and activities that for example may entail failure to supply the expected services. In our case, the measurements of customer-perceived quality – within the context of a highly competitive market like the one of mobile telecommunications in Greece – can provide a powerful tool for the managers of WIND. Furthermore, the measurement of quality should be more constructive as a channel for improvement than just data reflecting customer perspectives. Also, customer retention and growth appraisals seem to be very effective as performance indicators for evaluating quality enhancement efforts. As a result, such evaluations reveal the high importance of service quality in influencing customer retention and its subsequent influence on the overall performance of the company. Finally, the employment of quality assessment methods that make open reference to competition can bring the company into an advantageous position.

5.2. Conclusion

We conclude that a theoretical framework incorporating service-quality dimensions, factors that influence customer retention and an extended analysis of the WIND company could help managers to make successful decisions by projecting the impact of satisfaction and high quality on customer loyalty. From the research conducted, the impact of service quality on customer retention was investigated and the pros and cons of WIND were identified. It is obvious that service quality plays an extremely important role in building customer trust since good customer service and innovative services appear to be two of the advantages of WIND; reliability also achieved 60% regarding cultivating customer loyalty. Further, relatively to the previous conclusion, it is worth saying that a variable that had a strong impact on customer retention appeared to be the marketing communication mix. Repeated collection of customer data should allow the calibration of model parameters and the long-term assessment of the impact of quality on profitability measures in addition to growth measures. In a telecommunication company in which revenues from services constitute the largest part of its business, the concept of service quality may shift as a result of competitive market conditions, actions and the introduction of new lines of services. Consequently, service quality assessment should be examined and adjusted accordingly within rather short intervals and the management should make the necessary changes in training and duly reward employees while always remaining focused on customer satisfaction and the enhancement of customer loyalty.

5.3. Limitations

With regard to the current study, a number of limitations should be acknowledged. First of all, an important limitation lies within the rapid development of mobile technology, which causes several changes in the marketplace, either in the economic environment or the technological one. Structural changes in the market as well as changes in the competitive setting may tend to change how the market responds as well as how the company responds to those changes.

It is also necessary to be aware of the limitations that all statistical models entail. That is, models represent reality only roughly and cannot fully depict it since there are many aspects and complexities of human behaviour that can for example affect the service quality of a company. No statistical model can be as utterly inclusive and perfect as to manage and capture all the relevant constraints and complexities. Therefore, all statistical models are characterized by the limitation of failing to acknowledge and encompass fully the sum of the parameters that constitute human/customer behaviour.

References

Buzzell, R.D. and Gale, B.T. (1987), *The PIMS Principles – Linking Strategy to Performance*, New York, NY: Free Press.

Fornell, Claes (1992), "A national customer satisfaction barometre: The Swedish experience", *Journal of Marketing*, Vol. 56, January, pp. 6–21.

Ghobadian, A., Speller, S. and Jones, M. (1994), "Service quality, concepts and models", *International Journal of Quality and Reliability Management*, Vol. 11, No. 9, pp. 43–66, MCB University Press.

Grigoroudis, E., Kyriazopoulos, P., Siskos, G. and Samanta, I. (2005), "Competitive Environment and Customer Loyalty: The Case of Internet Providers", 17th National Conference of Hellenic Society of Operational Research, Patra, 16–18 June 2005.

Haywood-Farmer, J. (1988), "A conceptual model of service quality", *International Journal of Operations and Production Management*, Vol. 8, No. 6, pp. 19–29.

Johnston, R. (1995), "The determinants of service quality: Satisfiers and dissatisfiers", *International Journal of Service Industry Management*, Vol. 6, No. 5, pp. 53–71.

Kettinger, W. and Lee, G (1994), "Perceived service quality and user satisfaction with the information services function", *Decision Sciences*, Vol. 25, Nos 5–6, pp. 737–766.

Leisen, B. and Vance, C. (2001), "Cross-national assessment of service quality in the telecommunication industry: Evidence from the USA and Germany", *Managing Service Quality*, Vol. 11, No. 5, pp. 307–317.

Morgan, R.M. and Hunt S.D. (1994), "The commitment trust theory of relationship marketing", *Journal of Marketing*, Vol. 58, July, pp. 20–38.

Parasuraman, A., Zeithaml, V. and Berry, L. (1985), "A conceptual model of service quality and its implications for further research", *Journal of Marketing*, Vol. 48, Fall, pp. 41–50.

Samanta I. (2008) "Analysing the concept of Mass Customisation in banking services" 3rd Word Conference on Production and Operations Management, http://www.jomsa.jp/

Zeithaml, V.A., Berry, L.L. and Parasuraman, A. (1996), "The behavioural consequences of service quality", *Journal of Marketing*, Vol. 60, April, pp. 31–46.

In: HRM and Marketing Orientation in the New Era
Editor: Panagiotis Kyriazopoulos
ISBN: 978-1-62808-959-2

Chapter 17

REDEFINING SUSTAINABLE TOURISM IN INDIAN PERSPECTIVE: SEVEN STEPS APPROACH

Rahul Pratap Singh Kaurav*
VIM; HoD, VIILAS, Gwalior, India

ABSTRACT

This paper is about regular changes of tourism industry. It examines various changes that have taken place in politics, policy, development, conservation, human-environmental relations, and the convergence of these areas over the past 30 years, especially during the last 10 years. As the result of international cooperative scholarship, some old concepts of how the world works are shown to be giving way to a new focus. It discusses how, instead of managing tourism through attempting to maintain stability, new thought guided by close observations of reality, depicts in an environment full of uncertainty that is constantly changing and evolving, and where enhancing pliability to disturbance replaces the former focus on achieving stability. This is not a universal paradigm shift, but it is a shift nevertheless.

It shows how a new view is gradually supplanting the old. It suggests that this view and its leaders cannot be ignored. The paper also presents seven steps on the road to greater understanding of sustainable tourism, in the hope of enabling a more effective transition to sustainability.

Keywords: Sustainable tourism, Adaptive management, Complex adaptive systems, and Sustainability transition

New knowledge of the way in which systems function suggests that nature and human activity should be viewed and studied, not separately but as integrated, *complex adaptive systems,* also termed social-ecological systems (SESs). All living things, human and non-human, and their surroundings exist as communities and networks governed by their own particular behaviour and to a considerable extent they are structured by forces and interactions of complex systems themselves. It is the forces generated within systems that

* Rahul Pratap Singh Kaurav, is Asst. Professor, VIM; HoD, VIILAS, Gwalior. Email: rsinghkaurav@ yahoo.co.in; Mob: +91-9826569573.

produce continual uncertainty and unpredictability and confound those attempting management through rigid control. Although tourism practitioners may know something about social and ecological systems when looked at separately, in reality they know little if anything about complex systems or of merged SESs whose terrestrial landscapes are observed and experienced every day and that are largely the raison d'être of tourism (Holling and Sanderson, 1996).

While at school and university, students at various levels and after graduation in their daily lives, learn the well-established world-view that the Earth (nature, the economy, the stock market, personal health, political climate and tourism) is normally in balance and although there are disturbances, if treated properly things will ultimately return to expectable normality, a state of apparent equilibrium. This falsely optimistic principle has long governed the scientific study of nature as well as most of the social sciences, including economics and tourism.

But it is now known that people's lives are entangled in the interactions of mainly complex systems in every sphere of activity. These systems are periodically stable, but never permanently so. Events usually triggered by multiple causes have uncertain consequences, and because complex systems operate over a variety of *temporal* and *spatial scales,* little is likely to result simultaneously at the time expected or on the scale imagined. This is pivotal to any thoughts of achieving sustainability. Policy decisions may take from weeks to years for all goals to reach fruition. Those concerning human control of resources (like social policy) may cause cascades of surprising outcomes, some of which when they finally arrive may be quite out of proportion to the magnitude of the original inputs. Others, which take a long time to reveal themselves, may be recognized too late for us to do anything about them.

The nature of sustainability is vitally affected by these changes and this leads to the unhappy realization that present approaches to tourism serve students and researchers poorly, providing no more than a partial explanation with which to work. Each place or destination is unique in its combination of characteristics and its expressions of *self-organization:* the size, arrangement and character of lakes, coastal areas, transport net, habitations, schools and hospitals, shopping facilities, mountains, hotels, recreation facilities and areas, water supplies, agricultural resources, tourists and local population are all intricately connected in a network in which the alteration or disturbance of one component from within or without, may affect a hundred others. To assist readers to comprehend this new approach to sustainability and the common search for a *sustainability transition,* the discussion below takes the form of a series of steps: 'seven steps towards sustainability'.

Objectives of Study

In the coming era tourism is a very important emerging business opportunity. We want to explore various dimensions of tourism business. Following are the objectives of study:

- To explore different opportunities for emerging tourism business.
- To identify possibilities to formulate policies for developing this emerging business opportunities.
- To suggest ways and means for policy formulators to identify proper allocation and utilization of resources.

Some of this recent research runs counter to previous thinking and is not quickly assimilated. The aim here is to assist readers to grasp the basics of this new thinking and to understand how it affects sustainable development research, no matter from where it originates. The 'steps' in the title are not all sequential, but are believed to be important signposts on the road travelled.

These are by no means the only signposts, just the most salient points by way of an introduction to these new directions. The presentation is intended to be as simple as possible, and should readers develop an interest in what they read, the cited sources listed as references are a recommended supplementary, and easily available set of readings.

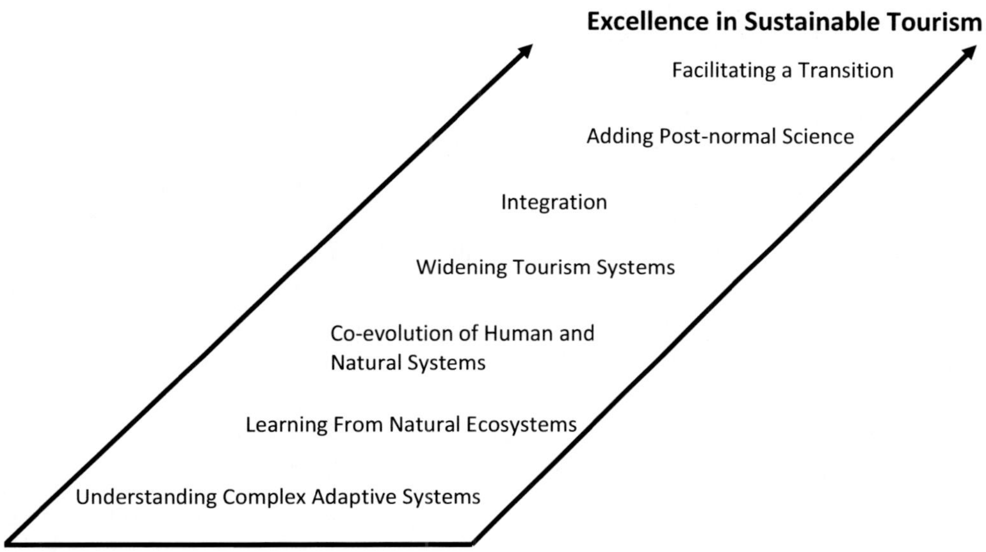

Figure 1. Seven Step Model for Sustainable Tourism (Proposed Model).

Step One: Understanding Complex Adaptive Systems

The first step begins with the recognition, understanding and acceptance of *complex adaptive systems* (SFE, 2004). Field observations and recent global change science indicate that they exist and are not humanly devised frameworks (ESA, 1995; GECP, 2001). Natural ecosystems and tourism systems are examples. They are dynamic, operational realities, being changeable, largely unpredictable, and only minimally explainable by linear cause and effect science. Once the threshold is crossed they flip from an existing condition to one that is less productive or rewarding, perhaps with unpredictable and possibly irreversible, cascading results (Holling, 1986; Marten, 2001).

An elementary working knowledge of complex systems and associated systems thinking are the key to understanding and implementing the next six steps.

Step Two: Learning from Natural Ecosystems

This step concerns *natural ecosystems.* These are complex adaptive systems, about which, as the result of many decades of research by ecosystem ecologists, more is known than appears to be the case with the social sciences. Ecosystems have been found to be driven, not by regular and expectable climatic controlled, vegetational succession, but by local variables. Now it is understood that continuing stability rather than being desirable, may indicate *ecosystem senescence* (in tourism an overly mature destination or part thereof), sharply reduced resilience and vulnerability to surprises, where an unexpected event may trigger collapse and a flip to a different dynamic state (tourist hostage taking, a severe hurricane, a SARS outbreak or a collapse in the economy of a major market area). As a consequence, it has become essential to manage ecosystems for uncertainty through *adaptive management,* whereby stakeholders co-manage on the basis of long understanding and reciprocal social learning (the passing of expertise on a particular ecosystem's behaviour from one generation to another) (Holling, 1978; Lee, 1993; Nyberg, 1999; Walters, 1986).

Natural ecosystems are a category of ecosystems dominated by natural processes and self-organisation (Holling *et al,* 1995). They develop their own changing character as complex systems and have enough in common with tourism systems to warrant close study.

Natural resource researchers have found that natural variability may obscure the effects of exploitation-induced stress and by the time those stress impacts are detectable they may very well be irreversible. Additionally, it is frequently assumed that the impact will simply increase gradually with the intensity of usage, but evidence suggests that this may not be the case. Ecosystems may not show signs of stress until suddenly a threshold is crossed when they collapse and flip to another state (Gunderson and Holling, 2002).

Step Three: Co-evolution of Human and Natural Systems

Social system or human behavioural research and theory provide valuable information about people and their constructions but, unfortunately, usually with little or no reference to natural ecosystems, despite knowledge that human and their structures have co-evolved with them. This is illustrated in the following example.

> Lake Arrowhead, California, has a population of 15-20,000, and it lies at over 5000 feet above sea level and the Los Angeles Basin, within the densely tree covered San Bernadino National Forest, well-known for its recreation and wildlife.
>
> A rigorously controlled leisure settlement surrounds the lake, which supports a thriving tourism industry. A pine dominated forest, a signature of the destination, exists within a sub-humid mountain climate. Drought is chronic and water conservation mandatory, yet building continues apace.
>
> The Lake Arrowhead Tourism Ecosystem is dysfunctional in the extreme but that is understood by very few. And in so doing, every component with its intensity of connections has played a part in the co-evolution of the whole.

Natural systems are, only one part of the equation. It is essential to understand social systems better in preparation for a more complete understanding of tourism systems. Humanly created networks and connections contribute to resilience by protecting against disturbance from outside causes.

All aspects of these connections effectively distance tourism from its other support connections and networks rather than contributing to the creation of a sustainable transition.

Step Four: Widening Tourism Systems

Tourism researchers frequently refer to systems in casual reference, sometimes as a framework for focused understanding, and very occasionally as a real entity. However, these are usually simple systems (referred to earlier), that are usually confined to tourism's industrial core, including relationships largely within the core with components that are mostly of economic origin.

In contrast to the bare-bones core system, this is a *comprehensive tourism system,* and it includes significant social, economic, geological and ecological components, along with the processes and functions that are essential for sustainability (Farrell and Twining-Ward, 2004). The comprehensive system is considered a basic unit for the study and management of tourism.

Step Five: Integration of Stimuli

Integration is essential and it takes several forms. First, there is the integration of the previous steps to effect sustainable development, including a now absent orientation towards complex systems, a greater understanding of natural ecosystems interconnecting with tourism components, a deep appreciation of the role of social systems and an integration of tourism theory with that of social science and ecosystem ecology. Secondly, because the highly connected system on the ground within a destination does not differentiate between the human and the biophysical or disciplinary divisions, scholarship should reflect this reality or risk disastrous misinterpretations (Berkes and Folke, 1998; Farrell and Twining-Ward, 2004; Twining-Ward and Farrell, 2005). Integration is as essential and important as complex systems, opens a new and revealing window on sustainability.

Step Six: Adding Post-Normal Science

Post-normal, or non-linear science, is an acceptable path that may be followed in addressing tourism study. It is far more appropriate than normal, regular, or orthodox science which is disciplinary, 'cause and effect' science, deterministic, quantitative, linear and the basis of present day scientific thinking and education.

It may be, that in time both normal and post-normal science, or parts of each, will merge and evolve as one. Post-normal science, largely governing all living complex adaptive systems, including tourism, is non-linear, uncertain, largely unpredictable, inductive, qualitative and concerned with the integration of parts rather than with high specialisation.

Step Seven: Facilitating a Transition

Sustainability transition is a term commonly used during the last decade by interdisciplinary scientific researchers to indicate not a management endpoint, but continual development towards biophysical and human well-being (Kates *et al,* 2001). Transition, without an endpoint of achievement, is one literal interpretation of the term sustainable development which can be seen as implying constant evolution and adaptation to site and region. This evolving view of development can never be completed. Imagine, for instance, a spike in tourist arrivals resulting in possible environmental stress, and the effects on ecosystem restoration, investment and reinvestment, infrastructure, competition for resources, and quality of life support systems, to mention only a few components which are likely to enter the mix. Each is evolving, always subject to change or disturbance, and each moves at its own pace. It bears repeating that at all other times, then the varying temporal and spatial scales involved in the interaction of subsystems within tourism systems, and the evolving aspirations and values of local people and their representative stakeholders involved in co-management, together with the probability of surprise from within or outside the system, will always prevent the uniform achievement of permanence.

Conclusion

The information presented here comes largely from the recent understanding of revised ecosystem ecology, global change science and the work of such groups as the Sustainability Science Forum (2009) and the Resilience Alliance (2011). All are outside tourism, all are international, and all are in the context of complex systems behaviour, integration and non-linear science (Steps 1-6). Movement towards a sustainability transition (Step 7) requires the identification of, and the combating of, an array of counter forces, including the ideological values of potent and powerful cultures, conservative elements within tourism, mono-disciplinary science, and linear tools and methods. Above all, it requires an entirely new outlook on the world, building on what has already been learned. Without this, transitions will never be achieved and future tourism will be handicapped and endangered by fragmentation, disunities, vulnerable management and inadequate knowledge of how to meet problems during the rest of this century.

Although the title, '*Sustainable Tourism: Breakdown or Breakthrough - Indian Perspective*' makes the task seem overly simple, it has been chosen only as an aid to learning and in the knowledge that *operationally* much has still to be learned. Every point raised brings forth questions, most of which have yet to be answered. Tourism has accumulated substantial resources, and it is argued here that if these resources are valuably complemented with knowledge of complex adaptive systems, natural ecosystems, co-evolution, a more inclusive tourism system, integrated social-ecological systems, and non-linear science, then tourism will be in a considerably better position to move towards a transition to sustainable tourism development than it is today.

References

Abel, T. (2000) The complex systems dynamics of a development frontier: The case of eco-tourism on the island of Bonaire, Netherland Antilles. Unpublished PhD Thesis, Department of Anthropology, University of Florida, Gainsville.

Abel, T. (2003) Understanding complex human ecosystems: The case of ecotourism on Bonaire. *Conservation Ecology* 7(3), 10. On WWW at http://www.consecol.org/vol7/iss3/artlO. Accessed 20.10.4.

Abel, T. and Stepp, J.R. (2003) A new ecosystem ecology for anthropology. *Conservation Ecology* 7(3),12. On WWW at http://www.consecol.org/vol7/iss3/artl2. Accessed 20.10.04.

Berkes, F. and Folke, C. (eds) (1998) *Linking Social and Ecological Systems: Management Practices and Social Mechanisms for Building Resilience.* Cambridge: Cambridge University Press.

Botkin, D. (1990) *Discordant Harmonies: A New Ecology for the Twenty-First-Century.* New York: Oxford.

Butler, R. (1980) The concept of a tourist area cycle of evolution: Implications for management of resources. *Canadian Ceographer* 24 (1), 5-12.

Ecological Society of America (ESA) (1995) *The Report of the Ecological Society of America Committee on the Scientific Basis of Ecosystem Management.* On WWW at http://esa.sdsc.edu/ecmtext.htm. Accessed 3.2.04.

Farrell, B.H. and Twining-Ward L. (2004) Reconceptualizing tourism. *Annals of Tourism Research* 31, (2), 274-95.

Faulkner, B. and Russell, R. (1997) Chaos and complexity in tourism: In search of a new perspective. *Pacific Tourism Review* 1, 93-102.

Folke, C, Carpenter, S., Elmqvist, T., Gunderson, L.H., Holling, C.S., Walker, B., Bengtsson, J., Berkes, F., Colding, J., Danell, K., Falkenmark, M., Gordon, L., Kasperson, R., Kautsky, N., Kinzig, A., Levin, S., Maker, K-G., Moberg, F., Ohlsson, L., Olsson, F., Ostrom, E., Reid, W., Rockstrom, J., Savenije, H. and Svedin, U. (2002) Resilience and sustainable development: Building adaptive capacity in a world of transformations.

Global Environmental Change Programme (GECP) (2001) Earth science system: An integrated approach. *Environment* 43 (8), 21-7.

Gunderson, L. and Holling, C. (eds) (2002) *Panarchy: Understanding Transformations in Human and Natural Systems.* Washington DC: Island.

Gunderson, L. Holling, C. and Light> S. (eds) (1995) *Barriers and Bridges to the Renewal of Ecosystems and Institutions.* New York: Columbia University Press.

Hein, W. (1997) Tourism and sustainable development: Empirical analysis and concepts of sustainability - A systems approach. In W. Hein (ed.) *Tourism and Sustainable Development* (pp. 359-400). Hamburg: Schriften des Deutschen Ubersee-Instituts, No. 41.

Holling, C. (1986) The resilience of terrestrial ecosystems: Local surprise and global change. In W. Clark, and R. Munn (eds) *Sustainable Development of the Biosphere* (pp. 292-317). Cambridge: Cambridge University Press.

Holling, C. (1995) What barriers? What bridges? In L. Gunderson, C. Holling and S. Light (eds) *Barriers and Bridges to the Renewal of Ecosystems and Institutions* (pp. 1-34). New York: Columbia University Press.

Holling, C. (ed.) (1978) *Adaptive Environmental Assessment and Management.* New York: John Wiley.

Holling, C. and Sanderson, S. (1996) Dynamics of (dis)harmony in ecological and social systems. In S. Harma, C. Folke, K. Maler and A. Jansson (eds) *Rights of Nature:*

Ecological, Economic, Cultural and Political Principles of Institutions fbr the Environment (pp. 57-86).

Kates, R., Clark, W., Corell, R., Hall, J., Jaeger, C, Lowe, I., McCarthy J., Schellnhuber, H., Bolin, B., Dickson, N., Faucheux, S., Gallopin, G., Grubler, A., Huntley, B., Jager, J., Jodha, N., Kasperson, R., Mabogunje, A., Matson, F., Mooney, H., Moore III, B., O'Riordan, T. and Svedin, U. (2001) Environment and development: Sustainability science. *Science* 292 (5517), 641-2.

Laws, E., Faulkner, B. and Moscardo, G. (1998) Embracing and managing change in tourism. In E. Laws, B. Faulkner and G. Moscardo (eds) *Embracing and Managing Change in Tourism: International Case Studies,* (pp. 1-10). New York: Routledge.

Lee, K. (1993) *Compass and Gyroscope: Integrating Science and Politics for the Environment.* Washington DC: Island.

Marten, G.G. (2001) *Human Ecology: Basic Concepts For Sustainable Development.* London: Earthscan.

McKercher, B. (1999) A chaos approach to tourism. *Tourism Management* 20 (4), 425-34.

Murphy, F.E. (1985) Tour: *A Community Approach.* London: Methuen.

National Research Council (NRC) Board on Sustainable Development (Policy Division) (1999) *Our Common Journey: A Transition Toward Sustainability.* Washington, DC: National Academy.

Nyberg, B. (1999) An introductory guide to adaptive management: For project leaders and participants. Victoria: British Columbia Forest Service. On WWW at http://www.for.gov.bc.ca/hfp/amhome/amhome.htm. Accessed 10.9.04.

Russell, R. and Faulkner, B. (1999) Movers and shakers: Chaos makers in tourism development. *Tourism Management* 20, 411-23.

Russell, R. and Faulkner, B. (2004) Entrepreneurship, chaos and the tourism area lifecycle. *Annals of Tourism Research* 31 (3), 556-79.

San Francisco Exploratorium (SFE) (2004) Complexity website. On WWW at http://www.exploratorium.edu/complexity/. Accessed 20.11.04.

Twining-Ward, L. and Farrell, B. (2004) Sustainable development. In G. Miller and L. Twining-Ward *Monitoring for a Sustainable Tourism Transition: The Challenge of Developing and Using Indicators.* London: CABI.

Walters, C. (1986) *Adaptive Management of Renewable Resources.* London and New York: Macmillan.

In: HRM and Marketing Orientation in the New Era
Editor: Panagiotis Kyriazopoulos
ISBN: 978-1-62808-959-2

Chapter 18

EXPERIENCES OF IMPLEMENTING QUALITY MANAGEMENT SYSTEMS: AN EMPIRICAL STUDY FOR MOTIVES AND BENEFITS

Evangelos Grigoroudis*
Department of Production Engineering and Management
Technical University of Crete
University Campus, Kounoupidiana, Chania, Greece

ABSTRACT

ISO 9001 attracts an increasing interest within both the business and the research community due to its wide acceptance by millions of organisations, as well as due to the effects that certified companies wield to their competitors and providers. Although sometimes it is considered as a sufficient condition towards the adoption of a Total Quality Management system, studies in the past have shown that certification is a necessary but not a sufficient condition for Total Quality Management. This creates the need for a more in depth analysis of the motives for certification and the resulting benefits, which constitutes the main aim of the study presented herein. To accomplish this aim, a questionnaire-based survey has been conducted among certified companies of the Attiki Prefecture in Greece. The analysis of the results reveals several aspects of the procedures before, during and after certification, and indicates that the factors primarily leading a company to certification are both internal and external. The limitations of the presented study, as well as future ways for extensions and enhancements are also discussed.

INTRODUCTION

The path of an organisation towards Total Quality Management (TQM) includes a number of transitional stages, where the development of a Quality Management System (QMS) plays a crucial role. To certify the development and adoption of a QMS system,

* Tel.: +30 28210 37346; Fax: +30 28210 69410; E-mail address: vangelis@ergasya.tuc.gr.

nowadays, there are available different international standards. From these, ISO 9001 quality standard is the most widely recognised and adopted. ISO 9001 specifies requirements for a quality management system where an organisation needs to demonstrate its ability to consistently provide products and services that meet customer requirements, and applies processes for the continual improvement of the system and the assurance of conformity to all applicable requirements, aiming to enhance customer satisfaction.

Despite some doubts regarding its true value, ISO 9001 attracts an increasing interest within both the business and the research community due to its wide acceptance by millions of organisations, as well as due to the effects that certified companies wield to their competitors and providers. The certifications according to ISO 9001 have recently increased, exceeding 1 million business organisations in 180 countries worldwide. This fact implies that, within the business world, there is a widespread view that the benefits resulting from its adoption are many and significant.

Despite the aforementioned widespread view, many researchers have proved that the mere compliance with the necessary certification requirements is not enough for the organisations willing to get the maximum possible benefits from the adoption of the standard. Additional requirements exist, which need to be traced and studied. Past surveys have also indicated that there is a confusion between the organisations' quality and the ISO 9001 certification, as well as between the certification motives and the benefits from the adoption of a TQM system. In short, it has been shown that certification is a necessary but not a sufficient condition for TQM. It is therefore necessary to study further and correlate the certification motives with the resulting benefits.

Starting from the above reasoning, the present paper aims to investigate and depict experiences from the application of ISO 9001, and study in more depth the relationship between the motives for certification and the resulting benefits. To this end, a questionnaire-based survey has been conducted in 1400 randomly chosen, ISO 9001 certified companies of the Attiki Prefecture in Greece. The questionnaire has been developed based on relevant literature information so as to focus in and cover all the important and timely issues, and has been analysed using descriptive statistics, segmentation and correlation analyses, as well as advanced ordinal regression techniques.

Following sections summarise the literature review based on which the questionnaire has been designed, and describe the survey and its results. A conclusions section at the end of the paper summarises the major findings of the study, discusses its limitations and suggests ways for future extensions and enhancements.

Literature Review

General Framework of Empirical Studies

Despite some doubts regarding its true value, ISO 9001 attracts an increasing interest within both the business and the research community due to its wide acceptance by millions of organisations, as well as due to the effects that certified companies wield to their competitors and providers.

In recent years, several research studies have dealt with the clarification of several factors that affect or are affected by the adoption of this standard such as the motives to certification, and the benefits and difficulties before and/or after certification. Common goal of all studies is to detect potential improvement margins and to investigate potential application problems, although they usually focus on different aspects of the standard and consider different parameters for their performed analyses.

The framework of the studies is usually limited to particular geographical areas or business sectors, while the parameters studied, refer mostly to one or more steps of the certification procedure. Figure 1 summarises the most important examined parameters.

The examination of the aforementioned factors is based, whenever possible, upon the main elements of the business operation, which include:

- management responsibility;
- customer satisfaction;
- relationship with providers;
- employees;
- internal quality assurance and documentation procedures;
- financial return.

To retrieve the most realistic conclusions, the examined parameters are usually correlated with the aforementioned elements of the business operation, and the utilised sample is delimited based on the size of the business organisation, the sector and the geographical area.

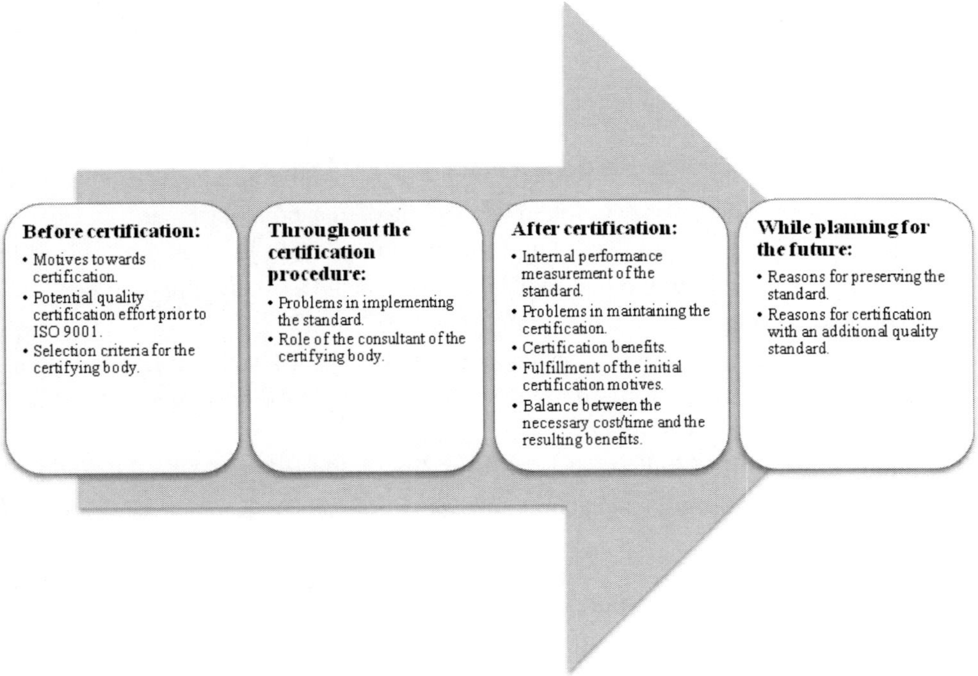

Figure 1. Factors examined in studies regarding the adoption of ISO 9001.

Motives for Implementing QMS

ISO 9001 has been primarily developed as a tool to support the provision of high quality from the certified organisations, as well as to improve their position in the market. As, however, the number of certified organisations increases, from a competitive advantage, certification tends to become a survival requirement.

Although there are several points of view regarding the certification motives, it is commonly agreed that it is the first and potentially the most significant step towards the adoption of a TQM system leading to the continuous improvement of an organisation's performance (Lee and Palmer 1999; Mezher et al. 2005). Within the relevant studies, the motives to certification are generally divided in two groups: internal and external motives. Internal motives relate mainly to the improvement of the inter-business organisation and performance, customer satisfaction and sales increase, while external motives relate to the needs of the organisation to improve its reputation (image) and marketing.

According to the majority of the past studies (Carlsson and Carlsson 1996; Lipovatz *et al.* 1999; Rayner and Porter1991; Withers and Ebrahimpour 2001), the external motives constitute the major push towards certification. Generally, however, the motives behind this need of organisations to certify their QMS relate mainly to the following (Arauz and Suzuki 2004; Beattie and Sohal 1999; Briscoe et al. 2005; Lipovatz *et al.* 1999; Mezher and Ramadan 1999; Poksinska et al. 2002; Subba Rao et al. 1997; Terlaak and King 2006; Tsiotras and Gotzamani 1996):

- Improvement of the business image and reputation and gain of international recognition.
- Improvement of financial performance through revenue increase and sales development via increase of market share and/or expansion in new markets.
- Increase of customer satisfaction through the offer of improved products/services resulting from a better orientation towards their needs and requirements.
- Increased control over cost and improvement of the quality of offered products/services through the reduction of defects and the improvement of the internal processes.
- Achievement of high level leadership in quality issues and creation of a quality culture to the organisation's employees so as for quality to comprise a significant part of the strategic planning of the organisation.
- Improvement in the relations of the organisation with its suppliers, and development of a quality-based supplier selection process.

In addition to the above, many researchers relate the certification motives with the business performance and profitability of a certified organisation, and pinpoint that in case of internal motives, business organisational benefits and improvement may be enforced (Buttle 1997; Jones *et al.* 1997; Tsiotras and Gotzamani 1996).

Benefits of Implementing QMS

No matter what their motives are, certified organisations seem to gain many benefits, which may be also divided in internal and external.

External benefits include (Buttle 1997; Casadesus and Gimenez 2000; Chow-Chua *et al.* 2003; Huarng *et al.* 1999; Mezher and Ramadan 1999; Tsiotras and Gotzamani 1996):

- Improvement of organisational image/reputation and increase of the level of trust across the different stakeholders.
- Fulfilment of customers' requirements and improvement of customer loyalty.
- Improvement of the quality of offered products/services.
- Gaining access to new markets by transforming the organisation to a more attractive supplier for other organisations.
- Achievement of competitive advantage through the use of certification as a promotion tool.

while internal gains include (Buttle 1997; Casadesus and Gimenez 2000; Chow-Chua *et al.* 2003; Corbett *et al.* 2004; Huarng *et al.* 1999; Lee and Palmer 1999; Lipovatz *et al.* 1999; Mezher and Ramadan 1999; Mezher *et al.* 2005; Tsiotras and Gotzamani 1996):

- Increase in sales, profits, and market share.
- Improvement of financial performance mainly due to the significant decrease in costs and reduction in defects, which is achieved with the improvement of the internal organisation and communication practices, as well as with their systematic reporting.
- Increase of the operational effectiveness due to better management, which is based on the definition, standardisation, continuous control and improvement of the organisation's processes.
- Improvement of suppliers' evaluation and selection processes.
- Productivity improvement due to the increased knowledge of operational problems and the gained employee commitment.
- Improvement of the understanding of the concept of quality, which is obtained through the continuous quality-related measurements.

Other Research Questions

Beyond the identification of the motives behind the organisations' decisions to obtain an ISO 9001 certificate and the examination of the benefits that a certification may have, there are other important issues also discussed in the relevant literature. These include the criteria for selecting the certifying body, as well as any potential problems during and/or after the certification process.

As far as the certifying body is concerned, the following factors and characteristics are usually considered as important for the selection:

- The international recognition and reliability.
- The involved costs.

- The experience as demonstrated by the clientele.
- The potential specialisation in particular production lines or services.
- The staff qualifications.
- The accreditation according to special relevant standards.
- The available software tools, which may facilitate the QMS implementation.

No matter, however, how experienced and qualified the selected certifying body is, the organisations, as mentioned earlier, may face several problems during and/or after the certification process. The majority of these problems relate to the organisational structure, and the most common of them include the following (Whalen and Rahim 1994):

- The lack of management participation.
- The resistance of the staff.
- The lack of employee training.
- The difficulty in developing an effective communication network.
- The difficulty in changing the organisational philosophy.

Generally, the relevant studies reveal the following issues, which may cause problems during and/or after certification (Chow-Chua et al. 2003; Douglas et al. 2003; Hong and Phitayawejwiwat 2005; Lipovatz et al. 1999; Mezher and Ramadan 1999; Singels et al. 2001; Tang and Kam 1999; Tsiotras and Gotzamani 1996; Wilson 1996):

- *Procedures developed without active participation of management and employees, and without interaction with customers.* As a consequence, the requirements of the standard are not understood and accepted by the organisation's staff. This problem appears usually in organisations that proceed to certification only to satisfy customers' requests.
- *Direct benefits seem to be only intangible.* The financial benefits appear only after a significant period of improved business performance.
- *The required time and cost for certification.* Cost continuous to be an issue that concerns organisations, even after certification. This is because, on the one hand, the required employee effort, especially during the first stages, is increased, and on the other hand, there are several cases where non-certified companies seem to have less operational costs, thus more net profits compared to the certified ones.
- *Certified organisations do not seem to follow adequately the procedures that constitute their QMS.* Thus, they fail to establish an effective internal auditing system. This problem appears, mainly, due to the lack of appropriately trained internal quality auditors.
- *It is very difficult to change the quality culture of the organisation.* In order to change the quality philosophy of employees, great effort is required by the management, since, in several cases, the usefulness of the necessary changes is not clear, while employees appear disappointed when problems occur in the new management system.

Finally, it should be mentioned that other notable problems relate to the selection of an unsuitable certifying body, as well as to the different opinions between those who develop the QMS and these that will finally use it (Tsiotras and Gotzamani 1996).

SURVEY

Questionnaire Design

The aim of the survey presented herein is to investigate and depict the experiences of ISO 9001 certified companies with the application of this particular QMS. Issues of interest include the motives for certification, the criteria employed for the selection of the certification body, the difficulties during the certification procedure, the resulting benefits, the problems in the maintaining the QMS, and the relation of certification with the adoption of the TQM principles.

Beyond the simple statistical analysis of the above issues, the survey aims also at revealing their interrelation with the company's profile, i.e. the size and type of activity, and at relating and comparing the motives for certification with the certification's final benefits.

The questionnaire developed for the purpose of this study consists of three main parts (Farasoglou 2010). The first one refers to the company profile and contains questions regarding the type of activity, the number of employees, as well as the time necessary for the certification of the company according to ISO 9001.

The second part of the questionnaire has been devoted to the certification motives, the criteria for selecting the certifying body, the preparations and the problems before the auditing process, as well as the certification benefits and the problems for maintaining the QMS. The examined certification motives constitute also the potential resulting benefits and include the following:

- Improvement of business image and reputation.
- Increase of the level of trust across different stakeholders.
- Improvement of customer relationships.
- Improvement of product/service quality.
- Increase of the B2B (Business-to-Business) sales.
- Increase of sales, profits and market share.
- Improvement of international competitive position.
- Increase of control over costs.
- Improvement of internal organisation and communication practices.
- Increase of the effectiveness of management decisions.
- Improvement of supplier relationships.
- Development and improvement of a TQM system.
- Creation of a quality culture for employees.

The importance of these factors has been measured using a 5-point Likert scale (not at all important-somewhat important-moderately important-important-very important).

Finally, in the third part of the questionnaire, the respondents have been asked to express their point of view in relation to six statements relating to their overall opinion for ISO 9001 and the basic principles of TQM, as well as their future plans, in a 5-point Likert scale (agree-somewhat agree-neither agree nor disagree- somewhat disagree-disagree).

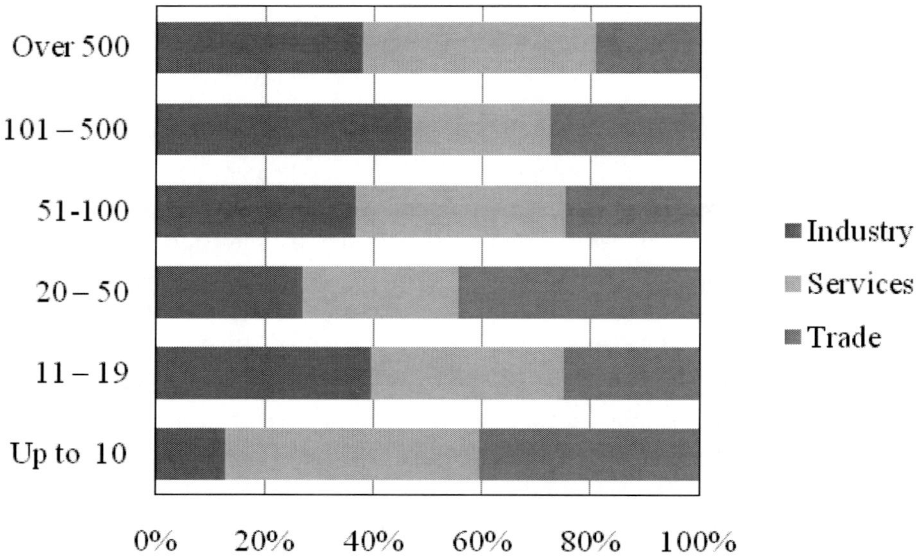

Figure 2. Distribution of surveyed companies according to size and type of activity.

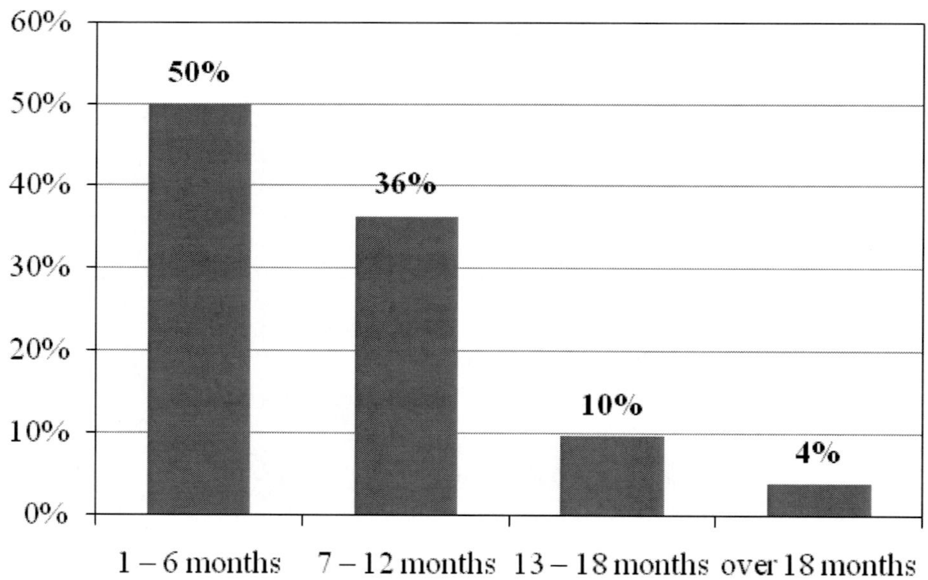

Figure 3. Time necessary for certification according to ISO 9001.

Survey Details and Sample Profile

The questionnaire was sent via e-mail, to the Quality Managers of 1400 randomly chosen, certified according to ISO 9001 companies of the Attiki Prefecture. The sample was identified from the ICAP 2009 Greek Financial Directory and the data collection process took place during the period December 2009-February 2010. The final sample consisted of 177 companies and the response rate (almost 13%) was considered satisfactory, given the type of the survey and the respondents' profile. The analysis of the first part of the questionnaire revealed that from the totally received 177 questionnaires, 64 came from the industrial sector, 79 from services and 51 from trade companies. Apparently, some companies declared more than one types of activities. Moreover, half of the surveyed companies were occupying 11-50 employees, while only 10 declared to occupy more than 500 employees. Figure 2 summarises the distribution of the surveyed companies according to their size and type of activity. In addition, as Figure 3 displays, the time necessary for certification did not exceed the period of 1 year for the majority of the sample (86%), while for only 4% of it, the corresponding time period exceeded the 18 months.

RESULTS

Descriptive Statistics

The analysis of the second and third part of the questionnaire revealed some useful conclusions regarding the application of the ISO 9001 QMS from the Greek companies, as well as their general attitude toward the TQM principles.

As shown in Table 1, the most important motive for certification seemed to be the improvement of business image and reputation, followed by the improvement of the internal organisation and communication. The increase of sales, profits, and market share, the control over costs, the effectiveness of managerial decisions, as well as the improvement of the suppliers' relationships did not seem to comprise significant motives. Notable is the fact that from all the investigated factors, the improvement of the competitive advantage of the company in the international market received the higher percentage of answers, which consider it as being non-important, although more than half of the sample considered it important or very important.

As far as the certifying body is concerned, it seems that its international recognition and reliability, as well as its experience, as demonstrated by its clientele, were the most important selection criteria. On the contrary, the software tools that may help the implementation of the QMS were not considered as being important. Table 2 summarises the corresponding results.

During the preparations for certification, the commonly followed procedures did not create significant problems to the sampled companies, with the exception of the change of the employees' culture and attitude, which created problems to more than half of the sampled companies, as Table 3 displays. After certification, the most important benefit for the companies was the improvement of their business image and reputation, followed by the increase of trust and the improvement of internal organisation and communication.

Table 1. Importance of certification motives (%)

Certification motives	Not at all Important	Somewhat Important	Moderately Important	Important	Very Important
Improvement of business image and reputation	0.6	1.7	8.0	32.4	57.4
Increase of the level of trust across different stakeholders	1.1	3.4	20.0	39.4	36.0
Improvement of customer relationships	1.1	8.0	23.9	39.2	27.8
Improvement of product/service quality	2.8	6.8	17.0	43.2	30.1
Increase of B2B sales	6.3	10.9	18.9	33.1	30.9
Increase of sales, profits and market share	7.4	13.1	33.0	34.7	11.9
Improvement of international competitive position	9.8	12.1	17.9	32.4	27.7
Increase of control over costs	9.2	14.4	31.0	25.3	20.1
Improvement of internal organisation and communication practices	0.6	4.6	16.6	40.0	38.3
Increase of the effectiveness of management decisions	3.4	10.3	28.6	44.6	13.1
Improvement of supplier relationships	5.7	13.8	23.6	43.1	13.8
Development and improvement of a TQM system	4.0	5.2	17.2	39.7	33.9
Creation of a quality culture for employees	2.9	8.1	23.7	38.7	26.6

Table 2. Importance of selection criteria for the certifying body (%)

Selection criteria	Not at all Important	Somewhat Important	Moderately Important	Important	Very Important
International recognition and reliability	0.6	2.9	5.7	31.6	59.2
Involved costs	2.8	5.1	26.7	43.2	22.2
Experience as demonstrated by the clientele	1.1	2.9	10.9	41.7	43.4
Specialisation in particular production lines or services	9.7	10.3	25.7	34.3	20.0
Staff qualifications	5.7	6.9	20.6	41.1	25.7
Accreditation according to special relevant standards	1.7	4.0	18.3	34.9	41.1
Software tools, which may facilitate the QMS implementation	5.7	6.3	24.6	38.3	25.1

Table 3. Importance of difficulties during the certification procedure (%)

Difficulties	Not at all Important	Somewhat Important	Moderately Important	Important	Very Important
Preparation of the quality manual	18.2	22.2	37.5	18.2	4.0
Development of the quality management documentation system	16.7	21.8	27.0	26.4	8.0
Development of a supplier selection and evaluation process	17.1	31.4	34.3	12.0	5.1
Work reengineering and task allocation	12.6	27.6	28.7	25.3	5.7
Adoption of new quality culture by employees	6.3	19.4	22.9	35.4	16.0
Calibration of tools and equipment	24.3	27.8	30.8	13.6	3.6
Training of managers	16.0	26.3	33.1	18.9	5.7
Training of other employees	12.1	27.7	26.6	27.7	5.8
Special laboratory equipment for quality measurement and control	45.1	21.0	17.9	11.1	4.9
Issues regarding environmental management, occupational health and safety	35.8	20.8	24.3	13.3	5.8

Table 4 summarises the relevant results. Notable is the fact that the sampled companies did not consider to have gained significant benefits relating to their financial performance (sales, profits, market share, production cost). Similarly they did not identify significant benefits for their access to new international markets as a consequence of their certification.

In addition to the above, companies were also asked to evaluate the overall importance of the certification benefits, and generally, more than 70% of the sample considered the application of ISO 9001 as being beneficial (26% very important, 48% important, 20% moderately important, 5% somewhat important, and 1% not at all important). As far as difficulties after certification are concerned, as Table 5 displays, with the exception of the adoption of a new quality culture by employees at all levels, as well as the need to follow the requirements of the QMS, the sampled companies did not report on significant problems in their effort to maintain the ISO 9001 certification. In addition, according to the analysis of the third part of the questionnaire, the majority of the sampled companies seemed to have realise and adopt the TQM philosophy and principles, while a 90% of them considered continuous training of staff as a prerequisite to ensure optimal quality. Finally, the majority of the sampled companies considered that the resulting benefits balanced the necessary quality costs, and included the maintenance of the standard among their future plans, while only a 44% of them considered further certifications according to other standards.

Table 4. Importance of certification benefits (%)

Certification benefits	Not at all Important	Somewhat Important	Moderately Important	Important	Very Important
Improvement of business image and reputation	1.7	6.3	10.8	43.2	38.1
Increase of the level of trust across different stakeholders	2.3	4.0	19.9	35.2	38.6
Improvement of customer relationships	4.0	4.0	27.6	33.9	30.5
Improvement of product/service quality	2.3	7.4	21.7	40.0	28.6
Increase of B2B sales	4.6	9.2	23.6	29.3	33.3
Increase of sales, profits and market share	5.7	21.1	37.7	23.4	12.0
Improvement of international competitive position	14.5	16.8	26.6	23.1	19.1
Increase of control over costs	6.9	20.1	33.3	27.0	12.6
Improvement of internal organisation and communication practices	2.3	8.6	19.0	47.1	23.0
Increase of the effectiveness of management decisions	5.7	15.4	33.1	33.1	12.6
Improvement of supplier relationships	5.7	15.4	29.1	30.9	18.9
Development and improvement of a TQM system	5.7	9.8	20.7	41.4	22.4
Creation of a quality culture for employees	2.9	8.0	32.2	37.4	19.5

Finally, in order to examine if the company profile characteristics differentiates the aforementioned results, a segmentation analysis was performed to the sampled companies. According to the results of this analysis, the type of activity did not seem to be related with the collected responses.

Table 5. Importance of difficulties after the certification procedure (%)

Difficulties	Not at all Important	Somewhat Important	Moderately Important	Important	Very Important
Documentation and data management	27.0	28.7	20.7	20.1	3.4
Management responsibilities	30.7	34.7	23.3	9.1	2.3
Corrective and preventive actions	22.4	33.3	25.9	14.4	4.0
Statistical techniques	26.1	28.4	29.5	13.1	2.8
Internal quality audits	29.1	27.4	31.4	11.4	0.6
Documentation procedures	28.6	28.6	30.9	10.9	1.1
Adoption of new quality culture by employees	10.9	34.3	28.0	21.1	5.7
Clarification of special requirements and critical items	19.0	33.3	28.7	16.7	2.3
Cost of quality	20.0	33.7	28.6	14.9	2.9
Customer complaint management	29.7	33.1	22.9	10.9	3.4
Collaboration with the certifying body	60.9	24.7	12.1	1.7	0.6
Non evidence for improved financial performance	18.4	36.2	33.3	9.2	2.9
Adoption of QMS requirement by employees	22.7	32.4	23.9	18.8	2.3
Measurement and testing laboratories	57.2	18.7	16.3	6.0	1.8

On the contrary, the size of the company had significant effects since, according to the results, larger companies, in contrast to the smaller ones:

- needed more time for certification,
- considered the majority of the reviewed motives as more important,
- considered the international recognition and reliability, as well as the experience of the certifying body as the most important factors for selection,
- rated, generally, more positive the partial, as well as the overall benefits resulting from certification,
- considered that the cost and time needed for certification were balanced by the resulting benefits, and
- considered maintenance of certification, as well as certification according to other standards among their future plans.

Comparative Analysis between Motives and Benefits

As already noted, the factors considered as motives for certification, were also examined as the main resulting benefits for the surveyed business organisations. It is important, therefore, to study the correlation between these certification motives and benefits, since the correlation can show if companies' expectations regarding the ISO 9001 standard were fulfilled. Table 6 shows the correlation coefficients of all factors that were considered both as motives and benefits. Given the ordinal nature of the collected data, the correlation analysis was based on Kendall's tau correlation coefficient, while casewise deletion was applied for missing data. According to the results of Table 6, all correlation coefficients are positive and significant (2-sided significance level is less than 0.001), meaning that the evaluation of a factor as motive is positively proportional to its evaluation as benefit.

Table 6. Correlation analysis between certification motives and benefits

Certification motives/benefits	Kendall's tau	N	p-level
Improvement of business image and reputation	0.519	176	0.000
Increase of the level of trust across different stakeholders	0.607	175	0.000
Improvement of customer relationships	0.549	174	0.000
Improvement of product/service quality	0.528	175	0.000
Increase of B2B sales	0.386	173	0.000
Increase of sales, profits and market share	0.618	175	0.000
Improvement of international competitive position	0.344	173	0.000
Increase of control over costs	0.547	173	0.000
Improvement of internal organisation and communication practices	0.516	173	0.000
Increase of the effectiveness of management decisions	0.583	174	0.000
Improvement of supplier relationships	0.613	173	0.000
Development and improvement of a TQM system	0.548	173	0.000
Creation of a quality culture for employees	0.614	172	0.000

In order to estimate the importance of these factors in a cardinal scale, different ordered weighted averaging operators were applied, given that these variables were measured using an ordinal scale (Likert scale of importance). In particular, two of the most widely used direct weight elicitation techniques were applied: the rank-sum (RS) approach and the rank-reciprocal (RR) approach.

In the RS scheme, the weights are obtained using the following formula:

$$w_i = \frac{n - r_i + 1}{\sum_{j=1}^{n}\left(n - r_j + 1\right)}$$

where w_i is the weight of the i-th factor, n is the number of factors, and r_i is the rank of the i-th factor. In the RR approach, the weights are computed as follows:

$$w_i = \frac{1/r_i}{\sum_{j=1}^{n}\left(1/r_i\right)}$$

These approximate weighting schemes preserve the rank order of attributes when the weights are arranged from the most important to the least important, which is the case of the presented survey. An analytical presentation of the RS and the RR methods, as well as other alternative weighting schemes and a detailed debate about the pros and cons of each approach may be found in the multicriteria decision analysis literature (see for example Ahn 2011; Ahn and Choi 2012; Barron and Barret 1996; Roberts and Goodwin 2003; Stillwell *et al.* 1981).

Table 7 summarises the results of the RS and the RR approaches and presents the estimated weights for the examined factors, averaging over all respondents. Although these alternative approaches gave different weighting schemes, the results show that the improvement of business image and reputation was the most important motive.

Table 7. Estimated importance of certification motives and benefits

Certification motives/benefits	Estimated importance			
	As motive (%)		As benefit (%)	
	RS	RR	RS	RR
Improvement of business image and reputation	8.223	10.791	8.100	9.596
Increase of the level of trust across different stakeholders	7.909	8.530	8.058	9.293
Improvement of customer relationships	7.819	7.791	7.809	8.375
Improvement of product/service quality	7.856	8.018	7.883	8.342
Increase of B2B sales	7.677	7.786	7.779	8.496
Increase of sales, profits and market share	7.461	6.194	7.409	6.148
Improvement of international competitive position	7.447	7.198	7.315	6.583
Increase of control over costs	7.353	6.419	7.380	6.286
Improvement of internal organisation and communication practices	7.916	8.801	7.790	8.144
Increase of the effectiveness of management decisions	7.537	6.555	7.510	6.574
Improvement of supplier relationships	7.432	6.358	7.587	7.045
Development and improvement of a TQM system	7.773	8.095	7.699	7.674
Creation of a quality culture for employees	7.596	7.464	7.683	7.445

Other important motives include the increase of trust, the improvement of customer relationships, and the improvement of product/service quality. On the contrary, the increase of control over costs, as well as the improvement of supplier relationships, and the increase of sales, profits, and market share were identified as the least important motives.

Similarly, the results indicate that the most significant certification benefits were also the improvement of business image and reputation, and the increase of trust. Less but yet important benefits include the improvement of customer relationships, and the improvement of product/service quality, while as least important benefits, the improvement of financial performance (sales, profits, market share), the improvement of international competitive position, and the increase of control over costs were identified.

A combined review of the results of Table 6 reveals a variation in the assessed importance of the factors when considered by the respondents as motives and as benefits. It should be noted that the estimated weights are relative degrees of importance, and thus the figures of Table 6 should be comparatively examined.

The most important result is the consistency among the estimated weights. The factors that are considered as both very important motives and benefits refer to the improvement of business image and reputation, the increase of trust, the improvement of customer relationships and the improvement of product/service quality. These factors should be considered as the main certification drivers and results and they can serve as push-pull factors for further promoting the application of QMSs.

On the other hand, the least important certification motives and benefits include the increase of sales, profits, and market share, the improvement of the international competitive position, and the increase of control over costs. These factors are related to financial and market variables. Their lower importance may be justified by the fact that these factors are affected by a large number of other exogenous variables, and thus the application of a QMS cannot ensure an improved performance on these areas.

The most significant gaps in the estimated weights of Table 7 relate to the improvement of internal organisation and communication. This particular factor is considered as a very important motive, but its estimated weight is lower when considered as a benefit. Similarly, the increase of B2B sales is considered as a very important benefit, but its assessed weight is relatively lower when considered as a motive. These factors reveal different examples of push and pull variables, respectively.

Consequently, it seems that the importance of certification motives and results are generally consistent, while the most important certification drivers and results contain both internal and external factors.

CONCLUSION

ISO 9001 attracts an increasing interest within both the business and the research community due to its wide acceptance by millions of organisations, as well as due to the effects that certified companies wield to their competitors and providers. ISO 9001 is sometimes considered as a sufficient condition towards the adoption of a TQM system. Past studies, though, have shown that certification is a necessary but not sufficient condition for TQM. This creates the need for a more in depth analysis of the motives for certification and the resulting benefits.

The major aim of this paper was to provide an in depth analysis of motives and benefits, through the study of companies that have been certified according to ISO 9001. The presented results have been based on a survey conducted to a sample of Greek certified companies and focus on the importance of all factors that may affect the procedure before, during and after certification.

One of the most important survey results is that the most significant certification motives and benefits are both internal and external, and include the improvement of business image and reputation, the increase of trust, the improved customer relationships, and the improvement of product/service quality.

Other important results include the following:

- Financial and market-related factors (sales, profits, or market share, international competitive position, and cost control) are considered as the least important certification motives/benefits, since they are affected by a large number of other exogenous variables.
- A positive correlation exists between the size of the company and the utility level. In particular all large companies aim at sustaining the ISO 9001 certification and believe that the effort in time and cost is balanced by the resulting benefits.
- The time necessary for certification, as well as the utility level seems to be lower for the companies with a less positive attitude towards the TQM principles.

The main limitation of the study refers to the small size of the sample compared to the total number of certified companies in the examined area. Moreover, non-response bias may affect the reliability of the results of the correlation and segmentation analyses, although the Attiki Prefecture is a representative geographical area regarding business activity in Greece. For these reasons, future research surveys may be focused on either a larger sample size or on a smaller but more specific sampling framework (e.g. companies of a particular size, type of activity or geographical region). Also, the analysis of the results may be combined with other particular variables such as financial data and business process measures, or in relation to other standards potentially adopted by the company.

REFERENCES

Ahn, B.S. (2011). "Compatible weighting method with rank order centroid: Maximum entropy ordered weighted averaging approach", European Journal of Operational Research 212(3), pp. 552-559.

Ahn, B.S. and Choi, S.H. (2012). "Aggregation of ordinal data using ordered weighted averaging operator weights", Annals of Operations Research 201(1), pp. 1-16.

Arauz, R. and Suzuki, H. (2004). "ISO 9000 performance in Japanese industries", Total Quality Management 15(1), pp. 3-33.

Barron, F.H. and Barret, B.E. (1996). "Decision quality using ranked attribute weights", Management Science 42(11), pp. 1515-1523.

Beattie, K.R. and Sohal, A.S. (1999). "Implementing ISO 9000: a study of its benefits among Australian organisations", Total Quality Management 10(1), pp. 95-106.

Briscoe, J.A., Fawcett, S.E., and Todd, R.H. (2005). "The implementation and impact of ISO 9000 among small manufacturing enterprises", Journal of Small Business Management 43(3), pp. 309-330.

Buttle, F. (1997). "ISO 9000: Marketing motivations and benefits", International Journal of Quality and Reliability Management 14(9), pp. 936-948.

Carlsson, M. and Carlsson, D. (1996). "Experiences of implementation ISO 9000 in Swedish industry". International Journal of Quality and Reliability Management 13(7), pp. 36-47.

Casadesus, M. and Gimenez, G. (2000). "The benefits of implementation of the ISO 9000 standard: empirical research in 288 Spanish companies", The TQM Magazine 12(6), pp. 432-441.

Chow-Chua, C., Goh, M., and Wan, T.B. (2003). "Does ISO 9000 Certification improve business performance?", International Journal of Quality and Reliability Management 20(8), pp. 936-953.

Corbett, C.J., Montes-Sancho, M.J., and Kirsch, D.A. (2004). "The financial impact of ISO 9000 certification in the US: An empirical analysis", Management Science 51(7), pp. 1046-1059.

Douglas, A., Coleman, S., and Oddy, R. (2003). "The case for ISO 9000", The TQM Magazine 15(5), pp. 316-324.

Farasoglou, E. (2010). "Quality management systems and Greek enterprises: Motives and application benefits", Diploma Thesis, Technical University of Crete, Chania, Greece (in Greek).

Hong, J.W., and Phitayawejwiwat, S. (2005). "The impact of ISO 9000 certification on quality management practices in Thailand", Journal of Industrial Technology 21(1), pp. 1-6.

Huarng, F., Horng, C., and Chen, C. (1999). "A study of ISO 9000 process, motivation and performance", Total Quality Management 10(7), pp. 1009-1026.

Jones, R., Arndt, G., and Kustin, R. (1997). "ISO 9000 among Australian companies: impact of time and reasons for seeking certification on perceptions of benefits received", International Journal of Quality and Reliability Management 14(7), pp. 650-660.

Lee, K.S. and Palmer, E. (1999). "An empirical examination of ISO 9000-registered companies in New Zealand", Total Quality Management 10(6), pp. 887-899.

Lipovatz, D., Stenos, F., and Vaka, A. (1999). "Implementation of ISO 9000 quality systems in Greek enterprises", International Journal of Quality and Reliability Management 16(6), pp. 534-551.

Mezher, T. and Ramadan, H. (1999). "The cost and benefits of getting the ISO 9000 certification in the manufacturing sector in Saudi Arabia", Quality Assurance 6(2), pp. 107-122.

Mezher, T., Abdul-Malak, M.A., Ghosn, I., and Ajam, M. (2005). "Knowledge management in mechanical and industrial engineering consulting: A case study", Journal of Management in Engineering 21(3), pp. 138-147.

Poksinska, B., Dahlgaard, J.J., and Antoni, M. (2002). "The state of ISO 9000 certification: A study of Swedish organizations", The TQM Magazine 14(5), pp. 297-306.

Rayner, P. and Porter, L. (1991). "BS5750/ISO9000 – The experience of small and medium-sized firms", International Journal of Quality and Reliability Management 8(6), pp. 16-28.

Roberts, R. and Goodwin, P. (2003). "Weight approximations in multi-attribute decision models", Journal of Multi-Criteria Decision Analysis 11(6), pp. 291-303.

Singels, J., Ruël, G., and van de Water, H. (2001). "ISO 9000 Series: Certification and performance", International Journal of Quality and Reliability Management 18(1), pp. 62-75.

Stillwell, W.G., Seaver, D.A., and Edwards, W. (1981). "A comparison of weight approximation techniques in multiattribute utility decision making", Organizational Behavior and Human Decision Processes, 28(1), pp.62-77.

Subba Rao, S.S., Ragu-Nathan, T.S., and Solis, L.E. (1997). "Does ISO 9000 have an effect on quality management practices? An international empirical study", Total Quality Management 8(6), pp. 335-346.

Tang, L.S. and Kam, W.C. (1999). "A survey of ISO 9001 implementation in engineering consultancies in Hong Kong", International Journal of Quality and Reliability Management 16(6), pp. 562-574.

Terlaak, A. and King, A.A. (2006), "The effect of certification with the ISO 9000 Quality Management Standard: A signaling approach", Journal of Economic Behavior and Organization 60(4), pp. 579-602.

Tsiotras, G. and Gotzamani, K. (1996). "ISO 9000 as an entry key to TQM: The case of Greek industry", International Journal of Quality and Reliability Management 13(4), pp. 64-76.

Whalen, M.J. and Rahim, M.A (1994). "Common barriers to implementation and development of a TQM Program", Industrial Management 36(2), pp. 19-21.

Wilson, L.A. (1996), "Eight-step process to successful ISO 9000 implementation: A quality management system approach", Quality Progress 29(1), pp. 37-40.

Withers, B.E. and Ebrahimpour, M. (2001). "Impacts of ISO 9000 registration on European firms: A case analysis", Integrated Manufacturing Systems 12(2), pp. 139-151.

BIOGRAPHICAL NOTE

Evangelos Grigoroudis is Assistant Professor on management of quality processes in the Department of Production Engineering and Management of the Technical University of Crete, Greece. He acts as reviewer for, and he is Editorial Board member of several scientific journals. He is author/editor of more than ten books on the measurement of service quality and the business development, operation and strategy, and of numerous research reports and papers in scientific journals and conference proceedings. His research interests include service quality measurement processes, customer and employee satisfaction, performance evaluation, business excellence, operational research, multicriteria decision analysis, data analysis, and marketing.

In: HRM and Marketing Orientation in the New Era
Editor: Panagiotis Kyriazopoulos
ISBN: 978-1-62808-959-2

Chapter 19

SELECTING PROMISING CUSTOMERS ON SOCIAL NETWORKS FOR PROMOTING NEW PRODUCTS IN PRESENCE OF RIVALS

Mossa. Anisa Khatun*[*1], Safique Ahmed Faruque[2,#] and Md. Saidur Rahman[2‡]

[1]Department of Operations Management, Faculty of Business Administration, American International University Bangladesh (AIUB), Dhaka, Bangladesh
[2]Graph Drawing and Information Visualization Laboratory, Department of Computer Science and Engineering, Bangladesh University of Engineering and Technology (BUET), Dhaka, Bangladesh

ABSTRACT

In the past couple of years, social media has become the most preferable marketing media. Viral marketing capitalized on word-of-mouth behavior which is properly suitable in social media. For introducing a new product into a competitive market in word-of-mouth strategy, managers consider using a program in which an initial group of customers, which is called a *seed*, receives the product early on so that their word of mouth begins to drive sales. In such a program, selection of appropriate seeds is a crucial step for being successful in business. In this paper we present three schemes for seeding strategy on social networks considering the presence of business rivals using graph algorithmic techniques.

[*] E-mail: anisa@aiub.edu.
[#] E-mail: safaruque@yahoo.com.
[‡] E-mail: saidurrahman@cse.buet.ac.bd

1. INTRODUCTION

Introducing a new product to the market is a challenging task for a business. Due to enourmous importance of launching new products, researchers have concentrated their attention in formulating successful strategies for promoting new products to the market (Di Benedetto 1999; Cooper 2000; El Houssi et al. 2005; Libai et al. 2010). In recent years many new product launch campaigns are adopting "word-of-mouth" strategy. In word-of-mouth strategy, for introducing a new product into a competitive market, managers consider a program in which an initial group of customers, which is called a *seed*, receives the product early on so that their word of mouth begins to drive sales (Libai et al., 2010). In such a program, selection of appropriate seed is a crucial step for being successful in business (Brown and Reingen 1987; Long and Wong 2011). Domingos and Richardson (Domingos and Richardson 2001; Richardson and Domingos 2002) posed a fundamental algorithmic problem for such systems as follows. Suppose that we have data on a social network, with estimates for the extent to which individuals influence one another we would like to market a new product that we hope to be adopted by a large fraction of the network. The premise of viral marketing is that by initially targeting a few "influential" members of the network, say, giving them free samples of the product, we can trigger a cascade of influence by which friends will recommend the product to other friends, and many individuals will ultimately try it. But how should we choose the initial individuals to use for seeding this process? In this paper we focus on selection of seeds for word-of-mouth marketing on social networks. Furthermore, we consider a competitive market and assume that some of the customers in a social network are already convinced by the product owners of business rivals.

Social diffusion phenomena play a significant role in selection of seeds for word-of-mouth marketing. In well studied models of social diffusion, some initial members of social network start diffusing ideas, innovations or information. According to the process of the models, information propagates through a social network. *Linear Threshold Model* (Goldenberg et al., 2001) and *Independent Cascading Model* (Granovetter 1978; Schelling 2006) are two well studied diffusion models which are relevant to our work. According to *Linear Threshold Model*, at each step, an inactive node becomes active if the sum of the weights of the edges with active neighbors exceeds predefined threshold. In general we can say, at each step, a neutral customer becomes influential customer if his/her acquaintances collectively have enough influence factors to convince him/her (Kempe et al., 2003). In the cascade model, each individual has a single, probabilistic chance to activate each inactive node for which he is a neighbor after becoming active himself. A very simple example is the independent cascade model, in which the probability that an individual is activated by a newly active neighbor is independent of the set of neighbors who have attempted to activate him in the past (Kempe et al. 2003; Wortman 2008).

We consider a scenario of having impact of business rivals in the network. We propose three schemes for the selection of seeds for word-of-mouth marketing motivated by the two diffusion models described above. Our first scheme is distance based, second scheme is influence based and the third one is a combination of them.

We now give an outline of our scenario. Assume that Company A wants to advertise its new product to prospective customers. First Company A finds out the people already convinced by other business rivals (competitors). We will call them *occupied* throughout the paper. According to *Linear Threshold Model* there is a high probability of person to be convinced for possessing any product that is already possessed by his/her acquaintances. So Company A wants to find out the list of persons who have less connection to the occupied persons. Figure 1 illustrates a social network where Bob and Tom are convinced customers of the rivals of Company A. It is likely that Mosby will be influenced by Bob or Tom. It will be difficult to convince Mosby. However, Ted and Penny are at a farthest distance from Bob and Tom, so it will be rather easy for Company A to convince them. So we consider Ted and Penny as prospective customers for Company A. Our goal is to find such prospective candidates in a social network. We define a graph model for the problem as follows.

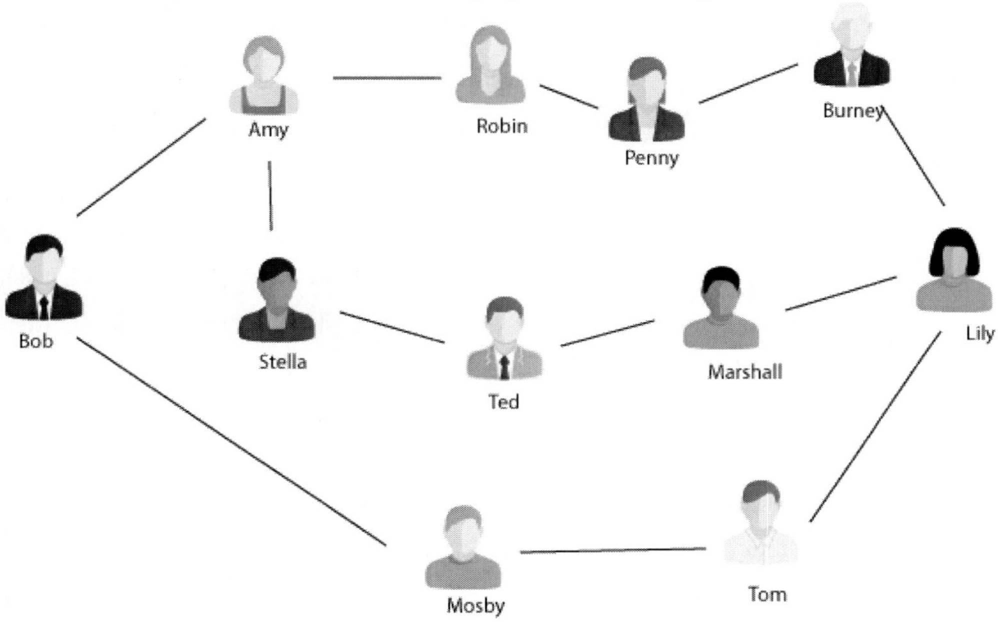

Figure 1. A social network.

Let $G = (V, E)$ be a simple graph representing the social network where each vertex $v \in V$ represents a customer and there exists an edge $(u, v) \in E$ if the customers corresponding to vertices u and v are acquainted with each other.

Let $C \subset V$ be the set of vertices corresponding to the persons convinced by rivals. Now the problem is to find k vertices in $V - C$ such that they are in longest distances from the vertices in C. Similar problems have been studied on Euclidian plane as "Voronoi diagrams" and "largest empty circle" for finding suitable location for new facilities where the distances are Euclidian distance (Okabe et al., 2009). However, our problem is different; in our case, we are studying the problem on social networks, namely on graphs.

The rest of the paper is organized as follows. In Section 2 we present some graph theoretic terminologies. In Section 3 we present our three schemes for selecting seeds for a word of mouth program on a social network. Finally Section 4 is a conclusion.

2. PRELIMINARIES

In this section we present graph theoretic terminologies which will be used in this paper. For interested readers we refer (Wilson 1996; West 2000; Nishizeki and Rahman 2004).

A *graph* G is a tuple (V, E) which consists of a finite set ***V*** of *vertices* and a finite set ***E*** of *edges*; each edge is an unordered pair of vertices. The set of vertices and the set of edges are often denoted by $V(G)$ and $E(G)$, respectively. We denote an edge joining vertices u and v of G by (u, v). If $(u, v) \in E$, then two vertices u and v are said to be *adjacent* in ***G***; *u* is a *neighbor* of v. The *degree* $d(v)$ of a vertex v in G is the number of edges incident to v in G. A *path* in a graph is a sequence of distinct vertices such that from each of its vertices there is an edge to the next vertex in the sequence.

Breath First Search is a technique used in graph to explore the vertices and edges of a graph. The search scans the adjacency lists of vertices in a first reached, first scanned manner. The search starts from a vertex v and visits all the neighbors of v. Then for each visited vertex u, all the unvisited neighbors of u are visited and the search continues in this way. A labeling of the vertices of G can be obtained based on breath first search as follows, which we call *BFS labeling*. We assign label 0 to the starting vertex v and 1 to all of the neighbors of v. We label 2 to the vertices which have not received label yet and are neighbors of a label 1 vertex. Clearly once we labeled the vertices of label 0, 1, …, i we can easily find the vertices of label $i + 1$: they are precisely the unlabeled vertices which are adjacent to label i vertices. Figure 2(b) illustrated BFS labeling of the graph in Figure 2(a). We call the start vertex the *source vertex*. Clearly the label of each vertex indicates the shortest distance from the source vertex.

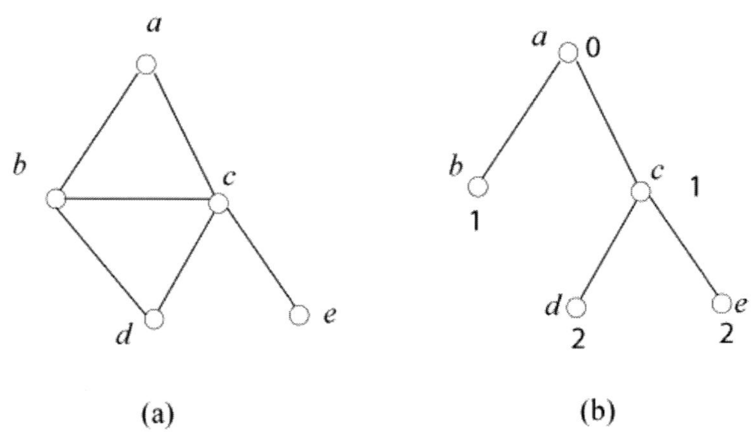

Figure 2. (a) A graph *G* and (b) a BFS labeling of *G*.

3. Selecting Promising Customers

In this section we present three schemes of selecting promising customers based on social network data and considering the presence of business rivals.

3.1. Distance Based Scheme

In this section we give an algorithm to rank promising customers using BFS labeling.

Let $G = (V, E)$ be a simple graph representing the social network where each vertex $v \in V$ represents a customer and there exist an edge $(u, v) \in E$ if the customers corresponding to vertices u and v are acquainted with each other.

Let $C \subset V$ be the set of vertices corresponding to the persons convinced by rivals. Now the problem is to find k vertices in $V - C$ such that they are having longest distances from the vertices in C.

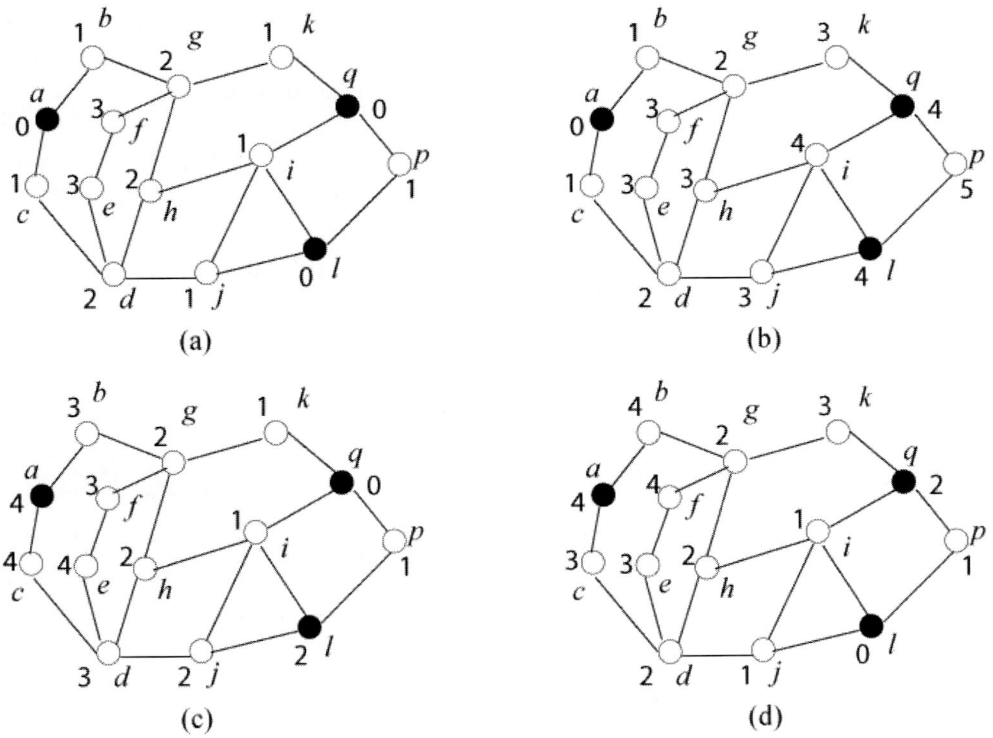

Figure 3. (a) A graph G with 3 occupied vertices a, l and q, (b) G with BFS labeling taking a as the source vertex (c) G with BFS labeling taking l as the source vertex, and (d) G with BFS labeling where q as the source vertex.

We first compute BFS labeling of the vertices of G taking each of the vertices of C as the source vertices. For each vertex we then choose the label which is minimum among all the labels obtained by taking the vertices in C as source vertices. In the graph in Figure 3(a) the vertices in C are a, l and q. BFS labeling of graph G is obtained by taking a as the source vertex in Figure 3(b). Similarly BFS labelings are obtained in Figures 3(c) and 3(d) by taking l and q as the source vertices, respectively. The minimum labels among the labels in Figures 3(b), 3(c) and 3(d) are shown in Figure 3(a). We consider the minimum label of each vertex as the rank of the vertex, and finally list the vertices in descending order of their rank.

3.2. Influence Based Scheme

According to *Independent Cascade* model, one active person u is given a single chance to activate each currently inactive neighbor *w*; it succeeds with a probability $p_{v,w}$. In general, people having more *social influence* have more probability to succeed. *Social influence* is a phenomenon that the actions of a user can induce his/her friends to behave in a similar way (Anagnostopoulos et al., 2008). Epidemiology studies indicate that vertex having more connection foster the spread of diseases (Anderson et al.,1992), which suggests in parallel that vertex having more connection should be more attractive for seeding viral marketing campaigns. Backstrom et al. (Backstrom et al., 2006) examined the membership problem in an online community. They observed correlation between the action of a user joining an online community and the number of friends who are already members of that community. From reverse perspective, we can say that users having more affiliation have more influence in social network. Here comes the necessity of user ranking considering degrees of vertices. We propose a scheme where we first delete the occupied vertices and then label the other vertices according to their degrees $l_u = d(u)$; here $d(u)$ is degree of vertex u after deleting the occupied vertices in the graph. Influence based labeling is illustrated in Figure 4; we label the vertices by their degrees after deleting the occupied vertices.

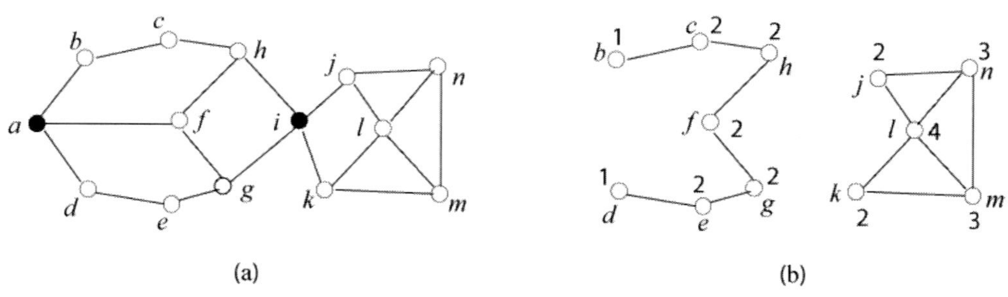

Figure 4. (a) A graph G with 2 occupied vertices and (b) influence based labeling after deleting the occupied vertices.

3.3. Distance and Influence Based Scheme

In this section we give a scheme for ranking promising clients that is a combination of the two schemes above. We consider the following three cases.

Case 1. *Some vertices are occupied by other business rivals.* We first compute a weight w_1 for a vertex u considering the distance based scheme as follows. Let L be the set of labels obtained by BFS labeling, let $max(L)$ be the maximum label in L and let the label of vertex u be l_u. Then we compute $w_1 = \frac{l_u}{max(L)}$ which can have value at most 1.

We now compute a weight w_2 considering influence based scheme. We first delete all the occupied vertices in the graph. Let Δ be the maximum degree of the graph after deleting the occupied vertices. We compute $w_2 = \frac{d(u)}{\Delta}$.

Taking weights w_1 and w_2 we finally formulate the function $f(r) = C_1 w_1 + C_2 w_2$ for ranking of vertices, where C_1 and C_2 are the variables satisfying the conditions $0 \leq C_1, C_2 \leq 1$ and $C_1 + C_2 = 1$. In different networks the values of C_1 and C_2 will vary. For a default case, we take $C_1 = C_2 = 0.5$.

Case 2. No vertex is occupied by other business rivals. In this case there is no source to start BFS labeling. Only degree of vertices considered for ranking of vertices.

Case 3. All the vertices are occupied by other business rivals. In this case, after BFS labeling we will get all the labels 0. Here also degree of vertices is considered for ranking of vertices.

In cases 2 and 3, we can choose a vertex of the maximum degree as a seed. But if we want multiple seeds, we choose the vertices that are far from each other to minimize the overlapping of their influence domain.

CONCLUSION

In this paper we have presented three schemes for selecting seeds for word of mouth marketing on social networks. Our distance based scheme works when there are some customers in the social network who are already convinced by the rival. The influence based scheme works fine even if no customer is convinced by rivals.

Launching a new product needs extensive marketing and to make it successful finding target market is mandatory. If the marketing media is social network which is widely used now a days, to find out the promising customers we can use this algorithm and start campaigning by making them convinced.

REFERENCES

Anagnostopoulos, A., Kumar, R., and Mahdian, M. (2008), "*Influence and correlation in social networks*", Proceedings of the 14th international conference on Knowledge discovery and data mining, ACM, pp.7–15.

Anderson, R. M., May, R. M., and Anderson, B. (1992), "*Infectious Diseases of Humans: Dynamics and Control*", volume 28, Wiley Online Library.

Backstrom, L., Huttenlocher, D., Kleinberg, J., and Lan, X. (2006), "*Group formation in large social networks: membership, growth, and evolution*", Proceedings of the 12th international conference on Knowledge discovery and data mining, ACM, pp.44–54.

Brown, J. J. and Reingen, P. H. (1987), "*Social ties and word-of-mouth referral behavior",* Journal of Consumer Research, 14(3), pp.350–362.

Cooper, L. G. (2000), "*Strategic marketing planning for radically new products"*, The Journal of Marketing, 64(1), pp.1–16.

Di Benedetto, C. A. (1999), "*Identifying the key success factors in new product launch*", Journal of product innovation management, 16(6), wiley, pp.530–544.

Domingos, P. and Richardson, M. (2001), "*Mining the network value of customers*". Proceedings of the seventh international conference on Knowledge discovery and data mining, ACM, pp 57–66.

El Houssi, A. A., Morel, K. P. N., and Hultink, E. J. (2005), "*Effectively communicating new product benefits to consumers: the use of analogy versus literal similarity*", Advances in Consumer Research, 32, pp.554.

Goldenberg, J., Libai, B., and Muller, E. (2001), "*Talk of the network: A complex systems look at the underlying process of word-of-mouth*", Marketing letters, 12(3), pp.211–223.

Granovetter, M. (1978). "*Threshold models of collective behavior*", American journal of sociology, 83(6), pp.1420–1443.

Kempe D., Kleinberg, J., and Tardos, É. (2003). "*Maximizing the spread of influence through a social network"*. Proceedings of the ninth ACM SIGKDD international conference on Knowledge discovery and data mining, ACM, pp.137–146.

Libai, B., Muller, E., and Peres, R. (2010), "*Sources of social value in word of mouth programs*", Marketing Science Institute working paper, pp.10–103.

Long, C. and Wong, R. C. W. (2011), "*Minimizing seed set for viral marketing*". Proc. of IEEE 11th International Conference on Data Mining, IEEE, pp.427–436.

Nishizeki, T. and Rahman, M. S. (2004), "*Planar Graph Drawing"*, World Scientific Publishing Company Incorporated.

Okabe, A., Boots, B., Sugihara, K., and Chiu, S. N. (2009), "*Spatial tessellations: concepts and applications of Voronoi diagrams"*, Wiley.

Richardson, M. and Domingos, P. (2002), "*Mining knowledge-sharing sites for viral marketing*", Proceedings of the eighth international conference on Knowledge discovery and data mining, ACM, pp.61–70.

Schelling, T. C. (2006), "*Micromotives and Macrobehavior"*, WW Norton.

West, D. B. (2000), "*Introduction to Graph Theory"*, Pearson, 2nd edition.

Wilson, R. J. (1996), "*Introduction to Graph Theory"*, Longman, 4th edition.

Wortman, J. (2008), "*Viral marketing and the diffusion of trends on social networks*", Technical Report MS-CIS-08-19, Department of Computer and Information Science, University of Pennsylvania.

In: HRM and Marketing Orientation in the New Era
Editor: Panagiotis Kyriazopoulos
ISBN: 978-1-62808-959-2

Chapter 20

TEAMWORK AND ITS CONTRIBUTION TO PERFORMANCE: EMPIRICAL FIELD EVIDENCE

Anderson Gwanyebit Kehbila*
Bediee School of Business, Simon Fraser University,
Vancouver, British Columbia, Canada

ABSTRACT

In order to establish what constitutes a high performing team, five interviews were conducted with diverse individuals in the following fields: legal, information technology management, stunt-entertainment, telecommunications product development, and transportation policy formation. Based on these interviews, several shared characteristics of high performing teams were identified. These characteristics have been itemized under the broad categories of inputs, processes, and outputs. They have been synthesized into a model which describes what it takes to make a highly performing team. Study results revealed that members of each team brought different and relevant skill sets that were mutually supportive and contributed to the success of the team within time constraints (either in the form of strict deadlines or general time constraints). These pre-established constraints helped to focus the efforts of the team into creating processes in order to generate outputs within a timely fashion while utilizing relevant technologies to facilitate interaction, process information, and dissemination of ideas.

Keywords: High performing team; interview; skill set; inputs; processes, outputs

1. INTRODUCTION

In light of today's virtual and multifaceted organizational structures (Kirschner and Bruggen, 2004), a growing interest in work group innovation (Anderson and west, 1995), and the emergence of group development theories in organizational management (Kass, 2010), the topic of team commitment to maximize quality of task performance has become increasingly important (West, 1990). In this paper, I seek to provide additional insight into the

* Corresponding author E-mail: kehbilaa@gmail.com.

nature and functioning of high performing teams and determine if these patterns are similar to previous studies, as given in the literature, or if they differ, in what ways. The paper builds on interviews conducted with five individuals, representing five different organizations, who have had experience working in high performing teams.

The first section of the interviews investigated the nature and structure of high performing teams (i.e. the inputs and outputs of extraordinary teams) while the second dwelled on the functioning of extraordinary teams (i.e. the processes of high performing teams). These characteristics have been itemized under the broad categories of inputs, processes, and outputs. They have been synthesized into a model which describes what it takes to make a highly performing team. The model is depicted in figure 1.

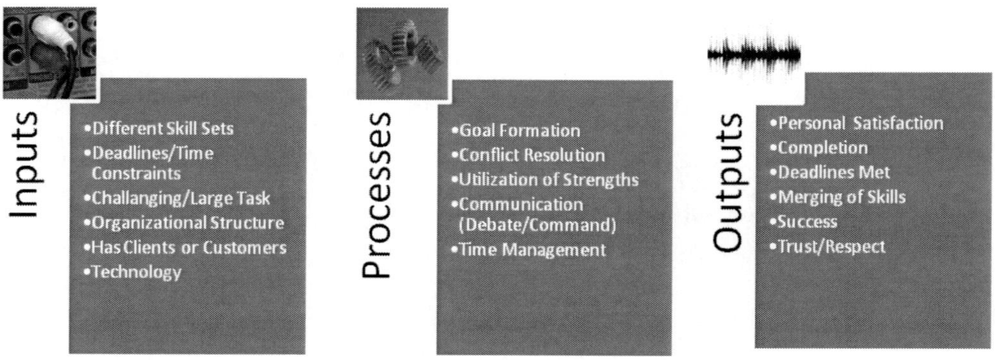

Figure 1. Nature and structure of high performing teams.

Inputs

Members of the group brought different and relevant skill sets. These skill sets were mutually supportive and contributed to the success of the team as a whole. Moreover, the members of the group represented the necessary skill sets, and helped to ensure that there were no unnecessary team members. As a second input, each team worked within time constraints (either in the form of strict deadlines or general time constraints). These pre-established constraints helped to focus the efforts of the team into creating processes in order to generate outputs within a timely fashion, and avoid a situation whereby locus of effort was diminished.

A third input was the nature of the task: the undertaken task was large in scope and content or challenging by its very nature. It is difficult to have an extraordinary result borne out of a mundane or simplistic task. Furthermore, the teams all had to report to others, and had either clients or customers. That is, the teams functioned under a hierarchy whereby team members had to report to another individual, either within their group or outside of the group. In addition, every team had clients or customers requiring the services of that team. Finally, in each instance the team utilized any relevant technological assets in order to facilitate interaction, process information, and to disseminate ideas.

Processes

Goal formation was imposed by team leaders in hierarchical group structures and established communally by more democratic teams. The groups would then establish and continually refine team goals in order to pursue desired outputs. Another process common to the five teams interviewed was conflict resolution: each team confronted and dealt with conflict.

Teams were able to utilize the expertise and specialties of each group member; this helped ensure optimized team performance. Clear communication among team members, as well as from teams to clients, was common to the extraordinary teams. Communication ranged from avid debate of issues to nonverbal signaling. Finally, each extraordinary team was able to manage time efficiently in order to achieve goals within the constraints or deadlines.

Outputs

Intangible outcomes included a sense of personal satisfaction, as well as trust and respect for team members. Tangible outcomes included not only completing the project, but also doing so within any established timelines. Furthermore, team members merged their individual skill sets to produce a deliverable. Finally, although each team defined success differently, success was met by each of the five teams interviewed. This success ranged from completion of the final task, to achievement of set goals, to satisfaction gained from being part of the team. The primary findings are now discussed and reflected upon throughout the remainder of the paper.

2. Analysis and Results

The findings of this study have been itemized under the broad categories of inputs (the nature and structure of high performing teams), processes (the functioning of high performing teams), and outputs (the nature and structure of high performing teams) as depicted in table 1 below. The key points raised under the three main categories, obtained from a list of 10 questions, are presented and discussed in order to facilitate the understanding of the results. All quotations and references are from the key informants who have delivered their ideas and experiences of working in high performing teams. Generally, study results observed lots of similarities with minor differences between survey results and those provided by the literature. To respect their anonymity the informants are referred to as interviewees A to E in this paper.

2.1. The Nature and Structure of High Performing Teams

2.1.1 Company and Team Characteristics

When asked about the nature of the teams, the interviewees provided a variety of responses to this concern, and ranged from legal counseling, information technology management, stunt-entertainment, telecommunications product development, and transportation policy formation (see table 2).

Table 1. Observations of High Performing Teams

	Interviewees				
Inputs	A	B	C	D	E
Different Skill Sets	✓	✓	✓	✓	✓
Deadlines or Timelines	✓	✓	✓	✓	✓
Challenging or Large Task	✓	✓	✓	✓	✓
Office Environment	✓		✓	✓	✓
One Team Leader		✓	✓	✓	✓
Reported to Others	✓	✓	✓	✓	✓
Had Clients or Customers	✓	✓	✓	✓	✓
Processes					
Goal Setting	✓	✓	✓	✓	✓
Discussion	✓	✓	✓		✓
Rewards or Incentives					
Conflict Resolution	✓	✓	✓	✓	✓
Idea Generation		✓			
Outputs					
High Effort	✓	✓	✓		✓
Completion of Project	✓	✓	✓	✓	✓
Deadlines Met	✓	✓	✓	✓	✓
Client Satisfaction	✓				
Personal Satisfaction	✓	✓			✓
Increased Knowledge			✓		
Merging of Skills	✓	✓	✓	✓	✓
Reliability or Trust	✓	✓	✓	✓	✓
Efficiency	✓				
Self Discipline	✓				
Listening		✓			✓

2.1.2. Inputs

Study results revealed that members of each team brought different and mutually supportive skill sets that contributed to the success of the team as a whole. Moreover, the members of each team represented the necessary skill sets, and helped to ensure that there were no unnecessary team members. These findings are indeed consistent with the results of a range of authors (Johnson and Johnson, 2009; Hackman, 2002; Stevens and Campion, 1994; Cannon-Bowers et al. 1995; Klimoski and Zukin, 1999; and Senior, 1997) who pointed to diverse task-relevant competencies and knowledge as the impetus of high performing teams.

Table 2. Companies' characteristics

Interviewees	Companies and teams' characteristics
A	This is a small litigation firm with four lawyers providing ongoing legal counsel for private clients. The firm typically teams up with lawyers from different firms to work on particular cases. Each team terminates after a court case.
B	This is a small company with 6 full-time staff providing Information Technology services to clients. It hired approximately 130 temporal staff, through an employment agency, to work during the 2010 Vancouver Olympics for a period of 5 months (i.e. November 2009 to March 2010). The team ended after the Olympics.
C	This is a small stunt-entertainment company with 14 artists providing stunt shows in theatres, parks, gyms.
D	This is a telecom product development company providing life line products to clients. The company assigned a 4-man team to provide telephone lines to low income and rural areas in Virginia, West Virginia, Maryland, and the District of Columbia. The team ended upon completion of the project and the final delivery of the outcome.
E	This is a board of a transportation company providing public transportation in Vancouver. The board is made up of directors with different skill sets including a lawyer, accountant, planner, economist, engineer, and a CEO.

In a similar vein, Ericksen and Dyer (2004) and Kass (2010) established a positive correlation between expertise and team performance in well developed productive teams. A comment from one of the interviewees that offers additional insight to this observation is, "A team is formed by bringing people from different firms whose skill sets fit well to a particular project with the overall objective of winning a case." A similar comment from another informant offers evidence to support this observation, "The team was made up of people with expertise, tremendous insight and dedication, capable of identifying and resolving critical issues well on time."

Apart from task-relevant competencies, which were regarded as important ingredients of high performing teams, fixed deadlines were equally cited by all the five interviewees as fundamental to the overall success of the teams. From that premise, each team had to work within pre-established time constraints to help focus the efforts of the team into creating processes that generate high-quality outputs in a timely manner. This submission supports Traci et al. (2006) and Keller's (2001) contention that high performing teams typically engage in collective supervision focused on monitoring performance and meeting tight deadlines. A comment from an interviewee that offers additional insight to this observation is, "We had a specific goal and knew the final deliverables were monthly, quarterly and one over 6 months." A comment from an another interviewee offers evidence to support this submission, "We are all very busy people with other jobs and the application of our talents had to be done in a way that maximized their efficacy while still being able to get things done on time."

Study results equally revealed that four of the five teams functioned under a hierarchy - a formal leadership structure - whereby team members had to report to another individual, either within their group or outside of the group. As one of the interviewees pointed out, "there was a very formal structure and the team functioned like any other board of directors with a chair overseeing everything and a committee structure to have in-depth look into issues. These submissions are buttressed by the findings of a range of authors (Traci et al. 2006; Johnson and Johnson, 2009; Bettenhausen and Murnighan, 1985; Hoyt and Blascovich, 2003; Van Dierendonck et al. 2004; and Manz, 1986) who argued that effective leadership represents a vital element of a group's performance and its ultimate success. Similarly, a study conducted by Zigurs (2003) pointed to self leadership as instrumental in the success of virtual teams. From that premise, effective leadership is critical to a team's effectiveness (Hackman, 1987; Wageman, 1998), requiring the performance of numerous and competing tasks concurrently (Dennison et al. 1995). A comment from an interviewee that offers evidence to support these results is, "Leadership is vital to having an effective team otherwise it will be rudderless and adrift without guidance; getting off track is very easy to do and having strong and experienced leadership ensures that this does not happen."

The nature of tasks also emerged as one of the main characteristics of all the teams, which were large in scope and content or challenging by their very nature. As an informant puts it, the project was very challenging for me because of its complex design; it required a lot of time, reading, and effort. This observation coincided with those of Locke and Latham (1990) who pointed to clear and compelling operational tasks as the initial inputs of high performing teams. As Ericksen and Dyer (2004) submit, "high performing teams do not incorporate initial operational tasks as one-time static inputs but, rather, as constantly evolving outputs that serve as revised inputs for subsequent phases of project team development". Further, study results revealed that every team had clients or customers requiring the services of that team. This focus on clients or customers requiring the services of teams have equally been observed in various other studies particularly with highly productive teams (Ancona and Caldwell, 1992; Keller, 2001).

An intriguing observation that emerged from this study is that each team utilized relevant technological assets in order to facilitate interaction, process information, and to disseminate ideas. Similar research, with similar results by Goodman et al. (1988), Campion et al. (1993), and Cohen and Ledford (1994) emphasized the use of equipments and materials as an essential resource for enhancing teams' performance. In fact, Johnson and Johnson (2009) cited information technologies as vital tools to facilitating group work between offices, and across geographically separated regions around the globe. A comment from an interviewee that offers evidence to support this submission is, "Technology was a tremendous bridge in working virtually in such pickup teams."

2.2. The Functioning of High Performing Teams

2.2.1. Processes

Study results revealed that goal formation was imposed by four of the team leaders in hierarchical group structures and established communally by one democratic team. The groups would then establish and continually refine team goals in order to pursue desired outputs. As an interviewee puts it, "Goal setting and constant feedbacks from team members were critical in the overall success of the team." These findings are consistent with those of Chong (2007) and Johnson and Johnson (2009) who emphasized the formation of comprehensible, operational, and measurable group goals as fundamental to accomplishing high-quality results. That said, the outcome of a team is dependent on common team goals with clear provisions of what a team seeks to accomplish (Edmondson, 1999; Ericksen and Dyer, 2004). A comment from an interviewee offers evidence to support this submission, "We tried something new each time with a lot of goal setting through open discussions and sharing of ideas." Another interviewee described this observation in similar terms, "We had a specific goal coming from the overall structure, which were set and could not be adjusted."

An intriguing observation that equally emerged from this study is that each team had to confront and deal with conflicts. This finding is not different from those of Johnson and Johnson (2009) who argued that "facing conflicts and engaging in integrative problem-solving negotiations to resolve them in constructive ways is crucial to the overall success of a team." A comment from an interviewee offers evidence to support this submission, "During the rehearsals on scenarios, there were lots of arguments with partners in sorting out the issues. But at the end, team members and I were very glad on our achievement in reaching agreeable solutions on all potential scenarios by all parties concerned." A similar comment from another interviewee that offers evidence to support this submission is, "The team worked together to get through conflict and brought in moderators when necessary."

Further, study results also indicated that teams were able to utilize the expertise and specialties of their members, which helped to ensure optimized team performance. As one of the interviewees puts it, "members knew each other's strength and respected their views". This observation coincides with those of Johnson and Johnson (2009), Edmondson (1999), and Chong (2007) who pointed to task-relevant competencies and knowledge as vital elements in ensuring that task behaviors of group members are mutually supportive in order to provide synergistic outcomes. As Kass (2010) and Chong (2007) submit, the positive correlation between tasks and maintenance roles and the emotional binding among team members are crucial for the success of high performing teams. From that premise, a successful team should be able to collectively monitor group's activities and move the group forward in a participative manner (Traci et al. 2006). A comment from an interviewee offers evidence to support these results, "The team created processes to enable team members to work with each other. That said, individuals who were not necessary working on particular tasks were able to bring in whatever they were able to contribute as on needed basis. Thus seniors leveraged their experiences in helping junior lawyers in critical situations such as cross examination". Another interviewee described this observation in similar terms, "The utilization of networks was a key element in ensuring that the best effort was put forward and the maximum efficiency was utilized to create results."

Clear communication among team members, as well as from teams to clients, was common to these teams, and ranged from avid debate of issues to nonverbal signalling. This submission has equally been observed by Barge and Hirokawa (1989) who pointed to effective communication as a vital ingredient for effective leadership. In a similar vein, Johnson and Johnson (2009) argued that "establishing effective two-way communication by which group members communicate their ideas and feelings accurately and clearly minimize misunderstandings and discord among group members." From that premise, group members who tend not to share their unique knowledge, because of fear of being criticized, pose major hurdles for group learning (Edmondson, 1999). As already mentioned, none of the interviewees cited communication hurdles with members of their teams. A comment from an interviewee offers evidence to support this submission, "Another vital ingredient is the ability to listen to each other and actually hear and incorporate what is being said and advised to make decisions, both from other board members as well as the managers." This submission is buttressed by another interviewee who pointed to team cooperation and internal information exchange as fundamental to the overall success of the team.

An intriguing observation that also emerged from this study is that all team members were able to manage time efficiently in order to achieve goals within deadlines. This observation is not different from those of Chong (2007) who pointed to good time management amongst team members as a vital ingredient for highly productive teams. As an interviewee puts it, "The people on the board were willing to devote huge amounts of time towards the project and that was an important thing as it showed how dedicated the team was to achieving results." This interviewee further pointed to planning and using time wisely as vital elements of a productive team.

2.3. The Nature and Structure of High Performing Teams

2.3.1. Outputs

Additional insights were gained by investigating how team members defined success. The interviewees provided a variety of responses to this concern. In particular, they varied to the extent and environment in which the teams operated. Interestingly, the first interviewee stated that an indicator of success is measured by the financial results of clients, whereby the costs of lawsuits are properly managed. He further remarked that success is defined by winning a case at a reasonable cost with the lawyer having a reasonable remuneration from the case. While success was defined by the third interviewee as delivering the best quality product, with minimal errors, within a specified timeframe, the second informant attributed success to the smooth running of the logistics and technical operations of the 2010 Vancouver Olympic Games with no major issues reported by the media. Besides, the fifth informant ascribed success to obtaining 130 million dollars in funding and running most of the major projects from inception to completion. As the third informant stated, "success was not about show completion; it was more about entertaining and growing the audience." Indeed, these submissions coincided with those of Johnson and Johnson (2009) who pointed to success as the ability of people to work in small groups and produce high-quality results.

Intangible outcomes such as a sense of personal satisfaction as well as trust and respect for team members' opinions emerged as vital ingredients for high performing teams. This appears to support Thomas and Bostrom's (2008) assertion of a positive correlation between trust and highly productive virtual teams. Indeed, these results are buttressed by Edmondson (1999) who argued that "coherent interpersonal climate within groups is characterized by the presence of a blend of trust, respect for each other's competence, and caring about each other as people." A comment from an interviewee that offers additional insight to this observation is: "Respect and trust are fundamental in a team; a team that does not respect other members' viewpoints is doomed to fail."

CONCLUSION

The main objective of this study was to provide additional insight into the nature and functioning of high performing teams and determine if these patterns are similar to previous studies, as given in the literature, or if they differ, in what ways. Based on interviews conducted with five individuals from five different organizations, several shared characteristics of high performing teams emerged (see table 1). Generally, study findings observed lots of similarities with minor differences between study results and those provided by the literature.

REFERENCES

Anderson, N.R., and West, MA. (1998). Measuring climate for work group innovation: development and validation of the team climate inventory. *Journal of organizational behavior*, 19, 235-258.

Ancona, D.G., Caldwell, D.F. (1992). Bridging the boundary: External activity and performance in organizational teams. *Administrative Science Quarterly*, 37(4), 634-665.

Barge, J.K., and Hirokawa R.Y. (1989). Toward a Communication Competency Model of Group Leadership. *Small Group Behavior* 20(2), 167–189.

Bettenhausen, K, and Murnighan, J.K. (1985). The emergence of norms in competitive decision-making groups. *Administrative Science Quarterly*, 30, 350-372.

Campion, M.A., Gina J.M, and A. Catherine, A.H. (1993). Relations between work group characteristics and effectiveness: Implications for designing effective work groups. *Personnel Psychology*, 46, 823-850.

Cannon-Bowers, J.L., Tannenbaum, S. I., Salas, E., and Volpe, C. E. (1995). Defining competencies and establishing team training requirements. In R. A. Guzzo, E. Salas, and Associates (eds.), *Team Effectiveness and Decision Making*, p. 333-380. San Francisco: Jossey-Bass.

Chong, E. (2007). Role balance and team development: A study of team role characteristics underlying high and low performing teams. *Journal of Behavioral and Applied Management,* 8(3), 202-217.

Cohen, S.G., and Gerald, E.L. (1994). The effectiveness of self managing teams: A quasi-experiment. *Human Relations*, 47, 13-43.

Denison, D.R., Hooijberg, R., and Quinn, R.E. (1995). Paradox and Performance: Toward a Theory of Behavioral Complexity in Managerial Leadership. *Organization Science* 6(5), 524–540.

Edmondson, A. (1999). Psychological safety and learning behavior in work teams. *Administrative Science Quarterly*, 44(2), 350-383.

Ericksen, J., Dyer, L. (2004). Right from the Start: Exploring the Effects of Early Team Events on Subsequent Project Team Development and Performance. *Administrative Science Quarterly,* 49 (3), 438-471.

Goodman, P, Devadas, S and Hughson T.L. (1988). Groups and productivity: Analyzing the effectiveness of self-managing teams." In J.P. Campbell, R. J. Campbell, and Associates (eds.), *Designing Effective Work Group*s, p. 295-327. San Francisco: Jossey-Bass.

Hackman, J.R. (2002). Leading Teams: Setting the Stage for Great Performances. Boston: *Harvard Business School Press.*

Hackman, J.R. (1987). The design of work teams. In J. Lorsch (ed.), *Handbook of Organizational Behavior*, p. 315-342. Englewood Cliffs, N J: Prentice-Hall.

Hoyt, C.L. and Blascovich, J. (2003). Transformational and Transactional Leadership in Virtual and Physical Environments. *Small Group Research* 34(6), 678–715.

Johnson, D.W., and Johnson, F.P. (2009). *Joining together: Group theory and group skills.* 10th edition. Boston, MA: Pearson education, Inc.

Kass, R. (2010). *Theories of small group development. 4th edition. The centre for human relations and community studies*, Montreal: Concordia University,

Keller, R.T. (2001). Cross-functional project groups in research and new product development: Diversity, communications, job stress and outcomes. *Academy of Management Journal*, 44, 547-556.

Kirschner, P. A., and Van Bruggen, J. (2004). Learning and understanding in virtual teams. *Cyberpsychology and Behavior*, 7, 135–140.

Klimoski, R. J., and Zukin, L.B. (1999). Selection and staffing for team effectiveness. In E. Sundstrom and Associates (eds.), *Supporting Work Team Effectiveness*, p. 63-94. San Francisco: Jossey-Bass.

Locke, E.A., and Latham, G.P. (1990). *A Theory of Goal Setting and Task Performance.* Englewood Cliffs, NJ: Prentice-Hall.

Manz, C.C. (1986). Self-Leadership: Toward an Expanded Theory of Self-Influence Processes in Organizations. *Academy of Management Review* 11, 585–600.

Senior, B. (1997). Team roles and team performance: Is there 'really' a link? *Journal of Occupational and Organizational Psychology*, 70(3), 241-258.

Stevens, M.J., and Campion, M.A. (1994). The knowledge, skill, and ability requirements for teamwork: Implications for human resource management. *Journal of Management*, 20: 503-530.

Thomas, D., Bostrom, R. (2008). Building Trust and Cooperation through Technology Adaptation in Virtual Teams: Empirical Field Evidence. *Information Systems Management,* 25(1),45 - 56

Traci, A., Chidambaram, L., Becker, A. (2006). Emergent Leadership in Self-Managed Virtual Teams: A Longitudinal Study of Concentrated and Shared Leadership Behaviors. *Group Decision and Negotiation*, 15(4), 323-343.

Van Dierendonck, D., Haynes, C. Borrill, C, and Stride, C. (2004). Leader Behavior and Subordinate Well Being. *Journal of Occupational Health Psychology* 9(2),165–175.

Wageman, R. (1998). The effects of team design and leader behavior on self managing teams: A field study." *Working paper, School of Business*, Columbia University.

West, M. A., and Farr, J. L. (1990). *Innovation and Creativity at Work: Psychological and Organizational Strategies,* Chichester: Wiley.

Zigurs, I. (2003). Leadership in Virtual Teams: Oxymoron or Opportunity? *Organizational Dynamics* 31(4), 339–351.

In: HRM and Marketing Orientation in the New Era
Editor: Panagiotis Kyriazopoulos
ISBN: 978-1-62808-959-2

Chapter 21

BUILDING BLOCKS OF ACCOUNTING–MARKETING INTEGRATION IN UK FINANCIAL SERVICES ORGANISATIONS

***Abdullah Promise Opute*[1]*, Evangelos Dedoussis*[2] *and Nikolaos Tzokas*[3,*]**

[1]Marketing and Management Consultant, gprom solutions ltd, Germany
[2]Management, American University in Dubai, UAE
[3]Marketing, University of East Anglia, UK

ABSTRACT

This paper reports the results from a research on the accounting-marketing integration and its antecedents in UK financial services organisations. The research was based on 162 responses, consisting of dyads from the accounting and marketing functions of the responding firms. Following a composite integration approach for the main construct our research identified the role of a number of antecedent factors, reflecting the type of managerial action required to achieve the required integration between accounting and marketing. The results of our study direct attention to the need for managerial interventions that capitalise on both the cultural fabric and the climate or structural properties of the firm. Our paper concludes with an appreciation of the theoretical and practical implications of this research and associated directions for further research.

1. INTRODUCTION

It is widely accepted that marketing oriented companies can sense changes in their customers' behaviour faster than other firms and as such adapt their offer so that they can generate superior customer value (Guenzi and Troilo 2006), which warrants sustainable competitive advantage. However, from sensing such changes in the market place to the development of attractive to customers value propositions, significant ground needs to be

[*] Corresponding author: Tel.: +44 1603 593537; E-mail: n.tzokas@uea.ac.uk.

covered, which in recent years has been acknowledged as requiring involvement by the whole of the organisation (e.g. Le Meunier-FitzHugh and Piercy 2007; Zinkhan and Verbrugge 2000) rather than few functional areas. This is very much in line with the essence of marketing orientation, where interfunctional coordination is critical in the ability of the firm to sense and translate market based learning into new products/services and complete value propositions that attract customer attention, facilitate buying behaviour and of course encourage long-term loyalty to the firm.

Within this tradition, while marketing's relationship with other departments/functions for instance, R&D, manufacturing, production and sales, and associated performance benefits is illuminated in literature (Parry and Song 1993), the relationship of marketing with the accounting function of the firm remains largely neglected.

This is quite peculiar mainly for two reasons. First, successful value propositions from a marketing perspective are reflected in product/service offers that capitalise on a unique set of the firm's capabilities and resources that allow the firm to a) claim competitive advantage, b) charge prices that create strong/superior value perceptions in their target market and c) charge prices that allow the firm to make and maintain a healthy stream of profits from its value propositions. Given the interplay of costs and benefits, areas primarily perceived under the influence of accounting and marketing respectively, the need for integration between the two functions is obvious. Second, despite the unquestionable need for integration between the two functions, considerable problems in the accounting/marketing interface have been flagged (Barker 2008; de Ruyter and Wetzels 2000). Therefore, the need to study and appreciate the nature of the accounting/marketing interface has been postulated by many authors (e.g. Langfield-Smith 2008; Wilson 2000; Zinkhan and Verbrugge 2000).

Responding to such calls for more research on this topic our study investigates the dimensions of accounting-marketing integration and their antecedents in financial services organisations of the UK. This distinction is motivated by the fact that integration relevance may be interface dependent, and identifying the key integration dimensions and interface features of various integrating mechanisms is essential (Griffin and Hauser 1996) for theory and policy development in this critical area of managerial activity. The study makes three unique contributions in the theory and practice surrounding current research debate as regards the accounting/marketing integration.

First, our study identifies a pool of managerial activities that can be used to enhance integration between accounting and marketing, and establishes their combined effect upon integration. In doing so it complements extant literature in that not only lists factors underlying integration but also their interrelationships.

The second contribution of our research lies in the recognition that both cultural and structural managerial interventions are required to achieve integration. In this context, top management support, formalisation and physical proximity figure highly in the agenda of firms that have achieved higher integration than their direct competitors.

Finally, our study highlights cultural differences between accounting and marketing and directs away from popular practices of role flexibility and rotation of employees within the two functions. On the basis of the three contributions the study draws clear managerial recommendations in order to achieve a higher degree of integration between accounting and marketing.

Below, we review the literature underlying our theoretical framework and hypotheses. This is followed by presenting the research methods used to test this framework alongside analysis. Finally, we draw conclusions and implications for theory and practice.

2. THEORETICAL FRAMEWORK AND HYPOTHESES

2.1. Integration and Integrating Mechanisms

As it was mentioned earlier several authors have identified a number of problem areas related to the accounting/marketing interface. These problems, classified in table 1, reflect attitudinal, cognitive, and organisational differences in the perceptions accounting and marketing have of their own and each other's role in the overall function of the firm.

As elaborated by Wilson (2000) accounting neither understands nor meets, in an accurate and timely manner, the information needs of the marketing function. Illuminating information sharing between marketing and accounting, Barker (2008:325) notes: "accountants view both the quality of shared information and its acceptability to the marketers and other recipients to be high", while "marketers see more contradiction in the information they receive, which raises quality concerns". Accounting has failed to firmly embrace the '*marketing concept*' and the direct implication is misdirection of marketing effort.

In addition to role shortcomings, the marketing/accounting interface is plagued by information sharing problems.

Table 1. The typical problems of the accounting/marketing interface

Classification of Problems	Definition of Problems
Cognitive	1. Accountants lack understanding of marketing principles and concepts. 2. Accountants lack understanding of marketing policies, problems, practices and 'marketing concept'.
Attitudinal	3. Inadequacy of accountants to identify and classify costs, and ineffective financial analysis of customers and distribution channels. Failure to understand information needs 4. Inaccurate and untimely accounting reporting 5. Accountants do not accept marketing as a distinct and separate managerial function 6. Accountants tend to over-emphasise cost control and are Production oriented 7. Lack of minimum acceptable goal criteria
Organisational	8. Inadequate informal communication between accountants and marketing decisions makers. 9. Multiple reporting responsibilities of accounting, leading to priority assignment prejudicial to marketing. 10. Information sharing problems
General Assessment	11. A general ineffective integration between the accounting and marketing functions, 12. Failure of accounting to understand the Marketing function. 13. Failure of Accounting to measure up to the information requirement of Marketing 14. There are serious integration issues between Accounting and Marketing

Source: The authors.

Integration, an essentially 'symbiotic interrelation', is the 'strategic linking' of functionally specialised groups, for corporate success and may be likened to a 'symphony orchestra', whose melody hinges on team blending (Plakoyiannaki and Tzokas 2002; Tzokas *et al.* 2004). Three typologies of integration have been identified in literature that is, 'Interaction' (Griffin and Hauser 1996), 'Collaboration' (Le Meunier-FitzHugh and Lane 2009; Le Meunier-FitzHugh and Piercy 2007), and 'Composite Integration' (interaction plus collaboration) (Guenzi and Troilo 2006; Parry and Song 1993).

In this study we approach integration as a three dimensional composite reflecting Information Sharing, Unified Effort, and Involvement.

The Degree of Information Sharing (DMIS) is the extent to which the departments' information sharing culture reflects: 1) firm awareness of the information need of each party, 2) timely and accurate information exchange, 3) use of understandable (not too technical) language, 4) awareness of the 'Marketing Concept', and 5) information sharing patterns that reflect common goals between the functions.

The Degree of Unified Effort (DUE) is contextualised to include 1) mutual support of each other, 2) give and take attitude, 3) openness to criticisms from each other, 4) swift resolve of conflicts, and 5) few disagreements in the strategic marketing efforts.

Finally, *the Degree of Involvement* (DINV) includes 1) direct involvement across the stages of the strategic marketing process, 2) open discussion of opposing views, 3) cross-functional role performance, 4) joint involvement in defining strategic marketing priorities, and 5) joint involvement in responding to market changes.

Substantial empirical insights exist about the antecedents of marketing's integration with other departments (see Le Meunier-FitzHugh and Piercy 2007; Parry and Song 1993; Xie *et al.* 2003, *inter alia*). With focus on the accounting-marketing interface, the hypothetical discussion draws largely from marketing-R&D literature, given the lacuna of accounting-marketing literature on antecedents of their integration. While we acknowledge activity contingency in integration (Garrett *et al.* 2006), this theoretical adaptation is methodologically valid, given that interfunctional relationships are: (1) based on interdependence relationships, and (2) driven by the need for goal congruity (Xie *et al.* 2003) towards corporate success. Based on this literature we identify the following building blocks of integration.

2.2. Building Blocks of Integration between Accounting and Marketing

2.2.1. Communication and Accounting/Marketing Integration

Though *communication* is critical in social systems as it enables focus and unity of purpose, facilitates interfunctional relationships, and enables better decision making, *communication gaps* are known to exist between accountants and marketers (Wilson 2000). Empirically, communication problems hinder marketing-R&D integration (Parry and Song 1993) and sales-marketing integration (Le Meunier-FitzHugh and Piercy, 2007). Communication barriers to R&D/Marketing integration (Song and Parry 1993) include inaccurate information, lack of communication, and too little information exchange. To optimise effectiveness (Lam and Chin 2005), information communication must be timely, accurate, and purpose-tailored to support role function, and to avoid collaboration conflict.

Extrapolating these findings to the accounting/marketing integration we provide the following hypothesis.

H1 (CG): The higher the communication gap between accounting and marketing the less accounting/marketing integration will be achieved.

2.2.2. Formalisation and Accounting/Marketing Integration

Formalisation is the extent to which explicit rules, regulations, policies and procedures govern organisational activities. Such 'organisational norms' (Shipilov and Danis, 2006) specify norms for decision making and performing tasks and enable achieved integration.

Empirically, the impact of formalisation on integration remains blurred, especially in the R&D-marketing literature. The sales-marketing perspective (Dewsnap and Jobber, 2002) supports the no significance evidence, but Parry and Song (1993) disagree that formalisation hinders achieved R&D-Marketing integration. Song and Parry (1993), reinforced by Mollenkopf *et al.* (2000), suggest the opposite. Interestingly, the marketing and logistics samples of the latter pictured negative and positive associations respectively.

However, a degree of formalisation has been found necessary for exercising meaningful managerial action and leadership in contemporary firms. Therefore, we expect that efforts to instigate a higher degree of integration between marketing and accounting will be relatively easier within organisations that have developed clear structures and therefore a degree of formalisation. As such we develop the following hypothesis.

H2 (FO): The higher the level of formalisation in an organisation, the greater the achieved level of accounting/marketing integration will be.

2.2.3. Top Management Support and Accounting/Marketing Integration

Research underlines *top management support* as a core cross-functional integration predictor (e.g. Le Meunier-FitzHugh and Lane 2009; Parry and Song 1993; Xie *et al.* 2003). No such evidence exists about the accounting-marketing integration.

However, we expect that top management support will enable cross-functional integration because such support provides focus and purpose in integration activities within the organisation. Moreover, as integration is a resource consuming activity requiring the devotion of time, energy and effort from employees in different function, top management support is imperative for channelling such resources, legitimising and encouraging such activity in the firm. On that logic, we offer the following hypothesis.

H3 (MS): The more top management supports accounting/marketing integration, the more the achieved integration between the functions will be.

2.2.4. Culture and Accounting/Marketing Integration

Different professions have *different cultures* (Wilson, 2000), and these influence their integration. Three core departmental differences that is, culture, perception, and orientation, shape interfunctional integration. Inter-firm relationship literature (Jaspers and van den Ende 2006) lends support to the view that cultural similarity aids higher integration.

Accounting/marketing interface literature suggests cultural differences between accountants and marketers. According to Wilson (2000), accountants' introspection differs from that of marketers in many ways. Barker, (2008) noticed that tension exists between accounting and marketing departments and that this situation may be attributed to cultural differences which cultivate interfuctional rivalry and misunderstandings.

Tension in teams made up of colleagues from different functions diminish the team interests thus culminating in 'goal incongruity', which hinders integration (Xie *et al.* 2003:242). Given the preceding discussion, we develop the following hypothesis.

H4 (COD): The more the perceived cultural differences between marketers and accountants the less the degree of achieved integration will be.

2.2.5. Role Flexibility and Accounting/Marketing Integration

Role flexibility, the movement of personnel beyond their functional domain, shapes interfunctional integration (Xie et al. 2003). Integrating partners would benefit from role flexibility, gain contextual knowledge (Jaspers and van den Ende 2006) for understanding why decisions are made (Griffin and Hauser 1996; Garrett et al. 2006), while comprehending each other's information needs. Therefore, we propose the following.

H5 (RF): The more the role flexibility between accounting and marketing personnel, the more the achieved accounting/marketing integration will be.

2.2.6. Physical Proximity and Accounting/Marketing Integration

Team work psychology theory presents *physical proximity* as a cross-functional integration facilitator. Spatial nearness facilitates interaction (Jaspers and van den Ende 2006), information transfer (Griffin and Hauser 1996), increased communication and performance (Xie *et al.* 2003; Dewsnap and Jobber 2002), and enables regular informal interactions (de Ruyter and Wetzels 2000).

Physical proximity enables '*socialisation*', a concept (Gupta and Govindarajan 2000) that refers to the level of interaction between, and communication of, various actors that leads to the building of personal familiarity, improved communication, and problem solving. Physical nearness of integrating functions will induce regular informal interactions, an outcome that promotes goodwill (Adler and Kwon 2002; Shipilov and Danis 2006). This should increase mutual understanding of common purpose and value thus helping to enhance integration. Therefore we propose the following.

H6 (NDP): The more the physical proximity of accounting and marketing, the more the integration between accounting and marketing will be.

The hypothesised relationships in our study are depicted in figure 1.

3. METHODOLOGY

The hypothesised relationships were tested on UK financial services organisations by means of a mail questionnaire. The measures used to tap the constructs were adapted from past studies. Scale development was refined through a pilot-testing with key informants, involving the use of exploratory, in-depth interviews and the actual testing of the questionnaire. After revision, the finalised questionnaire was mailed to the Accounting and Marketing heads of UK financial services organisations. To enhance response rate, a personalised letter, and a stamped, addressed reply envelope, were mailed along with the questionnaires.

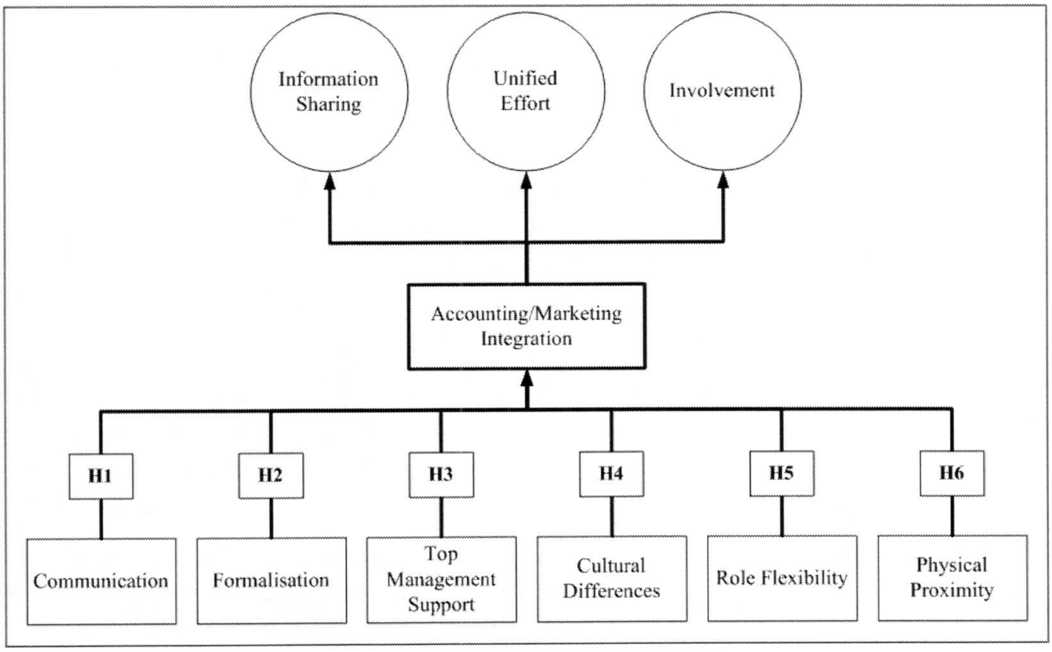

Figure 1. Accounting marketing integration and its antecedents.

3.1. Survey Sample and Response Rate

Participating companies (large/medium) satisfied the following criteria that is: (a) have separate accounting and marketing departments, (b) engage in strategic marketing activities, (c) operate in a competitive market, (d) have at least 100 employees, and (e) have their stock traded on the Stock Exchange market.

From the sampling frame of 1000 companies, collated from the 'FAME' Database, 320 companies were randomly sampled. 640 questionnaires were mailed out (proportionately dyadic distribution).

After three follow-up mailings, 162 (84 from marketing departments and 78 from accounting departments) questionnaires, reflecting 75 dyads, were eligible for further analysis. Compared with previous studies in inter-departmental relationships (e.g. Barker 2008), the response rate for the present study, standing at 27.34%, is acceptable.

Table 2 presents the sampled and respondent firms' distribution, while Table 3 shows the respondent managers' profile and employee statistics per department. For non-response bias test, statistical analyses were performed on annual turnover, operating profit, total number of employees, and total assets.

All t-tests for differences in respondent and non-respondent means as well as early and late respondents were not significant at the 10% level of confidence.

Table 2. Industry Sector representation and the Response Sample

	Numbers of Firms		
Industry Sector	Sampled	Participated[1]	Participated[2]
Insurance	100	30	24
Auditing and Accounting	50	16	11
Brokerage	40	15	13
Risk Assessment and Asset Management	60	21	14
TOTAL	320	99	76

Note: 1. At least one of the marketing and accounting managers participated. 2. Both marketing and accounting managers participated.

Table 3. Demographic profiles of respondents

Average		Marketing	Accounting
1	Age	41	45
2	Total work experience (Years)	22	23
3	Work experience with present company	15	12
4	Years worked with this company in present role	8	10
5	Bachelors Degree	75%	79%
6	MBA	2%	1%
7	Masters Degree	8.3%	7.4%
8	PhD Degree	1%	None
9	Accounting related Qualification	2.6%	82%
10	Marketing related Qualification	80.6%	1.4%
11	A member of a professional society	20.40%	46%
12	Associate Chartered Accountant	None	25%
13	Chartered Management Accountant	None	10%
14	Fellow Chartered Accountant	None	7%
15	Chartered Marketer	28.7%	None

3.2. Reliability of Constructs

Table 4 confirms reliability and validity of constructs. Principal axis factoring and Cronbach's alpha estimation was used for reliability, and exploratory plus (subsequently) confirmatory factor analyses for validity. These analyses produced satisfactory results, confirmed the first and second order nature of the variables used in this study and allowed us to progress with the application of multivariate analysis of variance (MANOVA) to test for the hypothesised relationships.

4. Findings and Discussion

Multivariate analysis of variance (MANOVA) was used to explore Figure 1. The regression statistics largely support our hypotheses (see Table 5).

The variance in achieved degree of accounting/marketing integration explained by the regression model was 49% [*Degree of Involvement*], 34% [*Degree of Unified Effort*], and

31% [*Degree of Mutual Information Sharing*]. For *Integration Total* (DINTTOT) 71% variance was explained, and five statistically significant relationships were found. More specifically for *Integration Total*: *Communication Gap*, and *Top Management Support*, had the most significant influence, at (beta = -.421; p<.000) and (beta = .208; p<.000) respectively; *Formalisation*, *Cultural Differences*, and *Physical Proximity* also showed significant levels. However, *Role Flexibility* was non-significant.

Table 4. Reliability and Validity Statistics for Factors

Factors	Factor Reliability Indices				Exploratory Factor Analysis Results		Model fit Summaries				
							Baseline Comparisons Stats			GFI Stats.	SRMR Stats
	Ite-ms	α	Mean	Std. Dev.	Eigen-value	Cumm. Var. Exp.	NFI	IFI	CFI	GFI	SRMR
Dependent											
DINTTOT		.71					.92	.95	.95	.88	.051
DINV	4	.90	3.71	0.94	3.1	26.19%	.97	.97	.97	.96	.027
DMIS	4	.93	4.05	0.92	2.8	23.39%	.98	.98	.98	.96	.023
DUE	4	.87	4.06	0.88	2.6	21.99%	.99	1.00	1.00	.99	.010
Independents											
CG	4	.92	2.87	0.96	3.2	80.99%	.99	.99	.99	.99	.010
FO	4	.86	4.26	0.94	2.8	70.60%	.92	.92	.92	.93	.060
COD	4	.89	4.04	0.96	3.0	76.91%	.96	.96	.96	.95	.042
MS	4	.92	4.13	0.96	3.2	81.19%	.98	.98	.98	.97	.019
RF	4	.81	2.31	0.96	2.6	66.06%	.95	.96	.96	.95	.065
NDP	4	.92	3.74	0.97	3.2	81.34%	.98	.98	.98	.97	.025

Table 5. Multivariable Regression Coefficients and Significance for Achieved Integration (Pooled sample. N = 162)

Variables	DINV		DUE		DMIS		DINTTOT		Collinearity Stats	
	Std. *B*	Sig.	Std. *B*	Sig.	Std. *B*	Sig.	Std. *B*	Sig.	Tolerance	VIF
CG	-.27a	.00	-.13	.15	-.39a	.00	-.42a	0	.5	2.0
FO	.08	.23	.04	.58	.10	.16	.12b	.01	.81	1.2
COD	-.06	.42	-.17c	.04	-.00	.95	-.12c	.03	.64	1.5
MS	.29a	.00	.022	.78	.07	.36	.21a	.00	.71	1.4
RF	-.03	.64	-.117	.11	.06	.42	-.04	.36	.82	1.2
NDP	.08	.27	-.258b	.00	-.07	.36	-.13b	.02	.67	1.5
R^2	.49		.34		.31		.71			
Adjusted R^2	.49		.29		.26		.69			
Regression F-Value	12.88 (.00)		7.14 (.00)		6.25 (.00)		33.73 (.00)			

Note: a. Correlation is significant at the .001 level (2-tailed). b. Correlation is significant at the .01 level (2-tailed), c. Correlation is significant at the .05 level (2-tailed).

As regards our hypotheses testing they are as follows:

H1 is confirmed reflecting a negative relationship of Communication Gap to achieved Integration (Total). This underscores once more the important role of communications amongst people from different functions.

H2 is supported showing that Formalisation correlates positively to achieved integration. Again this is in line with previous findings with a degree of formalisation creates platforms for communication and mutual appreciation of responsibility. This result reinforces Parry and Song (1993) who stated that if processes are formalised, the possibilities of ambiguities concerning tasks and role fulfilment and overall organisation procedures would be eliminated, thus aiding collaboration, through meaningful communication and appreciation of roles.

H3 is confirmed revealing a positive association of Top Management Support on achieved integration. This outline once more the need for orchestrated managerial action which is above and beyond structure. Indeed it reflects the need not only of resources to enable communication but the creation of a culture and climate which is motivated by top management's support towards integration and interfunctional coordination.

H4 is supported showing that the higher the Cultural differences the lower the level of integration. It is not surprising to find out that in cases where accounting and marketing exhibit considerable cultural differences the degree of integration is low. Once again this adds to the notion that perceptions of each other's roles, activities and contributions to the firms' overall objectives are important determinants of the degree of integration encouraged and attained.

H5 was not supported since Role flexibility has no significant relationship with achieved integration. It is important to note here that although insignificant, the Role Flexibility estimates may suggest that such a practice is not a feature of accounting-marketing integration. Strange as this finding may seem, it highlights the very sharp, water-tight boundaries that very often exist between accounting and marketing. An inspection of cross-functional role performance measures, and cross-functional knowledge backgrounds, suggests a strong functional dichotomy which is perpetuated by the knowledge background and associated views of the "business world" endemic to either accounting or marketing.

H6 was supported reinforcing a negative link between Physical proximity (distance) and achieved integration. In our study integration was lower in cases of firms with physically dispersed and distant accounting and marketing functions, whereas integration was at the highest in cases where both functions were situated closely to each other and as a minimum in the same building.

5. Conclusion, Implications and Directions for Further Research

This study's results support the views of Hatherly (2013) who has attributed the current financial crisis to, among other things, the lack of a close alignment between the accounting principles and practices used in financial institutions and their overarching business model. Indeed, the need for the accounting function of contemporary firms to understand the foundations of the business model used by the organization is paramount. In doing so the accounting function can inform, enable, monitor and report not only the performance of the firm as a whole but that of individual programmes and activities, thus safeguarding fit of practices and their close alignment to the objectives as well as the values of the organization as a whole. By the same token marketers in the marketing function, which is responsible for the identification, development and commercialization of products and services that fulfil customer needs while achieving organizational objectives, may be able to test their ideas and their influence upon the revenue streams of the organisation and their sustainability.

Our study reinforces the literature on integration in that it highlights once again the difference between accounting and marketing (Griffin and Hauser 1996). Indeed there are *Cultural and Orientation Differences* between accounting and marketing and these differences have a negative impact upon the integration of the two functions. Therefore, it is extremely important to identify the practices that can be used by researchers and managers alike to develop the building block that enhances integration.

5.1. Theoretical Implications

In researching the building block of integration between accounting and marketing our study confirmed the influential role of communications. Indeed where there is a communications gap between accounting and marketing the level of integration is reduced and problems of misunderstanding, misalignment of practice and unfocused joint effort emerge in the organisation making it difficult to develop and support a clear value proposition. Such misalignment and lack of integration can indeed have considerable consequences for the organisation as regards its internal fabric, its competitive posture as well as its image in the market place. While the negative consequences on the organisation's competitive posture and its image in the market place are easily understood since lack of integration affects performance, consequences on the internal fabric of the organisation need further attention. Indeed lack of inter-functional coordination can affect employee morale, give rise to antagonistic environments within the organisation and diminish trust and commitment to an internal services structure.

To avoid such negative effects, our study directs attention to the fact that the problems are embedded in cultural and orientation differences of the accounting and marketing function. However, this need not be the case as our research outlines clear practices that management can use to reduce the communications gap and facilitate mutual understanding between the two functions, thus strengthening integration between accounting and marketing. To this end our study shows that top management support coupled with a degree of formalisation that encourages and rewards communication and integration is an absolute must for organisations wishing to overcome the above mentioned problems. However our study underscores the fact that top management support and formalisation should be accompanied by a structure that facilitates interaction. In other words the closer the physical proximity of the two functions the more the chances that people will work closer with each other and develop closer working relationships.

It is important to outline once more that our study did not find role flexibility as contributing to higher level of integration. As it was explained earlier, this may be attributed to the fact that the two function not only have different world views of business but also a different portfolio of tools, practices and models they use to develop and test their hypotheses and outcomes of their activities. Cross-fertilisation of models in the two disciplines such as the balanced scorecard (Kaplan and Norton, 1996) or using real option in marketing (Adner and Levinthal, 2004) may alleviate some of these problems.

5.2. Practical Implications

From a practical perspective our study directs attention to the following issues.

First, it is encouraging to notice that there are specific blocks of managerial activity that can enhance integration among accounting and marketing despite cultural and orientation problems. Our study has revealed a portfolio of activities managers can use to develop and safeguard a level of integration among the accounting and marketing functions.

Second, our study reminds managers that their effort to enhance integration should be directed to both the culture and climate of their organisation. A culture-driven message is reflected in the top management support for integration as this will not only legitimise and authorise the use of resources for this purpose but also create an element of trust and credibility in the eyes of the employees thus enhancing its penetration in the organisational fabric. A climate-driven element is reflected in the degree of formalisation of integration practices and the physical proximity of the two functions in the organisation. We believe that culture and climate complement and reinforce each other in that they provide not only the impetus for integration but also a level of responsibility, ownership, and capability (resources) for achieving it.

Overall, therefore, our study conveys the message that managers wishing to enhance integration of accounting and marketing in their organisation they should be using a holistic perspective of its building blocks. This obviously provides them with a larger portfolio of intervention practices and as such it increases their chances for success.

5.3. Limitations and Further Research Directions

As a snapshot of financial organisations in the UK, our study has valid context specific limitations which reduce our ability to extrapolate our findings to other sectors in the UK or elsewhere in the world. As such more research seeking to replicate our study in other parts of the world and industries will help establish the application of our suggestions in different contexts. Such research will benefit from establishing factors critical to the implementation of the above mentioned managerial activities. Obviously this will require more qualitative research and preferably of a longitudinal nature to identify how managerial interventions towards integration of accounting and marketing change the culture and structure of the organisation leading to elimination of communication gaps and closer collaboration. Finally, a unique way to assess the efficiency and effectiveness of any integration structure is to feed specific critical pieces of information about the market and it customers in the accounting and marketing function and research how these pieces travel through accounting and marketing as well as how, in the course of this travel, they change to become managerially useful. The extent to which such changes can be traced back to accounting and marketing resources may help establish the degree of integration achieved in the organisation.

REFERENCES

Adler, P. and Kwon, S. (2002), "Social capital: Prospects for a new concept", *Academy of Management Review*, vol. 27, no. 1, January, pp. 17-40.

Adner, R. and Levinthal, D. (2004), "What is not a real option: Considering boundaries for the application of real options to business strategy", *Academy of Management Review*, vol. 29, no.1, pp. 74-85.

Barker, T. (2008), "Exploring the differences between accountants and marketers in terms of information sharing", *Marketing Intelligence and Planning*, vol. 26, no. 3, pp. 316-329.

de Ruyter, K. and Wetzels, M. (2000), "The marketing-finance interface: A relational exchange perspective", *Journal of Business Research*, vol. 50, issue 2, pp. 209-215.

Dewsnap, B. and Jobber, D. (2002), "A social psychological model of relations between marketing and sales", *European Journal of Marketing,* vol. 36, no. 7/8, pp. 874-894.

Garrett, T.C., Buisson, D.H. and Yap, C.M. (2006), "National culture and R&D and marketing integration mechanisms in new product development: A cross-cultural study between Singapore and New Zealand", *Industrial Marketing Management*, vol. 35, issue 3, pp. 293-307.

Griffin, A. and Hauser, J. (1996), "Integrating R&D and marketing: A review and analysis of the literature", *Journal of Product Innovation Management*, vol. 13, issue 3, May, pp. 191-215.

Guenzi, P. and Troilo, G. (2006), "Developing marketing capabilities for customer value creation through Marketing-Sales integration", *Industrial Marketing Management*, vol. 35, issue 8, pp. 974-988.

Gupta, A. and Govindarajan, V. (2000), "Knowledge flows within multinational corporations", *Strategic Management Journal*, vol. 21, issue 4, pp. 473-496.

Hatherly, D. (2013), "*The Failure and the Future of Accounting, Strategy, Stakeholders, and Business Value*", Gower Publishing Ltd., Surrey, UK.

Jaspers, F. and Van den Ende, J. (2006), "The organisational form of vertical relationships: Dimensions of integration", *Industrial Marketing Management*, vol. 35, issue 7, pp. 819-828.

Lam, P.K. and Chin, K.S. (2005), "Identifying and prioritizing critical success factors for conflict management in collaborative new product development", *Industrial Marketing Management,* vol. 34, issue 8, pp. 761-772.

Kaplan, R. and Norton, D. (1996) "Linking the balanced scoreboard to strategy", *California Management Review* vol. 39, no. 1, Fall, pp. 53-79.

Langfield-Smith, K. (2008), "Strategic management accounting: How far have we come in 25 years?", *Accounting, Auditing and Accountability*, vol. 21, no. 2, pp. 204-228.

Le Meunier-FitzHugh, K. and Lane, N. (2009), "Collaboration between sales and marketing, market orientation and business performance in business-to-business organisations", *Journal of Strategic Marketing*, vol. 17, no. 3, pp. 291-306.

Le Meunier-FitzHugh, K. and Piercy, N. (2007), "Exploring collaboration between sales and marketing", *European Journal of Marketing*, vol. 41, no. 7/8, pp. 939-955.

Mollenkopf, D., Gibson, A. and Ozanne, L. (2000), "Integration of marketing and logistics functions: An empirical examination of New Zealand", *Journal of Business Logistics*, vol. 21, no. 2, pp. 89-112.

Parry, M. and Song, M. (1993), "Determinants of R&D-Marketing integration in High-Tech Japanese firms", *Journal of Product Innovation Management*, vol. 10, issue 1, pp. 4-22.

Plakoyiannaki, M and Tzokas, N. (2002), "Customer relationship management: A capabilities portfolio perspective", *Journal of Database Marketing*, vol. 9 no. 3, pp. 228-237.

Shipilov, A. and Danis, W. (2006), "TMG social capital, strategic choice and firm performance", *European Management Journal*, vol. 24, no. 1, pp. 16-27.

Song, M. and Parry, M. (1993), "R&D-Marketing integration in Japanese High Technology firms: Hypotheses and empirical evidence", *Journal of Academy of Marketing Science*, vol. 21, no. 2, pp. 125-133.

Tzokas N., Hutlink, E. and Hart, S. (2004), "Navigating the new product development process", *Industrial Marketing Management*, vol. 33, issue 7, pp. 619-626.

Wilson, R.M.S. (2000), "*Some thoughts on Marketing Controllership*", Loughborough University Research Series Paper, 2000:4.

Xie, J., Song, M. and Stringfellow, A. (2003), "Antecedents and consequences of goal incongruity on new product development in five Countries: A marketing view", *Journal of Product Innovation Management*, vol. 20, issue 3, pp. 233-250.

Zinkhan, G. and Verbrugge, J. (2000), "The marketing/finance interface: Two divergent and complimentary views of the firm", *Journal of Business Research*, vol. 50 no. 2, pp. 143-148.

INDEX

#

A

B

C

D

F

G

H

I

J

K

L

M

N

O

P

Q

R

S

W

Y